IS U.S. GOVERNMENT DEBT DIFFERENT?

Penn Law
UNIVERSITY *of* PENNSYLVANIA LAW SCHOOL

Wharton
UNIVERSITY *of* PENNSYLVANIA
Financial Institutions Center

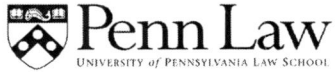

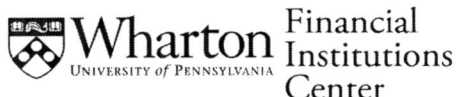

IS U.S. GOVERNMENT DEBT DIFFERENT?

EDITED BY
Franklin Allen
Anna Gelpern
Charles Mooney
David Skeel

AUTHORS
Donald S. Bernstein
William W. Bratton
Peter R. Fisher
Richard J. Herring
James R. Hines Jr.
Howell E. Jackson
Jeremy Kreisberg
James Kwak
Deborah Lucas
Michael W. McConnell
Jim Millstein
Charles W. Mooney Jr.
Kelley O'Mara
Zoltan Pozsar
Steven L. Schwarcz
Richard Squire
Richard Sylla

FIC Press
Philadelphia, USA

Published by FIC Press
2405 Steinberg Hall - Dietrich Hall
3620 Locust Walk
Philadelphia, PA 19104-6367
USA

First Published 2012

ISBN 978-0-9836469-9-0 (paperback)
ISBN 978-0-9836469-8-3 (e-book version)

Cover artwork, design and layout by Christopher Trollen

Contents

	The Contributors	ix
	Acknowledgments	xxi
	PREFACE by Anna Gelpern	xxiii
1	U.S. Government Debt Has Always Been Different! Richard Sylla	1
2	A World Without Treasuries? William W. Bratton	13
3	Default and the International Role of the Dollar Richard J. Herring	21
4	A Macro View of Shadow Banking: Do T-Bill Shortages Pose a New Triffin Dilemma? Zoltan Pozsar	35
5	Origins of the Fiscal Constitution Michael W. McConnell	45
6	The 2011 Debt Ceiling Impasse Revisited Howell E. Jackson	55
7	A Market for End-of-the-World Insurance? Credit Default Swaps on US Government Debt Richard Squire	69

8	Thoughts on Debt Sustainability: Supply and Demand Keynote Remarks *Peter R. Fisher*	87
9	The Federal Debt: Assessing the Capacity to Pay *Deborah Lucas*	101
10	The Tax Revenue Capacity of the U.S. Economy *James R. Hines Jr.*	113
11	Can the United States Achieve Fiscal Sustainability? Will We? *James Kwak*	129
12	Burning the Furniture to Heat the House – The Potential Role of Asset Sales in Funding the Federal Government's Deficits *Jim Millstein*	151
13	United States Sovereign Debt: A Thought Experiment On Default and Restructuring *Charles W. Mooney, Jr.*	169
14	A Comment on Professor Mooney's Thought Experiment: Can U.S. Debt Be Restructured? *Donald S. Bernstein*	237
15	Direct and Indirect U.S. Government Debt *Steven L. Schwarcz*	245

Appendix
The 2011 Debt Limit Impasse:
Treasury's Actions & The Counterfactual –
What Might Have Happened if the
National Debt Hit the Statutory Limit 255
Jeremy Kreisberg & Kelley O'Mara
(Under the Supervision of Professor Howell Jackson)

The Contributors

Franklin Allen
University of Pennsylvania
Franklin Allen is the Nippon Life Professor of Finance and Professor of Economics at the Wharton School of the University of Pennsylvania. He has been on the faculty since 1980. He is currently Co-Director of the Wharton Financial Institutions Center. He was formerly Vice Dean and Director of Wharton Doctoral Programs and Executive Editor of the Review of Financial Studies, one of the leading academic finance journals. He is a past President of the American Finance Association, the Western Finance Association, the Society for Financial Studies, and the Financial Intermediation Research Society, and a Fellow of the Econometric Society. He received his doctorate from Oxford University. Dr. Allen's main areas of interest are corporate finance, asset pricing, financial innovation, comparative financial systems, and financial crises. He is a co-author with Richard Brealey and Stewart Myers of the eighth through tenth editions of the textbook Principles of Corporate Finance.

Donald Bernstein
Davis Polk & Wardwell LLP
Donald Bernstein, who heads the Insolvency and Restructuring Practice at the international law firm Davis Polk & Wardwell LLP, is recognized as one of the world's leading insolvency lawyers. He has received numerous honors, including being elected Chair of the National Bankruptcy Conference, a non-partisan organization of leading academics, lawyers and judges seeking to improve bankruptcy law and administration in the United States. Mr. Bernstein's practice

includes representing debtors, creditors, liquidators, receivers and acquirers in major corporate restructurings and insolvency proceedings, as well as advising financial institutions and other clients regarding bank insolvency and resolution planning and the credit risks involved in derivatives, securities transactions, and other domestic and international financial transactions.

William Bratton
University of Pennsylvania
William Bratton is recognized internationally as a leading writer on business law. He brings an interdisciplinary perspective to a wide range of subject matters that encompass corporate governance, corporate finance, accounting, corporate legal history, and comparative corporate law. His work has appeared in the Cornell, Michigan, Northwestern, Pennsylvania, Stanford, and Virginia law reviews, and the Duke and Georgetown law journals, along with the American Journal of Comparative Law and the Common Market Law Review. His book, Corporate Finance: Cases and Materials (Foundation Press, 7th ed. 2012), is the leading law school text on the subject. Bratton is a Research Associate of the European Corporate Governance Institute. In 2009, he was installed as the Anton Philips Professor at the Faculty of Law of Tilburg University in The Netherlands, the fifth American academic to hold the chair.

Peter R. Fisher
BlackRock
Peter R. Fisher, Senior Managing Director, BlackRock, is head of BlackRock's Fixed Income Portfolio Management Group and a member of the firm's Global Executive Committee. Prior to joining BlackRock in 2004, Mr. Fisher served as Under Secretary of the U.S. Treasury for Domestic Finance from 2001 to 2003. Before joining the Treasury he worked at the Federal Reserve Bank of New York and at the Bank for International Settlements. He earned a B.A. in history for Harvard College in 1980 and a J.D. from Harvard Law School in 1985.

Anna Gelpern
American University Washington College of Law
Anna Gelpern is Professor of Law at American University Washington College of Law and Visiting Professor at Georgetown Law. She has published articles on financial integration, government debt, and regulation of financial institutions in law and social science journals, and has co-authored a textbook on International Finance. She has contributed to international initiatives on financial reform and sovereign borrowing. Professor Gelpern is a visiting fellow at the Peter G. Peterson Institute for International Economics, a fellow at the George Washington University School of Law Center for Law, Economics & Finance, and held a visiting appointment at the University of Pennsylvania Law School in Spring 2011. Earlier, she was on the faculty at Rutgers School of Law-Newark and Rutgers University Division of Global Affairs. Between 1996 and 2002, Professor Gelpern served in legal and policy positions at the U.S. Treasury Department.

Richard J. Herring
University of Pennsylvania
Richard J. Herring is Jacob Safra Professor of International Banking and Professor of Finance at The Wharton School, University of Pennsylvania, where he is also founding director of the Wharton Financial Institutions Center. From 2000 to 2006, he served as the Director of the Lauder Institute of International Management Studies and from 1995 to 2000, he served as Vice Dean and Director of Wharton's Undergraduate Division. During 2006, he was a Professorial Fellow at the Reserve Bank of New Zealand and Victoria University and during 2008 he was the Metzler Fellow at Johann Goethe University in Frankfurt. He is the author of more than 100 articles, monographs and books on various topics in financial regulation, international banking, and international finance. His most recent book, The Known, the Unknown & the Unknowable in Financial Risk Management (with F. Diebold and N. Doherty) has just been recognized as the most influential book published on the economics or risk management and insurance by the American Risk and Insurance Association. At various times his research has been funded by grants from the National Science Foundation, the Ford Foundation, the Brookings Institution, the Sloan Foundation, the Council on Foreign Relations, and the Royal Swedish Commis-

sion on Productivity. Outside the university, he is co-chair of the US Shadow Financial Regulatory Committee and Executive Director of the Financial Economist's Roundtable, a member of the Advisory Board of the European Banking Report in Rome, the Institute for Financial Studies in Frankfurt, and the International Centre for Financial Regulation in London. In addition, he is a member of the FDIC Systemic Risk Advisory Committee, the Systemic Risk Council and the Stanford University Hoover Institute Working Group on Resolution. He served as co-chair of the Multinational Banking seminar from 1992–2004 and was a Fellow of the World Economic Forum in Davos from 1992–95. Currently, he is an independent director of the DWS mutual fund complex, the Daiwa closed-end Funds, the Aberdeen Singapore closed-end fund, and Barclays Bank, Delaware. Herring received his undergraduate degree from Oberlin College in 1968 and his PhD from Princeton University in 1973. He has been a member of the Finance Department since 1972. He is married, with two children, and lives in Bryn Mawr, Pennsylvania.

James R. Hines Jr.
University of Michigan
James R. Hines Jr. is the L. Hart Wright Collegiate Professor of Law and co-director of the Law and Economics Program at the University of Michigan Law School. He is also the Richard A. Musgrave Collegiate Professor of Economics in the Department of Economics at Michigan, and serves as the research director of the Office of Tax Policy Research in the Stephen M. Ross School of Business. His research is focused on various aspects of taxation. Hines taught at Princeton and Harvard Universities prior to joining the Michigan faculty in 1997, and has held visiting appointments at Columbia University, the London School of Economics, the University of California, Berkeley, and Harvard Law School. He is a research associate of the National Bureau of Economic Research, research director of the International Tax Policy Forum, co-editor of the Journal of Public Economics, and once, long ago, served as an economist in the U.S. Department of Commerce. He holds a BA and MA from Yale University and a PhD from Harvard, all in economics.

Howell E. Jackson
Harvard Law School
Howell Jackson is the James S. Reid, Jr., Professor of Law at Harvard Law School. His research interests include financial regulation, international finance, consumer protection, federal budget policy, and entitlement reform. Professor Jackson has served as a consultant to the United States Treasury Department, the United Nations Development Program, and the World Bank/International Monetary Fund. He is a member of the National Academy on Social Insurance, a trustee of the College Retirement Equities Fund (CREF) and its affiliated TIAA-CREF investment companies, a member of the panel of outside scholars for the NBER Retirement Research Center, and a senior editor for Cambridge University Press Series on International Corporate Law and Financial Regulation. Professor Jackson frequently consults with government agencies on issues of financial regulation. He is co-editor of Fiscal Challenges: An Inter-Disciplinary Approach to Budget Policy (Cambridge University Press 2008), co-author of Analytical Methods for Lawyers (Foundation Press 2003) and Regulation of Financial Institutions (West 1999), and author of numerous scholarly articles. Before joining the Harvard Law School faculty in 1989, Professor Jackson was a law clerk for Associate Justice Thurgood Marshall and practiced law in Washington, D.C. Professor Jackson received J.D. and M.B.A. degrees from Harvard University in 1982 and a B.A. from Brown University in 1976.

Jeremy Kreisberg
J.D. candidate - Harvard Law School
Jeremy Kreisberg is a 2014 J.D. candidate at Harvard Law School and an editor of the Harvard Law Review. During his 1L summer, Mr. Kreisberg interned at the Office of Management & Budget. Mr. Kreisberg is a 2010 graduate of the University of Michigan.

James Kwak
University of Connecticut
James Kwak is an associate professor at the University of Connecticut School of Law. He is the co-author of The Baseline Scenario, a leading blog covering economics and public policy, and an online columnist for The Atlantic. He co-authored 13 Bankers: The Wall Street Take-

over and the Next Financial Meltdown, a New York Times bestseller chronicling the rise of the financial sector over the past three decades. His latest book, White House Burning: The Founding Fathers, Our National Debt, and Why It Matters To You is a history and analysis of government deficits and the national debt. James has an A.B. in social studies from Harvard, a Ph.D. in history from the University of California, Berkeley, and a J.D. from the Yale Law School. Before going to law school, he worked as a management consultant and co-founded Guidewire Software.

Deborah J. Lucas
MIT - Sloan School of Management
Deborah J. Lucas is the Sloan Distinguished Professor of Finance at MIT's Sloan School of Management. Her recent research has focused on the problem of measuring and accounting for the risk of government financial obligations. Her published papers cover a wide range of topics including the effect of idiosyncratic risk on asset prices and portfolio choice, dynamic models of corporate finance, financial institutions, and monetary economics. Previous appointments include Assistant Director at the Congressional Budget Office from 2009-2011; Donald C. Clark Professor of Finance at Northwestern University's Kellogg School of Management from 1996-2009; Chief Economist at the Congressional Budget Office from 2000 to 2001; senior economist at the Council of Economic Advisers from 1992 to 1993; and member of the Social Security Technical Advisory Panels of 1999-2000 and 2006–2007. Past editorial positions include co-editorship of the Journal of Money, Credit and Banking and associate editorships for a number of finance and economics journals. She is the co-organizer of the group Capital Markets and the Economy at the NBER, and a past director of the American Finance Association. She is an elected member of the National Academy of Social Insurance, a research associate of the NBER, and has served as a director on several corporate and non-profit boards. She received her B.A., M.A., and a Ph.D. in economics from the University of Chicago.

Michael W. McConnell
Stanford Law School
Michael W. McConnell is the Richard & Frances Mallery Professor and Director of the Constitutional Law Center at Stanford Law

School, as well as Senior Fellow at the Hoover Institution. He is a leading authority on freedom of speech and religion, the relation of individual rights to government structure, originalism, and various other aspects of constitutional history and constitutional law. He began his career as Assistant General Counsel of the Office of Management and Budget, where he dealt with issues involving the debt ceiling, the Budget Act, government shutdowns, and the like. He is author of numerous articles and co-author of two casebooks: THE CONSTITUTION OF THE UNITED STATES (Foundation Press) and RELIGION AND THE CONSTITUTION (Aspen). He is co-editor of CHRISTIAN PERSPECTIVES ON LEGAL THOUGHT (Yale Univ. Press). Since 1996, he has been a Fellow of the American Academy of Arts and Sciences. Professor McConnell brings wide practical experience to bear on his teaching and scholarship. Before joining Stanford in 2009, he served as a Circuit Judge on the U.S. Court of Appeals for the Tenth Circuit. He has argued thirteen cases in the United States Supreme Court, most recently CompuCredit v Greenwood, in 2011. Before his appointment to the bench, McConnell was Presidential Professor of Law at the S.J. Quinney College of Law at the University of Utah, and prior to that the William B. Graham Professor of Law at the University of Chicago Law School. He has taught six times as a visiting professor at Harvard Law School. McConnell served as law clerk to then Chief Judge J. Skelly Wright of the U.S. Court of Appeals for the District of Columbia Circuit, and to Justice William J. Brennan Jr. of the U.S. Supreme Court. He is a graduate of Michigan State University (1976) and the University of Chicago Law School (1979). He is of counsel to the law firm of Kirkland & Ellis.

Jim Millstein
Millstein & Co., LLC
Jim Millstein is the chairman of Millstein & Co., LLC, a financial advisory firm with offices in Washington, D.C. and New York City. Before forming Millstein & Co., Mr. Millstein was the Chief Restructuring Officer of the U.S. Department of the Treasury, where he was primarily responsible for the management and restructuring of the government's TARP investments in AIG and Ally Financial and was a senior advisor to the Secretary in the policy-making process that resulted in the Dodd-Frank Consumer Protection and Financial

Reform Bill. Before joining the Treasury in 2009, Mr. Millstein was the global co-head of Lazard's Restructuring Group, having joined Lazard in 2000 after an 18-year career at Cleary, Gottlieb, Steen & Hamilton, where he ran its Restructuring Practice. He received his bachelor's degree in politics from Princeton University in 1978, his master's degree in political science from the University of California at Berkeley in 1979 and his J.D. from Columbia University School of Law in 1982.

Charles Mooney Jr.
University of Pennsylvania
Charles W. Mooney Jr. is a leading legal scholar in the fields of commercial law and bankruptcy law. His book (with S. Harris) Security Interests in Personal Property (Foundation Press, 5th ed. 2011) is a widely adopted text used in law schools around the United States. Mooney was honored for his contributions to the uniform law process by the Oklahoma City School of Law and was awarded the Distinguished Service Award by the American College of Commercial Finance Lawyers. He also served as U.S. Delegate at the Diplomatic Conference for the Cape Town Convention on International Interests in Mobile Equipment and the Aircraft Protocol and for the Diplomatic Conference for the UNIDROIT (Geneva) Convention on Intermediated Securities. Mooney also served as a Co-Reporter for the Drafting Committee for the Revision of UCC Article 9 (Secured Transactions), as the ABA Liaison-Advisor to the Permanent Editorial Board for the UCC, and as a member of Council and Chair of the Committee on UCC of the ABA Business Law Section.

Kelley O'Mara
J.D. candidate - Harvard Law School
Kelley O'Mara is a 2014 J.D. candidate at Harvard Law School. Her research interests include financial regulation and federal budget policy. Prior to law school, Ms. O'Mara worked as a consultant at McKinsey & Company and a teacher with Teach for America. Ms. O'Mara is a 2007 graduate of the McIntire School of Commerce at the University of Virginia.

Zoltan Pozsar
International Monetary Fund
Zoltan Pozsar is a Visiting Scholar at the IMF advising on regulating the shadow banking system. Prior to joining the IMF, Mr. Pozsar was with the Federal Reserve Bank of New York's Markets Desk where he led the Bank's efforts to map and monitor the shadow banking system. Mr. Pozsar consulted policymakers globally about shadow banking including the U.S. Department of the Treasury, the White House, the BIS, the FSB, the FSA, the Bank of Canada and the Bank of England. During the financial crisis Mr. Pozsar was part of the Markets Desks' cross market monitoring efforts, informing FOMC members about global macro developments; was the point person between the Federal Reserve, finance companies, ABS syndicates and the ABS investor base; and was instrumental in designing and operationalizing the Fed's Term Asset-Backed Loan Facility (TALF). He and his wife live in New York City.

Steven L. Schwarcz
Duke University
Steven L. Schwarcz is the Stanley A. Star Professor of Law & Business at Duke University and Founding Director of Duke's interdisciplinary Global Capital Markets Center. His areas of research and scholarship include insolvency and bankruptcy law; international finance, capital markets, and systemic risk; and commercial law. (Links to his scholarship are at http://www.law.duke.edu/fac/schwarcz/.) Prior to joining the Duke faculty, he was a partner at two leading international law firms, where he represented top banks and other financial institutions in structuring innovative capital market financing transactions, both domestic and international. He also helped to pioneer the field of asset securitization, and his book, STRUCTURED FINANCE, A GUIDE TO THE PRINCIPLES OF ASSET SECURITIZATION (3d edition), is one of the most widely used texts in the field. Professor Schwarcz has been the Leverhulme Visiting Professor at the University of Oxford, Visiting Professor at the University of Geneva Faculty of Law, Senior Fellow at The University of Melbourne Law School, and an adviser to the United Nations. He has given numerous endowed or distinguished public lectures, including at The University of Hong Kong, the University of Oxford

(the Leverhulme Lectures 2010, available at http://www.law.ox.ac. uk/published/leverhulme2010.php), Georgetown University Law Center, National University of Singapore, and The National Assembly of the Republic of Korea. He also has given numerous keynote speeches, including at conferences of the European Central Bank, the Corporate Law Teachers Association of Australia, New Zealand, and Asia-Pacific, Moody's Corporation, and the Asian Securitisation Forum. Additionally, he has testified before the U.S. Congress on topics including systemic risk, securitization, credit rating agencies, and financial regulation and has advised several U.S. and foreign governmental institutions on the financial crisis. Professor Schwarcz is a Fellow of the American College of Bankruptcy, a Founding Member of the International Insolvency Institute, a Fellow of the American College of Commercial Finance Lawyers, and Business Law Advisor to the American Bar Association Section on Business Law.

David Skeel
University of Pennsylvania Law School
David Skeel is the S. Samuel Arsht Professor of Corporate Law at the University of Pennsylvania Law School. He is the author of The New Financial Deal: Understanding the Dodd-Frank Act and its (Unintended) Consequences (Wiley, 2011); Icarus in the Boardroom: The Fundamental Flaws in Corporate America and Where They Came From (Oxford University Press, 2005); Debt's Dominion: A History of Bankruptcy Law in America (Princeton University Press, 2001); and numerous articles on bankruptcy, corporate law, Christianity and law, and other topics. Professor Skeel has also written commentaries for the New York Times, Wall Street Journal, Books & Culture, The Weekly Standard, and other publications.

Richard Squire
Yale Law School
Richard Squire is currently the Florence Rogatz Visiting Professor of Law at Yale Law School. He is also an Associate Professor at Fordham Law School, where he has taught since 2006. Before joining academia, he practiced at Wachtell, Lipton, Rosen & Katz in New York City. Professor Squire received a J.D. from Harvard Law School, an M.B.A. from Harvard Business School, and a B.A. from Bowdoin College.

Richard Sylla
New York University
Richard Sylla is Henry Kaufman Professor of the History of Financial Institutions and Markets and Professor of Economics at the Stern School of Business, New York University. His Stern MBA courses include "Development of Financial Institutions and Markets," and "Global Perspectives on Enterprise Systems." Sylla is also a Research Associate of the National Bureau of Economic Research, with a current project on the development of the business corporation in the antebellum United States. Professor Sylla received the B.A., the M.A., and the Ph.D. from Harvard University. He is the author of The American Capital Market, 1846-1914 (1975); co-author of The Evolution of the American Economy (1993; 1st ed., 1980) and A History of Interest Rates, (4th ed., 2005; 3rd ed. Rev., 1996; 3rd ed., 1991); and co-editor of Patterns of European Industrialization—The Nineteenth Century (1991), The State, the Financial System, and Economic Modernization (1999); and Founding Choices: American Economic Policy in the 1790s (2011), as well as articles, essays, and reviews in business, economic, and financial history. Professor Sylla's research focus is on the financial history of the United States in comparative contexts. He is a former editor of The Journal of Economic History. Sylla has served as chairman of the board of trustees of the Cliometric Society, an association of quantitative historians; aspresident of the Economic History Association, the professional organization of economic historians in the United States; and as president of the Business History Conference (BHC), the leading professional association of business historians, which also presented its Lifetime Achievement Award to him in 2011. In 2012 he was named a Fellow of the American Academy of Arts & Sciences. Currently, Sylla serves as chairman of the board of trustees of the Museum of American Finance, a Smithsonian affiliate located at 48 Wall Street in New York.

Acknowledgments

We would like to thank all the people and institutions particularly the Penn Law School and the Wharton Financial Institutions Center that have helped to make the conference and the book possible. Our special thanks go to Tina Horowitz, Stephen Levy, and Christopher Trollen.

PREFACE

The Law School and the Wharton Financial Institution Center (FIC) at the University of Pennsylvania organized the conference "Is U.S. Government Debt Different?" in Philadelphia on May 4 and 5, 2012. The event was financed by a Sloan Foundation grant to the FIC. The conference was conceived against the background of skyrocketing U.S. government debt, the standoff over the statutory debt limit between the Congress and the President of the United States in the summer of 2011, and the ongoing debt crisis in the Eurozone. This confluence of shocks and near-misses impressed on us the urgent need to consider the unthinkable: default, restructuring, or a wholesale reassessment of the U.S. Treasury securities' place in the world. The conference brought together leading economists, historians, lawyers, market participants, and policy makers to discuss different aspects of U.S. government debt, including its role in the global financial markets, its constitutional, statutory and contractual basis, and its sustainability. Having laid the conceptual foundation, the conference ended with a discussion of a thought experiment, mapping out options for a hypothetical U.S. debt restructuring.

The opening panel explored the functions of U.S. Treasury instruments and the Treasury market in the United States and beyond. U.S. Treasuries play a unique role in the national and global economy. **Richard Sylla** put their current role in historical perspective, observing that U.S. government debt obligations from their birth in the revolutionary days have been much more than another means to finance the government: they cemented the political union, served as a currency, backed the banking system, and helped attract foreign capital. **William Bratton**, **Richard Herring**, and **Zoltan Pozsar** then discussed the Treasuries' role in the modern financial system, including corporate finance, banking and shadow banking in the United States and around the globe. While other reserve currencies and assets may eventually displace the U.S. dollar and the U.S. Treasuries, none are readily available at this time, and some that have served as substitutes in the past (notably agency securities) ultimately rely on the credit of the United States.

The second panel considered constitutional, statutory, and contractual dimensions of U.S. government debt. **Michael McConnell** opened with an examination of the U.S. Constitution as a fiscal framework based on legislative control of taxing, spending, and borrowing. **Howell Jackson** then returned to the statutory debt ceiling controversy, lifting the curtain on a plausible sequence of events had the President and the Congress failed to compromise as they did at the eleventh hour in the summer of 2011. In addition to Jackson's essay, this volume contains a policy brief by **Jeremy Kreisberg** and **Kelley O'Mara** detailing the Executive's options for honoring U.S. government payment obligations with the debt ceiling unchanged. **Richard Squire** concluded with thoughts on the market in credit default swaps on U.S. government debt.

Peter Fisher gave the luncheon keynote, where he brought his perspective as former U.S. government debt manager, central bank official, and market participant to bear on the themes of the conference. Echoing the first panel, his remarks urged closer attention to the sources of demand for U.S. Treasuries both at home and abroad. He surveyed the experience of Britain in the 19th century and Japan in the late 20th to identify some of the demand factors that help account for the ability of countries with very high debt burdens to avoid default. The focus on demand in the U.S. banking, shadow banking, and global financial systems suggests cautious optimism about the Treasuries' prospects going forward.

The first afternoon panel revisited the questions of U.S. ability and willingness to pay, which has been debated heavily in policy and academic circles. A sovereign's ability to pay is a function of its ability to generate revenues, which depends, among other things, on the economy's capacity to grow and on the government's political capacity to collect taxes. The line between ability and willingness to pay can be notoriously fuzzy. **Deborah Lucas** examined the structural sources and magnitudes of U.S. fiscal imbalances and the policy changes needed to avoid them. While conceivable, default remains unlikely; however, risks from rising healthcare costs, slow productivity growth, a spike in interest rates, and contingent liabilities can tip the outcome. **James Hines** observed that while the United States imposes a smaller tax burden than other large wealthy economies, its greatest unused tax capacity is in expenditure taxation that would alter the current distributional bargain. **James Kwak** put the U.S. fiscal challenge in historical and political perspectives, analyzing the structural and policy steps needed to address the debt problem, and the political capacity of the U.S. government to take these steps. **James Millstein** suggested that asset sales—such as sales of mineral rights—merit serious consideration as part of a package of debt reduction measures. His contribution drew on the history of sovereign asset sales, adapting it to the current needs of the United States.

The conference culminated in a panel discussion of a "thought experiment" laid out in **Charles Mooney's** contribution: what if the United States decided that it was in its interest to restructure U.S. Treasury debt? How might it go about it? What legal and policy options would the U.S. government have, what are the pros, cons, and likely consequences of taking any of these steps? His paper considers constitutional, statutory, market and transactional challenges to default and restructuring, and presents three options for a hypothetical operation. At the conference, he laid out the strategy for across-the-board and selective exchanges of outstanding U.S. Treasuries for new obligations, including the possible issuance of "Prosperity Shares," non-debt securities giving creditors a stake in future growth. **Donald Bernstein** and **Steven Schwarcz** offered comments on the paper. Bernstein was skeptical of recourse to the bankruptcy powers, and pointed to the many hard policy challenges, including loss distribution and policy reform, that would remain unsolved even with recourse to bankruptcy. Schwarcz noted further possibilities for restructuring, and obstacles to selective default. In addition, his contribution explored the problem of government financing through special purpose entities, and urged oversight to improve accountability.

Throughout the day, conference participants from different academic disciplines and backgrounds engaged in lively discussion. We did not strive for a policy consensus, nor did we achieve one. Our purpose in the volume, as it was in the conference, is to start a conversation long overdue. We hope it will continue. If the conference convinced us of one thing, it is that the stakes in the future of U.S. government debt are too high to confine serious analysis and informed debate to legislative back-rooms and disciplinary silos.

1
U.S. Government Debt Has Always Been Different!

Richard Sylla

1. Introduction: Opposed 18th-Century Views of Public Debts

At the time the U.S came into existence, conventional economic wisdom in Europe took a decidedly negative view of public debts. Writing in 1776, Adam Smith was a leading exponent of that wisdom. In the very last chapter of The Wealth of Nations, "Of Public Debts," Smith wrote as follows:

> *The progress of the enormous debts which at present oppress, and will in the long-run probably ruin, all the great nations of Europe, has been pretty uniform. Nations, like private men, have generally begun to borrow upon what may be called personal credit, without assigning or mortgaging any particular fund for the payment of the debt; and when this resource has failed them, they have gone on to borrow upon assignments or mortgages of particular funds....*
>
> *The practice of funding has gradually enfeebled every state which has adopted it.... Is it likely that in Great Britain alone a practice, which has brought either weakness or desolation into every other country, should prove altogether innocent?*[1]

---
1 Adam Smith, The Wealth of Nations, Modern Library edition (New York: Random House, 1937), Book V, Chap. III, pp. 863, 881.

Five years after Smith published his great work, an American soldier fighting against Great Britain on the other side of the Atlantic voiced a far more positive view of public debts than appeared in European conventional wisdom:

Speaking within moderate bounds our population will be doubled in thirty years; there will be a confluence of emigrants from all parts of the world; our commerce will have a proportionable progress, and of course our wealth and capacity for revenue. It will be a matter of choice, if we are not out of debt in twenty years, without at all encumbering the people.

A national debt if it is not excessive will be to us a national blessing; it will be a powerful cement of our union. It will also create a necessity for keeping up taxation to a degree which without being oppressive, will be a spur to industry.[2]

The writer was Lt. Col. Alexander Hamilton, a member of the Continental Army and the principal aide-de-camp to the commander, Gen. George Washington. Hamilton wrote to Robert Morris, one of America's leading merchants, who had recently been appointed by Congress to the position of Superintendent of Finance. Hamilton's optimistic view of the future and his positive view of national debts are remarkable because they were expressed in one of the darkest moments of the War of Independence. Over-issuance of paper Continental dollars had resulted in hyperinflation, and Morris had been called in to turn around the dire financial situation that threatened an American defeat in the war. Hamilton's long letter to Morris recommended a series of financial reforms that included a national bank. Morris was of a like mind, and began to implement versions of the reforms. Morris also used a French specie loan both to finance the crucial Yorktown campaign and to capitalize the first U.S. bank, the Bank of North America. But his plans to put the debts of Congress onto a sound footing failed because one state or another under the Articles of Confederation would not agree to revenue measures that might have provided the means to service them. So Morris re-

---

2 H. C. Syrett, ed., The Papers of Alexander Hamilton, Vol. II: 1779-1781 (New York: Columbia University Press, 1961), p.635. The letter is dated April 30, 1781.

signed from office in 1784, and during the 1780s the U.S. remained a nation in default on its debts.

2. Hamilton's Debt Restructuring and its Effects

By the end of the decade, Americans had scrapped the Articles in favor of the Constitution, and President Washington had named Alexander Hamilton to be the new nation's first Secretary of the Treasury. Congress used its new authority to pass revenue and debt legislation, and Hamilton acted quickly to turn the nation's debts into a national blessing. His measures included:

a. A voluntary exchange of old debt for a package of new debt consisting of a 6% bond, a 3% bond, and a 6% "deferred" bond that would pay no interest for the decade 1791-1800, and then 6% starting in 1801.
b. The package of new debt paid interest of 4% on par value, so investors making the exchange took what today would be called a haircut because the old debt had promised to pay 6%.
c. To compensate for the haircut, investors were given call protection: no more than 2 percent of main 6% security could be retired annually.
d. National debt principal was payable "at the pleasure of the government," which, like the interest haircut, recognized the limited resources of the Treasury and the uncertain outlook for revenues. The idea that debt should be repaid was an American departure from the contemporary European practice of making most public debts take the form of perpetuities that paid interest without a promise of redemption.
e. State debts were assumed into the national debt, based on the argument that they had been mostly incurred in the common cause of U.S. independence. But Hamilton also thought a larger national debt would constitute more cement for the union of states.
f. Interest in specie or specie equivalents commenced in 1791 for Congress's debts, and in 1792 for assumed state debts.
g. A sinking fund was established to channel surplus revenues into debt redemption, although its real purpose may have

been to allow the Treasury to intervene in the markets to stabilize market prices.

Active trading of the three new debt issues commenced in the securities markets of Boston, New York, and Philadelphia in 1791. This was the birth of the modern Treasury debt market, which is now well into its third century. By 1795, virtually all of the old debt had been exchanged for new debt.

Hamilton's positive views on the uses of public debt were manifested in several ways. He encouraged banks to accept U.S. debt as collateral for loans, which they quickly did and at increased values. When the 6% bonds first appeared in late 1790, they were accepted as loan collateral at 50 percent of par value. A year later their collateral value had risen to 90 percent of par, and by mid 1792 6%s were accepted as collateral at par.[3] The national debt thus created a liquid and bankable asset, solving many of the liquidity problems that previously had plagued the country.

At the end of 1790, with the debt restructuring program underway, Hamilton proposed that Congress create a national bank, the Bank of the United States, which it did in early 1791. Under the plan, the federal government took a 20-percent stake in the bank, paid for with a loan from the bank itself and to be repaid in annual installments over ten years. Private investors were offered the remaining 80 percent of the bank's shares, payable one fourth in specie and three fourths with U.S. 6% bonds. This design meant that the national bank would support the national debt, and vice versa. It had the effect of raising the market values of bank shares and public debt securities.

Hamilton had intended his program to have these effects. He wanted to encourage the states to charter more banks, and he wanted the market value of the U.S. debt to rise quickly so that foreign investors who bought it would transfer more capital from Europe to the United States. In his celebrated *Report on Manufactures* of December 1791, Hamilton stated, "It is ...evident that in a Country situated

---

3 See Richard Sylla, "U.S. Securities Markets and the Banking System, 1790-1840," Federal Reserve Bank of St. Louis Review 80 (May/June 1998), 83-98, at 89-90.

like the United States, with an infinite fund of resources yet to be unfolded, every farthing of foreign capital…is a precious acquisition."[4] By establishing the credit of the U.S. government, Hamilton's measures immediately attracted the interest of European investors. By 1803/1804, records of holdings of U.S. debt and other securities indicate that foreign investors—mostly English and Dutch—held more than half of the U.S. national debt and more than 60 percent of the shares of the Bank of the United States.[5] Large foreign holdings of U.S. debt are nothing new in the late 20th and early 21st centuries. They began shortly after the debt was restructured in the early 1790s.

The U.S., moreover, consciously acted to make its national debt appeal to foreign investors. In contrast with many later emerging market nations which have to borrow by issuing debt denominated in leading international currencies, after 1794 the U.S. issued debt denominated exclusively in U.S. dollars. But that was not a problem for foreign investors because Hamilton and Congress had made the dollar a convertible currency based on gold and silver, like the leading European currencies. Therefore, dollar-denominated securities had an implicit exchange clause or specie-convertibility guarantee.

A second innovation that made U.S. financial assets appeal to foreign investors was the making of arrangements with foreign banks and bankers to make interest payments on U.S. debt and dividend payments on shares of the Bank of the United States in foreign financial centers. Thus, U.S. assets were foreign-investor-friendly. Foreign investors likely were further encouraged to buy U.S. assets because they knew there were active markets for these assets in the United States. In contrast with many later emerging market nations, the main markets for American securities were always in the United States, not in foreign financial centers.[6]

The concern of the U.S. with making its national debt from the start an attractive asset for foreign investors was rewarded in many ways.

[4] H. C. Syrett, ed., Papers of Alexander Hamilton, vol. X, p. 276.
[5] See Richard Sylla, Jack W. Wilson and Robert E. Wright, "Integration of Trans-Atlantic Capital Markets, 1790-1845," Review of Finance 10, no. 4 (2006), 613-44.
[6] Ibid., 616-20.

One of the most significant was the Louisiana Purchase in 1803. In return for paying Bonaparte's France with $11.25 million of newly issued 6% bonds with a 15-year maturity and assuming $3.75 million of private American claims against France for cargo and ship seizures during the quasi-war of 1798-1800, the U.S. doubled the size of the country. France accepted the deal because the securities, the Louisiana 6s of 1803, had a ready market in Europe. The bonds were easily placed by Barings and Hopes, European investment banks, with investors in England and the Netherlands. While Jefferson sent Lewis and Clark to explore the new U.S. territorial acquisition, Bonaparte expended funds largely furnished by British investors to pursue his wars against Britain and other European countries. Such stories are what make financial history so interesting.

3. Paying Off the National Debt

Although Hamilton regarded a national debt as potentially a national blessing because it would lay the groundwork for a modern financial system and help to attract foreign capital to the U.S., most national policymakers after him thought differently. For them, as for Adam Smith, the less debt the better, and best of all would be no national debt at all. Europeans, as noted above, had another idea: debt in the form of perpetuities, requiring only interest payments without any obligation to pay back principal. That idea never caught on in the U.S.

There were several periods of substantial national debt reduction in the 19th and early 20th centuries. Thomas Jefferson (president, 1801-1809), who espoused "a wise and frugal government," and his successor, James Madison (1809-1817) reduced the national debt from $83 million to $45 million between 1801 and 1811. Since foreigners held the major part of the debt, this reversed Hamilton's policy of encouraging capital inflows. It was a popular policy, but the wisdom of it may be doubted. Americans could earn more than the 6% they paid foreign investors for the use of their capital, so why return that capital to them? Moreover, the frugality involved ill prepared the country for the War of 1812, which saw the national debt soar to $127 million in 1815. Penny-wise became pound-foolish.

After 1815, a generally prosperous and rapidly growing economy combined with high tariffs on many imported goods to generate budget surpluses that were used to reduce the national debt to zero by 1835. In this era, most of the debt was owned by Americans. When the federal government paid off the bondholders, they had to find something else to buy. State governments accommodated investor demand by issuing nearly $200 million of securities between 1815 and 1840 to finance so-called internal improvements, that is, transportation and banking projects. To the extent these were good projects, this substitution of state debts for federal debt might have been good for the country. But many of the projects turned out to be bad ones, and no fewer than nine states defaulted on their debts in 1841 and 1842. Paying off the national debt thus may have created a credit boom that ended up in a bust.

The next episode of large-scale debt retirement came after the Civil War. That war increased the national debt from $65 million in 1860 to $2,756 million in 1866. Rapid economic growth again combined with high tariffs on imports to swell federal revenues. There was a federal budget surplus every year from 1866 to 1893, and those surpluses allowed the national debt to be paid down to $961 million by the latter year. Once again, as in the 1820s and 1830s, federal bondholders who were paid off likely invested in other securities such as those of railroads, industrials, and state and local governments. That was probably good for capital formation and economic growth. But—see the next section—it created some monetary problems because the U.S. in the 1860s had come up with an innovative method of backing its currency with federal bonds before shrinking the amounts of those bonds outstanding.

The last episode of federal debt retirement came in the 1920s. During World War I, the national debt soared from $1.2 billion in 1914 to $25.5 billion in 1919. Then budget surpluses every year from 1920 to 1930 allowed the debt to be paid down to $16.2 billion in the latter year. No doubt the buoyancy of U.S. capital markets in the 1920s, and perhaps some of their excesses, was due in part to the federal government returning its budget surpluses to the markets via national debt retirements. The same thing happened in the 1820s and 1830s, and in the 1870s and 1880s.

For the first century and a half of U.S. history, from the 1780s to the 1930s, the prevailing sentiment was that national debt ought to be paid down whenever possible. The debt rose mostly in times of war, and was paid down in times of peace. The driving force, however, was less the sentiment that debts should be paid and more the rapid growth of the U.S. economy which swelled federal revenues, making debt reduction possible. Debt reduction probably added to capital formation, making the country grow even faster than it would have without paying down the national debt. In real terms, more was paid back at low prices in times of peace than was borrowed when prices were high in times of war. But debt reduction may itself have added to financial instabilities by creating credit booms and busts.

4. U.S. Debt as Backing for U.S. currency

The U.S. national debt served as backing for a large part of U.S. currency from the 1860s to the 1930s. Civil War legislation in 1863 and 1864 created the National Banking System and related legislation in 1865 taxed currency issued by state banks out of existence. The U.S. finally had a national currency issued either by the Treasury in the form of U.S. notes (greenbacks) or by national banks in the form of national bank notes. Both were liabilities of the federal government.

National bank notes were printed by the government, but stamped with the names of national banks that to issue notes had to buy government bonds and deposit them with a federal office, the Comptroller of the Currency, as collateral backing the notes. Then, if a bank failed, the holders of its notes would suffer no loss because the collateral would be liquidated and the proceeds would be used to pay off the note holders.

In principle, this was a good system for making the paper currency of the country safer than it had been when it was issued by thousands of independent banks before 1863. In fact, it was copied (although soon abandoned) by other countries such as Japan and Argentina. In the U.S., however, the policy of backing national bank notes with government bonds clashed with the policy of redeeming the national debt, which reduced the amount of collateral available for banks to purchase to back their currency issues. By the late 19th and early 20th centuries, the problem was described as an "inelastic" currency, a currency that did not expand and contract along with the needs of trade.

After the financial panic of 1907, which, among other things, featured a shortage or scarcity of currency, the problem of an inelastic currency was solved by the creation of the Federal Reserve System. The Fed could issue currency backed by general assets, which included so-called eligible paper (short-term private liabilities) as well as government debt. National bank notes continued to be issued into the 1930s. The Fed evolved by the 1960s to become the sole issuer of U.S. paper currency, replacing Treasury as well as national bank issues.

5. The Modern Treasury Debt Market

Kenneth Garbade's recent book, Birth of a Market, demonstrates that investor-friendly U.S. debt management policies that began with Alexander Hamilton in the early 1790s have continued in the 20th and early 21st centuries. He refers to "four pillars of the modern Treasury market," three of which emerged during the period 1914-1939 that he studied.[7] They are:

a) The Treasury Tax and Loan (TTL) system, which began in World War I with the establishment of War Loan Deposit Accounts. This system mitigates the potential adverse effects on the banking system and money markets that might arise from sudden, large payments into the Treasury. It works by creating a large network of financial institutions that receive tax and loan payments before they are called for by the Treasury.

b) Regular and predictable offerings and issuances of securities. These began during the 1920s when budget surpluses (see section 3 above) were channeled into debt reduction in an orderly way featuring early retirements, exchange offerings, cash redemptions, and regular quarterly refinancing. It continued in

---

[7] Kenneth Garbade, Birth of a Market: The U.S. Treasury Securities Market from the Great War to the Great Depression (Cambridge, Massachusetts: The MIT Press, 2012).

the 1930s when budget surpluses were replaced by a need to finance deficits and manage a growing debt. In the 1920s and 1930s, the Treasury also learned to tailor its offerings to a wide spectrum of market participants.

c) Auction offerings. Before 1914, the Treasury sold bonds by auction to finance projects such as the Spanish American War and the Panama Canal. But the national debt was small then, and banks—professional investors—were the main purchasers. In World War I, auctions were abandoned in favor of fixed-price offerings because the goal was to attract a wide range of buyers to a much larger Treasury market, and some of these buyers were afraid to purchase Treasury debt at auctions. Auctions came back beginning in 1929, when Treasury bills were first issued. By the late 1930s, Treasury bills were auctioned weekly, leading to a highly liquid short-term money market. By the 1970s, regular and predictable auctions were extended to Treasury notes and bonds.

The fourth pillar of the modern Treasury debt market, the book-entry system, arrived in the late 1960s. It took advantage of modern computer and information technologies to reduce much of the paper and paperwork of earlier systems of debt management.

Since the 1960s, the Treasury has taken or is considering more moves to tailor its offerings to the needs of a variety of potential purchasers of U.S. debt. TIPS (Treasury Inflation Protected Securities) arrived in the late 1990s. TIPS offer inflation protection by increasing the par value of securities by the annual rate of inflation. They have the additional advantage of providing a market-based estimate of investor expectations of inflation, which is the difference between the yields of non-inflation-protected and inflation-protected Treasury securities of the same maturity. This is useful because, as some have argued, the modern equivalent of the old gold standard is the careful management of inflation expectations by the central bank, the Fed.

In 2012, the Treasury has considered, but has not yet implemented, issuance of floating rate debt. The advantage for the Treasury of such a debt instrument is that it would lengthen the maturity of the national debt and reduce the need of the Treasury to come to the market as frequently and in the amounts it now has to do in its refinancing operations. Similarly, investors in such an instrument might be willing to purchase securities with, say, a two-year maturity instead of rolling over Treasury bills every three months.

The modern debt ceiling, an increase of which caused so much consternation in 2011, actually was introduced in 1939 as a measure to increase the latitude of the Treasury in managing the U.S. debt. Prior to 1939, Congress had established limits on the amounts of particular types of securities that could be issued by the Treasury, and limits on the amounts of particular types of securities that could be outstanding at any time. By introducing a ceiling on the overall amount of debt that could be issued, Congress reduced, even eliminated, previous constraints upon Treasury officials in deciding what types and amounts of securities to issue.

6. Conclusion

From Hamilton's time to the present, the U.S. national debt has been viewed as much more than a means to finance the government beyond the means offered by taxation and money printing. By creating a class of creditors dependent on the federal government for debt payments, it became a cement of the American union of states. It was a currency that could be used to pay for shares in the first central bank as well as for the purchase of the Louisiana territory. It attracted foreign capital to an initially capital-poor nation. It furnished an outlet to return federal budget surpluses to the nation's capital markets. It was used to back currency issues of national banks. It could be tailored to provide investors with appealing types of assets, to their own and the government's advantage.

In our own time, the U.S. debt is once again held widely around the world. Perhaps it could become a cement of the world economy, as it once was a cement of the American union. Such an outcome depends, however, on whether it is managed as carefully and creatively as it was during the first two centuries of U.S. history.

2
A World Without Treasuries?

William W. Bratton

Treasuries supply the risk free rate of return on which the valuation of all other assets builds. They accordingly are joined at the hip with corporate finance. What would we do without them? We would greatly suffer, said Timothy Geithner in a 2011 letter to Congressional leaders concerning the absolute necessity of raising the debt ceiling:

> A default would impose a substantial tax on all Americans. Because Treasuries represent the benchmark borrowing rate for all other sectors, default would raise all borrowing costs. Interest rates for state and local government, corporate and consumer borrowing, including home mortgage interest, would all rise sharply. Equity prices and home values would decline, reducing retirement savings and hurting the economic security of all Americans, leading to reductions in spending and investment, which would cause job losses and business failures on a significant scale.

A question arises regarding the accuracy of the Secretary's prediction. The question has been addressed before, but on an upside fact pattern. Between 1998 and 2000, an expanding economy combined with governmental fiscal responsibility caused a temporary decline in Treasury debt stock. By 2000 it was thought possible, if not probable, that the entire public Treasury stock could disappear in five or ten years. Actors in the government and in financial markets focused closely on the expected costs of a treasury-less world. Their projections bear on the present discussion.

Treasuries in Asset Pricing

Let us look first at asset pricing. Recall that under the capital asset pricing model, the expected return on an asset equals the risk free rate of return plus the return on the market times a volatility factor called beta. The model is theoretically parsimonious but surprisingly indeterminate as regards real world application. Most of the discussion goes to the robustness of beta as a risk measure. Let us put that to one side and go to the easier parts of the model. There are problems even there. The return on the market is a past return and so can be derived empirically. But there is no generally accepted calculus. Some use a geometric average, others use an arithmetic average. Terms of years also vary. Most use a 30 year past period, but others use shorter terms.

Current Treasury rates fill in the risk free return component. But there is variance in the practice even here. Most use a current short term bill rate. But some use a 30 year bond. Some use a blended rate of bills, notes, and bonds. Depending on yields, the choice among bills, notes, and bonds could mean a 100 or 200 basis point difference in a discount rate, and a huge difference at the bottom line of a real world valuation.

The point is that Treasuries' place in asset pricing is not quite as clear cut as first appears, even assuming that Treasuries really are risk free, which of course they are not. Once we fold in inflation and rate risk, Treasuries emerge as the most workable proxy for a risk free rate. If one adds liquidity risk and extraordinary conditions, they become problematic. That is one of the reasons why stories from the period 1998 to 2000 are interesting.

Economists who confronted the question as to what would happen if budget surpluses caused Treasuries to disappear answered that we would go from a close to complete asset market to a more incomplete one with a consequent welfare loss. Portfolio theory tells us that any combination of risk and return can be yielded in efficient portfolios that combine risk free Treasuries with risky assets. Without a risk free investment, the set of efficient choices shrinks, and large numbers of risk averse investors are put to less favorable risk-return tradeoffs and lower utility.

Antulio Bomfin, an economist at the Federal Reserve Board, conducted an empirical experiment to the end of quantifying the loss. (Antulio N. Bomfim, Optimal Portfolio Allocation in a World Without Treasury Securities, Working Paper 2001-11, FRB Finance and Economics Discussion Series.) He took actual recent returns and standard deviations from portfolios of six asset classes, including Treasuries (modeled as risky due to inflation and rate risk), and compared risks and returns available through portfolios containing Treasuries to risk and return combinations available without Treasuries. Taking out the Treasuries implied notable sacrifices: to get a 10 percent return with Treasuries was to accept a standard deviation of 9 ½; to get the same 10 percent in a Treasury-less world was to accept a standard deviation of 12 ½.

The experiment was assumption-laden, however. Two other FRB economists conducted a different experiment with existing portfolio return data and came up with less alarming results. (Vincent Reinhart & Brian Sack, The Economic Consequences of Disappearing Government Debt, Brookings Papers on Economic Activity, Vol. 2000, No. 2 (2000), pp. 163-220.) They assumed that corporate bonds would crowd in to replace the Treasury stock and held risk aversion constant. There resulted a claim that it would take only a six basis point increase in corporate yields to entice all investors to shift out of Treasuries and into corporates. However, as regarded other assets, including foreign government debt, yield increases would have had to be more substantial. And, unfortunately, liquidity was assumed away, and liquidity was the main problem so far as most people were concerned. The authors, confronting the bottom-line question whether an investment class completely lacking in default risk has some unique value, were left to suggest that progress in financial engineering could conceivably take up the slack and complete the markets in a world without Treasuries.

Treasuries in Debt and Money Markets

The question whether the markets could find a substitute investment to play Treasuries' unique role takes us to the main body of concern in the year 2000, which was not the role of Treasuries in asset pricing generally but their more particular functions in the debt and money markets.

Treasuries perform a bundle of significant functions in the markets: (1) They benchmark pricing and quotation in the bond markets; (2) they provide a key component of global bond indices used by money managers; (3) they are major instruments for hedging fixed -income positions in the U.S. dollar and in international markets; (4) they serve as collateral for financial transactions and (5) they are a primary tool in bank liquidity management.

Treasuries' minimal credit risk figures importantly in this functional picture, but financial markets and institutions also rely on Treasuries' deep, transparent, and cheap market structure along with the dense and broad yield curve they produce. Because, in normal markets, treasury prices change in response to public information, they provide a benchmark that allows the credit risk of other debt obligations to be distinguished from interest rate fluctuations. In normal times, there is also a high correlation between Treasury yields and private yields, which makes them useful for hedging. And as regards liquidity management, Treasuries provide a good substitute for deposits because they are auctioned every week with a very narrow bid-ask spread.

A combination of factors caused Treasuries to lose some of these reliable characteristics during the years in question.

Recall that 1998 saw a flight to quality triggered by a Russian debt default and then further stoked by the collapse of Long Term Capital Management. No sooner had those shocks worked their way through the system, than a further shock emanated from the Treasury Department itself. It decided, in view of its declining debt stock, to buy back long term Treasury bonds in order keep open room for Treasury bill issuance. Treasury yields quickly declined due to the step up in market demand even as corporate yields stayed more or less constant. Spreads widened. Liquidity declined, resulting in substantial haircuts in the repo market for some issues. Finally, increased demand for longer issues resulting from the Treasury Department's market intervention caused yields across different maturities first to flatten and ultimately to invert.

The shocks made Treasuries less reliable and more expensive, even as the Treasury market remained unmatched for liquidity.

Other issuers entered, offering substitutes. The agencies issued large amounts of long term noncallable bonds—Fannie Mae had Benchmark Notes in a 2 to 10 year range, Freddie Mac had Reference Notes, the FHL had a Tap Issuance Program. The agencies expanded their programs, adding callable notes, longer term notes, all issued in scheduled auctions. Fannie and Freddie eventually started weekly bill auctions. The market for these substitutes grew to around one-third the size of the Treasury market and bid-ask spreads on the substitutes narrowed. Ford Motor Credit and GMAC also entered, with more limited programs. The Fed Open Market Committee gave the Federal Reserve Bank of New York temporary authority to accept agency securities at the window and the commentators suggested that a more fundamental rethinking of open market policy was in order.

The substitute market seemed to be approaching functional equivalence to the Treasury market even as the substitutes' liquidity never matched that of Treasuries.

Here was the unavoidable question: Treasuries clearly served a public function as reliable near-monies and safe havens; could private securities substitute without sacrificing a part of the efficiency gains of modern finance? Two views circulated.

Some took the position that the substitutes would suffice. As regards Treasuries' benchmark role, the private debt markets already priced new issues by reference to the prices of existing private substitutes. The markets would manage. The repo markets already were accepting the substitute agency issues as collateral along with high grade corporates. On the other hand, it was expected that long term portfolio managers at pension funds and insurers would have a harder time finding a substitute. They were already shifting in more corporates, but were not happy about it. So they sent out the Bond Market Association to lobby in Washington with the suggestion that the Treasury should go right on issuing the 30 year bond, whether or not the government needed to borrow any money. As for the hedging function of Treasuries, it was thought that the swap market would be the substitute. Stepped up volume would mean more liquidity there. Of course, there was counterparty risk to worry about. But didn't the big market makers set up special AAA subsidiaries?

Finally, there was the shock absorber function. Some questioned whether we really needed the safe haven in bad times, suggesting that the flight to quality is itself distortionary and caused larger swings in the value of riskier assets than otherwise would be the case. Yes, Treasuries had been the anchor security for a broad range of financial activity. But the markets would adapt by shifting the anchor. Agency debt, high grade corporates, and bank liabilities would substitute.

To go back and look at these arguments today is to get the sense that those who made them thought of the projected shift of the anchor as a species of privatization—markets would be better off when weaned off their dependence on government borrowing. With the benefit of hindsight, we can see that privatization was not in the cards. If one removes high-grade corporate bonds from the list of substitutes, the remaining alternatives all derived their credibility from either the agencies' implicit federal guaranty or too big to fail assumptions respecting large financials.

The opposite view was that there are no substitutes for Treasuries in periods of stress. Actors in markets take risks on the assumption that Treasuries are there in the event they ever need to shed risk, and the U.S. government needed to take these market benefits into account in setting fiscal policy.

Conclusion

At the bottom line, and with the benefit of hindsight, it is pretty clear that the substitutes were inadequate and that the disappearance of Treasuries implicated a utility sacrifice.

3
Default and the International Role of the Dollar

Richard J. Herring[1]

The dollar plays a special role in world financial markets, the financing of world trade, and the provision of international foreign exchange reserves. For the moment, this role is unique and requires special consideration in analyzing motivations for and the consequences of any default on official dollar debt. I will begin with some general observations about the kinds of default and the differences between countries that are able to issue foreign debt denominated in their own currencies and those that cannot.

It is useful to distinguish between two kinds of default: a "hard default" and a "soft default." A hard default means that a country has missed or delayed the disbursement of a contractual interest or principal due past the contractual grace period (if any). Alternatively, it may have negotiated a distressed exchange in which the government offers creditors new or restructured debt that amounts to a lower present value than the original contractual payment or the creditor may have changed laws to reduce the value of debt to foreigners. Often, to obscure the accounting consequences for creditors, negotiated exchanges are designed to keep the nominal principal value con-

---

[1] I am grateful to Tina Horowitz for proofreading, Christopher Trollen for graphic design and Dominic Waltz for research assistance. None, of course, should be implicated in the errors that remain.

stant and simply reduce the interest payments due or extend principal repayments far into the future. So long as reporting conventions permit creditors to conceal the present value of their claims, this can soften the perceived blow on creditors, while giving the borrower the relief that it needs.

A soft default, in contrast, occurs when the borrower honors the terms of the contract, but reduces the present value of the creditors' claims by an unexpected burst of inflation, which may well be accompanied by a sharp depreciation of the exchange rate. So long as most of the debt has been contracted at fixed rates and has a reasonably long duration, this will provide the debtor with relief without setting off the legal sanctions that would permit debtors to take action to enforce their claims. These sanctions are of limited value with regard to sovereign debt because no international court has the power to enforce them.

The main motive for a sovereign debtor to honor its debts is the desire to continue borrowing. As Figure 1 shows, very few advanced industrial countries have issued substantial amounts of debt to foreign creditors; and, of those that have done so, only the United States, Canada, Britain and Japan have been able to denominate claims primarily in their own currency. Although many other advanced industrial countries have placed a higher proportion of their official debt with foreign creditors, most of these countries are members of the euro area and thus cannot issue their own currency. They must rely on decisions of the European Central Bank.

Sovereigns seldom choose a hard default if they have been able to issue a significant amount of debt to foreigners denominated in their own currency. The reason is obvious: they can almost always print enough domestic currency to service their debts in a timely manner. This avoids the legal consequences – which, although not usually enforceable in court, can amount to the threat of perpetual legal harassment in which any financial or physical asset that reaches a creditor-friendly country may be tied up in court proceedings. In practical terms, this constrains the ability of the defaulting debtor to engage in international trade under normal terms and its ability to participate in the global financial system. For most sovereigns, the ability to repay is seldom in question. Sovereigns can almost always sell sufficient assets to service their debts. While this may be technically possible, however, political constraints often limit or even prevent consideration of this option. But for sovereigns that have been able to issue claims in their own currency, the ability to print money avoids the politically-charged issue of selling assets to foreigners. Exceptions occur mainly when a new regime wishes to repudiate the obligations of the previous regime, which may involve the issuance of a new currency. Alternatively, countries that are especially inflation averse – often because they have experienced the pain of a hyper-inflation – may prefer the consequences of a default to those of increased inflation. Moody's (2011), in a survey of sovereign defaults from 1983 to 2010, notes only three defaults on domestic currency-denominated debt.[2] Of these, only the Russian default in August 1998 fits this mold. The Russians preferred the consequences of a hard default to the possibility of yet another bout of hyperinflation.

Figure 1: Vulnerability to foreign holdings of debt depends on whether denominated in a foreign currency or own currency

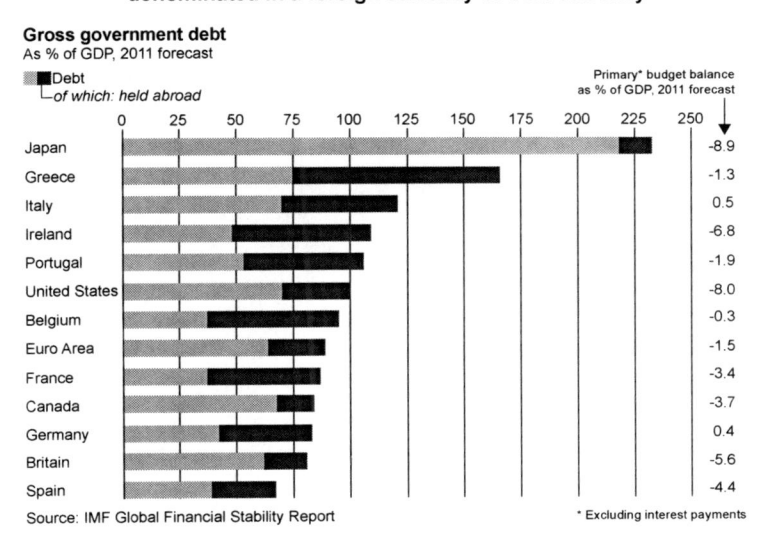

Gross government debt
As % of GDP, 2011 forecast

Country	Primary* budget balance as % of GDP, 2011 forecast
Japan	-8.9
Greece	-1.3
Italy	0.5
Ireland	-6.8
Portugal	-1.9
United States	-8.0
Belgium	-0.3
Euro Area	-1.5
France	-3.4
Canada	-3.7
Germany	0.4
Britain	-5.6
Spain	-4.4

Source: IMF Global Financial Stability Report   * Excluding interest payments

---

2 Historically, hard defaults on domestic currency debt have been much more common. Reinhart and Rogoff (2008) have identified sixty-eight instances of hard defaults on domestic currency debt since 1800. The mechanisms during these earlier defaults included forcible conversions, reductions in coupon rates, unilateral reductions in principal, and suspension of payments. But this number is small relative to the 250 hard defaults on foreign-currency-denominated debt that occurred over the same period.

The other two examples were entirely different. The first could be termed a default through incompetence. During 1998, Venezuela delayed interest payments by a week (on contracts that did not contain a grace period) simply because a bureaucrat forgot to initiate the payment process. The other default, by Turkey in 1999, was motivated by considerations of equity. The outstanding debt had been incurred at interest rates that reflected expectations of very high inflation rates and, after a successful stabilization program, politicians took the view that the resulting real interest rates were excessive. They imposed a retroactive withholding tax on interest payments that, in principle, maintained the real present value of its debt relative to the terms under which it was originally contracted.

Although defaults on domestic-currency debt have been quite rare over the past thirty years, it would be unwise to ignore the mounting pressures on government balance sheets in many of the largest industrial countries. (See Figure 2 for a stylized balance sheet in present-value terms.) Already many of these countries have substantial amounts of gross debt outstanding, and the net present value of future social expenditures is something few countries are willing to acknowledge fully, in part because pay-as-you go funding for such expenditures is simply not plausible in the face of declining population growth and rising dependency ratios. Defense expenditures are a major concern for only a very few countries, but they are difficult to predict in a multi-polar world where what were once considered isolated regional conflicts can easily have major international consequences. In many countries, the scope for increasing future tax revenues seems limited without distorting incentives to such an extent that it is counterproductive. In others, particularly the United States, the binding constraints are largely political, but no less difficult to resolve in the short to medium term. All countries own significant assets that could be sold, but political constraints are likely to intervene. Balance sheet identities can be fudged, but they cannot be denied. Pressures on government spending must ultimately be resolved by raising taxes, reducing expenditures, selling assets or reducing the value of debt.

Figure 2: Archetypal Government B/S

Assets	Liabilities
• Net present value of future tax revenues	• Net present value of future social expenditures
• Other financial assets such as loans, cash, etc.	• Net present value of future defense expenditures
• Equity holdings such as stakes in bailed out companies or financial institutions	• Gross debt
• Real assets such as land, buildings, military equipment, etc.	• Taxpayer Equity

As EU President Juncker of Luxemburg has wryly observed, politicians know the right thing to do, but they do not know how to do get re-elected if they do it. Thus, governments are likely to issue more debt so long as it can be placed on the market at acceptable terms. Inevitably, at some point, markets will judge new issues of debt to be unsustainable and, having run out of less painful options that could have been taken earlier, governments will be forced to take sharp, painful measures. Understandably, elected governments hope that such unpleasant choices can be deferred to their successors. The key issue then is how much debt will be judged by the markets to be unsustainable and when. This is difficult to answer because it is as much a political consideration as an economic one.

The United States enjoys an extra degree of freedom in this regard because of the international role of the dollar. Although Valery Giscard d'Estaing has described this as an "exorbitant privilege" enjoyed by the United States, this characterization is misleading. No official body decided to confer this "privilege" on the United States.[3] Rather, it was a convenient solution to an international problem that emerged slowly over a long time. It was the result of a number of decisions made independently by a wide variety of institutions, governments and investors.

The reserve currency system arose because the supply of gold could

---

3 Cooper (2009) draws the analogy with the adoption of English as an international language. Rather than being the result of some internationally negotiated agreement, it was the outcome of practice and experience.

not keep up with the needs of the growing world economy. Figure 3 shows that this trend, which began in the 19th century, was well underway by the 1920s. As world trade collapsed in the Great Depression and risk aversion intensified, gold increased in importance, but after World War II, as world trade recovered, gold quickly declined in importance relative to reserve currencies. The pound sterling was the first major reserve currency to emerge, but after World War I, the U.S. dollar began to displace it.

Figure 3: The Reserve Currency System Arose Because the Supply of Gold did not Grow Fast Enough to Support a Growing World Economy

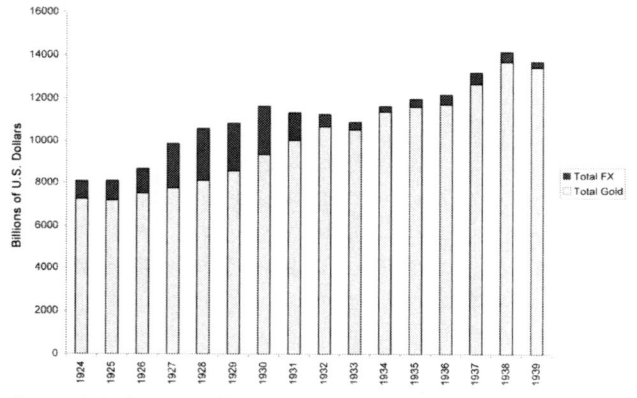

Source: Authors' estimates, based on Nurkse 1944 (gold and foreign exchange reserves pre-1932), Board of Governors of the Federal Reserve System (gold post 1932) and League of Nations *Memoranda on Central Banks* (foreign exchange reserves post 1932).

Source: Eichengreen & Flandreau, "The Rise & Fall of the Dollar or When did the Dollar Replace Sterling as the leading Reserve Currency?"

Figure 4 shows data painstakingly compiled by Eichengreen and Flandreau (2008) that indicate the dollar had surpassed the pound sterling in importance as a reserve currency in the mid-1920s. With the onset of the Great Depression and the Roosevelt Administration's decision to devalue the dollar from $20.67 to $35 per ounce, the dollar's importance as a reserve currency declined both in absolute terms and relative to the pound sterling.[4]

---

[4] The relative strength of the pound sterling in this era was mainly due to the use of the pound sterling within the British Commonwealth. After having abandoned the gold standard at the outbreak of World War I, an attempt was made to reintroduce a version of the gold standard in 1925 at the pre-war peg. This policy, however, was abandoned in September 1931, during the Great Depression.

Figure 4: The Rise & Fall of the $
(or the Power of the British Commonwealth)

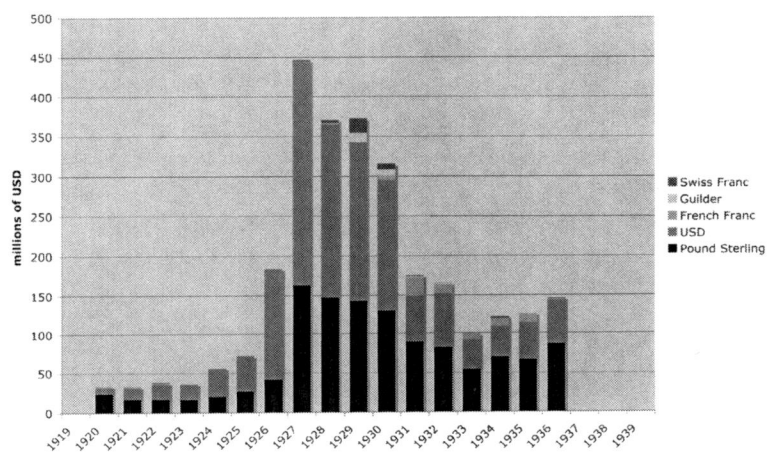

Source: Eichengreen & Flandreau, "The Rise & Fall of the Dollar or When did the Dollar Replace Sterling as the leading Reserve Currency?"

As Figure 5 shows, at $35/ounce, the dollar was not only as good as gold (because U.S. holdings of gold greatly exceeded dollar-denominated liabilities to foreign official institutions), it was unambiguously better than gold. After all, gold bears no yield (other than anticipated capital gains), it consumes storage and safekeeping costs, and it cannot be transformed at low cost into currencies that are useful for intervening in foreign exchange markets. The dollar provided a strong basis for the expansion of the international monetary system until the mid-1960s when foreign official holdings of dollars exceeded the U.S. stock of gold valued at $35/ounce. Several countries – most notably, France and Switzerland – began to redeem dollars for gold and the U.S. began to experience large capital outflows. President Nixon responded, on August 15, 1971, by closing the gold window, refusing to redeem dollar obligations to official institutions with gold. During December 1971, the U.S. increased the official price of gold to $38/ounce and then, during February 1973, to $42.22/ounce. But this was a very odd price: it was the price at which the U.S. would neither buy nor sell gold.

One might have expected that cutting the link between the dollar and gold would have reduced the official demand for dollars as a reserve currency. But that would have completely underestimated the advantages that dollar markets had gained relevant to all possible alternatives.[5] The U.S. offered short-term money markets that were incomparably broader, deeper, and more resilient than any alternative country or currency area. Official institutions could undertake large transactions at low cost, with little fear that their transactions would move prices against them. Equally important, the U.S. was free from the capital controls that constrained most other capital markets throughout the world during the 1970s and the dollar represented a relatively stable store of purchasing power that could be used to buy a broad range of goods and services. Thus, as Figure 6 makes clear, the official demand for dollars as a reserve currency actually accelerated after the "Nixon shocks." The network externalities achieved by the dollar are powerful and, to a certain extent, self-reinforcing.

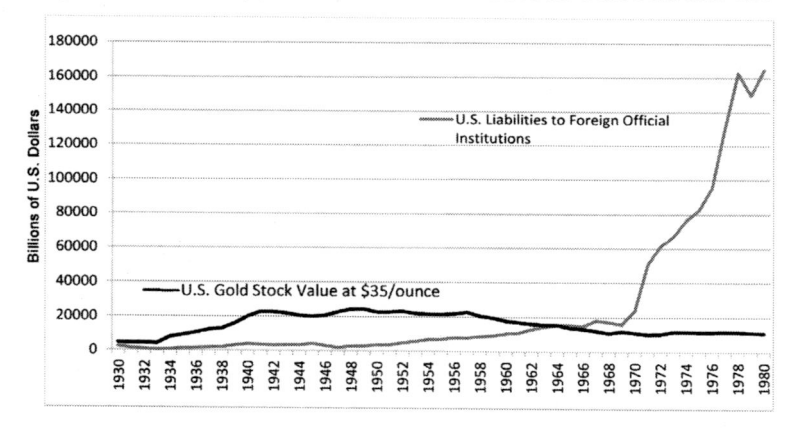

Figure 5: After WWII, $ Has Been Dominant: Good as Gold Until Mid '60s

Nonetheless, many other countries have continued to resent what Jacques Rueff described as "deficits without tears" – the ability of the U.S. to run current account deficits unconstrained by its stock of foreign exchange reserves. This resentment has led to attempts to introduce an artificial currency, the Special Drawing Rights, which might replace the dollar as a way of expanding the reserve base of the international monetary system.

---

5 Similarly, one might have expected the demand for dollars to fall when the rating on government obligations was dropped from AAA by Standard & Poor's. In fact, the inflow of dollars brought short-term rates to new lows.

Figure 6: Demand for Dollar Reserves Soars after Nixon Shock

US Liabilities to Foreign official institutions relative to Gold Stock - 1930-1980

In addition, the Japanese had plans to become a reserve currency – at least for Asian transactions. These plans ran aground, however, because the Japanese found it difficult to generate sufficient current account deficits and, more fundamentally, because of the near collapse of their financial system during the 1990s. Many countries, not least the members of the euro area, had hoped that the introduction of the euro, which provided purchasing power over an even larger array of goods and services than the U.S., would supplant the U.S. dollar as the principal reserve currency. Unfortunately, the euro area failed to develop financial markets that could approach the U.S. in terms of depth, breadth, and resiliency. These qualities are essential to holders of reserve currencies that may wish to make transactions as large as tens of billions of dollars at a time. Indeed, official holdings of the euro barely exceeded the proportion of international reserves that had been held in Deutsche Marks before the formation of the European Currency Union. Of course, the desire for an alternative to the dollar as a reserve currency is quite genuine, and some Europeans thought that the Chinese, in particular, would value the option of maintaining the euro as a viable alternative to the dollar to such an extent that they would be willing to make a large contribution to the European Financial Stability Fund. To a limited extent they were right. The Chinese were willing to contribute, but only if the IMF would bear the credit risk. The desire for an alternative to the dollar is genuine, but not at any price.

What are the actual advantages of "the exorbitant privilege" to the U.S.? First, and most obvious, is seignorage. About $500 billion in U.S. currency is held outside the U.S. (in some cases, one suspects, for nefarious purposes). Almost 70 per cent of $100 dollar notes and 60 per cent of $50 notes and $20 notes are held abroad. This means that foreigners have given up goods and services for dollar-denominated IOUs that offer a zero interest rate. While this benefit is certainly positive, it is by no means of overwhelming importance. If we were to pay a typical short-term rate of interest on these liabilities of, say 4 per cent, the magnitude of the benefit would be only $20 billion/year, a negligible fraction of a roughly $14.5 trillion GDP. The U.S. also benefits to the extent that it earns higher returns than it pays in interest on the borrowed funds that it employs. (Unfortunately, when foreign borrowings are used mainly to finance government deficits, this is a dubious bargain.) Some argue that it has permitted the U.S. to borrow much more relative to its GDP than would otherwise be possible, but this is not self-evident. Australia, for example, has borrowed even more relative to its GDP, but the Australian dollar plays no significant role in foreign exchange reserves. Others would argue that the reserve currency role provides the U.S. with profits and employment advantages for serving as a world financial center for dollar activitys, but the British have demonstrated that it is perfectly possible to retain these advantages without issuing the dominant reserve currency.

Moreover, the role of reserve currency does not come without costs. As provider of the reserve currency, the U.S. must run a passive foreign exchange policy – that is, the foreign exchange value of the dollar is determined by the intervention decisions of other countries. The resulting foreign exchange value of the dollar is probably higher than it might otherwise be, because many countries that intervene in foreign exchange markets prefer to maintain undervalued exchange rates to encourage their export sectors. Moreover, on occasion, the large external holdings of dollars must be factored into monetary policy and bank supervisory decisions – although, to be sure, this does not happen to the extent the rest of the world would prefer.

Most concerns about the reserve currency role of the dollar have focused on China, which has amassed more than $1.5 trillion in U.S.

Government bonds (see Figure 7). This has led to Chinese holdings of U.S. Government Treasury and Agency securities that approach 40% of the outstanding amount. The size and persistence of the imbalances between the U.S. and China, the two largest economies in the world, has led to mutual suspicion and discomfort. On the one hand, the Chinese are deeply ambivalent about their holdings of dollars. They are very concerned with maintaining the purchasing power of their huge stock of dollar assets and resent the pressure that dollar inflows put on their monetary policy, requiring increasingly aggressive measures to sterilize inflows to avoid a higher rate of inflation than they prefer. On the other hand, they are reluctant to let the yuan float because control over the exchange rate has been an important tool of stimulating growth and maintaining high levels of employment.

Figure 7: China has Accumulated huge holdings of US Government Bond

Chinese Holdings* of Treasury Securities

*Includes Chinese + United Kindgom Holdings

In contrast, factions in the U.S. hold two distinctly inconsistent views. One faction fears the potential leverage that might be inherent in such a heavy concentration of claims on the U.S. government held by one foreign government. They fear that a threat to disrupt financial markets might be used by the Chinese to gain political advantage. The other faction is concerned that the Chinese might suddenly decide to diversify their foreign exchange holdings for economic reasons, with the result that the U.S. might face much higher costs to finance its debt and deficits that it appears politically unable to manage fiscally – at least in the short run.

In my view, both the Chinese and U.S. views are misplaced. Interdependence on this scale tends to align incentives rather than exacerbate differences. Even with the depth, breadth, and resilience of U.S. financial markets, the Chinese would drive rates sharply against themselves if they tried to reallocate a large portion of their portfolio. And the question remains: reallocate to what? At the moment there is no credible alternative foreign currency market to place their funds. Countries with attractive currencies such as Switzerland or Singapore could not possibly absorb the magnitude of inflows, nor would they tolerate the consequent appreciation of their exchange rates. The euro area surely looks less promising as a refuge than the U.S. at present and the Chinese are likely to rule out the Japanese yen on a number of grounds.

The history of the pound sterling suggests that reserve currency status need not last forever. Nonetheless, it would take a dramatic shock to the system – much larger than the recent financial crisis – to eliminate the enormous network advantages the U.S. currently enjoys. Of course, a hard dollar default that is not cured immediately could be precisely that sort of shock. Although the benefits of issuing the predominant international reserve currency may not be overwhelmingly large, the costs of suddenly abandoning that role would have systemic consequences not only for the U.S., but equally for the rest of the world.

What other currency might ultimately challenge the dollar in its reserve currency role? The Chinese government is taking the first steps toward enhancing the international role of yuan. China has the natural advantage of an enormous, well-diversified economy, but, to date, the development of their financial markets has substantially lagged behind the development of their economy. In June 2011, however, the Chinese allowed most corporations to pay for imports in yuan. Then 365 Chinese companies were allowed to sell exports for yuan.

During August 2011, this privilege was extended to 67,359 companies. Not surprisingly, foreigners prefer to sell goods and services for yuan rather than to purchase Chinese exports with yuan. (Their presumption is that the yuan will inevitably appreciate relative to most other currencies.) The result is that there is an increasing offshore pool of yuan ('redbacks') held mainly in Hong Kong. A nascent offshore market in yuan-denominated bonds has emerged (the dim sum market) based mainly in Hong Kong, but with recent issues in London.

Nonetheless, all of this activity is far short of what would be required to launch the yuan as a major reserve currency. To do so, China would need to end its policies of financial repression and capital account controls – which have been important tools to sterilize reserve inflows and manage the economy. China would also need to give up setting its exchange rate, which has been a key policy tool, and permit itself to run sizeable current account deficits to accommodate the reserve currency demand for the yuan. This agenda is not impossible. Indeed, it would probably be in the best interests of China's citizens. But the difficulty in moving from China's current financial system to the open financial system necessary to sustain a reserve currency should not be underestimated. The measures necessary to open domestic capital markets might, indeed, undermine the current political structure.

What can be concluded from the preceding observations? First, if the U.S. should default on its obligations it is likely to be a soft default, not a hard default. The main risk that should concern foreign holders of dollars is the risk of diminished purchasing power that is not compensated for by higher nominal interest rates. Second, although the reserve currency role of the dollar is not overwhelmingly valuable, it cannot be renounced without global systemic impact. Third, in view of the substantial network advantages that the dollar has achieved, the loss of its role as the principal reserve currency would occur only if a viable substitute emerges slowly over time, or in the aftermath of a truly major shock such as a hard default on dollar obligations.

References

Casciani, Dominic, 2010, "Why criminals love the 500 euro note," BBC News http://news.bbc.co.uk/2/hi/8678979.stm.

Cooper, Richard N., 2009, "The Future of the Dollar," Policy Brief, Peterson Institute for International Economics, September.

Eichengreen, Barry and Marc Flandreau, 2008, "The Rise and Fall of the Dollar, or When did the Dollar Replace Sterling as the Leading Reserve Currency?" paper prepared for a conference in honor of Peter Temin, Cambridge, May 9.

Moody's Investors Service, 2011, "Sovereign Default and Recovery Rates, 1983-2010," May 10.

Reinhart, Carmen and Kenneth S. Rogoff, 2008, "The Forgotten History of Domestic Debt," Working Paper 13946, http://www.nber.org/papers/w13946.

4
A Macro View of Shadow Banking: Do T-Bill Shortages Pose a New Triffin Dilemma?

Zoltan Pozsar

The public safety net that has been embracing the U.S. banking system since the early 1900s has been tailored to retail cash investors, or depositors. The safety net made deposits "sticky" and the banking system less prone to runs. Institutional cash investors were not meant to benefit from this safety net, however. This was fine until the aggregate volume of cash balances managed by institutional cash investors grew to a size where runs by them could be destabilizing.

At its core, the U.S. financial crisis of 2007-09 was much more than a subprime mortgage crisis. It revealed the Achilles heel of the dollar-based international monetary system: namely, that for institutional investors the world over, the bulk of short-term dollar balances represent uninsured private claims on banks. In other words, prior to the crisis the dollar-based international monetary system was an uninsured private system, without any official backstops.

Of the funding base of the entire system, only "onshore" U.S. retail depositors were insured and everyone else was uninsured, effectively still living under conditions that existed before the creation of the Federal Reserve System and the FDIC. The financial crisis of 2007-09 was a crisis of the dollar-based international monetary system. The crisis brought to the fore fundamental questions about the ultimate reserve asset and the meaning of "cash" for institutional investors.

The answers to these questions underscore that U.S. sovereign debt is indeed different.

Banks' funding base is often assumed to consist mainly of retail cash investors, or depositors, and interbank loans. This was the case decades ago, but no longer. In recent decades, banks have been increasingly relying on institutional cash investors for funding. The rise of institutional cash investors as funding providers explains the rise of what is referred to as wholesale funding.

The aggregate volume of dollar-denominated institutional cash balances peaked at roughly $3.5 trillion prior to the financial crisis, compared to the volume of about $6 trillion in insured household deposits. In 1990, these figures were $100 billion and $3 trillion, respectively. Thus, at a macro level, the U.S. financial system's funding base has gone from nearly 100% government-insured and hence stable deposits to one where the sources of funding were roughly 2/3rd insured and stable and 1/3rd uninsured and instable. And the larger wholesale funding got as a share of the banking system's total funding base, the less effective the traditional banks' safety net was as a source of stability during systemic crises and during runs. Institutional cash investors effectively lived under 1907-like conditions prior to the crisis, without a safety net.

Institutional cash investors fall into three categories: (1) foreign official reserve managers; (2) global nonfinancial corporations; and (3) the asset management complex. Since the 1990s, all three categories have seen a dramatic increase in their volume of cash under management.

First, foreign official reserves have grown as Chinese and other Asian reserve managers pegged their currencies to the dollar as a part of their export-oriented, mercantilist policies. Second, global corporations, forming an integral cog of Asia's mercantilist policies, shifted their manufacturing activities to low-cost economies. Meanwhile their consumer base in developed markets embarked on a debt-fueled consumption boom. These dynamics drove a secular expansion in corporate profits, and led to the emergence of large, global corporations as net funding providers in the financial ecosystem. Third, given the problem of underfunded pensions and paltry returns before the crisis, real money accounts allocated an ever larger share of their portfolios to levered investment strategies. This drove the secular expansion of the hedge fund complex as providers of levered investment returns. Hedge funds' long-short equity, fixed income arbitrage and derivatives-based investment strategies drove an expansion in securities lending, securities financing and risk intermediation, respectively, each of which raised the cash intensity of the system for collateral and liquidity management purposes (see Pozsar, 2010).

Institutional cash investors' cash balances—or institutional cash pools—are very large. Just before the financial crisis, they averaged $400 billion for official accounts, over $75 billion for securities lenders, $50 billion for asset managers, and $25 billion for the most cash-rich of global corporations. These average sizes were far above pre-crisis deposit insurance limits of $100,000.

Institutional cash investors were challenged in trying to place their funds into safe, short-term liquid instruments or in instruments that offer guaranteed liquidity on demand and at par. They had three basic types of instruments to choose from: (1) government guaranteed instruments; (2) secured, privately guaranteed instruments; and (3) unsecured, unguaranteed instruments. These instruments represent the liabilities of the sovereign, the shadow banking system and traditional banks. Government guaranteed instruments include U.S. Treasury bills, Agency discount notes (or short-term paper issued by the housing GSEs) and insured deposits. Secured, privately guaranteed instruments include repurchase agreements and asset-backed commercial paper issued by broker-dealers and the now defunct SIVs and conduits, respectively. Unsecured instruments were uninsured deposits and commercial paper issued mainly by banks. Institutional cash investors held these instruments either directly or indirectly via money funds.

At a macro level the system was stretched between the two extremes of this product spectrum. Institutional cash investors' demand for government guaranteed instruments was significant. However, the supply of these instruments outpaced demand for them by nearly $2.5 trillion by the summer of 2007 (see Figure 3-1). On the other hand, institutional cash investors had only limited appetite for unsecured, uninsured instruments. The shadow banking system arose to fill the gap between the inelastic (and insufficient) supply of government guaranteed instruments and the inelastic (and limited) demand for unsecured, uninsured instruments via the issuance of secured, privately guaranteed instruments. The security of these instruments came from the collateral backing them and the associated credit, liquidity and par value guarantees were provided by AAA rated banks and insurers. According to this view, the rise of shadow banking was a substitution problem between government guaranteed and privately guaranteed claims.

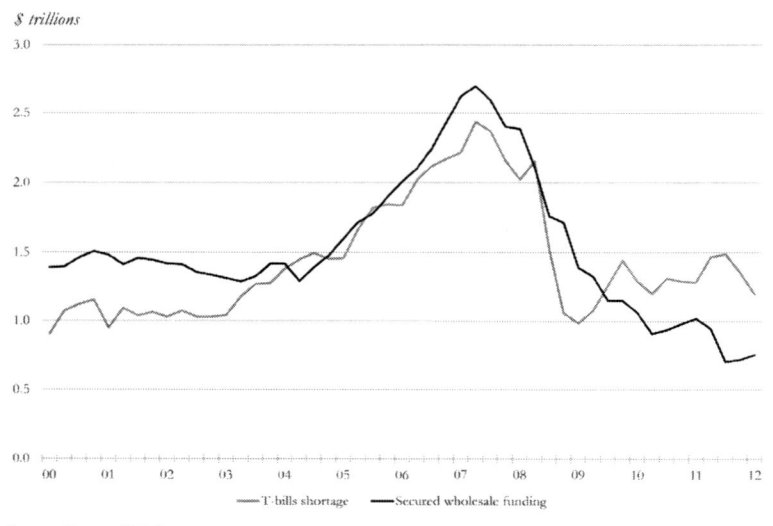

Figure 3-1 Filling the T-bills shortage with secured short-term debt

Source: Pozsar (2011)

Although the supply of shadow bank liabilities looks pro-cyclical, it is misleading to assume that this means wholesale funding itself—or more precisely, demand from institutional providers of wholesale funding for safe, short-term liquid assets supplied by the shadow banking system—was procyclical as well. It wasn't and after a collapse in the supply of shadow banking liabilities, it was absorbed by an increased supply of short-term government debt (in the form of Treasury bills, agency discount notes and increased deposit insurance limits). Taking into account these substitution flows, demand for dollar-denominated safe, short-term, liquid instruments looks stable, similar to the findings of Gorton, Lewellen and Metrick (2012) (see Figure 3-2). Thus, the shadow banking system should not be looked at in a vacuum but in the context of the broader money market which includes banks as well as sovereign issuers of short-term claims.

Figure 3-2 No pro cylicality in the demand for safe, short-term liquid assets

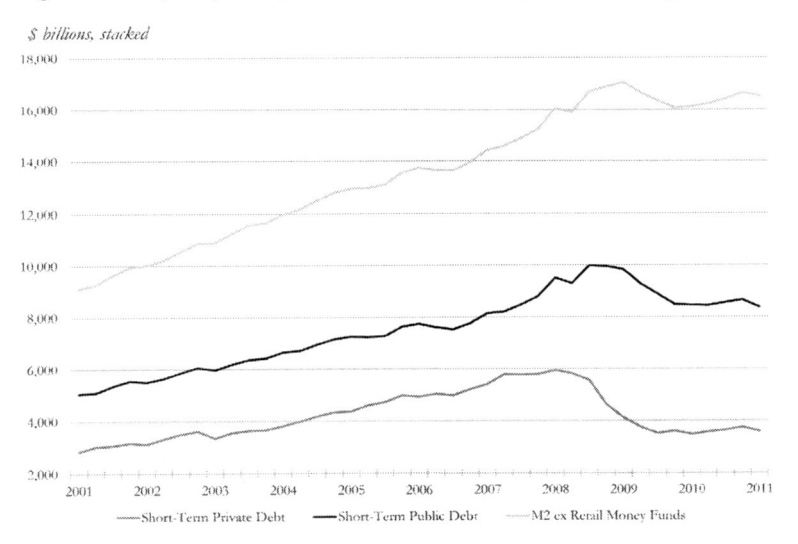

Source: Pozsar (2011)

The extremes of "unlimited" demand for government guaranteed instruments and limited demand for unsecured, uninsured deposits also puts the argument that "search for yield" was the dominant theme behind the rise of shadow banking into perspective. For example, the yield differential between 3 month negotiable CDs (large denomination, that is "institutional-class," uninsured CDs) and other money market instruments is instructive. What this shows is that, prior to the crisis, with the exception of Eurodollar deposits, all other instruments yielded less than CDs. Thus, while liabilities issued by shadow banks - repos and ABCP - yielded more than Treasury bills, they yielded less than uninsured deposits (see Figure 3-3)! Thus, if search for yield would have been the only consideration of investors, the system would all have migrated toward uninsured deposits. However, they did not, since they were constrained by safety concerns and risk management caps set on unsecured counterparty exposures. Therefore, investing in shadow bank liabilities was as much a story of search for yield relative to Treasury bills as it was of the inability to put one's hands on enough T-Bills given its supply constraints.

Figure 3-3 Search for yield with bounds

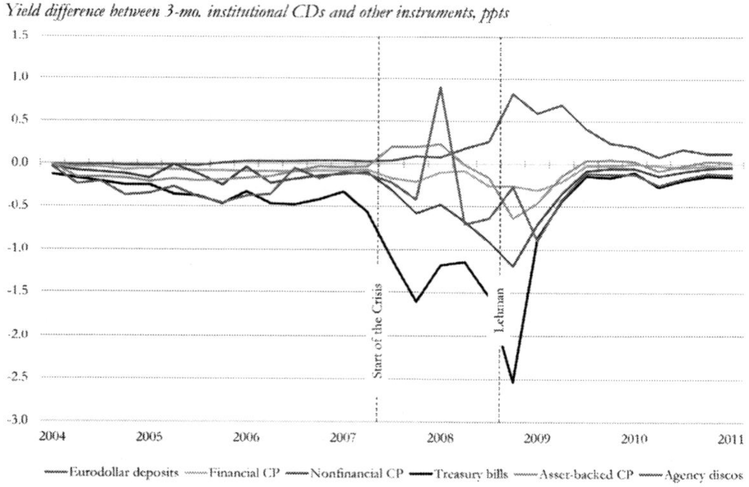

Yield difference between 3-mo. institutional CDs and other instruments, ppts

Source: Pozsar (2011)

The insight that there was a shortage of U.S. Treasury bills to invest in also puts in perspective the fact that the wisest money managers had the wisdom and foresight not to stray too far away from the ultimate safety of Treasury bills (if held directly) or government-only money funds (if held indirectly). Arguments that other managers "should have known their risks better" ignore the fact that, at the system level, given supply-demand balances, everyone would not have been able to invest their cash safely into the ultimately safe asset: U.S. Treasury bills. Of the three types of institutional cash investors, the rise of foreign reserve managers (the most safety conscious and yield inconsiderate of institutional cash investors) was a key reason for the reduction in the amount of U.S. Treasury bills left for private sector cash pools to invest in.

At a macro level, institutional cash investors faced a paradox of safe investing.

Perhaps the most important "macro-monetary" lesson of the crisis is that money creation is either a solely public or a public-private partnership. This observation offers a useful perspective to evaluate the money-ness of the four basic instruments that function as money in today's financial system. These are currency, insured deposits, and government-only and prime money funds. Of these currency is a public liability (issued against public debt by central banks); insured deposits are a public-private liability (issued against private loans and backed by Fed and FDIC backstops); government-only money funds are a private-public liability (issued against government guaranteed instruments (such as Treasury bills, etc.) but with private par and liquidity guarantees by money funds' sponsors); and prime money funds are a "private-private" liability (issued against secured, privately guaranteed instruments as well as unguaranteed instruments, and enhanced with private par and liquidity guarantees by money funds' sponsors).

During the crisis, the first three instruments were sources of stability and the last was a source of instability. From this angle, prime money funds, as purely private forms of money, should not exist as products offering monetary services, or guaranteed liquidity on demand, at par (see Pozsar and McCulley (2011)).

The problem revealed by the crisis was excessive private money-creation in response to an insufficient supply of Treasury bills. This private money creation in turn can be seen as a modern-day Triffin dilemma of the U.S. banking system. Just like the expanding role of the dollar as the international reserve currency came into conflict with the dollar's fixed exchange rate in the 1970s, the rise of institutional cash pools came into conflict with the U.S. banking system's (including its shadow banking sub-system) ability to provide them with guaranteed liquidity on demand and at par without an official backing. As institutional cash pools rose as a share of GDP and federal debt and the supply of U.S. Treasury bills barely changed, the U.S. banking system intermediated an ever larger share of institutional cash pools, trying to issue instruments for them just as safe as Treasury bills. But the more "private bills" they issued, the less safe they became. Just as the dollar's at par convertibility to gold became questionable in the 1970s, so did the convertibility of banks' and shadow banks' instruments on demand and at par.

One simple solution to this problem would be to increase the supply of Treasury bills to "crowd out" from money markets excessive volumes of wholesale funding raised by banks and shadow banks. This would influence the relative size of government-only and prime money funds so that funds would flow more into government-only funds and away from the riskier prime funds.

As others have argued (see Greenwood, Hanson and Stein (2010) and Krishnamurthy and Vissing-Jorgensen (2010)) Treasury bills are like money and are substitutes to bank deposits. In an "electronic" setting - the realm of institutional cash investors - Treasury bills essentially function as money. In fact for some large investors, cash is "U.S. Treasury bills in a segregated custodial account at a clearing bank" – hardly what comes to mind when one thinks of "cash".

The ultimate macro-prudential question around shadow banking is whether it is the banking system that should intermediate institutional cash balances under a strict supervision and regulation of private money creation or whether it is the U.S. Treasury that should intermediate them by issuing more Treasury bills. The latter solution would imply rollover risks from the system migrating from the (shadow) banking system to the balance sheet of the sovereign. That is an externality. However, it is a smaller externality than those associated with levered, uninsured maturity transformation and their flipside of forced sales during crises. In crises, the associated risks end up on the balance sheet of the sovereign anyway. The recognition of the inevitability of such contingent claims under regimes of excessive private money creation points to the benefits of internalizing some of these risks on the balance sheet of the sovereign ex ante.

While increased rollover risks for the sovereign are an externality, they are a less costly and disruptive externality than those associated with the alternative. Proposing that public debt management should incorporate considerations other than minimizing the cost of debt issuance may sound radical but so was the idea (pre-crisis) that central banks should focus on anything other than their inflation target. In the aftermath of the crisis, central banks today have an equally important mandate of focusing on financial stability as well. If Treasury bills are the closest it comes for institutional cash investors to "money" and their shortage leads to an excessive creation of private money claims, perhaps the management of the issuance volume of Treasury bills should be considered as an addition to the macro-prudential toolkit.

References:

Gorton, Gary, Stefan Lewellen, and Andrew Metrick. 2012. "The Safe Asset Share," NBER Working Paper No. 17777.

Greenwood, Robin, Samuel Hanson, and Jeremy Stein. 2010. "A Comparative Advantage Approach to Government Debt Maturity," HBS Working Paper 11-035.

Krishnamurthy, Arvind, and Annette Vissing-Jorgensen. 2010. "The Aggregate Demand for
Treasury Debt," NBER Working Paper No. 12881.

Pozsar, Zoltan, and Paul McCulley, 2011. "Why Banking Works One Large Confidence Trick," Financial Times, December 7, 2011.

———,. 2011. ""Institutional Cash Pools and the Triffin Dilemma of the U.S. Banking System," IMF Working Paper No. 11/190.

———, et al.. 2010. "Shadow Banking," Federal Reserve Bank of New York Staff Report No. 458, July.

5
Origins of the Fiscal Constitution

Michael W. McConnell

Congressional control over spending, taxing, and borrowing lies at the heart of the constitutional structure of the United States. Politicians and scholars who suggest that the President can solve a budget crisis unilaterally by raising the debt limit on his own authority[1] mistake our Constitution for some other. Born of the long constitutional struggle in Britain between Parliament and the King over who would control the purse strings, our Constitution clearly and unambiguously places the power over these matters in the hands of the representatives of the people – not the executive.

It is revealing to compare the history of the relevant clauses in Britain and the United States.

Taxation

Parliamentary control over taxation was the primordial authority that enabled the legislative branch to wrest power from the monarch over the course of centuries, and to become the supreme branch of government. Traditionally, the King had certain sources of revenue at his disposal, without need for parliamentary grant. These came from crown lands and certain ancient prerogative rights. But by the Seven-

---
1 See, e.g., Eric Posner & Adrian Vermeule, Obama Should Raise the Debt Ceiling On His Own, New York Times, July 22, 2012, http://www.nytimes.com/2011/07/22/opinion/22posner.html.

teenth Century they had become wholly inadequate to run a government, and especially to fight wars. Kings therefore had to go, hat in hand, to Parliament to request the grant of additional funds through taxation. This understandably gave Parliament leverage to question royal policy and to attach conditions to the grant of funds. Kings, also understandably, chafed at this interference. Matters came to a head under Charles I, who attempted to revive and expand certain feudal levies, and to imprison those who refused to comply. Many leading citizens resisted, and the affair led ultimately to the Civil War, and to Charles's execution.

American colonists regarded legislative control over taxation as the centerpiece of a free people, hence the revolutionary slogan "No Taxation Without Representation." The first of the Constitution's enumerations of congressional power – Article I, Section 8, Clause 1—confirms that Congress, not the President, has the power to levy taxes. This has ever since been one of the most jealously guarded of Congress's powers. To my knowledge, no one has suggested that President Obama could resolve a budgetary impasse by raising taxes on his own authority.

Spending

Legislative control over spending has a different history. The King had broad prerogative to spend, at least insofar as he had unconditioned sources of revenue. The United States Constitution conspicuously broke from that tradition. Not only did Article I, Section 8, Clause 1 impliedly grant Congress what is called the "Spending Power," but Article I, Section 9, Clause 7 provided that "[n]o money shall be drawn from Treasury, but in Consequence of Appropriations made by Law." This prohibits the executive from spending money without congressional appropriation – even money derived from sources other than taxation. It plugs the loophole that allowed the King to continue to enjoy some spending prerogative even into the modern period. As a matter of practice, however – and in marked contrast to the taxing power – Congress has tended to make appropriations in terms sufficiently general to enable the President to exercise considerable discretion in funding decisions.

Although the Constitution is explicit that the executive may not spend without congressional appropriation, it is less explicit about whether the executive can decline to spend funds that have been appropriated. For most of the nation's history, appropriations statutes were understood as more of a ceiling than a floor. For example, if Congress appropriated a certain sum for building a highway and the highway could be built for less, the executive returned the excess to the Treasury unspent. This discretion not to spend the entire appropriated sum is called "impoundment." Thomas Jefferson, for example, famously refused to spend money Congress appropriated for the purchase of gunboats on the ground that the Louisiana purchase made them unnecessary for their intended purpose of protecting access to the Mississippi. After Richard Nixon used impoundment authority abusively as a policy tool, Congress passed the Impoundment Control Act of 1974, which stripped the executive of this power, except with specific congressional acquiescence. As a technical matter, the President's legal obligation to spend all appropriated funds is best understood as a statutory duty rather than a constitutional mandate. If a President were to spend less than the appropriated amounts, he would be in violation of the Impoundment Control Act, not of the Constitution. That could be significant in a budgetary pinch, because the President's obligation to comply with the Constitution takes precedence over his obligation to comply with statutes.

Borrowing

The borrowing power had yet a different history. Prior to the Glorious Revolution of 1688, the King had unfettered legal authority to borrow funds, and often did so. But the loans were in effect personal to the king; Parliament was under no obligation to pay them back. Kings were notoriously unreliable creditors, and could borrow only at exorbitant rates of interest. Charles II, for example, could borrow money on the Amsterdam markets at about a 15% annual rate, while creditworthy private borrowers could obtain loans for a fraction of that. As part of the constitutional settlement of the Glorious Revolution, Parliament voted to curb the power of the King to borrow. This had the unintended effect of making the public debt backed by the full faith and credit of the nation, because borrowing was now authorized by statute rather than royal whim. This, along with the creation of the Bank of England, and decades of prudent financial management, led to what economic historians call the Financial Revolution. It enabled Britain to borrow vast sums of money at low rates – a critical advantage in the wars against France. It also converted the public debt into a reliable liquid asset, thus expanding the money supply and facilitating Britain's remarkable economic boom. The secret of Alexander Hamilton's financial plan for the new United States was to imitate the Financial Revolution in America.

The Constitution thus contains a clause replicating the Glorious Revolution's settlement of the borrowing question. Article I, Section 8, Clause 2 grants Congress – not the President – the authority "to borrow money on the credit of the United States." Originally, Congress exercised its borrowing power by authorizing each individual bond issue. During World War I, for the first time, Congress delegated discretionary authority to the executive to manage the specifics of the borrowing, within a certain limit, now called the debt ceiling. Congress has raised the limit 92 times since 1940. Often, this has been uncontroversial, but in recent years, when the Presidency and at least one House of Congress are controlled by different parties, the debt ceiling has become a political football. We have reached the crisis point with the ceiling three times: first, in 1985, under a Republican President with a Democratic House; second, in 1995-96, under a Democratic President with a Republican Congress; and now, in 2011, under a Democratic President with a Republican House. I point this out because some partisans like to claim that one or the other party is especially responsible for the brinkmanship. In fact, they behave symmetrically.

The so-called "debt ceiling" is not actually a statutory limitation on the executive's power to borrow. The statute containing the debt ceiling is a grant of authority the President would not otherwise have. When that authority runs out, it is the Constitution that prevents the President from attempting to borrow on the credit of the United States.

Some people wonder what prevents the President from ignoring the debt ceiling and simply borrowing more. Would the courts intervene? Who would have standing? The answer is that the bond markets are the check. Any loan to the government based solely on the President's say-so would not be backed by the full faith and credit of the United States. Indeed, in all likelihood, Treasury funds could not be used to repay any such illegal loans. It is doubtful that such bonds would sell, and if they did, bond traders would demand a significant risk premium to compensate for the lack of legal guarantee of payment. President Obama would find himself like Charles II, paying exorbitant rates of interest for loans not backed by the nation.

The general theme of the United States fiscal constitution is thus easily summarized: The President is powerless to tax, to spend, or to borrow without advance congressional authorization. Dreams of executive unilateralism are just that. Some may regard Congress's negotiating strategy as reckless, and others may regard it as a necessary means of procuring some measure of spending discipline from an unwilling executive, but either way Congress is acting within its constitutional authority. The President has no choice but to work with Congress on the political playing field established by the Constitution.

Default

Is default a constitutional option? Under the original Constitution, the answer is yes. Delegates at the Constitutional Convention debated proposals that would have effectively outlawed default on the public debt, but they were rejected – in favor of a provision, Article VI, which makes the pre-existing debt "as valid against the United States under the Constitution, as under the Confederation." Any wiggle room the United States had to default, it continued to have.

Some say that the Fourteenth Amendment changes all of this. Section Four of the Amendment states: "The validity of the public debt of the United States, authorized by law, including debts incurred for payment of pensions and bounties for services in suppressing insurrection or rebellion, shall not be questioned." This was designed to prevent a southern Democratic majority from repudiating the Civil

War debt. Beyond prohibiting the actual repudiation of the public debt, it is not clear exactly what it means, and how it would be enforced. Default is not the same as repudiation. If Congress repudiated the debt, it would be declaring that the debt is not owed. If Congress defaulted on the debt, the debt would still be owed; it would simply go (in part) unpaid. The Supreme Court has interpreted the provision only once, in *Perry v. United States*[2], the so-called Gold Clause Cases. The Court allowed Congress to renege on its contractual agreement to pay the debt in gold; this is when U.S. public debt became denominated in dollars. Effectively, this means that even if Section Four forbids Congress to declare a formal default, it could accomplish much the same thing by inflating the debt away.

During the debt-ceiling standoff, some commentators suggested that Section Four renders the debt ceiling unconstitutional, on the theory that because the debt ceiling creates the possibility of a default, it is unconstitutional.[3] This is a highly implausible interpretation – even assuming, which is far from clear, that a default would be unconstitutional in some sense. The debt ceiling does not limit the executive's ability to borrow; it is the top end of Congress's past authorization for the executive to borrow. Only Congress can authorize borrowing, and doing so requires an affirmative legislative act. It makes no more sense to say that Congress's decision to cap the amount to borrow is unconstitutional than to say that Congress's decision to cap the rates of taxation is unconstitutional. If anything, the language of Section Four reaffirms that the public debt of the United States is valid only insofar as it is "authorized by law," which means by act of Congress. Any borrowing above the amount authorized by law would not be part of the "valid" public debt.

In any event, hitting the debt ceiling is not the same as default. Even in the unlikely event that the political stand-off were not resolved, the Treasury would have more than enough money in new tax revenue to pay off principal and interest when due, as well as pensions.

---

2 294 U.S. 330 (1935).
3 See, e.g., Garrett Epps, The Speech Obama Could Give: "The Constituion Forbids Default," The Atlantic, April 28, 2011, http://www.theatlantic.com/politics/archive/2011/04/the-speech-obama-could-give-the-constitution-forbids-default/237977/.

(Social Security does not count as a "pension" under Section Four, but Congress has authorized the Treasury to sell notes in the Social Security Trust Fund to pay Social Security claims as they become due. So Social Security payments are not jeopardized by hitting the ceiling.) The practical effect of hitting the ceiling, in my opinion, is that the executive would be forced to prioritize expenditures in order to keep below the limit, by delaying expenditures that are the least urgent. To a certain extent, these delays are authorized under the Impoundment Control Act. But in any event, if Section Four means that a default would be unconstitutional, the only way the President could meet all his constitutional obligations would be to prioritize expenditures. If Section Four has any relevance to the current debate, it means that the President is under a constitutional, as well as a pragmatic, obligation to keep current on interest and principal, rather than continuing other spending with a mere statutory basis. This is what a prudent President would do in any event.

Some have urged that Section Four authorizes the President to borrow above the debt ceiling, in order to prevent default. I do not believe this is correct. The President has no constitutional power to borrow unilaterally, any more than to raise taxes unilaterally. The only latitude he has is to spend less, or more slowly.

Budgets

It is worth noting that the Budget Act of 1974 – passed in conjunction with the Impoundment Control Act – contains provisions that, if followed, would largely eliminate our periodic debt ceiling standoffs. The Act requires first the President, then both Houses of Congress, to pass budget resolutions estimating revenues, expenditures, and expected borrowing needs (including any need to raise the debt ceiling), all many months before the beginning of the fiscal year. These resolutions cannot be filibustered. If adopted, a budget resolution does not have the force of law, but it empowers the majority in Congress to make changes in taxes and spending through a budget reconciliation act, which cannot be filibustered. Unfortunately, in the last several years, the Senate leadership has declined to bring a budget resolution to the floor. This, in no small part, is the underlying cause of the brinkmanship and lack of fiscal prudence that we recently have experienced.

The Budget Act process has four great virtues. First, it forces action months before the fiscal year, thus giving all sides time to come to a resolution. Second, it disciplines congressional appropriations. Without a budget, congressional appropriators all feel free to spend money without taking into account competing fiscal needs (including the need to restrain growth of the public debt). The Budget Act reverses the process, requiring Congress to decide first how much money to spend and how to divide it up among various functional categories, and only then to allow appropriators to determine the details. Third, it provides expedited procedures, including the elimination of filibusters. And fourth, it increases transparency and public accountability. The Act requires public hearings, and "scoring" by the Congressional Budget Office under uniform scoring rules. This forces the various parties to the process to make their budget proposals public. We have seen the political mischief involved when the President and the congressional leadership negotiate in secret, while being able to make vague claims to the public about the contents of their proposals. The electorate cannot know whom to believe, and whom to blame.

Unfortunately, the Budget Act has no enforcement mechanism. The drafters of the Act assumed that congressional leaders would comply with its mandates. For the first quarter century of the Act, that was a correct assumption – budget resolutions were publicly debated and passed on time, and reconciliation bills conformed actual tax levels, spending levels, and borrowing to the budgets. When I was Assistant General Counsel of OMB in the early 1980s, the budget process, with its deadlines, was sacrosanct. But for the last three years, the Senate leadership has simply refused to consider a budget. When the Chair of the Senate Budget Committee, Kent Conrad, announced he would bring the Simpson-Bowles plan to a vote as the Senate budget, the Majority Leader intervened to prevent the vote. This signal piece of reform legislation may well have become a dead letter.

Conclusion

When most people think of the Constitution, they think of its inspiring guarantees of individual rights and its establishment of a framework for republican government based on democratic voting, federalism, and separation of powers. But the framers of the Constitution were no less concerned with establishing a workable fiscal regime, based on legislative control of taxing, spending, and borrowing. The recent debt ceiling stand-off rattled bond markets, but it was nothing new. The more fundamental problem we face is not the debt ceiling, but the sheer immensity of the annual deficit. There is no magic wand that will bring this under control. It will require Congress and the executive to work together with greater prudence and greater attention to the long-run public good.

6
The 2011 Debt Ceiling Impasse Revisited

Howell E. Jackson[1]

In 2011, the federal government came perilously close to reaching the statutory limit on public debt. For the first seven months of the year, the Obama Administration and congressional Republican leaders engaged in an elaborate sequence of press conferences and closed door negotiations. Straightforward measures to increase the public debt ceiling were caught up in partisan politics and larger questions of deficit reduction and fiscal policy. Only on the eve of crisis – on August 2, 2011 – when the federal government was within hours of being unable to pay its bills in a timely manner, did a compromise emerge in the form of the Budget Control Act of 2011, which established a three step process for raising the debt ceiling by at least $2.1 trillion. For the first time in a generation, policy analysts and budget scholars confronted the question of what would happen if political processes had in fact broken down and the debt ceiling had been reached.

---

[1] James S. Reid, Jr., Professor of Law, Harvard Law School. This essay draws on excellent research assistance from Jeremy Kreisberg and Kelley O'Mara, whose Budget Policy Briefing Paper, The 2011 Debt Limit Impasse: Treasury's Actions & the Counterfactual – What Might Have Happened if the National Debt Hit the Statutory Limit (Sept. 4, 2012) appears in Appendix A. Additional Budget Policy Briefing Papers appear at http://www.law.harvard.edu/faculty/hjackson/budget.php.

My goal in this essay is to explore that question. I begin by distinguishing several distinct phases of debt ceiling crises and then explore the dilemma that the Treasury Department would have faced in August 2011 had a compromise not been reached. At that point, the crisis would have transitioned from what I label a Phase One Debt Crisis, when the Executive manipulates federal accounts in what has become a stylized dance of creating additional borrowing capacity while political compromises are forged, into what I term a Phase Two Debt Crisis, when the debt ceiling is reached, no additional accounting shenanigans are available, and the Executive must determine which of the government's bills to pay and which bills to defer. As it turns out, the legal framework of a Phase Two Debt Crisis is not well defined. Though some scholars have suggested that the Public Debt Clause of the Fourteenth Amendment to the U.S. Constitution offers guidance under these circumstances, the constitutional constraints in a Phase Two Debt Crisis are far from clear. Conceivably, statutory provisions governing federal budget procedures may offer some guidance in defining how the Executive should proceed when federal commitments exceed cash on hand and additional borrowing is not authorized. But even these statutory guidelines are only useful by analogy, and ultimately the Executive retains considerable discretion as to the order in which federal obligations are liquidated during a Phase Two Debt Crisis.

The essay concludes with a series of suggestions as to how future Treasury Departments might proceed in the not entirely unimaginable possibility that the United States hits the public debt ceiling (perhaps in the first quarter of 2013) and confronts a genuine Phase Two Debt Crisis for the first time.

Phases of Debt Crisis

Debt crises arise when the federal government approaches the statutory limit on public debt, as it did in the first few months of 2011. When political forces threaten to delay approval for an increase, the Executive typically engages in a series of financial maneuvers designed to buy time to allow negotiations to proceed.[2] These responses are quite similar to what a commercial firm might do in the face of a

---

[2] The legal bases of these maneuvers are described in Part I.B. of Appendix A.

loss in liquidity. First, the Government can draw down its cash balances, as it did in the Spring of 2011 when the Treasury withdrew nearly $200 billion it had on deposit in a Supplementary Financing Account at the Federal Reserve. Second, the Treasury has statutory authority to suspend the issuance of Treasury securities, most importantly to various government retirement accounts, and thereby create an equivalent amount of borrowing headroom for new issuances of debt to the general public. In 2011, this maneuver created on the order of $250 billion of additional debt capacity, which was critical in allowing the government to function from May 16, 2011, until August 2, 2011, when a legislative compromise emerged. Third, the government could, in theory, liquidate assets to raise additional cash. While some outside analysts suggested that the Treasury could sell off gold reserves or student loan portfolios to delay the consequences of hitting the debt ceiling in the Summer of 2011, the Treasury Department chose not to pursue these options.

Financial maneuvering is the defining characteristic of a Phase One Debt Crisis. While in the past, these maneuvers have sometimes been criticized as unlawful, there is now a legal framework for many of the procedures that the Treasury Department employed in 2011. This framework includes express authority for the Treasury to suspend issuance of government securities to specific retirement accounts, as well as a statutory mandate that requires the Treasury to reissue those securities (with interest) once the debt ceiling has been increased. As a functional matter, these procedures convert government commitments to these funds into "exempt obligations" so that the government can obtain a limited amount of additional borrowing capacity until a political compromise can be reached. The obligations are exempt in the sense that they do not count towards the debt ceiling during this interim period, but they remain obligations in that the Executive is expected – indeed in many cases legally required – to restore them once borrowing capacity is restored. The recurring legal question during a Phase One Debt Crisis is how far the Executive can go in using ingenious strategies to create additional debt capacity out of clever manipulation of existing Executive powers. The most creative recommendation of the 2011 crisis was a proposal that the Treasury use its power to mint platinum coins to produce a trillion dollar specimen for deposit at the Federal Reserve. As coins do not count towards the public debt ceiling, this tactic would have produced the mother of all exempt obligations albeit with potentially considerable political repercussions and adverse market reactions.[3]

A Phase Two Debt Crisis begins when Phase One maneuvers run out and the debt ceiling becomes a binding constraint on government activities because the government's projected commitments to pay cash exceed its ability to make those payments. At that point, the implacable logic of cash-flow accounting poses a dilemma for federal fiscal management. In ordinary times, the federal government turns to the capital markets to manage imbalances between cash inflows and expenditures. When the government runs net cash surpluses, it can retire public debt; when it runs net cash outflows, public borrowing fills in the gap. In recent years, federal expenditures have substantially exceeded revenue. August 2011 is illustrative. In that month, the government received cash payments of $186 billion and paid out expenditures of $314 billion. In other words, inflows from sources of revenue covered slightly less than 60 percent of expenditures. The dilemma of a Phase Two debt crisis is devising a cash payment plan under these circumstances when access to public debt markets is precluded.

As Professor McConnell succinctly summarizes in his companion essay (Chapter 5), the complexity of Phase Two Debt Crises is that the Constitution vests the key fiscal powers with Congress: the power to spend, the power to tax, and the power to borrow. A Phase Two Debt Crisis occurs when Congress has exerted those powers into a mathematical inequality: authorized expenditures exceed authorized taxes plus permissible new borrowing. Under these uncomfortable circumstances, the Executive is forced to consider what options (if any) remain open and what discretion (if any) is available for choosing among those options.

A final characteristic of a Phase Two Debt Crisis is that the crisis is presumed to be temporary, to be followed in short order by a political compromise that restores liquidity to the federal government

---

[3] See Appendix A at note 163.

and provides resources for any pending federal obligations that have remained unpaid during the crisis. Though beyond the scope of this essay, one might also envision a Phase Three Debt Crisis when the United States follows the path of Argentina and other sovereign states that have intentionally and permanently defaulted on public obligations. In a Phase Two Debt Crisis, in contrast, the focus is on how best to manage funding shortfalls during an undefined, but presumably limited period, while political solutions are worked out.[4] While the economic and financial implications of a Phase Two Debt Crisis would no doubt be severe, the implications are less profound and legal framework quite different than would be the case with a fully blown Phase Three Debt Crisis.

Potential Executive Responses to a Phase Two Debt Crisis

From the extensive public debates of the Summer of 2011, as well as more limited prior academic writing on the subject, one can distill a variety of different postures that the Executive might take with respect to a Phase Two Debt Crisis. For ease of exegesis, I divide them into Theories of Executive Supremacy and Systems of Spending Prioritization.

A. Theories of Executive Supremacy

Some academic commentators and politicians have suggested that the Executive retains a wide degree of latitude in determining how to proceed in the face of a Phase Two Debt Crisis, including the authority to ignore the debt ceiling altogether. In some formulations, the source of Executive Authority stems from the Public Debt Clause of the Fourteenth Amendment:

> "The validity of the public debt of the United States, authorized by law, including debts incurred for payment of pensions and

---

[4] Thus conceived, Phase Two Debt Crises are similar to Phase One Debt Crises in that the presumption in both is that government obligations will all ultimately be honored. With the Phase Two Debt Crisis, however, the government lacks expressed statutory authority authorizing deferral. As a result, the delay of payment in Phase Two Debt Crises may result in additional legal liability (and costs) for the government beyond the accrual of additional interest. As discussed below, this liability will vary depending on the type of government payment being deferred.

bounties for services in suppressing insurrection or rebellion, shall not be questioned."

Finding strong support for Executive Supremacy in this clause runs into numerous interpretive challenges. First, it is not at all clear that the temporary delay of debt service constitutes questioning of the public debt of the sort that the Public Debt Clause proscribes. More importantly, even if deferred debt service is proscribed, the Executive could simply make those debt payments and forgo other expenditures. In August 2011, total debt service payments could easily have been accommodated within the government's monthly revenues without resort to new borrowings.[5] Finally, more extreme interpretations of the Public Debt Clause – claims that the provision invalidates congressional debt ceilings to the extent the ceiling inhibits the payment of a wide range of pension-like obligations and entitlements – run into what seem to me to be insuperable grammatical and historical difficulties, given that the Clause's reference to pensions and bounties is quite clearly limited to commitments arising out of the Civil War.

Somewhat more plausible arguments for Executive Supremacy proceed from the assumption that the Executive has some degree of inherent authority to decide how to proceed in the face of mutually inconsistent statutory mandates. So, the argument runs, if Congress specifies more spending than can be sustained by authorized taxes and borrowing, the Executive can choose how best to resolve the inequality, including the issuance of sufficient additional public debt to keep payments current. One could resist this assertion of inherent Executive powers, as Professor McConnell does, with the argument that not all fiscal dictates of Congress are equal and that spending provisions should be understood as less binding on the Executive than authorizations to tax or borrow. Or, as I outline below, one could divine from the larger body of statutory structures built into federal budgetary law crude congressional guidelines as to how the Executive is supposed to proceed in Phase Two Debt Crises.

---

5 Between August 2 and August 31, 2011, debt service payments totaled less than $40 billion whereas federal cash inflows were in excess of $186 billion.

While assertions of inherent Executive authority raise deep and unsettled questions of law, I am dubious that Treasury Department officials are likely to resort to these theories to ignore entirely a congressionally imposed debt ceiling in the face of a Phase Two Debt Ceiling crisis. The government officials who manage the public debt and would be required to defend their actions before Congress in the wake of a constitutional confrontation live and work within a system of well-defined rules and external controls. For personnel from the Office of Fiscal Service to invoke vague and untested theories of Executive Supremacy would require a considerable leap of faith into unfamiliar and uncomfortable territory. Moreover, unlike other contexts where the Executive has invoked emergency powers – covert operations and other matters of national security – debt ceiling crises are played out in the public eye and reactions to unilateral Executive action would provoke immediate and hostile responses. Finally, in the face of such controversies, one cannot be at all clear that the capital markets would find palatable the purchase of public debt issued in the absence of express congressional authorization. Whether that debt would be supported by the full faith and credit of the U.S. government and the implications for the secondary market pricing of previously issued government debt are imponderables that would further discourage most Treasury Department officials from venturing too deeply down the rabbit hole of inherent Executive powers.

B. Systems of Spending Prioritization

But if the Executive is unlikely to ignore the debt ceiling completely, how might it go about resolving an imbalance of expenditures and revenues in the face of a Phase Two Debt Crisis? In other words, if the government did lack sufficient cash resources to pay all of its bills as they came due, how might its available cash be allocated? A number of approaches are possible.[6]

1. FIFO and Other Mechanical Approaches

Perhaps the most commonly suggested approach to dealing with a Phase Two Crisis is a mechanical, "First in, First Out (FIFO)" rule, whereby the government simply pays its bills as they are received.

---
6 A more detailed discussion of these possibilities appears in Part II of Appendix A.

This is the approach that the Treasury Department usually (but not invariably) suggested it was going to apply in August 2011 had a compromise not been reached, and it has the bureaucratic advantage of providing a straightforward rule that would be relatively easy to administer.[7] Had the government been forced to follow a FIFO approach in August 2011, it would have been able to pay nearly 60 percent of its obligations over the course of the month and would have had about $127 billlion of unpaid bills pending by month's end, having deferred payment of both debt service (starting on August 2nd) and Social Security payments (starting on August 3rd).

Over the years, there has been debate over whether the government must adopt a FIFO payment plan in a Phase Two Crisis or whether the Treasury has discretion to adopt other systems of prioritization. The Executive has tended to favor the mechanical FIFO rule, both for its relative ease of administration and also for its political virtue of suggesting that congressional failure to raise the debt ceiling necessitates deferring payments across the board, including payments to key constituencies, such as Social Security beneficiaries and members of the armed service. Congressional leaders, in contrast, prefer to characterize the Executive as having greater latitude in prioritizing payment, thereby imposing on the Executive the responsibility (and political costs) of choosing which payments to defer.

While one could imagine other mechanical formulas for prioritizing payments – with pro rata distributions being an alternative method employed in various commercial contexts – FIFO prioritization is the dominant approach advanced in debt ceiling debates and represents something of a presumed default position for Government payments in a Phase Two Debt Crisis.

2. FIFO Informed by the Public Debt Clause

A potentially attractive variant on FIFO would be for the federal government to follow the basic FIFO rule for most payments but to prioritize a subset of expenditures based on special legal standing

---

[7] One complexity of administering even a FIFO prioritization scheme is that the Treasury Department does not actually control 100 percent of federal disbursements. See Appendix A, n. 198, and accompanying text.

of those payments. An obvious place to start would be to prioritize debt service payment in recognition of the privileged status those payments might be said to be entitled under the Public Debt Clause. Some unattributed comments from the Obama Administration in the final days of the 2011 debt crisis suggest that the Treasury may well have prioritized debt service had negotiations with Congress broken down and the debt ceiling been reached. During August of 2011, interest payments on public debt came to $38 billion over the course of the month. Had the Administration chosen to privilege those payments, only $148 billion of revenue would have remained available for other expenditures, implying that only 54 percent of other payments could have been made during that month.[8] Beyond arguable fidelity to the language of the Public Debt Clause, this modified version of FIFO would have advantages of assuaging (to some degree) adverse capital market reactions to a Phase Two Debt Ceiling crisis. Exactly how effective the approach would be in achieving this benefit is, of course, uncertain, and it is possible that non-performance with respect to payment of other obligations would still trigger significant adverse market reactions and could, among other things, constitute a credit event for the sake of credit default swaps on U.S. Treasuries, as well as other less easy to predict adverse consequences.

3. FIFO Informed by Special Authorities with Respect to Social Security Trust Funds

Scattered throughout the U.S. Code are a host of other provisions that might also conceivably be relevant to how the Treasury would administer FIFO payments in a Phase Two Crisis. For example, under 42 U.S.C. § 1320B–15, the Secretary of the Treasury arguably has power to redeem Social Security Trust Fund holdings of government securities in order to fund benefit payments.[9] The redemption

---

[8] This calculation assumes that the Treasury would roll over any principal payments on public debt. Had the government taken a broader interpretation of the Public Debt Clause and also prioritized Social Security and Medicare, the amount of revenue available for other government payments in August of 2011 would have dropped to 34 percent.
[9] The text of the provision reads:
PROTECTION OF SOCIAL SECURITY AND MEDICARE TRUST FUNDS (1996)

of these securities coupled with the issuance of an identical amount of new government securities into the public markets does not implicate the debt ceiling because government debt held by the Trust Funds and publicly held debt both count towards the debt ceiling. If the Secretary were to invoke his discretion to liquidate Trust Fund securities in this way, that might allow the government to stay current on Social Security obligations while treating other expenditures on a FIFO basis and possibly make similar adjustments from the Medicare trust funds, which are also covered by this provision.[10]

4. Discretionary Prioritization

An alternative approach would be for the Executive to make payments on a fully or largely discretionary basis, picking and choosing

> (a) In general. No officer or employee of the United States shall--
> (1) delay the deposit of any amount into (or delay the credit of any amount to) any Federal fund or otherwise vary from the normal terms, procedures, or timing for making such deposits or credits,
> (2) refrain from the investment in public debt obligations of amounts in any Federal fund, or
> (3) redeem prior to maturity amounts in any Federal fund which are invested in public debt obligations for any purpose other than the payment of benefits or administrative expenses from such Federal fund.
> (b) "Public debt obligation" defined. For purposes of this section, the term "public debt obligation" means any obligation subject to the public debt limit established under section 3101 of Title 31.
> (c) "Federal fund" defined. For purposes of this section, the term "Federal fund" means--
> (1) the Federal Old-Age and Survivors Insurance Trust Fund;
> (2) the Federal Disability Insurance Trust Fund;
> (3) the Federal Hospital Insurance Trust Fund; and
> (4) the Federal Supplementary Medical Insurance Trust Fund.

42 U.S.C. § 1320B–15. The provision is only arguably of relevance because the text takes the form of a limitation in subsection (a)(3) on how the proceeds of redeemed securities from the trust funds may be deployed. It is not, on its face, an authorization to redeem securities for this purpose, much less a mandate to do so in the case of a Phase Two Debt Crisis.

10 Exactly how such transactions would affect other government spending depends on how the transactions were structured. If the government were to redeem only enough securities to prevent any delay in entitlement payments, the benefit to other payees would be less than if the government redeemed enough securities to cover the full amount of entitlement spending.

which payments to prioritize as a Phase Two Debt Crisis proceeds. Back in 1985, congressional leaders solicited an opinion of the then-General Accounting Office to the effect that the Executive retains this broad discretionary power, but the opinion contains the most cursory of analysis and is not especially persuasive.[11] For reasons outlined above, Executive personnel would likely be reluctant to assume such discretionary authority since many of the choices to be made will be politically unpalatable and susceptible to public criticism. On the other hand, not all government payments have the same level of urgency, and one could imagine various rules of prioritization that would favor the needy or those payments whose delay might impose substantial subsequent costs on the federal government.[12]

11 See Letter from U.S. Government Accountability Office to Bob Packwood, Chairman, Committee on Finance, United States Senate (Oct. 9, 1985) (available at http://redbook.gao.gov/14/fl0065142.php). The letter, addressed to Senator Packwood states in full: "YOU HAVE REQUESTED OUR VIEWS ON WHETHER THE SECRETARY OF THE TREASURY HAS AUTHORITY TO DETERMINE THE ORDER IN WHICH OBLIGATIONS ARE TO BE PAID SHOULD THE CONGRESS FAIL TO RAISE THE STATUTORY LIMIT ON THE PUBLIC DEBT OR WHETHER TREASURY WOULD BE FORCED TO OPERATE ON A FIRST IN-FIRST-OUT BASIS. BECAUSE OF YOUR NEED FOR AN IMMEDIATE ANSWER, *OUR CONCLUSIONS MUST, OF NECESSITY, BE TENTATIVE, BEING BASED ON THE LIMITED RESEARCH* WE HAVE BEEN ABLE TO DO. IT IS OUR CONCLUSION THAT THE SECRETARY OF THE TREASURY DOES HAVE THE AUTHORITY TO CHOOSE THE ORDER IN WHICH TO PAY OBLIGATIONS OF THE UNITED STATES. ON A DAILY BASIS THE TREASURY DEPARTMENT RECEIVES A NORMAL FLOW OF REVENUES FROM TAXES AND OTHER SOURCES. AS THEY BECOME AVAILABLE IN THE OPERATING CASH BALANCE, TREASURY MAY USE THESE FUNDS TO PAY OBLIGATIONS OF THE GOVERNMENT AND TO REISSUE EXISTING DEBT AS IT MATURES. SEE GENERALLY H.R. REPT. NO. 31, 96TH CONG., 1ST SESS. 9-10 (1979). WE ARE AWARE OF NO STATUTE OR ANY OTHER BASIS FOR CONCLUDING THAT TREASURY IS REQUIRED TO PAY OUTSTANDING OBLIGATIONS IN THE ORDER IN WHICH THEY ARE PRESENTED FOR PAYMENT UNLESS IT CHOOSES TO DO SO. TREASURY IS FREE TO LIQUIDATE OBLIGATIONS IN ANY ORDER IT FINDS WILL BEST SERVE THE INTERESTS OF THE UNITED STATES. UNLESS IT IS RELEASED EARLIER OR WE HEAR OTHERWISE FROM YOU, THIS LETTER WILL BE AVAILABLE FOR RELEASE TO THE PUBLIC 30 DAYS FROM TODAY." (Capitalization in original; emphasis added).
12 For example, the Executive might be attentive to avoiding the deferral of payments that might trigger liquidated damages provisions or other adverse consequences. Given likely capital market reactions, deferral of debt service payments

5. Potentially Applicable Federal Budget Laws

Often overlooked but potentially relevant to discussions of spending prioritization are a series of federal budget laws that might be used to legitimate, if not guide, Executive spending decisions during a Phase Two Debt Crisis. Most important, I think, are the provisions of the Impoundment Control Act, which grant the Executive the power to "withhold or defer the obligation or expenditure of budget authority" in the face of "contingencies." By claiming that a Phase Two Debt Crisis constitutes a qualifying contingency, the Executive could delay making payments through the end of the current fiscal year, which would have been September 30, 2011, in the case of the 2011 debt ceiling controversy. At a minimum, this authority would have offered the Executive a statutory mechanism for delaying payments – which is what FIFO entails – for two months in the Summer of 2011, and even longer were a future debt crisis to arise earlier in the fiscal year. The existence of these Impoundment Act deferral mechanisms are important both because they offer a plausible legal framework for imposing FIFO payments procedures or other more elaborate systems of payment prioritization, and also because they offer a congressionally sanctioned way out of the apparent conflict between revenue, spending, and borrowing decisions (at least for an interim period).

Two other arguably useful pieces of federal budget law involve Government Shutdown procedures and OMB-supervised procedures for apportioning appropriations throughout the fiscal year. Both of these legal structures are designed to restrain the obligation of federal expenditures (that is, the incurring of legal commitments) rather than the liquidation of existing obligations, which is the essence of a Phase Two Debt Crisis. But both mechanisms suggest congressionally-sanctioned procedures for slowing the rate at which federal obligations accrue and thus might be used to limit to some degree the level of federal expenditures during the course of a Phase Two Debt Crisis, pending political resolution. Conceivably, the Treasury could adapt one or both of these procedures to slow the accrual of commitments in the face of a Phase Two Debt Crisis.

---

is one example of this phenomenon, but there are likely many other contexts – for example, payments on procurement contracts, in which the government could incur substantial future costs from payment deferrals.

Concluding Thoughts

One of the paradoxes of debt ceiling crises is that the part of the government best equipped to engage in advance planning for the conduct of government business in a Phase Two Debt Crisis has strong political incentives to avoid any public discussion of sensible planning procedures. In the months and weeks leading up to a debt ceiling crisis, the Executive's primary goal is to force congressional compromises by suggesting that the consequences of failing to raise the public debt ceiling will be unpredictable and unpalatable to a wide range of important constituencies. However, should the debt ceiling ever actually be reached and should a Phase Two Debt Crisis ensue, the incentives of the Executive will transform overnight. Rather than raising the specter of dire consequences, the focus of government policy would then be to convey to the general public and the capital markets that a prudent, legally-defensible, and economically-efficient plan for addressing government payments is in place and capable of preserving fiscal stability while the political branches work out a longer-term compromise.

In my view, payment rules derived solely from obscure Reconstruction Era constitutional provisions or controversial theories of inherent authority are unlikely to have the desired effect. Rather a sensible system of prioritization – likely built off of a FIFO payment plan adjusted to honor debt service payments under the Public Debt Clause as well as Social Security and perhaps other trust fund payments under 42 U.S.C. § 1320B–15 – is the most attractive path. To the extent that the prioritization decisions are supported through invocation of the Impoundment Act's rules of deferral and other potentially applicable federal budget laws, so much the better. While one might wish that we lived in a country where Phase Two Debt Crises were impossible to imagine, we no longer inhabit that world. Thus, we have no choice but to plan for crisis in a manner that is as consistent as possible with the rule of law, and to map out a course of governmental action that will minimize disruption and uncertainty. The dynamics of political brinksmanship may make it difficult for the Executive to plan for a Phase Two Debt Crisis in the public view, but the academic community and independent analysts are under no such constraints and should not hesitate to debate publicly how best to allocate limited government resources in the face of a binding debt ceiling.

7
A Market for End-of-the-World Insurance? Credit Default Swaps on US Government Debt

Richard Squire*

Introduction

While a default on United States Treasury debt is to many investors unthinkable, a market exists to insure against that very possibility. The insurance takes the form of the credit default swap (singular or plural: CDS), a type of financial derivative used to protect against, or speculate on, the risk of default by a borrower such as a corporation or government. In a CDS contract, a protection buyer makes quarterly payments to a protection seller, who in exchange agrees to make a payout if a default occurs on a debt instrument referenced in the contract. The amount of the payout equals the difference between the reference debt's face value and its post-default market value. While the majority of CDS are written to protect against default risk on corporate bonds, a large market for government-debt CDS exists as well: when Greece restructured its sovereign debt in March of this year, Greek sovereign-debt CDS with a face value of more than $70 billion was then outstanding.

---

* Associate Professor, Fordham Law School. I am grateful to Foteini Teloni for excellent research assistance.

Currently, a much smaller percentage of US government debt is covered by CDS than is the debt of other large sovereign borrowers. To many observers, the relative paucity of CDS on US Treasury debt—called here "CDS on USA"—has a simple explanation: counterparty credit risk. CDS protection sellers tend to be large financial institutions, many of which might end up insolvent if the US ever defaulted on its national debt. The implication is that CDS on USA is like end-of-the-world insurance sold by Earth-bound insurers. If the world actually blew up, surely it would take the insurers with it.

While this standard explanation for the relative scarcity of CDS on USA has a superficial appeal, it is based on a misunderstanding of what actually happens under US insolvency law when a firm with open derivatives positions fails. Rather than recovering nothing, the firm's derivatives counterparties enjoy preferential treatment that typically ensures them substantial payouts on their claims. Thus, even if there is a strong correlation between the risk that liability on a CDS contract will be triggered and the risk that the protection seller will then be insolvent, it does not follow that the contract has no value. The explanation for the unusual thinness of the market for CDS on USA seems to lie elsewhere.

A high correlation between the liability risk on a CDS contract and the protection seller's insolvency risk does, however, have a different—and more troubling—implication. The shareholders of such a protection seller enjoy the upside from the CDS sale, as the fees charged to the protection buyer augment the seller's profits. And the shareholders are indifferent to the possibility that liability on the contract will be triggered, because by assumption the seller will then be insolvent anyway. Thus, the downside on the contract is borne not by the seller's shareholders but rather by its general creditors, whose recoveries from the protection seller's bankruptcy estate are diluted by the protection buyer's recovery. Besides transferring expected value from creditors to shareholders, CDS sales of this type can distort markets, causing CDS prices to understate the probability of default on the reference debt, and CDS liability to be concentrated in a handful of systemically important firms.

So far, there is little evidence that such "correlation-seeking" activity is occurring in the market for CDS on USA. But regulators should be aware of the hazard and monitor protection sellers accordingly, rather than proceeding under a mistaken assumption that a tight link between the solvency of the US Treasury and the solvency of protection sellers means that demand for CDS on USA will always be negligible.

The Size and Function of Markets for CDS on Government Debt

At the end of 2011, the gross notional value of outstanding CDS contracts worldwide was $28.6 trillion.[1] Of this amount, only $3.0 trillion, or 10.5%, referenced government debt.[2] If, however, we look at the market in terms of reference entities (that is, the borrowers whose debts are referenced in the contracts), sovereign debt becomes more important: in weekly lists of the ten largest reference entities by notional amounts, sovereign borrowers consistently represent a large majority.[3] Protection sellers, in turn, tend to be large financial institutions, with just over half of all government-debt CDS written by five firms: Deutsche Bank, Goldman Sachs, Barclays, Citigroup and Bank of America.[4]

Government-debt CDS serves several potential functions for protection buyers, including the following:

- *Regulatory capital compliance:* Banks that operate under minimum capital regulations may be required to hold more capital if, instead of investing in assets deemed safe, they invest in sovereign debt with a low credit rating. This regulatory penalty can be avoided, however, if the bank "covers" the debt by purchasing CDS from a highly rated protection seller.[5] By definition, this

---

1 Bank for International Settlements, Credit default swaps, by sector (2011), http://www.bis.org/statistics/otcder/dt25.pdf. The "gross notional" amount is the total face value of outstanding CDS contracts without accounting for offsetting positions.
2 Id.
3 Depository Trust & Clearing Corporation (DTCC), Trade Information Warehouse Data (Section IV), http://www.dtcc.com/products/derivserv/data_table_iv.php (last visited Oct. 25. 2012).
4 Creditflux, CDS League Tables (2011), http://www.creditflux.com/Data/.
5 D. Andrew Austin & Rena S. Miller, *Treasury Securities and the US Sovereign Credit Default Swap Market*, Congressional Research Service Report for Congress (Aug. 15, 2011), http://www.fas.org/sgp/crs/misc/R41932.pdf.

function does not apply to CDS on high-grade government debt such as that of the US and Germany.

- *Investment-risk hedging:* Some observers have argued that investors may be able to create a position that mimics the safety of US debt but provides higher returns by purchasing high-yield, emerging-country sovereign debt and then covering it with CDS from a low-risk protection seller.[6] Once again, this function does not apply to CDS on low-yield government debt such as that of the US.

- *"Pure play"* default speculation: CDS permits investors to focus their exposure, separating default risk from other factors that affect bond yields, such as prepayment risk and—especially if the CDS and the reference debt are denominated in different currencies, as is often the case—inflation risk.

In addition to these more conventional explanations for demand for government-debt CDS, there is a fourth potential explanation that bank regulators should keep in mind:

- *Exploitation of opportunism-induced underpricing:* If a CDS protection seller's managers are motivated to maximize shareholder profits, and they believe that the risk that liability on the CDS will be triggered is highly correlated with their firm's insolvency risk, then they face an incentive to increase CDS sales by cutting the price charged to protection buyers below the expected liability on the contracts. This incentive arises because most of the expected liability on such contracts is borne by the firm's general creditors rather than by its shareholders. Protection buyers will then be able to profit through the difference between prices and expected payouts.

Besides these private functions of CDS on government debt, such contracts can provide a public benefit. An important component of the market price of a CDS contract is an estimate of the likelihood

---

[6] Id. Why arbitrage would not eliminate the profitability of such positions is unclear.

that the reference entity will default before the contract expires. Market observers and regulators can thus use CDS market prices as an additional indicator—beyond the yield on the reference debt itself—of the reference entity's solvency.

The usefulness of CDS prices as default predictors is somewhat attenuated by the fact that default risk is only one factor that can affect CDS prices, and not all of the other factors are directly observable. Factors that are not directly observable include: the expected percentage payout on the contract if a default occurs; a risk premium that compensates the protection seller for the systematic (non-diversifiable) risk it bears; and the protection seller's own default risk.[7] Observers must estimate these variables in order to use a CDS market price to derive an implied default probability for the reference entity. Despite the potential for error in such estimates, CDS markets can serve a valuable discovery function, which means that any market dynamic that distorts CDS prices can generate a public cost.

CDS Performance in the Greek Restructuring

On March 8, 2012, the Greek finance ministry announced that a restructuring of the country's sovereign debt had been negotiated with private investors.[8] This announcement raised two important questions about the Greek sovereign-debt CDS contracts then outstanding. The first was whether a negotiated restructuring of this type would trigger payouts on the CDS, permitting the contracts to serve their function of protecting bondholders against default risk. And the second was whether, if payouts were triggered, the resulting liability would be large enough to create financial distress for systemically important protection sellers.

Concerns that outstanding CDS contracts would fail to serve their bondholder-protection function arose from the manner in which Greece had written down its debt. Rather than simply declaring a default or missing a coupon payment, Greece had negotiated a workout in which private bondholders agreed to exchange their bonds for

---
[7] Another factor, which is observable, is the time value of money.
[8] Steve Schaefer, *Greece Seals Restructuring Deal to Evade Default, for Now*, FORBES (March 9, 2012, 8:47 AM), available at http://www.forbes.com.

new debt instruments with lower face values, lower interest rates, and longer maturities.[9] The overall effect was to write down 74% of the value of the surrendered bonds.[10] To discourage holdouts, on February 27, 2012, the Greek government had retroactively inserted collective-action clauses into the outstanding bonds. These clauses provided that a restructuring would be binding on all bondholders if holders of at least 75% of the outstanding bonds agreed to the exchange.[11] On March 1, 2012, the International Swaps and Derivatives Association (ISDA)—a private trade organization authorized to define terms used in standard CDS contracts—had announced that the insertion of the collective-action clauses did not constitute a "credit event" that triggered liability for protection sellers.[12] This announcement fed concerns that a *de facto* sovereign debt default could be structured in a manner that avoided CDS liability, rendering CDS on government debt effectively worthless.

Such concerns were quickly allayed, however, when the Greek finance ministry announced on March 8 that the completion of the workout had caused the collective-action clauses to be triggered. Within 24 hours, ISDA declared that a credit event had at that point occurred.[13] ISDA further announced that an auction would be held on March 19 to determine how large a percentage payout each protection buyer would receive. Concerns at that point shifted to whether liability on Greek sovereign-debt CDS would be large enough to threaten the solvency of the banks that served as the main protection sellers. This concern was greatest among observers who focused on the outstanding contracts' gross notional value, which at the time of the restructuring was about $70 billion.[14]

---

9 Michael Steininger, *Biggest debt restructuring in history buys Greece only 'a bit of time'*, CHRISTIAN SCIENCE MONITOR, March 9, 2012, available at http://www.csmonitor.com.
10 Id.
11 Kerin Hope et al., *Greek bond swap deal on a knife-edge*, FINANCIAL TIMES (March 4, 2012, 9:06 PM), available at http://www.ft.com/home/us.
12 News release, ISDA EMEA Determinations Committee, *Credit Event Has Not Occurred with Respect to Recent Questions on The Hellenic Republic Restructuring* (March 1, 2012).
13 News Release, ISDA EMEA Determinations Committee, *Credit Event Has Occurred with Respect to Recent Questions on The Hellenic Republic Restructuring*, (March 9, 2012).
14 *Bloomberg View: Credit Default Swaps Work (See Greece); Eyes in the Sky vs. Privacy*, BLOOMBERG BUSINESSWEEK (March 15, 2012), available at http://www.businessweek.com.

In fact, the gross notional figure greatly overstated protection sellers' exposure because it did not account for setoffs. Thus, most sovereign-debt CDS positions are hedged, with protection sellers also holding offsetting positions as buyers. It turned out that the *net* notional amount on the contracts—the remaining liability for all protection sellers after offsetting positions were cancelled—was only $4 billion. When the March 19 auction set the payout ratio at 78.5%, only $3 billion changed hands,[15] a level of liability the financial sector easily absorbed.

Overall, how well did the CDS market perform in the Greek debt restructuring? One part of the answer has already been noted: the triggering of the CDS contracts generated no obvious systemic shocks, suggesting that the contracts may have helped diffuse the restructuring's impact. And the CDS market had in fact evolved toward a more diffuse structure in the years leading up to the March 2012 credit event. Between October 2008 and October 2011, the gross notional amount of outstanding CDS on Greek sovereign debt more than doubled, from $34 billion to $74 billion. But over the same period, the net notional amount fell by half, from $8 billion to $4 billion.[16] Thus, as the perceived likelihood of default rose, protection sellers increasingly hedged their positions, reducing systemic risk despite the growth of the market in gross terms.

A second aspect of the CDS market's performance is the accuracy of the CDS prices as predictors of near-term default. As noted previously, CDS market prices can be used to calculate an implied default probability for the reference debt. Thus, on April 1, 2011—less than one year before the restructuring occurred—the market price for 5-year CDS on Greek sovereign debt was 986.3 basis points per year. This figure means that, to obtain five years' worth of default coverage on a given principal amount of Greek sovereign debt, a protection buyer had to pay, annually, 986.3 basis points times that principal amount. To derive a default probability from this price, an assumption must be made about the expected payout percentage on the CDS if a default were to occur.

---

15 Id.; see also *Greek CDS Auction Sees Bond Price at 21.5 Cents*, CNBC (March 19, 2012, 12:04 PM), http://m.cnbc.com/us_news/46781134.
16 DTCC.

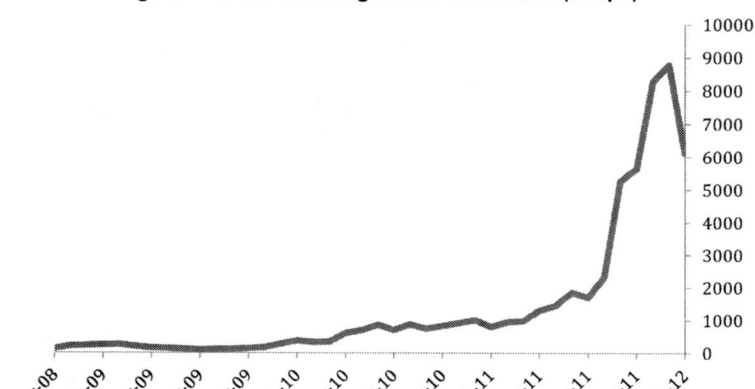

Figure 1: Greek Sovereign Debt CDS Prices (in bps)

Source: Bloomberg

The actual percentage payout when the CDS on Greek sovereign debt were triggered was, as noted above, 78.5%. Using this figure, the CDS market price on April 1, 2011, implies a probability of default within the next year of 12.0%.[17] Given that actual default was less than one year away, this implied probability is surprisingly low, raising questions about the accuracy of CDS prices as default predictors, except perhaps in the very short term. (As Figure 1 indicates, prices did begin a rapid ascent in the summer of 2011.[18]) Although one possible explanation for this seemingly low probability is that investors underestimated the payout percentage, a more modest payout percentage of 40% raises the implied annual default probability

---

17 The implied default probability is calculated here as the probability that causes the expected present value of the premium payments over five years to equal the present value of the expected payout if the reference debt defaults. A higher default probability increases the expected payout value, and it also decreases the expected premium payments given that no payments are made after a payout occurs. For a formal derivation of this formula, see Deutsche Bank Research, *Sovereign default probabilities online – Extracting implied default probabilities from CDS spreads,* http://www.dbresearch.com/PROD/DBR_INTERNET_EN-PROD/PROD0000000000183612.PDF. The figures presented here were calculated using US Treasury yields for the time value of money. See U.S. Dep't of the Treasury, http://www.treasury.gov/resource-center/data-chart-center/interest-rates/Pages/Historic-Yield-Data-Visualization.aspx. As noted in the text, the risk premium is ignored, as is counterparty default risk, the implications of which are discussed below.
18 On October 3, 2011, the price had risen to 5273.0 basis points, which assuming the actual payout percentage of 78.5% implies a default probability of 52.1% within one year.

to only 22.6%. Thus in retrospect, Greek sovereign-debt CDS look like a bargain through much of 2011.

A limitation of the method used here for calculating implied default probabilities is that it does not adjust for the likely value of the risk premium in CDS prices.[19] Such a premium would reflect an expectation that the risk of a credit event correlates positively with the risk of a general market downturn, leading CDS protection sellers to demand additional compensation for the non-diversifiable risk they bear on the contracts. Conversely, protection buyers should be willing to pay a premium for a CDS contract's capacity to hedge systematic risk in their own investment portfolios. The bottom line is that, by ignoring a potential risk premium, the figures given above overstate market estimates of default probabilities on Greek sovereign debt. To be sure, the degree of overstatement is less than it would for CDS on the debt of a country such as Germany or the US, which play larger roles than Greece in the world economy. Nonetheless, including an estimated risk premium would only heighten the appearance that the market for CDS on Greek sovereign debt was too rosy on April 1, 2011, given the size of the default that was to occur less than a year later.

Shockingly Thin? The Market for CDS on USA

Following the Greek CDS credit event, it is natural to ask whether CDS on USA would perform similarly if the US Treasury ever restructured its obligations. At least in nominal terms, the two markets look similar: in late 2011, the net notional value of CDS on Greek debt was $4 billion, comparable to a figure of $5 billion at that point for CDS on USA.[20] But of course this comparison ignores the massive difference in the countries' outstanding debt levels. A better comparison comes from looking at what we might call "coverage ratios": net notional CDS amounts divided by reference debt held by the public. On this measure, the market for CDS on USA is remarkably thin, compared not just to the Greek market but also to markets for other large government borrowers.

---

19 DTCC
20 DTCC.

Table 1: Government-Debt CDS Market Data

	CDS Net Notional (Bil. US$)	Government Debt (Bil. US$)	Coverage Ratio (%)	CDS Price (BPS)
Portugal	$5.05	$243.12	2.08	1051
Ireland	$3.52	$223.29	1.58	588
Spain	$14.72	$969.56	1.52	501
Italy	$19.75	$2,502.76	0.79	463
Greece	$3.70	$491.66	0.75	3137
Germany	$19.16	$2,755.11	0.70	87
UK	$11.42	$2,041.47	0.56	63
USA	$5.03	$10,858.15	0.05	31

Note: All figures are for 4/20/2012 except Greece, which are for 10/28/2011

Sources: Depository Trust & Clearing Corporation (DTCC), Eurostat, Bloomberg

The earlier discussion of the private functions of government-debt CDS suggests a few reasons why the US coverage ratio is lower than the ratios for Greece and for other higher-risk sovereign borrowers. CDS on USA serves no regulatory capital function since US Treasury debt is highly rated. And the low yields on US Treasury debt suggest that CDS on USA does not have an important role as an investment hedge either.

What is remarkable about the US coverage ratio is not how low it is compared to Greece's, but how low it is compared to the ratios of countries whose government debt is considered safe. As Table 1 indicates, the US ratio is an order of magnitude smaller than the ratios for Germany and the UK. This is despite the fact that CDS prices for those countries' debt are comparable to the price of CDS on USA, and are themselves an order of magnitude lower than CDS prices for the debt of sovereign Eurozone borrowers that, after Greece, are considered riskiest: Ireland, Italy, Portugal and Spain. Thus, the low US coverage ratio cannot be explained solely in terms of the perceived relative safety of US Treasury debt.

End-of-the-World Insurance, Bankruptcy, and Dodd-Frank

Other commentators have also observed that the market for CDS on USA is remarkably thin in relative terms. To try to explain why, they have cited a factor that, in addition to those already discussed, can affect the value of a CDS contract: the risk that the protection seller will default. An economic report from the Congressional Research Service named this type of counterparty risk as the primary reason that CDS on USA is scarce, arguing as follows: "Were a serious Treasury default to occur, major US banks could face severe deterioration in their capital bases, leaving their ability to make CDS payments in doubt."[21] Along the same lines, an article in *The Daily Beast* by Daniel Gross offered an analogy:

> Does it make sense to buy insurance against, say, a nuclear attack on Washington—if all the insurance providers' headquarters are inside the Beltway? Of course not. So why do investors buy insurance on US government debt?[22]

Indeed, the real question for Gross was not why the market for CDS on USA is so thin, but rather why anyone would buy such insurance at all.[23]

While the metaphor of a nuclear attack is vivid, it is also misleading. When a financial firm fails it does not disappear in a cloud of dust. Rather, it is unwound in an insolvency proceeding that distributes its assets to its creditors. And at least under US law, counterparties of a failed CDS protection seller enjoy a preferred position in the distribution queue.[24] Thus, CDS positions tend to be collateralized, and several provisions of the US Bankruptcy Code protect the ability of derivatives counterparties to seize and liquidate posted collateral. First, the Code exempts counterparties from bankrutcy's automatic stay, permitting them to terminate their contracts and liquidate posted collateral immediately.[25] Second, the counterparties are exempt

---

21 Austin & Miller, note 5 above.
22 Daniel Gross, *The World's Strangest Financial Instrument*, THE DAILY BEAST (March 16, 2010, 8:00 PM), available at http://www.thedailybeast.com.
23 Id. (asking, "Why does anyone buy insurance policies that pay off only if the US goes bankrupt?").
24 See David A. Skeel, Jr. & Thomas H. Jackson, *Transaction Consistency and the New Finance in Bankruptcy*, 112 COLUM. L. REV. 152, 154 (2012) (describing the "privileged status of derivatives and repos" under US bankruptcy law); Edward R. Morrison & Joerg Riegel, *Financial Contracts and the New Bankruptcy Code: Insulating Markets from Bankrupt Debtors and Bankruptcy Judges*, 13 AM. BANKR. INST. L. REV. 641 (2005).
25 11 U.S.C. § 362(b)(17).

from rules on fraudulent and preferential transfers, which means that CDS buyers generally cannot be forced to return collateral that a protection seller posted before it filed for bankruptcy.[26] And third, the Code permits CDS buyers to exercise setoff rights immediately rather than having to follow the normal procedure of obtaining the bankruptcy court's permission.[27]

If a failed protection seller is a "systemically important financial institution"—which, in today's CDS market, would almost certainly be the case—then the 2010 Dodd-Frank Act creates the possibility that its unwinding will be overseen not by a bankruptcy court but rather by the FDIC under its new "orderly liquidation authority."[28] Yet Congress was careful to specify that derivatives counterparties will enjoy the same general advantages in this receivership process that they enjoy under the Bankruptcy Code. Thus, Dodd-Frank provides that derivatives counterparties of a firm in receivership are exempt from rules requiring the return of fraudulent and preferential transfers,[29] and also that they can exercise contractual rights to terminate and liquidate their positions if a day has passed since the receivership began and their contracts have not been transferred to another financial institution.[30] In addition, the FDIC has indicated that it intends to manage the receivership process in a way that will insulate derivatives counterparties from losses. Thus, the FDIC has stated that one of its primary goals in exercising its liquidation authority will be to prevent a firm's failure from putting "the financial system itself at risk."[31] This concern with systemic risk was among Congress's ostensible justifications for privileging derivatives counterparties in the Bankruptcy Code,[32] a choice of stabilization mechanisms that the FDIC seems unlikely to second-guess. Moreover, the FDIC has

---

26 11 U.S.C. § 546(g).
27 11 U.S.C. § 561.
28 Dodd Frank Wall Street Reform and Consumer Protection Act (2010) ("Dodd-Frank"), § 201 et seq., 12 U.S.C. § 5381 et seq.
29 Id. at § 210(c)(8)(C), 12 U.S.C. § 5390(c)(8)(C).
30 Id. at § 210(c)(8)(A), 12 U.S.C. § 5390(c)(8)(A); id. at § 210(c)(10)(B), 12 U.S.C. § 5390(c)(10)(B).
31 Remarks by Martin J. Gruenberg, Acting Chairman, FDIC, to the Federal Reserve Bank of Chicago Bank Structure Conference, Chicago, IL (May 10, 2012), http://www.fdic.gov/news/news/speeches/chairman/.
32 See Skeel & Jackson, note 24 above, at 162.

announced that in liquidating a systemically important firm it will concentrate losses on the shareholders and creditors of the parent company rather than on the creditors of the operating subsidiaries,[33] which presumably would include any CDS protection buyers.

Of course, not all CDS protection sellers are based in the US, and foreign insolvency regimes may be less favorable to CDS counterparties. But this consideration is a reason why CDS on USA might be sold primarily by US-based firms notwithstanding the potentially higher correlations between the firms' insolvency risks and the risk that liability on the contracts will be triggered.

In combination, these observations suggest that buyers of CDS on USA would receive significant payouts on their claims under the US legal system even if their protection sellers were insolvent. While the buyers certainly are not guaranteed 100 cents on the dollar, the risk of an insolvency-related "haircut" should not undermine the market for CDS on USA so long as the risk is foreseeable and can be priced into the contracts ex ante. Counterparty risk is thus a reason why CDS on USA might be priced at a discount, but it is not a reason why, assuming that market-clearing prices can be charged, the *volume* of contracts demanded should be unusually low as well.

In analyzing counterparty risk on sovereign-debt CDS, a complicating factor is the push by regulators since the crisis of 2008 for trading in CDS contracts to be moved through centralized counterparties known as clearinghouses. When a derivative contract is traded through a clearinghouse, the clearinghouse assumes the counterparty credit risk that the two parties to the contract would otherwise bear directly. The Dodd-Frank Act contains a general mandate that swap contracts be centrally cleared, and it directs US regulators to decide which specific categories of swaps will be subject to the mandate.[34] If CDS on USA were traded through a clearinghouse, protection buyers would bear the credit risk not of the particular protection sellers who originally wrote their contracts, but rather that of the clearinghouse itself.

---

33 Remarks by Martin J. Gruenberg, note 31 above.
34 Dodd-Frank, §§ 723(a), 763(a); 7 U.S.C. § 2(H), 15 U.S.C. § 78c-3(a).

To date, the only categories of CDS that regulators have proposed to subject to the clearing mandate reference pools of corporate borrowers.[35] Whether the regulators are likely in the future to consider CDS on USA a good candidate for mandatory clearing is questionable. As a general matter, clearinghouses seem particularly likely to suffer financial distress if the US Treasury ever defaulted on its debt. Clearinghouses rely heavily on posted collateral to protect themselves against counterparty risk, and by necessity a large portion of such collateral is US Treasury debt and other securities whose value is highly correlated with that of US Treasury debt. Moreover, clearinghouses do not post collateral *to* their counterparties, who therefore are exposed fully to the credit risk of the clearinghouse itself. In a "bilateral" (uncleared) CDS contract, by contrast, the protection seller posts collateral directly to the protection buyer, and that collateral can be selected for its likely resilience in the face of a US Treasury default. For these reasons, market demand for centrally cleared CDS on USA seems unlikely to emerge, and without such demand regulators are unlikely to make central clearing of that particular type of swap mandatory.[36]

While the thinness of the market for CDS on USA is not readily explained by counterparty risk as that term is normally defined, another factor that is peculiar to US government debt might be relevant. Given the central role that US government debt plays in the world economic system, market participants might fear that a US Treasury default is highly likely to accompany a political or social crisis that threatens the rule of law and leaves the enforceability of all contracts in doubt. Put another way, CDS on USA is valuable only in a future state of the world in which a US Treasury default does not occasion a general breakdown of social order, and the probability of such a future state is difficult to estimate.

---

35 See Commodity Futures Trading Organization, Clearing Requirement Determination Under Section 2(h) of the CEA, 17 C.F.R. Part 50 (Aug. 7, 2012).

36 Strictly speaking, US regulators could subject a category of CDS contract to the clearing mandate even if no clearinghouse has announced a willingness to accept the contract for clearing. As a practical matter, however, regulators seem unlikely to take such a step. For a useful discussion, see Mark Jickling & Kathleen Ann Ruane, *The Dodd-Frank Wall Street Reform and Consumer Protection Act: Title VII, Derivatives*, Congressional Research Service Report for Congress (Aug. 30, 2010), http://www.llsdc.org/attachments/files/239/CRS-R41398.pdf.

CDS on USA and Correlation-Seeking

There is a type of investment strategy that, counter-intuitively, could make firms whose insolvency risk is highly correlated with that of the US Treasury *more* likely to sell CDS on USA. This strategy, which elsewhere I have termed "correlation-seeking,"[37] is a form of debtor opportunism in which a firm's managers use contingent liabilities—such as those created by CDS—to transfer value from the firm's unsecured creditors to its shareholders.[38] Correlation-seeking in the market for CDS on USA could cause the contracts to be underpriced and the liability risk to be over-concentrated. To date, there is no direct evidence that correlation-seeking is occurring in this market. But the likelihood that the solvency of many large financial institutions is tied to that of the US Treasury suggests that correlation-seeking is nonetheless a hazard, and that regulators should monitor for signs of its emergence.

In general terms, correlation-seeking occurs when a firm sells contingent claims against itself whose risk of being triggered is strongly correlated with the firm's insolvency risk. The fees collected from the sales enrich the firm's shareholders as long as the firm remains solvent. And if conditions arise that cause the contingent liabilities to be triggered, the high likelihood that the firm will then be insolvent means that the liabilities will probably be borne not by the shareholders, but rather by the firm's general creditors, whose recoveries in the insolvency proceeding will thereby be diluted. To be sure, the fees collected from the sales may be part of the firm's estate and hence may augment creditor recoveries. But it can be shown as a matter of simple arithmetic that the fees will be inadequate to offset the expected dilutive impact on unsecured creditors as long as the firm's insolvency risk and the contingency risk are positively correlated.[39] In this way, the sales of the contingent claims transfer expected value from the firm's general creditors to its shareholders. Unsecured credi-

---

37 Richard Squire, *Shareholder Opportunism in a World of Risky Debt*, 123 HARV. L. REV. 1151 (2010).
38 A simple and prevalent example of correlation-seeking occurs when a parent corporation issues a guarantee on the debt of a subsidiary whose equity is among the parent's primary assets. See Richard Squire, *Strategic Liability in the Corporate Group*, 78 U. CHI. L. REV. 605 (2011).
39 See Squire, note 37 above, at 1159.

tors can deter this kind of behavior by writing loan covenants that prohibit it, but this remedy may be impractical due to monitoring costs and collective-action problems.[40]

Besides its distributional impact on investors, correlation-seeking in the market for CDS on USA would generate social costs. Because the protection sellers' shareholders would bear little of the expected liability on the CDS contracts, managers whose goal is to maximize shareholder wealth would be willing to cause their firms to sell the contracts at artificially low prices, thereby undermining the market's discovery function. The distortion would be especially severe given that the protection sellers would lack the normal incentive to charge a premium for systematic risk. Underpricing could also cause CDS sales to be concentrated in those firms whose solvency is most tightly linked with that of the US Treasury and which therefore can profit most from correlation-seeking.

The possibility of risk concentration suggests that the market for CDS on USA could evolve to look quite different from the market for CDS on Greek sovereign debt pre-March 2012. As noted above, the Greek credit event seems not to have impaired the solvency of the protection sellers, implying a market in which risk was well diffused. A contrast is offered by the 2008 financial crisis, in which three firms that had sold insurance on the default risk on mortgage-backed securities—AIG, Fannie Mae and Freddie Mac—suffered losses that would have bankrupted them but for large government bailouts. Losses at these firms were so severe because each had assumed a concentrated position in the mortgage market. Thus, besides selling CDS on mortgage-backed securities, AIG had invested large sums in such securities directly.[41] And Fannie Mae and Freddie Mac, in addition to selling guarantees on mortgage-backed securities, owned extensive mortgage portfolios.[42] Of course, firms that concentrate risk in this way are more likely to fail if the risk materializes, with systemic implications through their relationships with counterparties.

To this point, the relative scarcity of CDS on USA suggests that little if any correlation-seeking is occurring in that market. This does not

---

40 Id. at 1182.
41 Id. at 1186-87.
42 Id. at 1192-96.

mean, however, that the hazard could not manifest in the future. Notably, the US coverage ratio is growing relative to the ratios for other large government borrowers, albeit from a much lower starting point.

Table Two: Changes in Government-Debt CDS Coverage Ratios

	10/30/08	4/20/12	% Change
United Kingdom	0.22%	0.56%	155%
United States	0.02%	0.05%	109%
Germany	0.50%	0.70%	40%
Italy	0.84%	0.79%	-7%
Portugal	3.47%	2.08%	-40%
Spain	2.74%	1.52%	-45%
Ireland	3.87%	1.58%	-59%
Greece	2.37%	0.75%*	-68%

*Figure for 10/28/11

Sources: DTCC, Eurostat

As Table 2 indicates, coverage ratios have increased in recent years for high-grade government debt, and have decreased for sovereign debt deemed riskier. For the riskier countries, the decrease has occurred through reductions in net rather than gross CDS notional amounts.

Were correlation-seeking to occur in a particular government-debt CDS market, we might expect the net notional amount to hold steady or even rise, as the market became increasingly dominated by protection sellers assuming large unhedged positions.

Figure 2: Outstanding Government Debt CDS Net Notional/Gross Notional

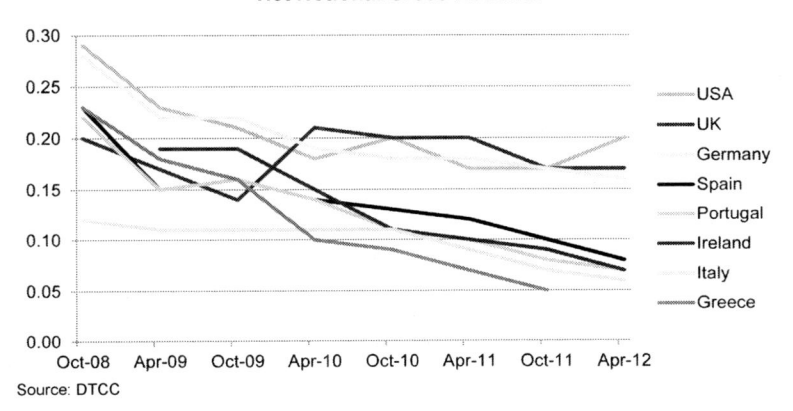

Source: DTCC

Conclusion

The market for CDS on US government debt is remarkably thin. If we compare the net value of sovereign-debt CDS outstanding with reference debt levels, we see that the US market is an order of magnitude smaller than the markets for other large government borrowers, including those that also have high credit ratings. The prevailing explanation for the thinness of the US market is counterparty risk, but this explanation is difficult to reconcile with the privileged position that derivatives counterparties enjoy under US insolvency law. Moreover, the strong correlation between the insolvency risk of the US Treasury and that of many banking firms means that sales of CDS on USA could be used opportunistically to transfer expected value from a protection seller's general creditors to its shareholders. While there is no direct evidence of such conduct in the current market, regulators should not disregard this hazard, which if realized could distort CDS prices and over-concentrate contingent liabilities, thereby producing conditions similar to those in the market for mortgage-backed securities in the years leading up to the 2008 financial crisis.

8
Thoughts on Debt Sustainability: Supply and Demand
Keynote Remarks

Peter R. Fisher

Under what conditions do sovereign borrowers default? Under what conditions do sovereigns with very high levels of indebtedness not default? Can we draw any useful insights from contrasting these two sets of conditions to address the question of whether U.S. government debt is different or to illuminate the likelihood of a U.S. default?

By phrasing the questions this way, I should confess that I am already anticipating my conclusion: in the analysis of sovereign debt sustainability there is too much attention given to measures of supply and too little attention to the sources of demand. That which is easy to measure distracts us from that which is important. Measures of the current (and projected) level of U.S. government indebtedness (relative to measures of the size of the economy) distracts us from the more difficult and important task of understanding the sources of, and behavior of, demand for federal debt.

The sources and behavior of demand are to be found in the pool of savings that can be drawn upon to purchase the debt. In particular, they are to be found in the banking system that intermediates between sources and uses of savings and that creates the "money" that is available to buy the debt. Our predecessors in the 19th century would have understood that a discussion of the banking system was not about branches and tellers but, rather, was about the "money question" – what gets to be money and who gets to create it? Today, we have lost touch with that way of thinking about our banking system and, thus, our understanding of "money and banking" and the dynamics of debt and money are correspondingly limited.

In drawing attention to the demand side of the equation, and particularly to the banking system, I am not trying to ignore the high level of federal indebtedness in order to be comforting or to suggest that we need not worry. On the contrary, given how close we came to blowing up our banking system in 2008, I find it deeply disturbing to think how dependent we are on our banking system to deliver the demand that sustains federal borrowing. We are now watching Europe come even closer to undermining the sustainability of sovereign borrowing through the fragility of their banking system.

First, let me offer a personal reflection on the mistake of focusing on the supply of federal debt without giving comparable consideration to the sources and motivation of demand. Then I will outline the conditions under which sovereigns with high levels of indebtedness do not default, comparing conditions in the United Kingdom in the 19th century and Japan in the 21st century with current conditions in the United States. Finally, I will offer a personal reflection as a former sovereign debt manager.

What a difference ten years can make

Almost ten years ago, when I was serving as the Under Secretary of the Treasury for Domestic Finance, I gave a speech about the long-run fiscal outlook. I said: "Think of the federal government as a gigantic insurance company (with a side line business in national defense and homeland security) which only does its accounting on a cash basis - only counting premiums and payouts as they go in and out the door. An insurance company with cash accounting is not really an insurance company at all. It is an accident waiting to happen." ("Beyond Borrowing: Meeting the Government's Financial Challenges in the 21st Century", Nov. 14, 2002[1]) I was trying to draw attention to our unfunded retirement and health care commitments and to suggest that more attention be paid to the actuarial position of the federal government. Draw attention I did, as pundits and journalists picked up on the stark comments of the senior Treasury official responsible for federal debt.

As gloomy as I was then, looking back ten years, I could not have imagined that over the next decade we would (1) triple federal debt outstanding, (2) have the federal government explicitly assume the liabilities of Fannie Mae and Freddie Mac as wards of the state, and (3) vastly expand unfunded health care liabilities through both the Medicare drug benefit and universal coverage in the recent health care reform and the result would be that yields on the ten-year U.S. Treasury security would *fall* from 4.05 percent at the time of my speech to below 2 percent today.

I could not have imagined that outcome because of how trapped I would have been in a model that focused on supply. I would have assumed that demand is roughly constant and that the risk to sustainability, or the risk of higher yields, would come from supply "overwhelming" demand. With the benefit of hindsight we can see that while the current projected supply of federal debt is much greater, yields are lower not higher.

The difference must be the behavior of demand. Contributing factors appear to include (a) higher household and corporate savings, (b) stronger demand for the relative safety of Treasuries, (c) a much lower supply of other "highly-rated" assets – as less credit is created elsewhere in the economy, (d) weaker expected growth – in part because of the high level of debt, and (e) a much lower expected path of short-term interest rates.

---

[1] Remarks to the Columbus Council on World Affairs Columbus, Ohio, November 14, 2002, available at http://www.truthinaccounting.org/national_reports/listing_article.asp?section=439&section2=458&page=458&CatID=7&ArticleSource=396.

So let us all try to shed our predisposition to focus on the easy-to-measure supply of sovereign debt and open ourselves up to a model that looks at both supply and at the more elusive, and harder-to-measure, concept of demand.

Sovereigns that default and sovereigns that don't

Under what conditions do sovereigns default? I will leave it to you to read Carmen Reinhart and Ken Rogoff's book *This Time is Different – Eight Centuries of Financial Folly* (2009) – if you have not already done so. While their focus is on the (high) levels of sovereign and total indebtedness that lead to sovereign defaults, they were mindful of the importance of the demand as indicated by the title of their preamble: "Some initial intuitions on financial fragility and the fickle nature of confidence." But most of their book focuses on various measures of internal and external debt to gross national product (GNP), tending to the view that levels of debt to GNP in excess of 90 percent create much greater risks of default.

So I will assume that this audience has read Reinhart and Rogoff to answer the question - under what conditions do sovereigns default - and, now, turn to my second question: Under what conditions do sovereigns with very high debt levels not default?

The experience of the United Kingdom in the 19th century provides a useful example of what it takes to survive very high debt levels. To outline the U.K. experience, I rely on James Macdonald's account (chapter 8) in his wonderful book *A Free Nation Deep in Debt – The Financial Roots of Democracy* (2003), which I commend to you. (Both Macdonald's book on fiscal policy, as well as David Hackett Fischer's book on inflation *The Great Wave: Price Revolutions and the Rhythm of History* (1996), provide wonderful complements to Reinhart and Rogoff).

19th century UK: Prospering with almost 300 percent debt-to-GNP

At the end of the Napoleonic Wars, the U.K. had nominal debt to GNP of almost 300 percent. Not only did they avoid default, the

U.K. prospered greatly for the next one hundred years. What went right? While there are a number of factors, I would focus on five things.

First, the U.K. had "sources of income somewhat in excess of apparent GNP" – that is, they had an empire or, at least, they were building one. However one measures the size of the U.K. economy in the early 19th century, my hunch is that we underestimate the benefit they derived from their expanding empire.

Second, they had a "big pool of savings" - much of it already invested in government borrowing to finance the war effort.

Third, they had the "dominant wealth storage and transfer technology" of the day, in the form of the U.K. banking system (supported by the Bank of England), to efficiently intermediate between sources and uses of that pool of savings.

Fourth, they had "creditor-friendly government policies" in a government sympathetic to the interests of the creditor class.

And, finally, as a consequence of that creditor-friendly attitude, they explicitly adopted a policy of deflation, as Parliament made the conscious choice of seeking a return to the pre-war price level. The deflation that they engineered had a profound effect on English society and politics (recall the Corn Laws) but it certainly proved beneficial to bond holders.

Japan: Getting by with 200 percent debt-to-GDP

Now, let's briefly compare these five factors to the recent history of Japan, with debt-to-GDP level of just over 200 percent.

First, Japan's current account surplus provides it with the modern equivalent of "sources of income in excess of apparent GNP." While Japan's current account position may begin to shift against them, it certainly has been one reason that Japan has been able to sustain its high level of sovereign indebtedness with extremely low yields.

Second, Japan has a big pool of domestic savings. So, yes, check this box.

Third, we would be hard pressed to call the Japanese banking system "healthy" or the "dominant wealth storage technology." But while Japanese banks have not been particularly strong, the Japanese have at least had an efficient means of channeling savings into government borrowing. Since the banking crisis of the late 1990s, Japan Post has been brutally efficient in converting savings into government financing as it became the preferred destination for household deposits and was effectively restricted to holding JGBs on the asset side of its balance sheet.

Fourth, while low interest rates in Japan have not been good for savers, Japanese government policies have been reasonably friendly to creditors – perhaps most noticeably in its policies toward its banks as Japan resisted the recommendations of foreign observers and critics in the late 1990s to force banks to absorb losses and raise capital more quickly.

Finally, while it does not appear that it did so intentionally, Japan has experienced outright deflation so the purchasing power of savings stored in JGBs has been rising in real terms, even if nominal yields are extremely low.

How does the U.S. Look? A Mixed Bag.

Now let's turn to the United States and see how we fare today on each of these five different measures, which I will take up in a different sequence.

Creditor-friendly policies. Here, at best, I would suggest we get a mixed score. The Fed is certainly trying to do what it can to be supportive of credit intermediaries. But, for the most part, our Congress and our regulators are at something of a loss to decide whether they want to beat up the bankers and make it harder and more expensive to lend money or whether they want to make it easier to lend money. I fear the Fed's efforts are being – and will be – overwhelmed by the forces that wish to punish the lenders for their bad behavior.

Sources of income beyond apparent GNP. We score poorly here. We are running a significant current account deficit so we are relying on foreign savers to finance our borrowing. However, I am one of a few who think that our position is not as bad as widely assumed.

For one, I suspect that we overestimate our current account deficit because we're not as good at counting soft exports (like services and chip designs) as we are counting at hard imports (like how many iPads arrive at the port of Long Beach, California). Our tax code further encourages anyone doing a global business to claim as much of the value-add as originating outside the U.S. as possible. We also have a lot of wealth that is apparently stored outside the United States, recorded as owned by Americans and American companies, which end up in dollar assets (and even Treasury securities): if you happen to own Apple stock, you are sitting on a large pile of cash that is "resident" in places like Ireland. So, while our current account deficit is a negative for us, I don't think it is as big a negative as we measure it to be.

Deflation. We don't seem to have deflation; at least, not yet or not apparently. If we had been using house prices rather than owner-equivalent rent in the calculation of the Consumer Price Index we would now be experiencing measured deflation. Investors are certainly behaving as if they feared deflation more than they fear inflation, as evidenced by the negative real yields they are willing to accept and the pronounced preference of both corporate and household savers for cash. So while we don't seem to be experiencing measured deflation, perhaps we should understand our current ability to sustain our high levels of federal debt at low interest rates as reflecting the benefit (in debt sustainable terms) of investors' anticipation of deflation.

A big pool of savings. Contrary to popular mythology (about Americans "living beyond their means"), we do have a big pool of savings but we must be careful to distinguish stocks and flows. The net wealth of the American household sector is $58 trillion dollars. Liquid net wealth – the financial assets of the household sector (not counting hard assets like housing) less all debt– is $35 trillion. We are the wealthiest society in the history of mankind; we're just not getting wealthier at the same rate that we were accustomed to. (Federal Reserve Flow of Funds, Fourth Quarter 2001, p. 106).

There is also the pool of foreign savings that ends up in dollar assets. This is the source of demand that is feared will "dry up," leaving us with higher interest rates or an inability to rollover our debt. So, is it a weakness or a source of strength that foreigners keep buying our sovereign debt?

Let me mention two stories. First, in the mid-1990s, the Prime Minister of Japan came to New York and, in a speech, threatened to sell their holdings of U.S. Treasury securities; since then Japan has more than doubled its holdings of U.S. Treasury securities. Second, in the run-up to the launch of the Euro, I was speaking in Madrid and I was asked the question: "How do you Americans trick us into buying so many dollars?" Had I not been asked such an odd, blunt question I doubt I would have come up with as good a rejoinder, which was: "If it was a trick it wouldn't be very interesting; What's interesting is: Why do you do it of your own free will?"

Let me turn to the flows. As already mentioned, we run a current account deficit and this is a problem. The household sector savings rate was declining but has risen a bit since the financial crisis. But focusing strictly on the flows – indeed, on the Fed's Flow of Funds data – the household sector is currently a net saver equal to 2.8% of GDP. The non-financial corporate sector is a net saver of 2.5% of GDP and the non-financial business sector a further 2.9% of GDP. Foreigners are net savers in dollars equal to 3.6% of U.S. GDP. When you add those up, it's pretty easy for the government sector to borrow about 10% of GDP.

Those who worry about yields backing up, or a U.S. default, usually invoke fears of "foreign flows" into the dollar "drying up" and, thus, creating conditions when the supply of Treasury borrowing "overwhelms demand." I have two reactions to this line of reasoning.

First, *when* some combination of households, non-financial corporations and foreigners *save less*, they will be *borrowing more* and this will lead to greater competition for funds with government borrowing and yields will rise (as we see private borrowing "crowding in" with public borrowing). Particularly when the corporate sector becomes a net borrower, this will mean that we have more private borrowing and, in all likelihood, we will view this as the "good news" that the economy is expanding more robustly. So, yes, yields will rise and that will provide a higher return on the savings that are invested in U.S. Treasury securities, which will draw in (some) more savings. This will not be a problem; it will be the successful demonstration of the adjustment mechanism in action.

Second, (as Richard Herring mentioned in Chapter 1), our bilateral relationship with China is reciprocal – with flows running in both directions, not just one. I have always been baffled by the "savings glut hypothesis" because it imagines that, somehow, there is an exogenous source of savings that is falling down on the U.S. that might stop and, then where would we be? This ignores the fact that the so-called savings glut in Asia originated with a "glut" of U.S. consumption in excess of income. If we curtail our consumption, and save more (as we are now doing), we will need to worry less about how we finance our borrowing from foreign saving.

In sum, there is a large pool of savings available to finance U.S. government borrowing – some of it domestic, some of it foreign.

<u>The U.S. banking system.</u> Our banking system is the mechanism that delivers that pool of savings to the market for federal debt. Our banking system also uses federal debt as the base asset – the low volatility, core holding – in building their balance sheets. Their balance sheets are the source of "money" that we all can use to buy federal debt. (While banks have to deliver "Fed Funds" to settle purchases of U.S. Treasury securities, the rest of us buy Treasury securities with balances at our banks.) If these balance sheets are healthy (sound, stable) there will be a persistent supply of "money" to buy the supply of debt. So, I think of our banking system as the most critical component in sustaining demand for federal debt.

Much like the U.K. banking system in the 19th century, the U.S. banking system today is the dominant wealth storage and transfer technology on the planet.

The speed with which the U.S. authorities moved to recapitalize the major U.S. banks in 2008 and 2009 was hugely important in stabilizing the U.S. and world economy – and in ensuring the sustainability of financing for federal debt.

Think about the difference between the American and the European bank stress tests. The critical difference is not to be found in the technicalities of the tests themselves. Rather, the key difference is that Secretary Geithner wisely announced in advance of the 2009 stress tests which (19) banks he was going to save and that he was running the stress tests to figure out how much capital they needed (and if they could not raise the additional capital themselves he was going to inject whatever capital was necessary). As Europe is now discovering, their mistake has been to run stress tests and then simply ask the market: "So, what do you think?" This has put continued pressure on all banks to de-lever, with corresponding adverse consequences for government bond markets – as banks reduce their demand for sovereign debt, the easiest market in which to adjust their balance sheets.

Banking, money and "monetary arrangements"

I mentioned earlier that our 19th century predecessors would have immediately recognized a discussion of the banking system as being about the money question: what constitutes money and who gets to create it? This topic is also connected to the issue of reserve currency status and to an important piece of central bank mythology that needs to be debunked.

Reserve currency status is not about the "unit of account" but, rather, is about the reserve asset. The dollar's popularity as a notation in accounts – as a measurement and reference unit – is not what makes it a reserve currency. Rather, the fact that the world's principal reserve asset, U.S. Treasury securities, is denominated and traded in dollars makes the dollar a popular unit of account.

Central bank mythology would have us believe that central bank liabilities, in this case those of the Federal Reserve, are the base asset in our monetary regime. Central bank reserves are "high-powered money" that banks hold as their reserve asset and use as the starting point for the money multiplier underpinning the process of creating money with which financial institutions can buy more assets.

The myth is that central banks do not and should not monetize sovereign debt. The myth continues that the central banks' liabilities are "the real thing." The fact is that central banks can and do monetize sovereign debt and that central bank reserves are a "second-best" substitute for sovereign debt, rather than the other way around. This is particularly so for U.S. Treasury securities because of the extraordinary depth, liquidity and breadth of this market.

This creates an awkward reality for central banks. If sovereign debt is the base asset in our monetary regime (and central bank liabilities are not), then finance ministries and treasuries are in charge of the quantity of the monetary base through the accident of fiscal policy decisions about spending and taxes. This would mean that central banks do not control the quantity of the monetary base; they only influence its price. That is exactly what is going on.

Once you recognize that central banks' key tool is their influence over sovereign debt pricing it is easier to understand why the ECB felt bound to intervene in Spanish and Italian bond markets last year: because if a central bank loses its influence over the pricing of the sovereign yield curve it has lost its principal means of conducting monetary policy. This also provides the context for understanding why the Federal Reserve feels compelled to tell us that they are likely to hold short-term rates extremely low through 2014: they are using their direct control over short-term rates to influence our expectations about the future path of short-term rates in order to influence the pricing of long-term Treasury debt.

To be clear, central bank liabilities are a "pretty good" substitute for sovereign debt and central banks can and do liquefy sovereign debt.

But they are not the real thing. The duration issues, discussed in previous chapters, are important. But given the extraordinary liquidity of sovereign debt markets, this only underscores the return advantage sovereign debt has in contrast with central bank liabilities.

The role of sovereign debt as the base asset is not determined by logic or principle but by experience and practice. The status can be lost – as Greece, Portugal, Ireland and other European countries are now finding out. This sad history betrays one of the original sins of the Euro: from the creation, they maintained the Deutsche Bundesbank's pretense that they would not monetize sovereign debt but in their operations they then doubled-down on the Basel Committee's zero-risk weight for sovereign debt by giving all Euro-area member nations' sovereign debt identical margin treatment in the European Central Bank's repo operations, treating them all as assets of identical, riskless characteristics.

The preeminent role of Treasury securities as the base asset in the U.S. monetary system, rather than Federal Reserve liabilities, partially reflects a curious legacy of the Glass-Steagall Act. Since the separation of commercial banking and investment banking in the 1930s, the only institutions with access to accounts at Federal Reserve Banks have been commercial banks. Most countries would not dream of preventing important financial intermediaries from having direct access to accounts at the central bank.

But because of the hangover from Glass-Steagall, it seems natural to us to limit access to accounts at the Federal Reserve to "real" banks – or at least those that the Fed deems to be real banks. So a broad range of financial intermediaries – all our non-bank financial intermediaries – cannot directly hold central bank liabilities at all and, thus, need to hold U.S. Treasury securities as a low volatility, base asset on their balance sheets. By definition, the market for Treasury securities is wider than the market for Fed Funds.

Before one even considers the dollar's role as a reserve currency, and the financial intermediaries outside of the U.S. who actively manage both sides of their balance sheets, our shadow banking system provides a persistent source of demand for Treasury securities.[2]

A final word about demand

Let me conclude with another observation as a former debt manager.

If you ask Treasury or finance ministry officials responsible for debt management "What keeps you up at night?" the only candid reply will be: the risk of not being able to rollover their debt at the next auction. In practice, debt sustainability is about rollover risk: the risk that demand at an auction will drop precipitously from recent, prior auctions. Of course, at the moment that the worry surfaces one can wish, one can imagine, having a lower amount to rollover and this permits you, in your imagination, to cover the auction despite the fewer bids. But that is a mere counterfactual. What you worry about is a failure of demand.

If we peel back the question of sovereign debt sustainability to the question of whether there is the "political will" to sustain high debt burdens, we should recognize that this is not a question of political will in the abstract. Rather, it will involve a concrete choice between whether to try to roll over your debt or not to try to roll over your debt. The actual policy choice is a practical one among the consequences of (a) not rolling over your debt, and all that default entails, (b) trying to roll over your debt at increasing cost and (c) trying to roll over your debt and failing do so and, thereby, defaulting.

---

2 Who is holding the federal debt? According to the Federal Reserve's Flow of Funds data, at the end of 2011, the Fed held 14 percent of the total outstanding amount of Treasury, Agency debt and agency mortgage-backed securities, up from 7 percent for 2005, but down from 17 percent in 1975. So the Fed is monetizing less as a share of the total than it was in 1975, but double what it was in 2005. Unsurprisingly, the holdings of foreign authorities, or "the rest of the world" as the Fed puts it, equaled 32 percent at the end of 2011, up from 28 percent in 2005 and 12 percent in 1975. The holdings of the household (and nonprofit) sector were at a mere six percent in 2011, down from nine percent in 2005 and from 22 percent in 1975. Most interestingly, the group of institutions that we would broadly lump together as non-bank intermediaries (money market mutual funds, mutual funds, closed-end funds, exchange-traded funds, government-sponsored enterprises, asset-backed securities issuers and broker-dealers) held 18 percent in 2011, down from 19 percent in 2005 but up from a mere one percent in 1975.

Watching the current Greek drama unfold has helped sharpen my thinking about this choice. For present purposes, let's put aside the question of Greece withdrawing from the Euro and simply consider the question of whether, if you had to play the part of the Greek government, would you default on your debt (by not rolling it over or by falling out of the Euro – either way) or would you try to keep rolling it over at higher interest costs. What are the differences between defaulting and not defaulting?

First, if you default you will lower your debt burden and improve your economic prospects. If you do not default you will continue to incur your high debt burden. Second, if you default you are going to destroy a great deal of wealth and, in all likelihood, destroy the efficacy of your banking system and its ability, in the near term, to help you finance your debt in the future. If you don't choose to default, you are choosing to continue to rely on your banking system to help you finance your debt. Since the benefits of reducing your debt burden are obvious, it strikes me that the critical issue is whether, in a country with extremely high debt, your banking system is already so severely impaired that it is not capable of helping you finance your debt. If your banking system is already impaired, then you are more likely to default because you have already incurred the major cost of default. However, if you can find a way to default without impairing your banking system, by somehow shielding your banks from the consequences of default, then the attractiveness of default goes up.

Which brings me to my final point. Sovereign defaults are not likely to happen when there is "too much" money but, rather, when there is "too little" money. These are opposite conditions. So while I fully understand that one can impair the real value of a bond through inflation as well as through default, the former central banker in me rebels against describing as parallel the condition of there being too much money around (and its spilling over into inflation) and the condition of there not being enough money.

9
The Federal Debt: Assessing the Capacity to Pay

Deborah Lucas

In this chapter, I focus on fiscal imbalances — their structural sources and magnitudes; the types of policy changes that will be needed to address them; and some of the risks to the fiscal outlook that make an eventual default on Treasury debt a conceivable, although unlikely, outcome. I emphasize the fiscal outlook because the odds that the U.S. will find itself in a position where it is unable or unwilling to meet its debt obligations depend critically on the paths of future taxes and spending.

While the future paths of taxes and spending will be affected by many uncertain economic and political developments, there is little doubt that current fiscal policy is on an unsustainable trajectory. Fortunately there are well understood and economically feasible policy options, which if implemented, would in all likelihood avert a future debt crisis. At the same time, there are significant downside risks that could significantly erode the economic capacity and political will to pay. Those include the realization of higher-than-anticipated health care cost growth, sharp increases in borrowing costs, a significant slowdown in productivity growth, losses on contingent financial liabilities or other large spending or revenue shocks — and perhaps most important, the difficulty of reaching a political consensus that will allow the necessary policy changes to be made in a timely fashion.

Effects of Aging

Lower birth rates and longer life expectancies than in the past make population aging inevitable, both in the U.S. and abroad. One of the most salient statistics is the old-age dependency ratio — the percentage of people over age 65 relative to the size of the working-age population. That ratio is expected to climb rapidly over coming decades, from 21.6 in 2010 to 39.0 by 2040 for the U.S., and by similar amounts in the rest of the world. With significantly fewer workers per retiree, living standards will improve more slowly than in the past, unless productivity growth turns out to be high enough to compensate. Nevertheless, in the absence of the pressures created by aging on the federal budget, many experts predict that population aging would have modest effects on the macro economy.[1]

However, because the costs of the largest federal expenditure programs are tied to the number of retirees, projections of increased federal spending as a share of the economy can be largely attributed to the effects of population aging. For example, absent the effect of aging (and excess health care cost growth), federal spending on its major health care programs such as Medicare and Medicaid and on Social Security would remain steady at about 10 percent of gross domestic product through 2035 (see Figure 1). Population aging will also affect the revenue side of the ledger, lowering payroll and income tax collections, and perhaps making it less feasible to raise tax rates on earnings because discouraging work effort will be more costly to society.

---

1 For a detailed analysis, see National Research Council (2012). *Aging and the Macroeconomy. Long-Term Implications of an Older Population.* Committee on the Long-Run Macro-Economic Effects of the Aging U.S. Population. Board on Mathematical Sciences and their Applications, Division on Engineering and Physical Sciences, and Committee on Population, Division of Behavioral and Social Sciences and Education. Washington, DC: National Academies Press.

Projected Size of Deficits and Debt

Most long-term fiscal projections show imbalances between spending and taxes that continue to grow indefinitely into the future, but the path of projected deficits varies significantly depending on the underlying assumptions about future policies, prices, and interest rates. For example, the Extended Baseline Projection made by CBO, which is the basis for congressional deliberations about the budget, assumes that current law will remain unchanged.[2] CBO is further required by law to assume that for discretionary programs (which include defense) costs will grow at the rate of inflation. Those rules understate expected future deficits and debts because they imply the continuation of money-saving policies that most observers believe are unlikely to remain in place. For example, current law includes an expiration of the Bush tax cuts, no reduction in the growing coverage of the alternative minimum tax, and effective caps on compensation to Medicare health care providers. Under those assumptions, the primary deficit — the deficit not including interest payments — is close to zero through 2035 (see the top panel of Figure 2). To provide a more plausible alternative, CBO constructs an "Alternative Fiscal Scenario," which takes into account tax and spending changes that seem highly probable. Under that alternative, the projected primary deficit is projected to grow to over 6 percent by 2035 (see the bottom panel of Figure 2).

The deficits shown in Figure 2, together with projected interest payments, imply the future levels of debt held by the public shown in Figure 3. There is a wide difference in accumulated debt in 2050 between the Extended Baseline Scenario and the Alternative Fiscal Scenario: over 200 percent in the first case versus less than 50 percent in the latter. The difference underscores the sensitivity of fiscal projections to the assumptions made about highly uncertain policies. My own conclusions from having worked on and studied many of these sorts of analyses are on the one hand optimistic: There are non-draconian combinations of tax increases and spending cuts that would stabilize the debt at sustainable levels. On the other hand,

---

2 See, for example, Congressional Budget Office, CBO's 2011 Long-Term Budget Outlook, June 2011.

the Alternative Fiscal Scenario is far from the worst conceivable outcome, as discussed below.

Restoring Balance

The ongoing accumulation of debt implies that the size of the necessary adjustments and the accompanying pain will be greater the longer policymakers wait to act. But in any case, avoiding an explosive accumulation of debt will probably require lawmakers to enact a combination of benefit cuts and tax increases rather than relying on either one alone. Nevertheless, a number of proposals call for closing the gap using a unilateral approach. For example, a plan proposed by Congressman Paul Ryan would reduce the projected debt held by the public to less than 20 percent of GDP in 2050 without raising taxes (see Figure 3); by contrast, the Center for American Progress recommends narrowing the fiscal gap largely with taxes and avoids any significant cuts in spending on social insurance programs. The obvious advantage of a mixed approach is that it could avoid the very deep spending cuts or large tax increases that would be necessary using either mechanism alone. As an indication of the size of adjustments needed under a unilateral approach, under the Ryan plan federal spending for Medicaid, children's health insurance and exchange subsidies for health care would account for about 1 percent of GDP in 2050, versus over 4 percent of GDP under either of the CBO scenarios discussed above.

Because the gap to be filled is so large and the majority of federal spending is for social insurance programs and defense, proposals that call for addressing fiscal problems solely by eliminating inefficiencies in government operations or by ending smaller discretionary programs are unrealistic. As a result, most plans to restore fiscal balance emphasize changes to Social Security and Medicare.

Social Security is an example of a large program where a combination of relatively modest tax increases and spending cuts would put the program on a sustainable path and maintain its basic structure and function, even though, under current law, the value of projected benefits greatly exceeds the value of projected future program tax revenues. In fact, many plans for how to restore balance have been proposed and analyzed.[3] The basic elements generally include gradual increases in the normal retirement age (possibly linked to longevity changes), benefit cuts or higher taxation of benefits for wealthier beneficiaries, removal of the annual cap on payroll tax collections, and moderate increases in the payroll tax. An important theme in such analyses is that acting sooner, or at least having a credible plan, has the advantage that it gives people more time to prepare for the changes and ultimately allows smaller adjustments to be made.

The rising cost of Medicare, and to some extent of Medicaid, is driven by the excess cost growth in medical services, and also by the aging of the population. Lowering the growth rate of federal health care spending is almost certainly a prerequisite for achieving fiscal balance. Unlike for Social Security, there is little agreement about what the solution should look like. Some favor price controls on medical services; others fear those measures would degrade the quality of care and stifle innovation. Rather, they see the need to harness competitive forces to create incentives for providers to control costs. Some would like to limit Medicare benefits for higher income households; others believe that greater use of means testing would undermine political support for the program. Some would like to privatize Medicare and provide vouchers to low-income retirees to buy private insurance; others fear it would create a two-tier system with insufficient care for the poor. Such debates have been raging for decades and there are no signs of an emerging consensus. Nevertheless, because the rising cost to the government of health care is too large to be tolerated for much longer, I believe that something will be done to change that trajectory (although I would not like to wager on what the approach will look like).

Risks to the Fiscal Outlook

Thus far, I have argued that, despite the impediments to restoring balance, the most likely paths for future fiscal policy will avoid a fiscal crisis and the accompanying risk of default. However, there

---

[3] For a survey of policy options and their quantitative implications, see Congressional Budget Office, "Social Security Policy Options," July 2010.

are significant risks to that outlook that, if realized, could reverse that conclusion, and those possibilities deserve more consideration, at least by way of a warning, than they often receive. Those risks include higher-than-expected health care cost growth; a slow-down in productivity growth; large increases in Treasury's borrowing costs; losses on contingent financial liabilities like deposit insurance and pension guarantees; and pressures from fiscal imbalances at the state and local level.

Health care cost growth. The deficit and debt projections in Figures 2 and 3 are based on projections of federal health care cost growth that are considerably more optimistic than historical experience. Figure 3 compares the projections of Medicare spending used in various government projections with Medicare spending if historical rates of excess health care cost growth were to continue. The difference is significant: Medicare spending would rise to over 10.5 percent of GDP by 2050 if historical trends continue, to about two percentage points higher than under the CBO Alternative Baseline.

Productivity growth. The capacity to repay the debt is related to the size of the economic pie, which over long horizons depends critically on the growth rate of productivity — the value of output that is produced per unit of labor and capital inputs. The determinants of productivity growth are not well understood, and, historically, productivity growth has varied widely. Some are concerned that productivity growth will be slowed by the aging of the population, or that higher taxes and spending cuts will lower productivity growth. However, there is little empirical evidence to support those views. Some observers believe that higher productivity growth is the best way to resolve fiscal problems, but it is not a dependable approach because we know so little about how to encourage it, and because the necessary growth is so unlikely to be attainable. In fact, even if growth proves to be somewhat above its expected path, the salutary effect on spending will be dampened by the positive correlation between productivity and program costs.

Interest rates. As the debt grows, so does the importance of the level of interest rates on its affordability. The U.S. currently benefits greatly from the global desirability of Treasury debt as a safe store of value and very low borrowing costs. As economic and financial market conditions improve, and if investors become nervous about future inflationary pressures, those borrowing costs could increase sharply. Table 1 shows the sensitivity of interest payments as a share of GDP to the average interest rate.

Contingent Financial Liabilities. Treasury debt currently stands at over $10 trillion dollars. However, that represents only about half of the explicit financial obligations of the U.S. government that are firmly committed today.[4] Those other obligations include over $5 trillion in debt and mortgage guarantees of Fannie Mae and Freddie Mac, government sponsored enterprises that are now in federal conservatorship; about $2.7 trillion of direct government loans and loan guarantees; over $6 trillion of insured deposits, and over $2 trillion in pension insurance. In the event of a further downturn in housing prices or another large wave of financial institution failures, the cost of meeting those liabilities could make it significantly more difficult to meet all of the government's financial obligations.

As well as explicit financial liabilities, implicit guarantees expose the Treasury to additional large losses. In evaluating the capacity of the U.S. economy to pay the debt, some argue that it is the total level of indebtedness, not only federal obligations, that should be taken into account. For example, state and local pension systems are, as a group, severely underfunded, and if those costs fall to the federal government, they will be a further source of fiscal strain.

---

4 Deborah Lucas, "Credit Policy as Fiscal Policy," MIT working paper, 2012.

Figure 1: Sources of Growth in Federal Spending on Major Mandatory Health Care Programs and Social Security, 2011 to 2035
(Percentage of gross domestic product)

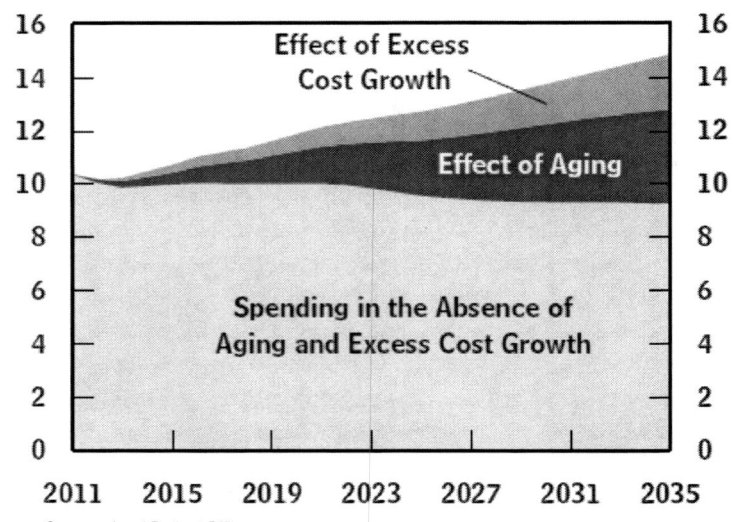

Effect of Excess Cost Growth

Effect of Aging

Spending in the Absence of Aging and Excess Cost Growth

Source: Congressional Budget Office

Figure 2: Primary Spending and Revenues, by Category, Under CBO's Long-Term Budget Scenarios
(Percentage of gross domestic product)

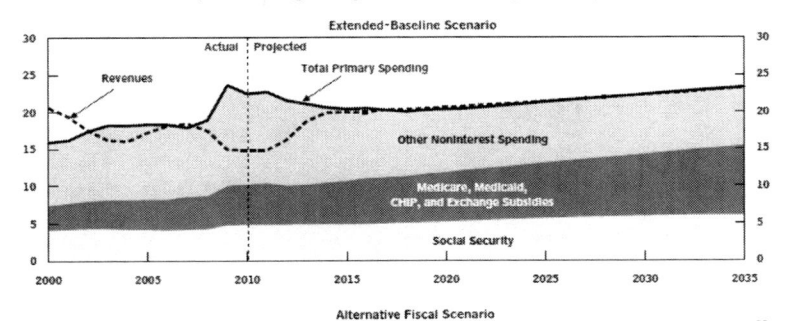

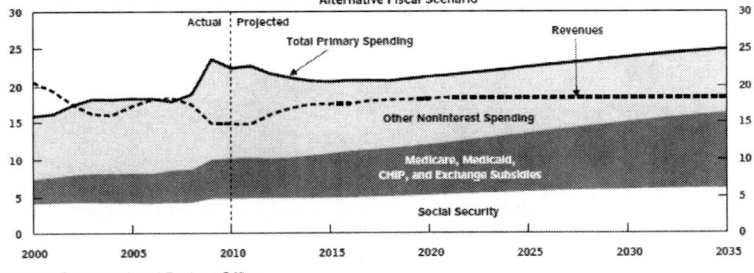

Source: Congressional Budget Office

Notes: Primary spending refers to all spending other than interest payments on federal debt.
The extended-baseline scenario adheres closely to current law, following CBO's 10-year baseline budget projections through 2021 and then extending the baseline concept for the rest of the long-term projection period. The alternative fiscal scenario incorporates several changes to current law that are widely expected to occur or that would modify some provisions that might be difficult to sustain for a long period. (For details, see Table 1-1 on page 4.)

CHIP= Children's Health Insurance Program.

Figure 3: Debt Held by the Public
(Percentage of gross domestic product)

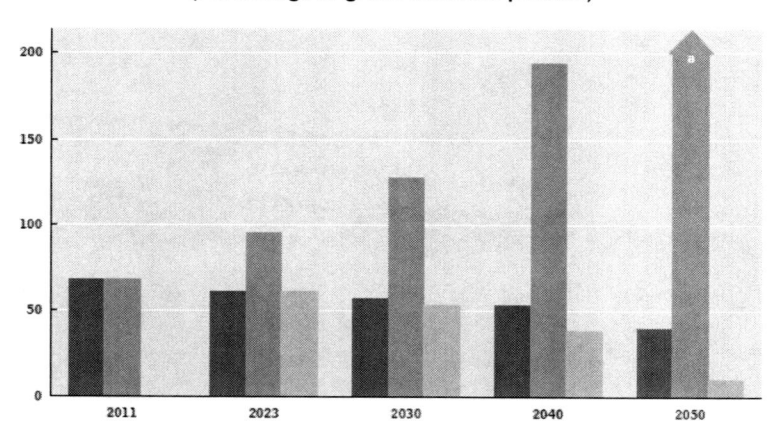

■ Extended Baseline Scenario (Interim)[b]

■ Extended Alternative Fiscal Scenario (Interim)[b]

■ Paths Specified by Chairman Ryan and His Staff[c]

Source: Congressional Budget Office

a. Debt would be greater than 200 percent of gross domestic product.
b. The extended baseline scenario and extended alternative fiscal scenario reflect projections through 2022 from *Updated Budget Projections: Fiscal Years 2012 to 2022* (March 2012) extrapolated into future years using rates of interest and growth rates for revenues and spending from *CBO's 2011 Long-Term Budget Outlook* (June 2011).
c. Amounts of revenues and spending for 2012 through 2022 were provided by Chairman Ryan and his staff. The specified paths of revenues and spending thereafter would set federal spending for major health care programs according to specified formulas, leave Social Security spending as it would be under current law, and set all other spending (excluding interest) and revenues on the basis of specified growth rates or specified percentages of GDP. For all years, the Chairman specified that there would be no spending for subsidies to purchase health insurance through new exchanges established by the Affordable Care Act.

Figure 4: Medicare Spending Projections

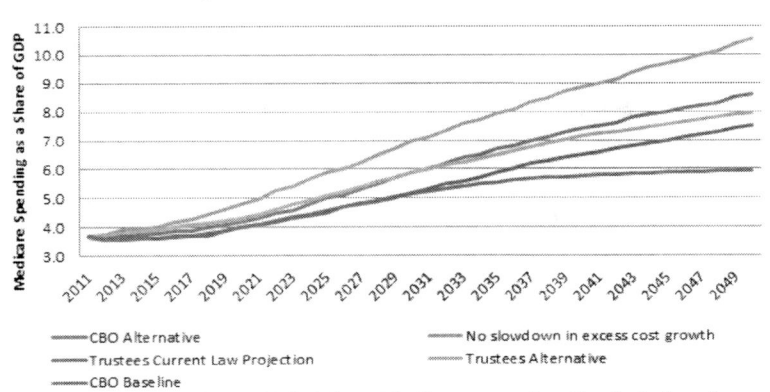

Legend:
- CBO Alternative
- No slowdown in excess cost growth
- Trustees Current Law Projection
- Trustees Alternative
- CBO Baseline

Source: National Research Council (2012). *Aging and the Macroeconomy. Long-Term Implications of an Older Population.* Committee on the Long-Run Macro-Economic Effects of the Aging U.S. Population.

Table 1: Interest Burden as Percent of GDP

Rate / Debt to GDP	2%	5%	8%
50%	1%	3%	4%
100%	2%	5%	8%
150%	3%	8%	12%
200%	4%	10%	16%

Source: Author's calculations.

10
The Tax Revenue Capacity of the U.S. Economy

James R. Hines Jr.

Summary: The United States imposes smaller tax burdens than do other large high-income countries, its 24.8 percent ratio of tax collections to GDP in 2010 representing the lowest fraction among the G-7. The United States also differs from other G-7 countries in relying relatively little on expenditure-type taxes. It follows that there is significant unused tax capacity in the United States that could be deployed to pay the country's debts, but that the most promising source of additional tax revenue is expenditure taxation that is widely perceived to have very different distributional features than the income taxes on which the U.S. government currently relies. The extent to which the country is able, politically and economically, to incur greater tax burdens to pay its debts may therefore depend on its willingness to adopt a tax system that more heavily emphasizes taxing expenditures.

1. Introduction

Politics famously impedes cogent discussion of long-run government budget issues, but for all of the partisan controversy over U.S. fiscal policy, there is little dispute over the plain fact that the United States government rapidly accumulated debt following the crash of 2008. At year-end 2007, the value of U.S. government debt held by the public was equal to 36.3 percent of U.S. GDP.[1] By year-end 2011, that figure had risen to 67.7 percent of GDP, and, in March 2012, the Congressional Budget Office (2012) estimated that, in their "alternative fiscal scenario" intended to offer an optimistic but nonetheless more realistic projection than official baselines, U.S. debt held by the public would rise from 73.3 percent of GDP at year-end 2012 to 93.2 percent of GDP by year-end 2022. This accumulation of U.S. public debt reflects the impact of the recession that followed the crash of 2008, including the accompanying tax cuts and spending increases. Deficits are projected to average 5.3 percent of GDP over the 2012-2022 decade; and these figures generally understate total obligations, since debt held by the public is only a portion (69.7 percent as of 2012) of total U.S. government indebtedness.

This very rapid accumulation of U.S. government debt is troubling to many observers, who worry about the political and economic repercussions of shifting burdens to future generations of taxpayers, the macroeconomic consequences of large amounts of debt, the efficiency cost of raising taxes to meet future interest and principal payments, and simply whether the U.S. economy is capable of generating sufficient tax revenues to satisfy debt obligations along with financing annual expenditures. The purpose of this paper is to evaluate the ability of the U.S. economy to meet current and future government funding needs, and the implications for tax policy of actually undertaking to do so.

Some comfort can be found in the experiences of other G-7 countries, all of which collect significantly greater tax revenues as a fraction of GDP than does the United States. To the extent that these countries offer reasonable guides to the type of policy the United States might adopt, it follows that there is ample ability of the United States to finance projected interest and principle payments on its debt. This is not to say that addressing U.S. fiscal imbalances could be easily accomplished. Other G-7 countries that raise significant tax

---

1 These estimates and others are drawn from data provided by the Congressional Budget Office, www.cbo.gov, and in which years are U.S. government fiscal years. March 2012 projections are reported in Congressional Budget Office (2012).

revenue rely on expenditure-basis taxes that differ significantly from the income taxes that are the mainstay of U.S. federal tax collections. Furthermore, the greater government expenditures that typically accompany higher taxes in these countries make the taxes more tolerable politically than they would be simply in the service of debt repayment.

Tax policies ultimately represent the outcomes of political processes that express the willingness of citizens to subject themselves to taxation. Tax alternatives differ in the extent to which they distort economies and in the distribution of their burdens. As aggregate burdens rise, the consequences of inefficient taxes become increasingly severe, thereby moving even intractable political processes in the direction of adopting efficient taxes. This is evident in the widespread use of consumption-based taxes in most of the world. It is a sad reality that countries must be forced by events to undertake efficient tax reforms – though this pattern may carry promising implications for U.S. policy as the country confronts its own debt burdens.

2. U.S. Taxation in Global Perspective

Throughout the modern era, the United States has maintained a smaller public sector than the other large high-income countries in the G-7 (Canada, France, Germany, Italy, Japan, and the United Kingdom). This entails correspondingly lower total tax burdens. The large U.S. deficits of 2007-2012 are the products of declining tax collections and rising government expenditures, but even prior to the crash of 2008, or for that matter prior to the 2000s, U.S. tax collections were low compared to those of other high income countries.

Table 1 presents OECD statistics on total (federal plus subnational) tax revenues as a fraction of GDP in G-7 countries in 2006 and 2010, which are representative years before and after 2008.[2] In 2006 U.S. tax revenues were 27.9 percent of GDP, representing the lowest fraction among G-7 countries. Japan was a close second at 28.0 percent, Canada third at 33.3 percent, and others higher. By 2010

---

2 These and other OECD tax data presented in Tables 1-5 are available at: http://www.oecd-ilibrary.org/taxation/data/revenue-statistics_ctpa-rev-data-en.

U.S. tax revenues had fallen to 24.8 percent of GDP, still the lowest among the G-7 countries, the 3.1 percent of GDP U.S. tax revenue drop between 2006 and 2010 also representing the greatest percentage decline of all the G-7 countries.

Table 1: Total Tax Revenue as a Percentage of GDP

Country	2006	2010
Canada	33.3	31.0
France	44.4	42.9
Germany	35.6	36.3
Italy	42.3	43.0
Japan	28.0	26.9
United Kingdom	36.4	35.0
United States	27.9	24.8

Source: OECD StatExtracts, http://stats.oecd.org/Index.aspx?QueryId=21699.
Note to Table 1: The entries represent ratios of total government (federal, state and local) tax collections to national GDPs in 2006 and 2010.

The United States, which had relatively modest tax collections prior to 2008, responded to the crash by reducing taxes more significantly than did the other G-7 countries. Falling incomes due to the crash had the effect of reducing both GDP and tax collections, with taxes typically declining more than GDP, due to the progressive nature of taxes in these countries and the sensitivity of business profits to macroeconomic conditions. Furthermore, all of these countries enacted tax cuts and delayed tax increases in efforts to stimulate their economies. That these tax-cutting efforts are reversible has been demonstrated by the United Kingdom and others subsequently talking steps to address long-run fiscal balance.

The most obvious difference between U.S. tax policy and the policies of other G-7 countries – indeed, the tax policies of almost any other country in the world – is that there is no U.S. value added tax (VAT).[3] A VAT is a sophisticated form of a sales tax, and has proven immensely popular among governments around the world; since 1966, more than 150 countries have adopted VATs. Among the high-income OECD countries, 33 out of 34 have VATs; the United

[3] While there has never been a U.S. federal VAT, for a period of time the state of Michigan imposed a business tax with many VAT-like features (Hines, 2003).

States is the lone exception. A VAT has the attractive property of not taxing the return to saving and investing, and thereby not discouraging business formation or expansion; furthermore, VATs are commonly believed to be more easily enforced than are other taxes. Despite these features, the U.S. federal government has consistently resisted adopting a VAT, reflecting liberal concerns that the VAT is insufficiently progressive and conservative concerns that the VAT too readily facilitates the tax collections necessary to support big government.

Despite its aversion to VATs, the United States uses some expenditure-based taxes. Most U.S. states impose general sales taxes at rates that are significantly below VAT rates in other countries. Furthermore, there are federal and state excise taxes on specific goods and services, such as gasoline, cigarettes, and alcohol; but overall U.S. taxes on goods and services are low compared to equivalent tax rates in other countries.[4]

Table 2 presents ratios of taxes on goods and services to GDP for G-7 countries in 2006 and 2010. The numerator includes VAT, sales, and excise tax revenues. The United States has the lowest ratio, collecting 4.5 percent of GDP in goods and services taxes in 2010. Japan is the next lowest country at 5.1 percent, Canada follows at 7.5 percent, and the European G-7 countries are all above 10 percent. It indeed appears that VATs can be used effectively to collect significant revenues from expenditures on goods and services.

U.S. taxes on goods and services declined from 4.8 percent of GDP in 2006 to 4.5 percent in 2010, but this was much more modest than the drop in total tax revenues. Expenditure taxes offer revenue streams that are more stable over the business cycle than are the revenue streams produced by many income tax alternatives. Legislative changes actually increased the fraction of GDP collected by expenditure taxes in some other G-7 countries between 2006 and 2010, with only Canada and France showing declines of comparable magnitude to the U.S. change.

---

4 Hines (2007) reviews the history and impact of U.S. sales and excise taxation.

Table 2: Taxes on Goods and Services as a Percentage of GDP

Country	2006	2010
Canada	8.1	7.5
France	11.1	10.7
Germany	10.1	10.7
Italy	11.1	11.1
Japan	5.2	5.1
United Kingdom	10.6	10.8
United States	4.8	4.5

Source: OECD StatExtracts, http://stats.oecd.org/Index.aspx?QueryId=21699.
Note to Table 2: The entries represent ratios of total government (federal, state and local) tax collections on goods and services to national GDPs, expressed as percentages, in 2006 and 2010.

Other governments, particularly those of high-tax continental Europe, finance significant portions of their expenditures with social insurance taxes. These taxes are typically imposed at flat rates, and only on labor-type income; their revenues are dedicated to certain categories of social expenditures. As a result of their flat-rate structure, these social insurance taxes appear to be much less progressive than income tax alternatives (though the expenditures they fund tend to be highly progressive). The comparatively small size of U.S. old-age social insurance programs, together with a reluctance to use flat-rate taxes to finance general social expenditures, means that the United States relies much less than do some other countries on social insurance taxes.

Table 3 presents statistics on the use of social insurance taxes by G-7 countries. Canada, the United States and the United Kingdom rely the least on social insurance taxes, as measured by tax collections as a fraction of GDP. In 2010, the United States collected social insurance taxes equal to 6.5 percent of GDP, Canada collected taxes equal to 4.8 percent of GDP, and the United Kingdom collected taxes equal to 6.7 percent of GDP, all of these ratios roughly unchanged since 2006. All four of Japan, Italy, Germany and France in 2010 collected social insurance taxes equal to 11 percent or more of GDP.

Table 3: Social Security Taxes as a Percentage of GDP

Country	2006	2010
Canada	4.9	4.8
France	16.4	16.6
Germany	13.7	14.2
Italy	12.5	13.6
Japan	10.2	11.0
United Kingdom	6.7	6.7
United States	6.6	6.5

Source: OECD StatExtracts, http://stats.oecd.org/Index.aspx?QueryId=21699.
Note to Table 3: The entries represent ratios of total government (federal, state and local) social insurance tax collections to national GDPs, expressed as percentages, in 2006 and 2010.

The United States relies relatively heavily on personal income taxes, and to a lesser extent on corporate income taxes. As a result, U.S. tax collections from these sources, measured as a fraction of GDP, look similar to those of other countries, despite the significantly smaller size of the U.S. government. Personal – and particularly corporate – tax collections move over time with the business cycle, but in general the United States does not differ sharply from other G-7 countries in total income tax collections as a fraction of GDP.

Table 4 presents personal income tax collections as a fraction of GDP. In 2006, U.S. personal income tax collections were 10.1 percent of GDP, a ratio greater than those of France, Germany, and Italy, and thereby representing the median ratio for the G-7 that year. By 2010 U.S. tax cuts had reduced personal tax collections to 8.0 percent of GDP, leaving only Japan and France with smaller ratios.

Table 5 presents corporate tax collections as a fraction of GDP. In 2006, U.S. corporate tax collections represented 3.4 percent of GDP, exceeding the ratios of Germany and France, and equaling that of Italy. Between 2006 and 2010, corporate tax collections fell as a fraction of GDP in every G-7 country, reflecting primarily the decline in corporate profits associated with the recession that followed the crash of 2008, and to a much smaller extent the reactions of government policies. By 2010, U.S. corporate tax collections were only 2.7 percent of GDP, still ahead of Germany and France, very close to Italy and Japan at 2.8 percent, and not far behind the United Kingdom and Canada.

Table 4: Individual Income Tax Revenue as a Percentage of GDP

Country	2006	2010
Canada	11.9	10.8
France	7.8	7.3
Germany	8.6	8.9
Italy	10.7	11.7
Japan	5.2	5.2
United Kingdom	10.5	10.0
United States	10.1	8.0

Source: OECD StatExtracts, http://stats.oecd.org/Index.aspx?QueryId=21699.
Note to Table 4: The entries represent ratios of total government (federal, state and local) individual income tax collections to national GDPs, expressed as percentages, in 2006 and 2010.

Table 5: Corporate Tax Revenue as a Percentage of GDP

Country	2006	2010
Canada	3.8	3.3
France	3.0	2.1
Germany	2.2	1.5
Italy	3.4	2.8
Japan	4.7	2.8
United Kingdom	3.9	3.1
United States	3.4	2.7

Source: OECD StatExtracts, http://stats.oecd.org/Index.aspx?QueryId=21699.
Note to Table 5: The entries represent ratios of total government (federal, state and local) corporate tax collections to national GDPs, expressed as percentages, in 2006 and 2010.

3. *Implications for Future U.S. Tax Policy*

It is clear that U.S. government finances differ significantly from those of other large high-income countries. To the extent that valid inferences can be drawn from cross-country comparisons, the experiences of other G-7 countries suggest that there is significant untapped federal tax revenue capacity in the United States, particularly among expenditure and social insurance taxes. While there are differences between the U.S. economy and the economies of other G-7 countries, these differences carry no obvious implications for their relative abilities to generate tax revenue. Lower U.S. tax revenue as a fraction of GDP is the product of deliberate policy choices made by successive U.S. governments, and reflects an unwillingness to incur the tax cost of supporting a larger public sector. There are certainly impediments to increasing U.S. tax collections, but these largely fall into the category of considerations that raise the cost of greater taxation, not factors that prevent the government from generating higher levels of tax revenue.

Tax compliance is an important ingredient in producing significant tax collections. The United States currently has among the lowest measured tax evasion rates in the world, with a shadow economy – the part of the economy not reported to tax authorities – estimated to account for between between 8 and 16 percent of GDP (Schneider et al., 2010; Slemrod, 2007). In the cross-country estimates offered by Schneider et al., U.S. underground activity represents just 8.6 percent of the economy, the second lowest fraction in the world (Switzerland is the lowest at 8.5 percent). The other G-7 economies have significantly larger underground sectors, including Canada, at 15.7 percent of GDP, Germany, at 16.0 percent, and Italy, much higher at 27.0 percent. The very low U.S. tax evasion rate makes it possible to obtain greater tax revenue than would otherwise be available, though tax evasion rates are apt to rise with higher tax rates.

It is one thing to have the ability to raise taxes, another to have the willingness. There are significant political costs associated with higher taxes, particularly if the higher taxes are not accompanied by greater spending on social or other programs that the electorate values. This is not to say that the country is unwilling to incur these costs. The history of U.S. federal government debt is one of accumulation during wartime and decline during the subsequent peace. Indeed, the first U.S. federal taxes were excises imposed early in the Washington administration to pay off debts from the revolutionary war, a process that, together with land sales, led ultimately to the extinguishment of the federal debt by 1837. Subsequent debt accumulations during the Civil War, the Spanish-American War, World War I, and World War II were likewise, albeit not quite as dramatically, diminished by frugality after these wars. There may be reason for concern that U.S. politics has evolved to a point at which it is difficult to summon the political will to impose short-term costs in the service of long-run sound fiscal management; though the focus of this essay is not on the politics of debt repayment, but instead on the underlying economics of the options facing the U.S. government.

The potential economic consequences of greater taxation include discouraging labor supply, saving, investment, business formation, efficient asset allocation, and other choices that affect the performance of the economy. The cost of lost economic efficiency associated with higher taxation depends critically on which taxes the government chooses to deploy in order to raise revenue. Feldstein (2006) estimates that an across-the-board increase in U.S. personal income taxes would be associated with an efficiency cost of 76 cents per dollar of additional tax revenue. This figure is based on estimates of the responsiveness of taxable income to changes in tax rates, a method that is controversial, and which some critics argue overstates the magnitude of deadweight loss (Saez et al., 2012), though it is clear that higher U.S. personal income taxes would generate economic distortions of significant magnitude.

The U.S. government could raise additional revenue without resorting to higher personal income taxes. VATs, social insurance taxes, and carefully chosen excise taxes have the potential to generate significant tax revenues at considerably smaller cost to the economy than a general expansion in the personal income tax, since these tax alternatives have flatter rates than the personal income tax, and effectively tax the return to saving little if at all. Whether the United States would have an interest in a significant expansion of these taxes in preference to the individual income tax turns largely on the perceived tradeoff between the distributional objectives of the tax system and the desire to maintain efficient incentives.

Countries differ in the extent to which taxes are apt to distort their economies. Higher tax collections are generally associated with greater economic costs of raising additional tax revenues, since the efficiency cost of taxation rises roughly proportionately with the square of tax rates (Auerbach and Hines, 2002). Consequently, countries with the greatest tax revenue needs will tax themselves to the point that additional tax revenue is associated with significant economic distortions. These high-tax countries stand to benefit the most from adopting efficient tax structures, typically consisting of a combination of expenditure taxes and income taxes with relatively flat tax rates. In practice, tax system design appears to be sensitive to the costs of economic distortions. Lindert (2004) reports that countries with large government sectors tend to have less progressive tax systems than countries with small government sectors, reflecting the cost of high-rate progressive taxes. There is also almost a mechanical relationship between tax collections and the extent of measured tax progressivity. Consider an extreme case in which the government represents 99 percent of the economy, and is financed by income taxes. The tax system would need to extract virtually all of private income, in which case income tax rates must average 99 percent, and would therefore have a nearly flat structure. This is obviously a fanciful example, but it illustrates that the decline of tax progressivity at high tax collection levels is a function not only of the rising economic cost of collecting tax revenue, but also of the need for broad-based taxes to support large governments.

Factors that contribute to the economic cost of heavy taxation include not only high tax rates themselves, but also a high degree of responsiveness of economic activity to taxation. There is ample evidence that, in the modern era, economic activity has become considerably more responsive than before to taxation, this sensitivity being attributable in large part to technology changes and the globalization of the world economy. Firms seeking to maximize after-tax returns have extensive options among production locations, suppliers, and final markets, all located in jurisdictions with potentially very different taxes. High tax rates discourage economic activity in part by encouraging the activity to relocate to tax-friendlier jurisdictions.

Governments attempting to raise significant tax revenue in this environment are understandably loath to do so with taxes that have the effect of driving businesses to other locations. As a result, the range of attractive tax options narrows to those whose burdens are largely borne by fixed local factors, specifically land and labor, as land is unable to relocate and labor is often not much more mobile than land. Given that land is simply not valuable enough for land taxes to finance much of the needs of modern governments, it follows that labor taxes are instead likely to represent the mainstay of modern government finance. Labor income can be taxed in many guises, including by personal income taxes, social insurance contributions, and expenditure taxes. Of these, personal income taxes bear only partly on labor income, as personal income that forms the tax base commonly includes returns to saving and investing. By contrast, social insurance taxes are usually flat-rate taxes on wages and salaries, and expenditure taxes do not (in present value) tax the expected return to saving and investing, so effectively tax labor income. Consequently, modern developments give governments strong incentives to rely on social insurance and expenditure taxes.

There is evidence that governments have responded to these incentives. Small countries, whose economies depend to the greatest extent on international trade and foreign investment, and who therefore have long faced more elastic tax bases than larger countries, rely on corporate and personal taxes much less than do large countries. Small countries largely use expenditure taxes instead of income taxes. In a cross-sectional study of national tax patterns in 1999, Hines and Summers (2009) report that a ten percent smaller national population is associated with a one percent smaller ratio of personal and corporate income tax collections to total tax revenues. Over time, the experience of small countries is likely to become the experience of all countries, as technological advances, and accompanying globalization, increase the elasticity of economic activity to taxation, pushing governments ever more strongly in the direction of taxing fixed labor rather than mobile business capital.

4. Conclusion

Throughout the modern era, the United States has maintained a smaller government sector than have other large high-income countries, and consequently U.S. tax collections have represented a relatively small fraction of national income. This pattern can be viewed in two ways. From one perspective, there appears to be significant unused tax capacity in the United States, so the tax increases necessary to finance significant U.S. government debts are well within the capacity of the U.S. economy. From another perspective, the United States in recent decades has demonstrated that it is unwilling to demand of its residents large tax payments. This tension, between the capacity of the economy and the realities of political decision making, leaves the course of future policy far from certain.

Some aspects of future tax policy have predictable features. It is unlikely that business and personal income taxes will be used to generate significant additional future tax revenues, since current economic forces, if anything, put downward pressure on these taxes. Since the United States has relied to a greater extent on income taxation than have other high-income countries, reducing reliance on income taxes entails a significant restructuring of revenue sources. The additional resources necessary to pay the country's debts are likely to come instead from social insurance and expenditure taxes. Consequently, greater U.S. tax collections in the future will almost surely entail a tax system that is less progressive than is the current U.S. system. This reality generates considerable political anguish, which may be a good part of the reason why the country has for so long put off dealing with its fiscal imbalances.

References

Auerbach, Alan J. and James R. Hines Jr., Taxation and economic efficiency, in Alan J. Auerbach and Martin Feldstein, eds. *Handbook of public economics*, Volume 3 (Amsterdam: North-Holland, 2002), 1347-1421.

Congressional Budget Office, Updated budget projections: Fiscal years 2012 to 2022, March 2012.

Feldstein, Martin S., The effect of taxes on efficiency and growth, National Bureau of Economic Research Working Paper No. 12201, May 2006.

Hines, James R., Jr., Michigan's flirtation with the Single Business Tax, in Charles L. Ballard, Paul N. Courant, Douglas C. Drake, Ronald C. Fisher, and Elisabeth R. Gerber, eds. *Michigan at the millennium* (East Lansing, MI: Michigan State University Press, 2003), 603-628.

Hines, James R., Jr., Taxing consumption and other sins, *Journal of Economic Perspectives*, 21 (1), Winter 2007, 49-68.

Hines, James R., Jr. and Lawrence H. Summers, How globalization affects tax design, in Jeffrey R. Brown and James M. Poterba, eds. *Tax Policy and the Economy*, Volume 23 (Chicago: University of Chicago Press, 2009), 123-157.

Lindert, Peter H., *Growing public: Social spending and economic growth since the eighteenth century* (Cambridge, U.K.: Cambridge University Press, 2004).

Saez, Emmanuel, Joel Slemrod and Seth H. Giertz, The elasticity of taxable income with respect to marginal tax rates: A critical review, *Journal of Economic Literature*, 50 (1), March 2012, 3-50.

Schneider, Friedrich, Andreas Buehn and Claudio E. Montenegro, Shadow economies all over the world: New estimates for 162 countries from 1999 to 2007 (revised version), World Bank Policy Research Working Paper No. 5356, July 2010.

Slemrod, Joel, Cheating ourselves: The economics of tax evasion, *Journal of Economic Perspectives*, 21 (1), Winter 2007, 25-48.

11
Can the United States Achieve Fiscal Sustainability? Will We?

James Kwak

By any conventional measure, the fiscal outlook for the United States has deteriorated significantly in the past four years. In the wake of the global financial crisis that began in 2007 and peaked in 2008, official Congressional Budget Office (CBO) projections of the national debt increased by more than forty percentage points of GDP, largely due to a decline in tax revenues because of the economic downturn.[1] The federal government ran annual deficits well above $1 trillion in 2009, 2010, and 2011—at 10.1 percent, 9.0, and 8.7 percent of GDP, respectively, the largest deficits since World War II.[2] The financial crisis and ensuing recession accelerated a long-term increase in the national debt that had already been expected because of an ag-

---

1 The CBO's baseline projection for publicly held national debt at the end of the 2018 fiscal year increased from 22.6 percent of GDP in January 2008 to 67.0 percent in August 2009. CBO, *The Budget and Economic Outlook: Fiscal Years 2008 to 2018*, January 2008, Summary Table 1, p. xii; CBO, *The Budget and Economic Outlook: An Update*, August 2009, Summary Table 1, p. x. As of January 2012, even after the passage of the Budget Control Act of 2011, the 2018 debt projection was still at 66.8 percent of GDP. CBO, *The Budget and Economic Outlook: Fiscal Years 2012 to 2022*, January 2012, Table 1-3, p. 10. By law, the CBO baseline projection must follow certain rules that make it unrealistic. Because these rules are consistent, however, the CBO baseline projection is often the best way to compare the government's fiscal position at different points in time.
2 OMB, *Fiscal Year 2013 Budget of the U.S. Government: Historical Tables*, Tables 1.1, 1.2.

ing population and rising health care costs. According to the CBO's most recent long-range forecast, by 2035 the federal budget deficit will exceed 15 percent of GDP and the national debt will be approaching 200 percent of GDP.[3]

Yet, according to bond market investors (the once-feared "bond vigilantes"), the United States government has only become a better credit risk. The yield on 10-year Treasury bonds, which averaged 4.9 percent in the decade preceding the financial crisis (1998–2007), fell to 3.2 percent in 2009 and in 2010.[4] In the summer of 2011, when a standoff over raising the debt ceiling brought the federal government within a few days or weeks of default, interest rates continued to fall, and they fell further after Standard & Poor's downgraded the Treasury Department in early August, hovering around 2 percent for the rest of the year.[5]

Clearly, buyers of Treasury bonds expect to get their money back, with interest (though not much of it)—despite large annual deficits, slow economic growth, looming Social Security, Medicare, and Medicaid obligations, and a political system that seems incapable of either raising taxes or significantly cutting spending. Are they right to have such confidence?

Whether or not a country will pay off its debts depends on a sequence of factors. First, its economy must be large enough to divert resources to needed government spending and debt service without impoverishing the population. Second, the central government must have the administrative capacity necessary to collect taxes. Third, the government must have both the legitimacy and the political will to impose sufficient taxes—or, in the alternative, to reduce spending on existing government services.

At the end of the seventeenth century, Great Britain and France began a contest for predominance in Europe that lasted for more than

---
3 CBO, *CBO's 2011 Long-Term Budget Outlook, June 2011*, Table 1-2, p. 8.
4 Federal Reserve Statistical Release H.15.
5 Yields on the 10-year bond averaged 2.0 percent from September through December. *Ibid.*

one hundred years.[6] At the time, Great Britain had a smaller population, smaller economy, and smaller military.[7] Yet Britain was more than France's equal, containing Louis XIV and his successors on the Continent while seizing many of France's overseas colonies, and ultimately it was the Bourbon Monarchy that collapsed under the fiscal strain of repeated wars in 1789. Great Britain's crucial advantage was its superior ability to raise money through borrowing, amassing debts that seem staggering even by today's standards, exceeding 150 percent of GDP in the 1750s and again in the 1780s.[8] Following the American Revolutionary War, Britain had a larger debt than France; in 1782, interest on the debt consumed 70 percent of government expenditures.[9] Yet Britain still paid lower interest rates than France, which enabled it to bring its debt under control, while France's inability to finance its debts led directly to the French Revolution.[10]

Great Britain's fiscal advantage was not due to a larger economy, but to the second and third factors listed above: administrative capacity and political will. It could collect taxes much more efficiently thanks to a modern centralized bureaucracy, while the French state depended on a host of intermediaries as well as the sale of offices.[11] Furthermore, the British government had the legitimacy necessary to impose higher taxes than those in France because the economic elites

---

6 For a slightly longer discussion of eighteenth-century Great Britain and France, see Simon Johnson and James Kwak, *White House Burning: The Founding Fathers, Our National Debt, and Why It Matters To You* (Pantheon, 2012), pp. 17–20.
7 Paul Kennedy, *The Rise and Fall of the Great Powers: Economic Change and Military Conflict from 1500 to 2000* (Vintage, 1989), p. 99; Angus Maddison, "Historical Statistics: Statistics on World Population, GDP, and Per Capita GDP, 1–2008 A.D.," available at http://www.ggdc.net/maddison/Maddison.htm.
8 "Time Series Chart of UK Public Spending," ukpublicspending.co.uk.
9 Kathryn Norberg, "The French Fiscal Crisis of 1788 and the Financial Origins of the Revolution of 1789," chapter 7 in Philip T. Hoffman and Kathryn Norberg, eds., *Fiscal Crises, Liberty, and Representative Government, 1450–1789* (Stanford University Press, 1994), p. 272; Richard Bonney, "France, 1494–1815," chapter 4 in Richard Bonney, ed., *The Rise of the Fiscal State in Europe, c. 1200–1815* (Oxford University Press, 1999), p. 148.
10 Norberg, note 9, above, p. 292; Bonney, note 9, above, p. 148; David D. Bien, "Offices, Corps, and a System of State Credit," chapter 6 in Keith Michael Baker, ed., *The French Revolution and the Creation of Modern Political Culture, vol. 1, The Political Culture of the Old Regime* (Pergamon Press, 1987), p. 90.
11 John Brewer, *The Sinews of Power: War, Money and the English State, 1688–1783* (Harvard University Press, 1990), especially chapter 4; Norberg, note 9, above, pp. 265–66.

who would pay those taxes were part of the dominant coalition in Parliament, and therefore had control over both spending and taxation.[12] It was Britain's political system that enabled it to raise the vast sums of money necessary to fight the wars of the eighteenth century and ultimately to defeat Napoleon.

The United States began its life in a serious fiscal crisis, missing payments due to foreign governments repeatedly in the 1780s.[13] This should not have been a surprise; the central government lacked both the authority to levy taxes (a power reserved by the states under the Articles of Confederation) and any administrative apparatus to collect them. The fiscal crisis was a major motivation for the Constitutional Convention of 1787 and the ratification of the new Constitution, which gave the federal government the power to impose and collect taxes.[14] This made it possible for Treasury Secretary Alexander Hamilton to restructure the national debt, effectively swapping outstanding obligations for new bonds that had lower interest rates but were now backed by both tariffs and excise taxes.[15] The fast-growing American economy could generate the resources necessary to pay off the national debt; once the government had the ability to levy taxes and showed the willingness to do so, investors quickly became convinced that it was a good credit risk.[16]

Only two decades later, however, the federal government was facing another fiscal crisis. In 1812, at President James Madison's request, the Democratic-Republican majority in Congress declared war against Great Britain. Since taking power in 1801, however, the Democratic-Republicans had lowered taxes and cut defense spending; when war broke out, the U.S. Navy had seventeen ships, while

---

12 Steven C.A. Pincus and James A. Robinson, "What Really Happened During the Glorious Revolution?" NBER Working Paper 17206, July 2011, pp. 30–36.
13 Davis Rich Dewey, *Financial History of the United States,* 2nd ed. (Longmans, Green, and Co., 1903), p. 89. For a longer discussion of early American finances, see Johnson and Kwak, note 6, above, pp. 20–33.
14 Sidney Homer and Richard Sylla, *A History of Interest Rates,* 4th ed. (John Wiley & Sons, 2005), p. 274.
15 Dewey, note 13, above, pp. 94–96.
16 On economic growth rates, see Louis Johnston and Samuel H. Williamson, "What Was the U.S. GDP Then?" MeasuringWorth, 2011, available at http://www.measuringworth.com/usgdp. On market reception of the restructured debt, see Dewey, note 13, above, p. 96.

the Royal Navy had over one thousand.[17] Nevertheless, Congress refused to vote for the new excise taxes requested by Treasury Secretary Albert Gallatin. As a result, the government struggled to borrow enough money to fight the War of 1812, and in 1813 the Treasury Department had to be bailed out by private banker Stephen Girard, who personally underwrote a loan after it failed to attract enough subscribers.[18] The United States was barely able to keep its forces supplied through the end of the war in early 1815.[19]

This time, the United States lacked neither the economic potential nor the legal and administrative capacity necessary to raise the money it needed to support its borrowing. U.S. GDP in 1812 was almost $800 million, about three times as high as in 1790; despite more than two years of war, the national debt only grew to 15 percent of GDP by 1816, less than half the level that Hamilton had confronted when taking office.[20] Furthermore, the country had established the administrative apparatus needed to collect both tariffs on external trade and excise taxes on internal commerce. Instead, Congress in 1812 lacked the political will necessary to impose taxes—in particular, because the Democratic-Republicans feared the political consequences of reinstating excise taxes that they had eliminated upon taking power a decade before.[21] This was the fundamental cause of the fiscal crisis of 1813.

Political willingness to pay is, once again, the shadow hanging over the federal government's credit today. The United States may not be able to regain the levels of economic growth of the three decades following World War II. According to mainstream forecasts, how-

---

17 Donald R. Hickey, *The War of 1812: A Forgotten Conflict* (University of Illinois Press, 1995), pp. 90–92.
18 Robert D. Hormats, *The Price of Liberty: Paying for America's Wars from the Revolution to the War on Terror* (Times Books, 2007), pp. 43–44; John Steele Gordon, *Hamilton's Blessing: The Extraordinary Life and Times of Our National Debt*, revised ed. (Walker, 2010), pp. 46–48.
19 Alan Taylor, *The Civil War of 1812: American Citizens, British Subjects, Irish Rebels, & Indian Allies* (Vintage, 2011), pp. 416–17.
20 Treasury Department, " Historical Debt Outstanding—Annual," available at http://www.treasurydirect.gov/govt/reports/pd/histdebt/histdebt.htm.; Johnston and Williamson, note 16, above. Includes gross government debt.
21 Hickey, note 17, above, p. 50; Hormats, note 18, above, pp. 38–39.

ever, the country should be able to sustain levels of economic activity necessary to finance its current debt levels, even given projected increases in government spending. The IMF forecasts that Italy will average real GDP growth of only 0.3 percent from 2012 through 2017, while Spain will average growth of only 0.8 percent, so those countries will need large primary surpluses simply to stabilize their national debt levels. The United States, by contrast, is expected to see real GDP growth of 2.9 percent per year.[22] Since the federal government currently pays a nominal effective interest rate of only 2.1 percent,[23] this means that it could run modest annual deficits while still bringing down the national debt as a percentage of GDP.

The same is true over the longer term, at least according to commonly cited forecasts. Discussions of the United States' fiscal sustainability often begin with the CBO's long-term alternative fiscal scenario. In contrast to the CBO's extended-baseline scenario, which is closely based on current law, the alternative fiscal scenario incorporates several assumptions intended to make it more realistic.[24] According to the most recent alternative fiscal scenario, published in June 2011, the national debt will rise to 187 percent of GDP by 2035; updated to incorporate subsequent legislative changes and economic re-estimates, this figure is now 142 percent of GDP, as shown in Figure 1—still high by any standards.[25] (The most important reason for the decline in projected debt levels is the limits on discretionary spending imposed by the Budget Control Act of 2011.)

---

22 IMF World Economic Outlook Database, April 2012.
23 Projected net interest payments for 2012, divided by the average year-end debt levels for 2011 and 2012. CBO, *The Budget and Economic Outlook: Fiscal Years 2012 to 2022*, January 2012, Table 1-3, p. 10.
24 For example, the alternative fiscal scenario assumes that various tax cuts will be extended rather than allowed to expire; Medicare payment rates will remain at current levels rather than falling as under current law; and the drawdown of troops from Afghanistan will progress as currently scheduled. Somewhat more controversially, it also assumes that tax revenues will remain constant as a share of GDP in the long term. CBO, *CBO's 2011 Long-Term Budget Outlook*, June 2011, pp. 3–7.
25 The CBO's long-term forecasts are extensions of its ten-year forecasts. I have updated the June 2011 long-term alternative fiscal scenario by incorporating the ten-year forecast from the CBO's January 2011 *Budget and Economic Outlook*, using similar assumptions to those in the June 2011 *Long-Term Budget Outlook*.

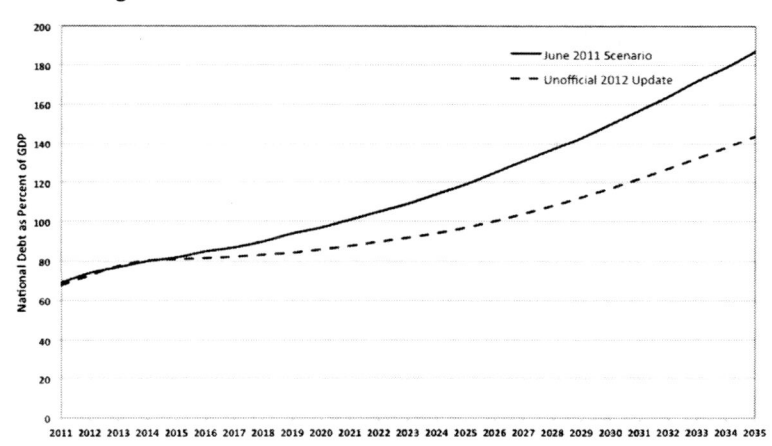

Figure 1: National Debt in CBO Alternative Fiscal Scenario

Source: CBO, *CBO's 2011 Long-Term Budget Outlook*, June 2011; CBO, *The Budget and Economic Outlook: Fiscal Years 2012 to 2022*, January 2012; analysis by the author.

If we take government spending policy as given, however, this high projected debt level is a direct result of the United States' comparatively low tax levels. For the decade from 2000 through 2009, total taxes in the United States averaged 26.9 percent of GDP: 17.6 percent collected by the federal government and 9.3 percent collected by other levels of government.[26] In the OECD as a whole, total taxes over the same period averaged 34.7 percent of GDP—7.8 percentage points higher than in the United States. Increasing federal taxes by 7.8 percentage points would bring them to 25.4 percent of GDP. If federal tax revenues were to stabilize at this level, rather than at the 18.1 percent of GDP specified in my updated version of the alternative fiscal scenario, the national debt in 2035 would be only 45 percent of GDP and falling—even assuming the exact same Social Security, Medicare, and Medicaid obligations that exist today.[27]

---

26 Total tax level is from the OECD.StatExtracts database, Revenue Statistics—Comparative Series. Federal tax level is from OMB, note 2, above, Table 1.2.
27 In the CBO's June 2011 long-term alternative fiscal scenario, tax revenues remain constant after 2021 at their 2021 level of 18.4 percent of GDP. I updated the alternative fiscal scenario by incorporating the ten-year forecast published in January 2012, which goes out through 2022; in that year, tax revenues are now projected to be 18.1 percent of GDP (assuming the same adjustments as those in the CBO's alternative fiscal scenario). So my updated alternative fiscal scenario keeps tax revenues stable at 18.1 percent of GDP after 2022.

The general relationship between federal tax levels and the future national debt can be seen in Figure 2, which plots debt levels in 2035 and 2050 against different levels of federal tax revenues. In each case, I assume that government spending policy is the same as in the CBO's alternative fiscal scenario. I also assume that tax policy is the same as in the alternative fiscal scenario through 2022; that is, the tax level on the X-axis does not take effect until 2023. Even so, it is clear that the national debt could be kept at moderate levels given tax revenues that are only average by international standards. This is not to say that increasing our taxes to these levels is necessarily good policy. My point is simply that the American economy generates sufficient resources such that, with average tax levels, the United States could manage its current debt levels even given expected growth in entitlement spending.[28]

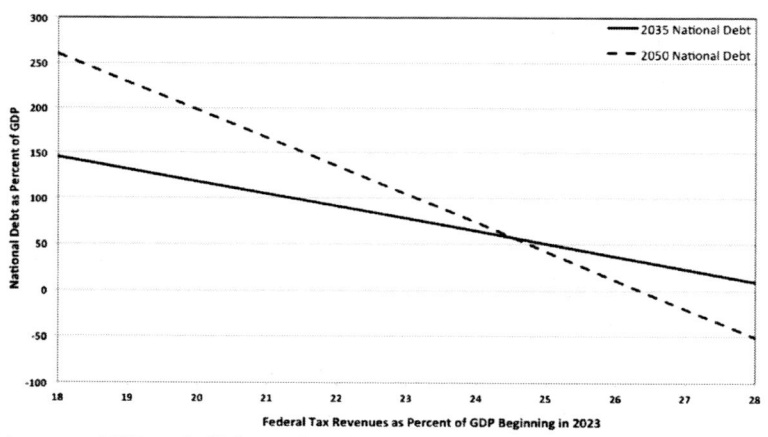

Figure 2: Impact of Tax Level on National Debt

Assumes: real GDP growth of 2.2 percent beginning in 2023; effective real interest rate of 2.7 percent beginning in 2027.
Source: CBO, *CBO's 2011 Long-Term Budget Outlook*, June 2011; CBO, *The Budget and Economic Outlook: Fiscal Years 2012 to 2022*, January 2012; analysis by the author.

Figure 2 incorporates the basic macroeconomic assumptions of the CBO's 2011 long-term forecast: a real interest rate of 2.7 percent and

---

[28] Note that this analysis does not incorporate any potential macroeconomic effects of higher tax levels; this is consistent with usual CBO practice. Higher tax rates could reduce economic growth by changing the incentives facing individuals. That said, tax revenues could be increased significantly by eliminating tax expenditures, which function like government spending programs implemented through the tax code. Eliminating tax expenditures should reduce economic distortions and should not adversely affect incentives to generate income.

a real growth rate of 2.2 percent.[29] Given historical experience, these seem like reasonably conservative assumptions. From 1948 through 2011, the average real effective interest rate paid by the Treasury Department was 1.7 percent; the real interest rate has not exceeded 2.5 percent since 2002.[30] From 1982 through 2011, however, the average rate was 3.6 percent, significantly above the CBO's long-term forecast. This implies that we should attempt to estimate the sensitivity of future debt levels to interest rates. Figure 3 shows the 2050 national debt level as a function of the long-term average real interest rate, assuming real growth of 2.2 percent and a tax level of 25 percent of GDP (the federal tax level that would raise overall taxes to the OECD overage).[31] As can be seen from the figure, higher long-term real interest rates do have a significant impact on future debt levels, but even with interest rates at 4 or 4.5 percent, the 2050 debt remains around current levels.

Figure 3: Impact of Long-Term Interest Rate on 2050 National Debt

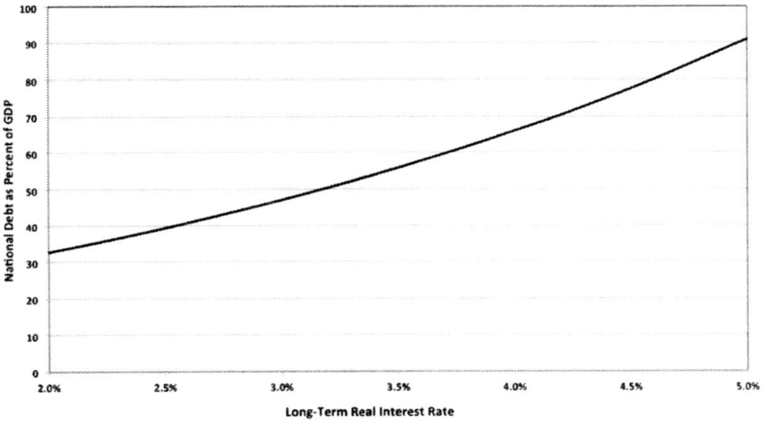

Assumes: federal tax revenues of 25 percent beginning in 2023; real GDP growth of 2.2 percent beginning in 2023.
Source: CBO, *CBO's 2011 Long-Term Budget Outlook*, June 2011; CBO, *The Budget and Economic Outlook: Fiscal Years 2012 to 2022*, January 2012; analysis by the author.

---

29 CBO, *CBO's 2011 Long-Term Budget Outlook*, June 2011, pp. 24–25.
30 Calculated as net interest payments in year N divided by the average of debt held by the public at the end of years N-1 and N, deflated by the annual change in the GDP price index. OMB, note 2, above, Tables 3.1, 7.1; BEA, National Income and Product Accounts, Table 1.1.4.
31 Through 2022, I use the effective interest rate produced by the CBO's alternative ten-year forecast. After that point, I modify the interest rate linearly until it reaches the specified long-term rate (on the X-axis of Figure 2) in 2027. Note that this analysis incorporates only the impact of higher interest rates on the financing of the national debt, not their impact on the overall economy.

The CBO's projected annual real growth rate of 2.2 percent is also consistent with historical experience. From 1948 through 2011, real growth averaged 3.2 percent per year; from 1982 through 2011, growth still averaged 2.7 percent.[32] The CBO projects lower growth in the future because of its assumptions regarding demographic variables and productivity growth. Its demographic variables are taken from the Board of Trustees of the Social Security trust funds, except that it expects immigration to remain at historical rates; the CBO also expects total factor productivity to grow at an annual rate of 1.3 percent.[33] These assumptions could turn out to be overly optimistic. For the purposes of this paper, however, there is no easy way to estimate the sensitivity of future debt levels to different estimates of GDP growth because lower growth levels would have many complicated effects on the federal government's finances.

In summary, the United States appears to have a large enough economy to sustain the federal government's current spending habits at levels of taxation that are unremarkable by international standards. The economy can reasonably be expected to grow fast enough to keep the national debt at a manageable level, despite the demographic changes and health care inflation that are expected to boost spending in the long term, again assuming tax levels around the OECD average.

The United States also has the administrative apparatus necessary to collect those taxes. In different years, the federal government has collected as much as 10.2 percent of GDP in individual income taxes, 7.2 percent of GDP in corporate income taxes, 6.8 percent of GDP in social insurance contributions, and 3.1 percent of GDP in excise taxes, for a potential total of over 27 percent of GDP.[34] While it might not be good policy to increase all of those taxes to those levels, the government has shown the practical ability to collect the revenue necessary to finance its current debts and future spending.

This brings us to the question of political will: are politicians in Washington willing to increase taxes or reduce spending enough to

---

32 BEA, National Income and Product Accounts, Table 1.1.1.
33 CBO, *CBO's 2011 Long-Term Budget Outlook*, pp. 23, 26.
34 OMB, note 2, above, Table 2.3.

keep the national debt at a sustainable level? This is a difficult question to answer, in part because it is not enough for individual politicians to be willing to reduce deficits on their terms; what matters is whether the political system as whole can generate a set of policies that will achieve fiscal sustainability.

One possible approach is to use historical data to assess whether a country is likely to make the fiscal adjustments necessary to manage its debt successfully. In a recent paper, Jonathan D. Ostry, Atish R. Ghosh, Jun I. Kim, and Mahvash S. Qureshi of the IMF used different countries' past willingness to pay—that is, to improve primary budget balances in the face of rising debts—in estimating the "fiscal space" available to them today.[35] The core of their analysis is a "fiscal reaction function" that shows how the primary balance responds to changes in debt levels: over some range of debt levels, as debt increases, countries tend to increase their primary balances in response, which has the effect of lowering the debt. Beyond some point, however, it gets harder and harder to raise taxes or to cut spending further; as a result, improvements in the primary balance will not be large enough to compensate for rising interest payments, and the debt will therefore continue to increase indefinitely. Because creditors are aware of this possibility, they will demand higher interest rates as the debt approaches this point, compounding the problem. Ostry et al. define a country's debt limit as the level of debt (as a percentage of GDP) beyond which debt becomes unsustainable. Fiscal space is the difference between this debt limit and the current level of debt.

Ostry et al. use the fiscal reaction function to estimate the debt limit for twenty-three different countries. For the United States, they estimate the debt limit to be between 160 and 183 percent of GDP.[36] These figures are based on general government debt, including obligations of state and local governments (but not intra-governmental

---

35 Jonathan D. Ostry, Atish R. Ghosh, Jun I. Kim, and Mahvash S. Qureshi, "Fiscal Space," IMF Staff Position Note SPN/10/11, September 1, 2010.
36 The estimates differ depending on whether they use market interest rates for government debt or a model that estimates how the interest rates will rise as debt approaches the debt limit. In the former case, they calculate the debt limit using both historical and projected interest rates. *Ibid.*, pp. 11–12.

debt holdings), which is larger than federal government debt.[37] Still, however, the IMF estimates that general government gross debt will only reach 113 percent of GDP by 2017, apparently leaving a considerable buffer.[38] The fiscal space estimate in Ostry et al. means that, given its past record of responding to debt increases by improving its primary balance,[39] the United States is likely to bring its debt under control so long as it does not exceed 160 percent of GDP. Participants in the credit markets realize this, and therefore they will not demand sharply higher interest rates on Treasury debt until the national debt approaches that level.

From here, however, it is still a long way to conclude that the United States will find the political willingness to pay its debts. As Ostry et al. emphasize, the fiscal reaction function is estimated based on historical data; that is, it projects future responses to increasing debt levels based on past political performance. Therefore, this approach necessarily fails to reflect recent changes in domestic political systems. In particular, if there has been a change in the political dynamics of taxes and spending in the past few decades, this change will not be fully incorporated in the estimated debt limit. The federal government may not respond to increasing debt levels as effectively as it has in the past; market participants may be aware of this change, and may demand higher interest rates at lower debt levels than predicted by Ostry et al. For these reasons, this attempt to estimate fiscal space based on historical performance must be complemented by an analysis of current political dynamics.

Since the midterm elections of November 2010, deficits and the national debt have been at or near the top of the political agenda in Washington. At various times, both parties have agreed on the importance of reducing deficits and bringing the debt under control.

---

37 Correspondence with the authors.
38 IMF World Economic Outlook Database, April 2012.
39 Ostry et al. do not estimate a separate fiscal reaction function for each country. Instead, they estimate a single fiscal reaction function using observations for all countries. This function includes country-level fixed effects and also includes a number of independent variables that vary across countries such as demographic profile, political stability level, openness to trade, etc. Ostry et al., note 35, above, p. 12.

Republicans have seized on the issue in reaction to what many see as excessive spending by the federal government, urged on by the Tea Party movement. For much of 2011, President Obama agreed to focus on deficit reduction, to the chagrin of some more liberal Democrats, who argued that generating economic growth and reducing unemployment should have been a higher priority. But even with both parties agreeing on the goal, they were unable to make much progress toward either increasing taxes or reducing long-term spending significantly. This should lead us to question whether America's elected leaders will collectively be able to muster the political will necessary to pay off our growing debts.

When it comes to fiscal policy, the 111th Congress's main accomplishment since taking office in January 2011 is the Budget Control Act of 2011,[40] enacted in early August in order to avert the potential government default that could have been caused by a failure to raise the statutory debt ceiling. The Budget Control Act imposed statutory limits on discretionary spending in 2012 through 2021, reducing expected outlays by $917 billion over that period. It also created a Joint Select Committee on Deficit Reduction that was mandated to produce a plan to reduce deficits by $1.2 trillion over the same period; because that committee failed to reach agreement, the Budget Control Act required automatic sequesters that reduce spending by almost $1.2 trillion over the 2013–2022 period.[41] Together, these two provisions should reduce spending in 2021 by almost 1.3 percent of GDP (including lower interest payments). Whether they will do so is open to question, however. Whatever Congress can do, Congress can also undo, and both parties have already proposed measures that would undo the automatic sequesters (while replacing them with other deficit-reduction measures).[42] The CBO includes the elimination of these automatic sequesters in its alternative fiscal scenario for the next ten years.[43]

---

40 Pub. L. 112-25, 125 Stat. 240 (2011).
41 CBO, Letter to the Honorable John A. Boehner and the Honorable Harry Reid, August 1, 2011, Table 3; CBO, *The Budget and Economic Outlook: Fiscal Years 2012 to 2022*, January 2012, Table 1-6, pp. 18–19.
42 Suzy Khimm, "How Obama Wants To Soften the Blow of the Debt Ceiling Deal," Wonkblog by Ezra Klein, *The Washington Post*, February 14, 2012; Pete Kasperowicz, "Ryan Offers Bill To End Sequester in Bid To Stop Automatic Defense Cuts," *The Hill*, May 1, 2012.
43 CBO, *The Budget and Economic Outlook: Fiscal Years 2012 to 2022*, January

Even if the spending limits in the Budget Control Act take full effect, they apply mainly to discretionary spending (subject to annual appropriations). All of the projected long-term growth in government spending, however, occurs in the much larger category of mandatory spending (required by law until explicitly repealed or amended), which includes Social Security and most government healthcare programs. In addition, given the scale of the United States' deficits, 1.3 percent of GDP is a relatively small reduction. In December 2010, just months before the debt ceiling standoff, Congress extended through 2012 the George W. Bush income and estate tax cuts (initially passed in 2001 and 2003) and some of the tax cuts contained in the 2009 American Recovery and Reinvestment Act, while also adding a payroll tax cut through 2011; that payroll tax cut was later extended through 2012. Those tax cuts, if extended again, will be worth 3.2 percent of GDP in 2021 (including higher interest payments), dwarfing the savings from the Budget Control Act.[44]

Again, this does not necessarily mean that the December 2010 tax cut was bad policy, or that the Budget Control Act should have mandated larger spending cuts. It simply shows that Congress and the White House, while publicly emphasizing the importance of cutting the deficit, have been unable to achieve significant long-term reductions in the national debt. What reductions they have achieved have been outweighed by other measures that are likely to increase the national debt.

What accounts for this wide gulf between words and deeds? One possible explanation is that politicians in Washington have no interest in fiscal sustainability and only pay it lip service for political reasons, and there is no doubt some truth to that. At least since President Reagan in the 1980s, politicians have railed against deficits while enacting policies that increase deficits. But President Barack Obama and House Speaker John Boehner went to considerable lengths last summer attempting to forge a large, bipartisan deficit

---

2012, pp. 1–2.
44 *Ibid.*, Table 1-6, pp. 18–19. This figure includes the effect of extending the 2001 and 2003 tax cuts and indexing the AMT for inflation; it does not include extension of the payroll tax cut.

reduction package.[45] Furthermore, the "it's all politics" explanation only raises the question of why politicians believe it is in their interests to avoid doing anything about the national debt, even when it has become a front-page issue. Deficits and the national debt are routinely considered one of the top two economic issues facing the United States (along with "jobs" or "the economy"),[46] and leaders of both parties have gone out of their way to elevate their perceived importance among the public. If politicians nevertheless believe that they are better served by doing little or nothing about the issue, there must be some factors in the political environment that make inaction the smart strategy.

Logically speaking, there are two main ways to reduce deficits and therefore the national debt: increasing taxes and reducing spending. At present, there are powerful political constraints against increasing taxes and against reducing the most important categories of government spending. The political dynamics are particularly clear on the tax side. Opposition to tax increases, as well as support for tax cuts whenever possible, has become the central unifying feature of the Republican Party. This goes beyond mere ideology. The party's legislators have effectively committed to block any tax increase by signing the Taxpayer Protection Pledge, conceived of and monitored by Grover Norquist and Americans for Tax Reform, which requires them to oppose any bill that would increase tax rates or tax revenues. At present, a clear majority of the House of Representatives and more than forty members of the Senate have signed the pledge, effectively blocking tax increases in either chamber. The pledge is enforced by the threat to "primary" a legislator who breaks it—that is, to support a right-wing challenger in the next Republican primary election.[47] This is a credible threat because Americans for Tax Reform and likeminded groups such as the Club for Growth and Americans for Pros-

---

[45] See Peter Wallsten, Lori Montgomery, and Scott Wilson, "Obama's Evolution: Behind the Failed 'Grand Bargain' on the Debt," *The Washington Post*, March 17, 2012; Matt Bai, "Obama vs. Boehner: Who Killed the Debt Deal?," *The New York Times*, March 28, 2012.

[46] See, e.g., Lydia Saad, "Americans' Worries About Economy, Budget Top Other Issues," Gallup, March 21, 2011; Frank Newport, "Americans' Economic Worries: Jobs, Debt, and Politicians," Gallup, January 12, 2012.

[47] See Jacob S. Hacker and Paul Pierson, *Off Center: The Republican Revolution and the Erosion of American Democracy* (Yale University Press, 2005), chapters 4–5.

perity can mobilize large amounts of money to support challenges to Republicans whom they consider insufficiently conservative. In 2010, candidates associated with the Tea Party upset Republican incumbents or establishment candidates in six Senate primaries; although breaking the Taxpayer Protection Pledge was not an issue in those elections, this performance showed the political costs of failing to toe the conservative line.[48]

As a result, proposals that would increase tax revenues are effectively off the table in Washington. During the debt ceiling negotiations, Boehner at one point offered $800 billion in higher tax revenues over ten years, but this tax "increase" came with two big caveats. Much of those revenues were created by the assumption that lower tax rates would generate additional economic growth[49]—an assumption that many economists question. In addition, the $800 billion was only an increase from a baseline that assumed the extension of the 2001 and 2003 Bush tax cuts, which were (and are) scheduled to expire at the end of 2012. In other words, Boehner's offer was for a large tax cut relative to current law. There is controversy about exactly what happened, but it appears that Obama asked for an additional $400 billion in tax revenues, which Boehner said he could not get his caucus to approve; Obama then decided to settle for $800 billion at the last minute, which Boehner also rejected. In the "supercommittee" negotiations that followed the passage of the Budget Control Act, Republican members proposed $300 billion in additional tax revenues, but thirty-three Republican senators insisted that there should be no net tax increase and powerful House Majority Leader Eric Cantor refused to endorse the proposal.[50] Even that $300 billion offer was only possible because of the impending expiration of the Bush tax cuts, which made it possible for Republicans to frame it as a way to avoid a large tax increase.[51]

---

48 The Senate primaries were those in Alaska, Delaware, Florida, Kentucky, Nevada, and Utah.
49 Wallsten, Montgomery, and Wilson, note 45, above.
50 Jennifer Steinhauer and Robert Pear, "G.O.P. Is Optimistic but Democrats Are Glum on Deficit Panel," *The New York Times*, November 15, 2011; Robert Pear, "G.O.P. Senators' Letter Clouds Talks on Deficit," *The New York Times*, November 3, 2011.
51 Robert Pear, "Deficit Panel Seeks To Defer Details on Raising Taxes," *The New York Times*, November 13, 2011.

The bottom line is that few people think it would be possible to pass more than a modest tax increase, and any such increase would be from the low baseline set by the 2001 and 2003 tax cuts. This is why major bipartisan budget reduction proposals such as Domenici-Rivlin and Simpson-Bowles reduce tax rates even further from current (George W. Bush) levels; they claim to increase taxes, but tax revenues would remain closer to George W. Bush levels than to the Bill Clinton levels that are scheduled to resume in 2013.[52] Once the fate of the 2001 and 2003 tax cuts is resolved, it is likely that even the small amount of flexibility Republicans have shown during the past year would vanish, since they will no longer be able to excuse a small tax increase on the grounds that it is better than the expiration of those tax cuts. For these reasons, the idea that future budget deficits can be reduced through significant tax increases seems farfetched.

There is no political bar against spending cuts analogous to the Republicans' commitment to oppose tax increases, but the prospects of significant reductions in future spending are also relatively bleak. The underlying constraint is that most government spending programs are popular. Majorities of Americans oppose cutting spending not only on Social Security and Medicare, but also on anti-poverty programs and even funding for the arts and sciences.[53] Despite this, it is politically feasible to reduce discretionary spending. Because discretionary spending is subject to annual appropriations, Congress does not have to affirmatively vote to eliminate or cut back a popular program; instead, it can simply appropriate less money for that program. This is why the Budget Control Act placed caps on discretionary spending in future years.

The problem, from the standpoint of fiscal sustainability, is that there is not that much discretionary spending, and it is declining already.

---

52 Bipartisan Policy Center Debt Reduction Task Force, *Restoring America's Future: Reviving the Economy, Cutting Spending and Debt, and Creating a Simple, Pro-Growth Tax System*, November 2010 ("Domenici-Rivlin"), p. 30 ($435 billion in tax increases over 2012–2020, relative to a baseline in which all expiring tax cuts are extended); National Commission on Fiscal Responsibility and Reform, *The Moment of Truth*, December 2010 ("Simpson-Bowles"), p. 30 ($180 billion dedicated to deficit reduction in 2020, relative to a baseline in which all expiring tax cuts are extended). According to the CBO, the total impact of extending all expiring tax cuts is $4.7 trillion over 2012–2020 and $800 billion in 2020. CBO, *The Budget and Economic Outlook: An Update*, August 2011, Table 1-8, pp. 26–27.
53 Frank Newport and Lydia Saad, "Americans Oppose Cuts in Education, Social Security, Defense," Gallup, January 26, 2011.

Discretionary spending averaged 12.5 percent of GDP in 1962–1969 but only 7.5 percent of GDP in 2000–2009;[54] even before the Budget Control Act, it was already projected to fall to 6.1 percent of GDP in 2021.[55] Deep cuts in defense spending, which currently makes up more than half of all discretionary spending, are also politically difficult. All of the projected growth in government spending comes in mandatory programs, particularly in Social Security and in federal health care programs, including Medicare, Medicaid, and the new health insurance subsidies mandated by the Affordable Care Act of 2010. Reducing this spending is always politically treacherous. These programs are very popular—especially Social Security and Medicare, which benefit large numbers of people and are widely seen as earned entitlements. In addition, their benefits are set by law for decades into the future, so reducing spending requires a politically dangerous vote to cut those benefits.

Focusing on the two most important entitlement programs, Social Security and Medicare, recent history has amply demonstrated the political hurdles standing in the way of significant spending cuts. The most recent attempt to modify Social Security was undertaken by President George W. Bush in 2005. While no final proposal was ever released, the administration floated the idea of diverting a portion of workers' payroll taxes into individual accounts, with a corresponding reduction in their statutory benefits. This proposal would have required large amounts of additional borrowing in the short term (to pay benefits to current retirees) but might have improved the program's long-term financial outlook by reducing its mandatory obligations. Opponents easily attacked the proposal as reducing benefits and shifting investment risk onto individual workers; despite majorities in both the House and the Senate, Republican congressional leaders declined to bring the issue to the floor.

Medicare provides an even clearer example of the difficulty of reducing entitlement spending. In order to pay for its expanded coverage

---

54 OMB, note 2, above, Table 8.4.
55 CBO, *The Budget and Economic Outlook: Fiscal Years 2011 to 2021*, January 2011, Tables 1-4, 1-7, pp. 15, 22–23. I deducted from baseline discretionary spending the adjustment for the projected reduction in spending on overseas contingency operations (primarily Iraq and Afghanistan).

provisions, including health insurance subsidies and an expansion of Medicaid eligibility, the Affordable Care Act of 2010 included several provisions that would reduce growth in Medicare spending by about $400 billion over ten years.[56] Among others, these included a reduction in payments to Medicare Advantage plans, changes to the formulas for calculating reimbursement rates, increasing Part B premiums for higher-income beneficiaries, and reducing payments to disproportionate share hospitals.[57] Before and since its passage, Republicans have attacked the Affordable Care Act for cutting Medicare, with presidential nominee Mitt Romney recently claiming that President Obama "has taken a series of steps that end Medicare as we know it."[58]

In 2011, the House Budget Committee, led by Representative Paul Ryan, proposed converting Medicare into a program where beneficiaries would receive vouchers they could use to buy coverage from private insurers—but the vouchers would grow in value considerably more slowly than likely health care inflation, shifting both costs and risks onto beneficiaries. In 2012, the same committee issued a slightly modified proposal in which vouchers would increase in value with growth in per capita GDP plus 0.5 percent points, again more slowly than expected health care inflation.[59] After Romney endorsed the Ryan plan, President Obama responded by saying that the plan would "end Medicare as we know it."[60]

This is not the place to discuss which Medicare proposal is better policy. The point here is that each party positively relishes the opportunity to attack the other for cutting Medicare. When Romney first signaled his support for the Ryan plan, one Democratic operative's response to a reporter was: "Rejoicing."[61] And so far, it seems to

---

56 CBO, Letter to the Honorable Nancy Pelosi, March 20, 2010, Table 5.
57 Kaiser Family Foundation, "Summary of New Health Reform Law," April 15, 2011.
58 "Mitt Romney Delivers Remarks to the Newspaper Association of America," Boston, Massachusetts, April 4, 2012, available at http://www.mittromney.com/news/press/2012/04/mitt-romney-delivers-remarks-newspaper-association-america.
59 CBO, "The Long-Term Budgetary Impact of Paths for Federal Revenues and Spending Specified by Chairman Ryan," March 2012, p. 3.
60 "Remarks by the President at the Associated Press Luncheon," Washington, D.C., April 3, 2012.
61 Greg Sargent, "Mitt Romney Fully Embraces Paul Ryan's Medicare Plan," The Plum Line, *The Washington Post*, December 8, 2011.

be a viable strategy. Republicans successfully used Medicare spending cuts (among other things) to demonize the Affordable Care Act, which helped them win the November 2010 midterm elections. In May 2011, Democrat Kathy Hochul won a seat in Congress from a conservative New York district, coming from far behind by making the special election all about the recently released Ryan plan.[62] These are only individual data points, but there seems little reason to believe that significant cuts to Medicare spending, no matter how principled or well thought out, can be a winning political issue. This is all the more true given the increasingly negative tone of American political campaigns in the super PAC era, when attacking your opponent as a cold-hearted scourge of the elderly—or having an "independent organization" attack her for you—is a familiar formula for electoral success.

For these reasons, the prospects for major reductions in future entitlement spending seem slim. Ultimately, this is not simply a matter of clever politicking. Medicare, as well as Social Security and even Medicaid, is a very popular program. Furthermore, many people see it as a benefit that they earn by paying payroll taxes, even though a typical person's lifetime contributions do not come close to covering the actuarially fair value of Medicare coverage. (Medicare Parts B and D are largely funded by contributions from general revenues.) The fact that Medicare has a dedicated funding mechanism (payroll taxes and beneficiary premiums) that is insufficient to cover its costs may have created the perverse situation where participants feel as entitled as if they were paying their full costs, even though they are paying only a modest fraction of those costs directly.

There are real reasons to worry about whether our elected officials can muster the political will necessary to increases taxes or cut spending sufficiently to put the national debt on a sustainable footing. Washington's failure to address the national debt reflects the attitude of the American electorate at large, which stands ready to punish politicians either for raising taxes or for slashing popular social insurance programs.

---

62 Raymond Hernandez, "Democrat Wins G.O.P. Seat: Rebuke Seen to Medicare Plan," *The New York Times*, May 24, 2011.

Despite these political constraints, the United States is unlikely to explicitly default on its debts anytime soon. If the fiscal situation deteriorates, some sort of debt restructuring deal would be the most likely outcome. If all else fails, the Federal Reserve could resort to monetizing the debt, because it is denominated in dollars.

The more pressing question is whether the United States will adopt policies that make the national debt sustainable without experiencing a deep fiscal crisis that would require negotiations with creditors or sharp austerity measures. Current political dynamics do not appear encouraging, since there appears to be an insuperable barrier preventing tax increases and a strong presumption against significant cuts in entitlement spending. Still, as mentioned earlier, the credit markets remain remarkably sanguine about U.S. debt, with the yield on 30-year Treasury bonds barely above 3 percent.[63] It is possible that interest rates are so low because of "non-economic" investors, such as foreign central banks, that are primarily concerned with safety and liquidity and do not see other promising places to stash their money. It is also possible that investors are relying on the saying attributed to Winston Churchill: "We can always count on the Americans to do the right thing, after they have exhausted all the other possibilities." Markets may be betting that today's levels of polarization and gridlock cannot continue in the face of growing debts.

In the current political environment, if there is to be a solution, it is more likely to be along Republican lines than Democratic ones. In the Taxpayer Protection Pledge and the threat of attack from well-funded conservative groups, anti-tax advocates have found an effective way of locking the Republican Party into a "no new taxes" position; Democrats have no such device to protect entitlement programs. Furthermore, early anecdotal evidence implies that recent changes in campaign finance law are likely only to strengthen the position of conservative pressure groups, making it even harder to increase tax revenues. The growing national debt may also make reductions in those programs more politically feasible. In 1995, a Republican proposal to partially privatize Medicare was a major reason

---

[63] Federal Reserve Statistical Release H.15.

for their defeat in the budget showdown with President Clinton;[64] today, at least some party leaders have decided that a similar proposal has political potential. Still, there have been numerous political realignments in American history, and the specter of the national debt could provide the motivating force for another one in the next decade or two. It is the contours of the American political system that will determine whether and how the United States deals with its long-term debt problem.

---

64 Iwan Morgan, *The Age of Deficits: Presidents and Unbalanced Budgets from Jimmy Carter to George W. Bush* (University Press of Kansas, 2009), pp. 183–87.

12
Burning the Furniture to Heat the House – The Potential Role of Asset Sales in Funding the Federal Government's Deficits

Jim Millstein*

"And that claim is by the right of our manifest destiny to overspread and to possess the whole of the continent which Providence has given us for the development of the great experiment of liberty and federated self-government entrusted to us." – John L. O'Sullivan[1]

Introduction

Washington's inability to bring its deficits under control is the product of a political stalemate, now entering its second decade, that threatens the long-term solvency of the Federal Government. One political party is committed to "starving the beast," the other to keeping in place post-retirement benefits designed when Americans lived

---

* Jim Millstein served as Chief Restructuring Officer of the US Department of the Treasury from 2009 to 2011 and is now the Chairman and CEO of Millstein & Co., L.P., a financial services firm.
1 *New York Morning News,* Dec. 27, 1845, quoted in McCrisken, Trevor B., *Exceptionalism: Manifest Destiny*, in Encyclopedia of American Foreign Policy, Vol. 2, p. 68, 2002.

much shorter lives. The only budgetary priority that garners bipartisan support is military spending that now exceeds the defense outlays of the next ten largest economies combined.[2] As a result of this fiscal stalemate, annual federal deficits exceeding 5% of GDP stretch out as far as the Congressional Budget Office is willing to project.

That the cost of servicing the $8 trillion of publicly-held debt that the last three Administrations have racked up remains manageable is largely a result of the Federal Reserve's intervention in Treasury markets and its maintenance of low interest rates for what is now an unprecedented period of time. If the Federal Reserve is ultimately forced to unwind its monetary expansion and move rates higher, the increased cost of servicing the Federal debt will crowd out private capital formation and productive government investment, constraining economic growth and undermining the US government's future ability to meet fiscal burdens going forward. Budgetary discipline is required.

This chapter explores the role that asset sales could play in facilitating the inevitable political compromise that is needed to right our fiscal ship. In the absence of policymakers' willingness both to raise taxes and to cut entitlement and military spending, selling off the Federal Government's substantial landholdings and mineral rights to the highest bidders and applying the proceeds to reduce our debt to more sustainable levels may be the path of least political resistance, however embarrassing it may be to a once proud empire.

The Risk of a Bond Market Revolt

Policymakers in Washington, DC seem unwilling or unable to make hard decisions to bring US fiscal imbalances to a sustainable path. While some deficit hawks see as a blessing the imminancy of the "fiscal cliff" (where the combination of expiring tax cuts and mandatory spending cuts will automatically kick in next year without further Congressional action), seasoned Washington observers see "going over the cliff" as nothing more than a set up for each side to re-claim

---

[2] Stockholm International Peace Research Institute, SIPRI Military Expenditure Database, available at http://www.sipri.org.

its spending and tax cutting credentials with its core constituency once the Congress re-convenes in 2013. In short, the cliff is more likely to be a small step down.

Restoring some of the automatic spending cuts would be a good outcome for the economy in the short run. However, it increases the likelihood that the Congressional Budget Office's (CBO) "alternative scenario" fiscal projection will be realized: deficits averaging 5.4 percent of GDP over the 2013-2022 period, and debt held by the public increasing to 94 percent of GDP by 2022.[3]

While deficits and debt levels of such magnitude would normally attract higher borrowing rates, a Federal Reserve dedicated to avoiding a deflationary debt spiral and the safe-haven status of Treasury securities for European investors confronting a more imminent sovereign debt crisis have combined to mute the bond market vigilantes. But we should not be lulled into a false sense of complacency: The Federal Reserve's recent intervention in Treasury markets has been unprecedented in the post WWII era. Between 2009 and 2011, the US Department of the Treasury issued $5.8 trillion of interest-bearing marketable debt to finance record deficits and the Federal Reserve purchased $1.3 trillion of those securities in the secondary market, $772 billion in 2011 alone—equivalent to 48 percent of the amount Treasury issued into the market that year.

These purchases by the Federal Reserve held down Treasury's borrowing costs and allowed Treasury to extend the average maturity of its portfolio from 4.1 years to 5.2 years over the last three years, despite a worsening fiscal position.

---

3 Congressional Budget Office, 2011 Long-Term Budget Outlook, Feb. 29, 2012 (assumes tax cuts implemented by President Bush apart from payroll tax reduction are extended, the alternative minimum tax is indexed for inflation after 2011, Medicare payment rates for physicians remain at current levels, and the automatic discretionary spending reductions required by the Budget Control Act do not take effect).

Figure 1: U.S. Treasury Maturity Schedule and Federal Reserve Holdings

Federal Reserve Holdings of Treasury Securities

Average Maturity

Sources: Federal Reserve; Treasury; Bloomberg.
Notes: Maturity schedule as of April 30, 2012.

Figure 2: Issuance and Interest Rates

- Treasury Issuance (LHS)
- Fed Purchases (LHS)
- Avg Int Rate* (RHS)

Sources: Federal Reserve; Treasury; Bloomberg.
Notes: Average interest rate on marketable interest-bearing securities.

While safe-haven flows will likely persist in the near term given Europe's woes, the Federal Reserve's willingness to monetize fiscal deficits will likely not. First of all, the Federal Reserve is getting less bang for its buck. The federal funds rate has been close to zero for four years, and the Federal Reserve has engaged in three rounds of quantitative easing. Yet growth remains weak. Moreover, according to the central bank's Senior Loan Officer Opinion Survey on Bank Lending Practices data, access to credit is still constrained. Small businesses—which are most sensitive to changes in bank lending practices—overwhelmingly point to poor sales, taxes, and government regulations as the most important problem they face, not credit.[4] In short, an accommodative monetary policy unprecedented in scope and duration is having at best only a muted impact on the US economy.

Second, the threat of inflation and of currency depreciation from the Federal Reserve's expanding balance sheet is significant, at least in the medium term. While the Federal Reserve insists that it has tools to contract the money supply when the economy begins to recover—selling Treasury securities, increasing the rate of interest on reserve balances, offering term deposits, engaging in reverse repurchase agreements[5]—the sheer amount of stimulus it must withdraw is massive, and the reduction in money supply likely necessary to avoid inflation down the road is unprecedented. It will be nothing short of miraculous if the transition from an accommodative monetary policy of unprecedented proportions to a contractionary monetary stance can be effectuated without a significant increase in Federal borrowing costs.

Moreover, for the dollar to remain a viable reserve currency over the long run, interest rates in the US must exceed expected inflation. Confidence that the dollar can achieve that equilibrium over the long run is waning. Its trade-weighted value has fallen roughly 20 percent over the past 10 years, and its share of official reserves and foreign currency transactions has gradually declined.

---

4 Dunkelberg, W., Wade, H., NFIB Small Business Economic Trends, p. 18, Jun. 2012.
5 Bernanke, B., Testimony Before the House Financial Services Committee, Feb. 10, 2010.

Figure 3: The Federal Reserve Cannot Defy Economic Gravity Forever

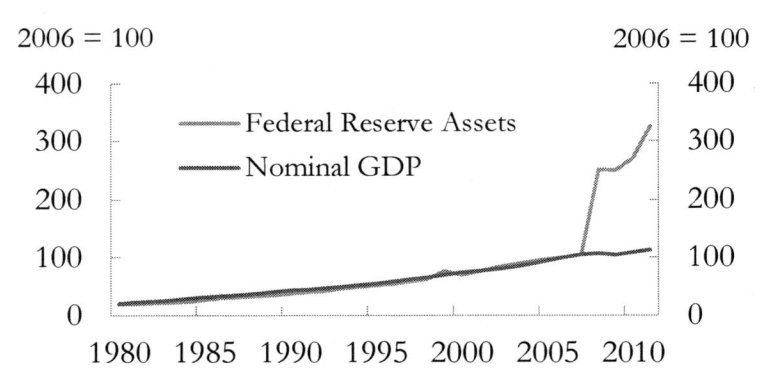

Sources: Federal Reserve; Bureau of Economic Analysis.

Figure 4: U.S. Dollar Losing Prominence and Value

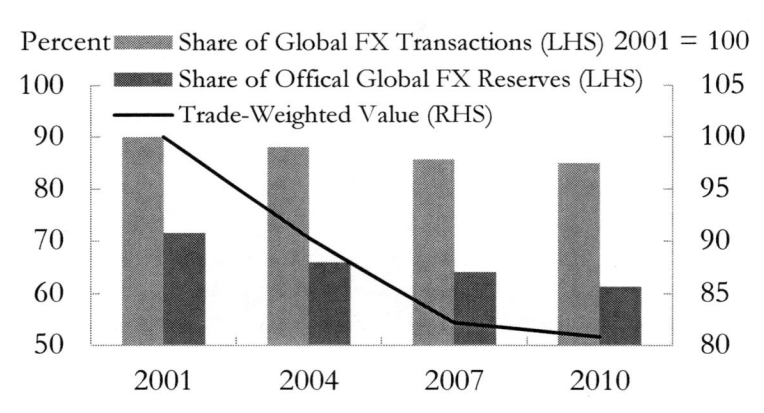

Sources: Bank for International Settlements; International Monetary Fund; Federal Reserve.

Declining confidence in the dollar (itself a by-product of our fiscal stalemate) and Federal Reserve actions to reduce its balance sheet and contract the money supply will create significant headwinds for US government financing. Sales by the Federal Reserve of its now substantial portfolio of Treasury securities will reduce prices and increase Treasury borrowing rates; the offering of term deposits will compete with demand for Treasury bills;[6] the offering of higher rates

---

6 Goodfriend, M., *Central Banking in the Credit Turmoil: An Assessment of Federal Reserve Practices,* Journal of Monetary Economics, pp. 1-12, Jan. 2011.

on reserve balances will also decrease bank demand for short-term Treasury securities. And if inflation does in fact pick up or the dollar depreciates, investors will demand higher rates to protect real returns and compensate for returns available elsewhere.

There is also a feedback loop that will constrain further Federal Reserve monetization of US debt. Woodford and Sims argue that prices will naturally rise if fiscal authorities continue to run excessive deficits while the central bank restrains growth in the money supply.[7] Unless policymakers begin to exercise fiscal discipline, we could enter a vicious cycle of inflationary pressure and monetary tightening.

The combination of an increasing sovereign debt burden, increasing benchmark interest rates, and a falling dollar could drive Federal Government borrowing costs up significantly. It is entirely possible that we could return to Federal borrowing rates last seen in the 1990s and 1980s. If so, Federal Government interest costs would average between seven and nine percent on new issues, compared with less than three percent at which the Government is borrowing on average today. The threat of public debt service crowding out private capital formation and government spending on productive activities would be even more severe if the CBO's alternative scenario projection came to pass, in which the ratio of debt held by the public would reach 82 percent by 2015 and the deficit still remain elevated at five percent of GDP. If markets forced Treasury borrowing costs to return to the average of where they were during the stagflating 1980s—9.1 percent—debt service would reach 70 percent of total government outlays projected by the CBO in 2016.

---

[7] Woodford, M., *Price-Level Determinancy Without Control of a Monetary Aggregate*, Carnegie-Rochester Conference Series on Public Policy, 43, pp. 1-46, 1995; Sims, C.A., *A Simple Model for Study of the Determination of the Price Level and Interaction of Monetary and Fiscal Policy*, Economic Theory, 4, pp. 381-399, 1994.

Figure 5: U.S. Debt Service Costs

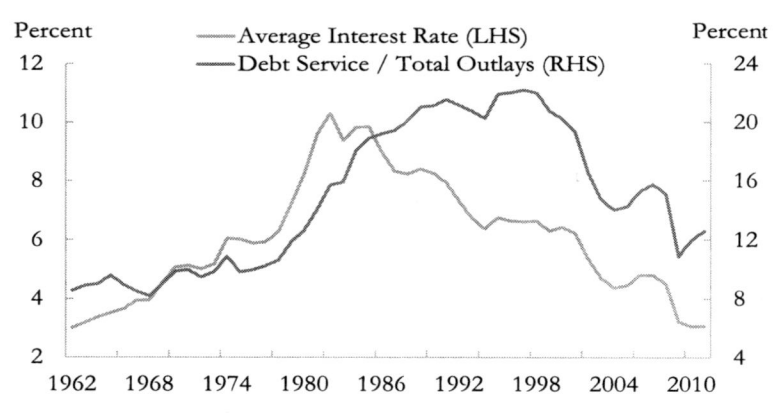

— Average Interest Rate (LHS)
— Debt Service / Total Outlays (RHS)

Sources: Office of Management and Budget, President's Budget for FY2013, Historical Tables; Treasury.
Notes: Average interest rate on total interest-bearing debt

Table 1: Interest Rate Sensitivity

	Average Interest Rate	*Implications for Servicing Today's Debt*	
Period	Rate	Service/ Total Outlays	Service/ GDP
Today	2.7%	11.1%	2.7%
2000s	4.9%	20.0%	4.8%
1990s	7.0%	28.5%	6.9%
1980s	9.1%	37.3%	9.0%

Sources: Office of Management and Budget, President's Budget for FY2013, Historical Tables; Treasury.
Notes: Sensitivity calculations use debt service, total outlays, and GDP for 2011.

Options for Skinning the Debt Cat

Before any of these scenarios come to pass, policymakers must toss the mantle of Hamlet aside and act to reduce our ongoing deficits and put the federal government's finances back on a sustainable path.

There are six basic options to skin the debt cat, and only two are viable without significant economic dislocation in the transition. The full list of options includes fiscal austerity (some combination of increased tax revenues and reduced spending phased in over the medium term), asset sales, stimulus (which produces higher tax revenues and reduced social welfare spending through enhanced economic growth), default, monetizing or inflating away debt, or financial repression. The two best options to reduce deficits in the medium term and to promote growth in the long term are fiscal austerity and asset sales.

Before exploring how much of the burden asset sales can handle, I will briefly explain why four of the options are not viable.

Some have argued that large-scale fiscal stimulus is the way out of the debt trap.[8] The logic is that tax revenue from higher growth will more than offset the lifetime cost of additional near-term borrowing to finance the stimulus. Looking only at the current low interest rate environment, this argument may have some appeal. However, recent experience suggests that Keynesian multipliers on spending programs may be significantly less than advocates of this approach would have us believe. If, as Cogan, Cwik, Taylor, and Wieland convincingly argue, the multiplier is less than one, then stimulus offers a bad trade.[9] Policymakers would simply pull forward economic resources at a premium. Moreover, they would add to a debt burden already approaching levels historically correlated with lower growth[10] and at which the borrowing rate dynamic could change. It should therefore be unsurprising that countries rarely grow their way out of debt problems.[11]

---

8 Summers, L. and Delong, B., *Fiscal Policy in a Depressed Economy*, Brookings Paper on Economic Activity, Mar. 2012; Krugman, P., *Fiscal Policy Works*, The New York Times, The Conscience of a Liberal Blog, Dec. 24, 2011.
9 Cogan, J. et al., *New Keynsian Versus Old Keynsian Government Spending Multipliers*, Journal of Economic Dynamics and Control, Vol. 34, Issue 3, pp. 281-295, Mar. 2010.
10 Reinhart, C. and Rogoff, K., *Growth in a Time of Debt*, American Economic Review: Papers & Proceedings 2010, 100:2, pp. 1-9 (demonstrating that median growth rates for countries with public debt over roughly 90 percent of GDP are about one percent lower than otherwise and average growth rates are several percent lower).
11 *Id.*

Outright default or restructuring or attempting to implement capital controls would generate a severe credit shock in the US and abroad. Investors in US securities across the risk spectrum would flee, provoking a severe credit contraction and sinking prices along with the dollar. Moreover, impairing recoveries on Treasury securities would reduce the value of a large proportion of the assets on balance sheets of US financial and non-financial companies alike. Domestic providers of credit—banks, mortgage finance companies, life insurance companies—would all retrench, slowing economic activity. The capital buffers that US banks have built up since the crisis would likely be eliminated, requiring government re-intervention to shore up the financial sector at the worst possible time. Moreover, it is unlikely that the US could effectively implement capital controls to prevent capital flight, given how open its economy is today.

Using inflation to reduce the US government's real burden of debt service would run directly contrary to one of the Federal Reserve's two core mandates. And if Congress proved desperate enough to revise the central bank's charter to force it to abandon price stability as a target, markets would revolt. Inflation would reduce real returns not only on Treasury securities, but all US securities. The dollar would again sink. And borrowing costs for the Federal Government would skyrocket.

That leaves budgetary austerity and asset sales. Political compromise to reach agreement on serious long-term budgetary austerity is unlikely in the near term for two reasons. First, the majority of serious debt reduction proposals call for both lower expenditures and tax increases.[12] As Alexander explains, leading proposals reflect very different if not irreconcilable political priorities, which make it difficult to achieve consensus on long-term reform.[13] For example, there are

---

[12] President Obama's FY2013 Budget, the LaTourette-Cooper Plan modeled after proposals from the Bowles-Simpson Commission and the Domenici-Rivlin Task Force, and the Progressive Caucus proposed budget, all feature combinations of lower expenditures and tax increases. The Ryan Plan calls for lowering expenditures and taxes.

[13] Alexander, L., *Near-Term Fiscal Challenges for the US*, Nomura Policy Watch, Jun. 26, 2012 (comparing the Ryan plan, which would shrink federal transfer programs without directly increasing aggregate tax revenues, with the Progressive Caucus plan, which increase the progressivity of the tax system to accommodate rising healthcare costs).

fundamental disagreements over the appropriate level of expenditures in social security, health care, and defense—by far the largest contributors to Federal spending. Second, US policymakers share the same fear as their European peers: tightening too fast, too quickly would likely send the economy into another recession. Each side of the political aisle highlights that risk in defending its refusal to cut spending, on the one side, and in refusing to raise taxes, on the other. As a result, we are left with a budgetary stalemate and seemingly no alternative but to sell assets to bring our debt levels down to sustainable levels in the medium term.

Brief History of Sovereign Asset Sales

Sovereigns have long relied on asset sales to raise revenue and adjust fiscal balances, and more recently to promote economic efficiency, competition, and the development of their capital markets.

Land sales are the most dramatic examples. In the 12th century, King Richard I sold real property throughout England to finance his Crusade, famously stating: "I would sell London, if I could find a purchaser." In the 19th century, Napoleon sold the Louisiana Territory to pay off debts incurred to fund his military campaigns, while Russia sold the Alaska Territory to avoid spending money to have to defend it against the British.

Mineral rights, including oil and gas rights, have become increasingly valuable over the past century and an alternative to outright land sales. For example, Colombia has granted foreign corporations oil exploration and production rights on over 90 million acres of land, as well as mining rights on another 12 million acres and farming rights on other land. That represents mineral and agricultural rights on 40 percent of the country's land. In order to fuel its economic growth and satisfy its growing demand for industrial inputs, China has provided cheap funding to its nascent private sector and to its state-owned enterprises to obtain significant mineral rights in Africa, Latin America, Southeast Asia, Iran, and Russia.

Over 100 countries have auctioned off state-owned enterprises (SOEs) since World War II ended.[14] The Federal Republic of Germany under Adenauer sold majority stakes in Volkswagen in 1961 and in VEBA in 1965. Privatization took deeper root in the early 1980s, most famously under Thatcher's UK government which sold stakes in British Telecom, British Aerospace, and Cable and Wireless. And the fall of communism in Eastern Europe and Russia brought waves of SOE sales.[15]

Asset sales are also playing a role in addressing the current European sovereign debt crisis. The troika of the European Union, European Central Bank, and International Monetary Fund are requiring asset sales from Greece, Portugal, and Ireland in exchange for bailout funds. Italy has pledged to raise €15 billion from real-estate sales by 2015.

However, states do not part with assets lightly, in particular with land and mineral rights. National pride in ownership can be a large obstacle, as can security and environmental concerns. There is also a danger that a sovereign will attempt to re-trade an asset physically located in its territory. Venezuela and Argentina offer recent examples. Voiding past sales impairs the value of future sales, as investors, once bitten, will be twice shy. It can also damage other private capital flows and lead to cross-border political turmoil.

Also, in theory, and other things equal, the sale price of an asset should equal the present value of future income derived from the operation or exploitation of that asset. If the discount rate is equal to a sovereign's cost of borrowing and the objective is to raise revenue to repay debt, then the state may be equally well off financing against the asset value as it would be in selling it.

---

14 *See generally* Organisation for Economic Co-Operation and Development, *Privatising State-Owned Enterprises, An Overview of Policies and Practices in OECD Countries*, 2003; Megginson, W. and Netter, J., *From State to Market: A Survey of Empirical Studies on Privatization*, Journal of Economic Literature, Jun. 2001.

15 *See, e.g.*, Freeland, C., Sale of the Century: Russia's Wild Ride from Communism to Capitalism, 2000.

However, other things may not be equal. For example, it may be politically divisive to extract minerals in environmentally-protected areas. It may simply be easier to sell such an asset to a third party, pocket the proceeds as debt reduction and stand by and watch that party seek to balance the competing interests that have stalemated the exploitation of much of the value of the Federal Government's mineral rights for the past 40 years.

Sale of The 21St Century – What Could the U.S. Raise Through Asset Sales?

The US government has substantial saleable assets. It owns over 650 million acres of land, representing 29 percent of total land in the country.[16] Most Federal land is located in western states and Alaska. For example, the US government owns 85 percent of land in Nevada, 69 percent of Alaska, and 45 percent of land in California, while it owns less than one percent of land in New York and roughly two percent of land in Texas.[17]

The US government also has a wealth of mineral rights, including oil, natural gas, coal, and iron. Many are currently off limits to development, including the Eastern Gulf of Mexico, portions of the Rocky Mountains, and the Atlantic and Pacific Outer Continental Shelf. According to Wood Mackenzie, those areas could in the aggregate yield nearly 100 billion barrels of oil equivalent.[18]

According to the Office of Management and Budget (OMB), the aggregate book value of these and other Federal Government assets was $4 trillion at the end of 2011.[19] Approximately $1.4 trillion was financial assets with various degrees of liquidity, and $900 billion was defense-related fixed reproducible capital. The agency attributed only $942 billion of the total to land and mineral rights: $463 billion

---

16 U.S. General Services Administration, Federal Real Property Profile 2004.
17 *Id.*
18 Energy Policy at a Crossroads: An Assessment of the Impacts of Increased Access Versus Higher Taxes on US Oil and Natural Gas Production, Government Revenue, and Employment 2011 [hereinafter Wood Mackenzie, Energy Policy at a Crossroads].
19 President's Budget for Fiscal Year 2013, Analytical Perspectives, p. 491.

for land and $479 billion for minerals, and implied that the market value of the Federal Government's land and mineral rights could be considerably higher.[20]

Figure 6: Resource Estimates of U.S. Areas Currently Off Limits

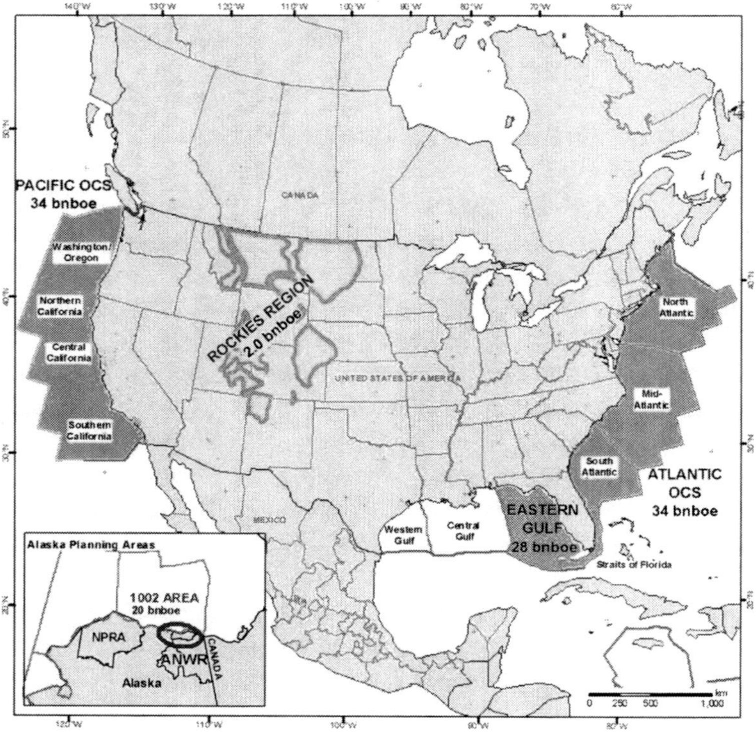

Source: Wood Mackenzie

Alaskan land alone could yield between $500 billion and $1.5 trillion. The US government owns over 240 million acres of land in the state, representing 37 percent of all Federal land holdings. Much of it is along the coast, including parkland and fishing grounds. Assuming that recent OMB estimates of US government land values are on the mark and that all Federal parcels across the country are equally valuable, selling that land could raise $171 billion. However, revenues from timber, fishing, and tourism, among other industries,

---

20 OMB concedes that the estimates for land and mineral rights in the President's Budget do not reflect market values. *Id.* at 492.

would likely command a premium to that estimate if it was sold to private companies.

The US government could do even better selling its mineral rights in the states. Recent political debate has focused on whether to exploit resources located under the Coastal Plain of the Arctic National Wildlife Refuge. According to Arctic Power, a non-profit organization of Alaskan companies in a variety of industries, lease sale revenues, royalties, and taxes to the Federal government from developing the Coastal Plain could be between $89 billion and $244 billion.[21] The US Chamber of Commerce puts the upper estimate at $167 billion.[22] In 1985, Boskin et al. estimated that the value of all Federal oil and gas rights in Alaska was $335 billion,[23] an estimate that must be viewed as conservative, given discoveries and improvements in extraction technology since.

So $500 billion to $600 billion would appear to be the minimum the Federal Government could obtain from the sale of all Federal land and mineral rights in Alaska. If applied to the reduction of the Federal Government's outstanding indebtedness, that would represent about five percent of the $10.9 trillion of US debt currently held by the public, reducing debt as a share of GDP to 64 percent.

The US government could take a more aggressive approach to Alaska's mineral and land rights. The state's share of oil revenues is between 2 to 2.5 times the Federal government's share. If the Federal government expropriated the state's mineral rights as well, then the combined public mineral rights could be valued between $1 trillion to $1.2 trillion. Similarly, land rights currently held by the State could be worth between $100 billion and $150 billion. Transferring federal sovereignty over the territory as a whole therefore might gar-

---

21 See anwr.org. The organization also argues that developing the Coastal Plain could further decrease US reliance on oil imports and create between 250,000 and 750,000 jobs.
22 Issue Advertisment, Feb. 28, 2012, available at http://www.uschamber.com/ads/mr-president-make-american-energy-next-big-thing.
23 Boskin, M. et al., *New Estimates of the Value of Federal Mineral Rights and Land*, American Economic Review, 75, pp. 923-936, 1985; *see also* Boskin, M. and Robinson, M., T*he Value of Federal Mineral Rights, Correction and Update*, American Economic Review, 77, pp.1073-1074, 1987.

ner additional revenue.[24] These additional actions, if legal, could generate aggregate proceeds of between $1.3 trillion and $1.5 trillion, or 13 to 14 percent of US debt held by the public. That would be substantially more than the two cents per acre price that the US paid Russia in 1867, or more than a tenfold return on the $110 million in today's dollars that was then referred to as Seward's Folly.

Beyond the Coastal Plain in Alaska, oil and gas reserves in Federal lands currently off limits to development might generate an additional $350 billion through 2030.[25] Because these areas would continue to produce significant flows beyond 2030, the US government may be able to obtain as much as $1 trillion if it were to sell them now.

Liquidating the US government's entire portfolio of land and mineral rights might therefore generate closer to $2.5 to $3.5 trillion. On top of that, selling the assets in the Federal Government's financial portfolio could yield $1 trillion. The nearly $900 billion in defense assets would probably continue to be viewed as off limits, but selling non-defense fixed reproducible capital and inventories could yield an additional $800 billion.

The aggregate sales price of all of these non-defense assets could be between $4.3 and $5.4 trillion, which, if applied to debt reduction, could decrease publicly-held debt as a share of GDP to between 36 and 43 percent—well below the 90 percent threshold associated with slower growth[26] and in line with AAA-rated Sweden.

Conclusion

In looking for solutions to the US debt problem, serious consideration should be given to asset sales. The US has a wealth of assets. Selling those assets could turn around a dangerously weakening balance sheet.

---

24 The State of Alaska currently has $30 billion in obligations, which would offset at least some of a premium that sovereignty transfer could provide.
25 Wood Mackenzie, Energy Policy at a Crossroads, note 18 above.
26 Reinhart and Rogoff, note 10 above.

There will inevitably be objections to the downsizing of a nation that was largely assembled through annexation and purchase over the past two hundred and fifty years. But the reality of the current political stalemate between the parties has put into question our ability to fund the "manifest destiny" to which generations of Americans have subscribed. And so, before we find ourselves forced to sell these assets under duress, policymakers should consider developing a plan to sell them in an orderly fashion to obtain their maximum value, bring our debt down, and put our budget on a sustainable footing.

13
United States Sovereign Debt: A Thought Experiment On Default And Restructuring

Charles W. Mooney, Jr.*

I. Introduction

I have quite self-consciously styled this essay a "thought experiment" on the default and restructuring of United States (U.S.) sovereign debt. The U.S. debt addressed here is the obligation of the U.S. on its Treasury Securities. I make no claim that a default by the U.S on its Treasuries is likely or imminent. Nor do I argue that a restructuring, whether based on bilateral or multilateral negotiations or on unilateral imposition, would be in the interest of the U.S. if a default were likely or imminent or in any other circumstances. Instead, this essay assumes, without demonstrating, that at some time in the future conditions might be such that restructuring of U.S. obligations

---

* Charles A. Heimbold, Jr. Professor of Law, University of Pennsylvania Law School. I wish to thank Haley Wojdowski, J.D. 2012, University of Pennsylvania Law School, for excellent research assistance. This paper was prepared in connection with "Is U.S. Government Debt Different?", a conference sponsored by the Wharton Financial Institutions Center of the University of Pennsylvania and the University of Pennsylvania Law School which was held on May 5, 2012 (the "Conference"). I also wish to thank Donald S. Bernstein, William W. Bratton, Steven L. Schwarcz, David A. Skeel, the other participants at the Conference, and the participants at the University of Pennsylvania Law School 2012 annual faculty retreat for helpful comments on a draft of this paper.

on Treasuries *might* be in the interest of the U.S. I also do not claim that the hypothetical approaches to a restructuring discussed here are optimal. These exemplary approaches are adopted and analyzed solely for the purpose of exploring the feasibility of *any* restructuring.

By "restructuring," I mean a process resulting in an adjustment (*i.e.*, reduction) of the principal amount of the U.S. Treasury obligations. As I use the term, it includes both a reduction of debt as a legal matter, such as by consensual agreement, or a selective intentional default by the U.S. on a portion of its Treasury obligations with the stated intention not to pay the relevant debt. Given the difficulties attendant to the actual enforcement of the obligations on Treasuries, the latter approach may be considered a de facto reduction of principal.

The central assumption that a restructuring conceivably might be in the U.S. interest at some time in the future necessarily raises important questions. First, what are the economic and political circumstances that could give rise to a need for a beneficial restructuring of U.S. debt? It seems obvious that such a restructuring would make sense only in extremely dire economic circumstances. Part II of the essay sketches a scenario in which such circumstances might exist and how such a situation might come about. Nevertheless, no attempt is made here to analyze in detail the circumstances or possible events that might give rise to the need for a restructuring. One working assumption is that, in the face of an economic emergency, Congress would be highly motivated to find a solution. Another is that either Congress could eliminate the possibility that a domestic U.S. court could determine the legality of a restructuring or that the Court of Federal Claims[1] as well as the Supreme Court[2] would be amenable to approving a Congressional solution if at all possible.[3]

---

1 *See* note 134, *infra* (discussing jurisdiction of Court of Federal Claims).
2 It is possible that the legal issues implicated by a restructuring could never properly be presented before a court sitting in the U.S. However, much of the analysis assumes that, in some fashion, these issues could be before the Court.
3 It might make good sense for the U.S. to explore a restructuring before, and in anticipation of, a financial crisis. But I suspect that approach would not be feasible, given political realities.

Second, would any type of material restructuring of U.S. debt involving a material haircut of principal be feasible? This essay directly addresses this question. Part III examines the informational, logistical, and legal impediments to effecting any restructuring of the type considered here. To my knowledge, this specific topic of the feasibility of a restructuring of U.S. Treasury obligations and the issues that it raises largely have been unexplored in the literature. Of course, I must concede that it is possible that behind closed doors at the Department of Treasury and within the Federal Reserve System (Fed) the relevant issues have been pondered and analyzed in depth. For obvious reasons, such investigations, even if purely theoretical, would not be made public as they might trigger a crisis of confidence in the dollar and U.S. Treasuries. It is one thing for pointy-headed academics to offer thoughts on the subject and quite another for the U.S. and its central bankers to indicate that they may see default and restructuring as a real possibility. But I suspect that no such investigations have taken place. The statements and behavior of Treasury and the Fed during the period of 2007 to 2009 appear to reflect a classic case of denial. Exploring a U.S. default or restructuring would be much out of their institutional character. For that reason, I offer this essay as a modest initial step toward the needed investigation and analysis.

II. Imagining the (Im)Possible: A Journey Forward in Time and a Doomsday Scenario.

The following scenario taking place in the year 2018 is fiction.[4] Whether it is possible, I leave to others. It is inspired by the very real notion that if we are worrying only about what we believe is possible, we are almost surely missing something important. Almost two decades ago, I offered similar musings about attempting to anticipate and predict future developments in information technology. Consider the following (necessarily dated) passage:

> [T]he Frequent Change and Unpredictability attributes[5] also are apt descriptions of the financial markets generally in recent

---
4 It is not yet 2018.
5 These attributes are a part of a taxonomy of attributes of information technology which I explored.

years, where most of the significant events were thought to have been impossible shortly before they occurred. The following come to mind: a prime rate of 21 percent; the *de facto* failure of Continental Bank brought on by purchasing participations in loans generated by an Oklahoma City shopping center bank; a more than 500-point fall in the Dow Jones Industrial Average in one day; a $24 billion leveraged buyout (RJR Nabisco); allowing hundreds of insolvent S & Ls to continue operations; Texaco's Chapter 11 filing brought on by a single tort judgment; and the failure of Drexel, Burnham, Lambert, the high-flying securities firm darling of the 1980s. As the realization emerges that the "impossible" is the "normal" in the financial markets, perhaps the same realization will increasingly be seen as applicable to information technology.[6]

On to the story—

It is now March 2018. President Palin has announced that she will not run for reelection for a second term in 2020 in order to devote her complete attention to the worsening global economic crisis— especially to the U.S. economy and the U.S. monetary and fiscal policies (shades of LBJ). Vice President Ryan, Palin's go-to person on all things economic, has made a similar pledge and vow. Congress, Treasury, and the Fed, however, seem paralyzed and helpless.

As was the case a bit more than a decade ago, the usual suspects (Treasury and the Fed) failed to see that in 2012 the real financial bubble (much bigger than the housing bubble of 2007 to 2008) was just about to burst. It is now typical to blame the first Obama administration for the huge increases in U.S. debt and deficits from 2008 to 2012 because it failed to see the impending crisis. But it is likely that had McCain's "No we can't" approach prevailed in 2008, the result would have been essentially the same. Given Congress, Treasury, and the Fed as it was (and is), the U.S. government was trapped in an imagination-challenged debt spiral. Others, of course, outside of government and the conventional financial market par-

---

[6] Charles W. Mooney, Jr., *Property, Credit, and Regulation Meet Information Technology: Clearance and Settlement in the Securities Markets*, 55 L. & Contemp. Probs. 131, 158 (1992).

ticipants, did see what was on the immediate horizon. They issued appropriate warnings, but they were not heeded.

As the economy entered (or reentered) a recession by the first or second quarter of 2013 (which quarter is not very important, looking back about five years), the U.S. deficit continued to grow apace. U.S. Treasuries continued to roll at every auction but at ever increasing interest yields. The largest holders of U.S. Treasuries (such as the Chinese and Japanese governments) began to question more openly the ability of the U.S. to continue to finance its growing debt burden. Eventually, it appeared that the time was approaching when the U.S. would not be able to continue to roll the increases in debt necessary for the debt service.

The U.S. government's response was to "monetize" its debt (an oversimplification, but sufficient for this sketch). Conventionally, the Fed continued to provide more and more funds to banks which, conventionally, increased the money supply through increased lending. But Congress, surprisingly, took a bolder step of directly creating more money by firing up the printing presses. Not surprisingly, Congress took the less bold approach of continuing to spend the increasing money supply beyond its available revenues and to refuse meaningful tax increases. While this spending did provide benefits, such as increased employment and enhanced infrastructure, the net result of the U.S. strategy was negative. Cutting to the chase, the result has been hyperinflation which now approaches 60% per year in the U.S. (shades of Germany and Austria almost a century ago). The U.S. has good company in 2018, as many other states face similar situations. The dollar remains a reserve currency, although a distant second to the Euro, only because of the relative size of the U.S. economy, the large volume of U.S. dollars, and the dollar's liquidity. Nonetheless, since 2012, the dollar's value against a typical basket of other currencies has fallen by about 70%.

So far, the principal benefit of the U.S. strategy has been to avoid a technical (i.e., actual) default on its debt. Even now, in this precarious situation in 2018, the conventional wisdom (in the U.S. and elsewhere) remains that a U.S. default is unthinkable. As it turns out, "unthinking" may be a better characterization for the conventional wisdom. Nevertheless, it has become clear to many, including a majority of members of Congress, that continuing to print money to pay U.S. obligations is not sound monetary policy.

Today at a cabinet meeting in the White House, the prospect for a bold new approach surfaced. Following a briefing on the economy and the U.S. fiscal situation by the Treasury Secretary, the Attorney General asked a simple question: "Secretary Cain, I understand that the U.S. now is a distressed debtor. Could you tell us about your contingency plans for restructuring our debt?" The AG, clearly, was now the proverbial "skunk at the picnic." But the Treasury Secretary was at first speechless. There were no plans, of course. Speaking of default and restructuring of U.S. debt had always been taboo. But the AG, a former Circuit Judge, District Judge, and bankruptcy lawyer, was undeterred. The AG pressed her case, but the Treasury Secretary's only response was the unsurprising: "Seems to me that you are asking me a legal question." Following this exchange, the President asked the AG to come up with a plan.

The remainder of this paper focuses primarily on default and restructuring from the standpoint of the AG.

Of course, the benefits of reducing the U.S. obligations on Treasuries would be offset against the resulting costs. A default and restructuring could result in increases in the cost of borrowing by the U.S. in the future or even fundamental damage to the Treasuries market. Perhaps the most significant specter posed by a default would be the loss of continued access to the capital markets. Moreover, the significance of the Treasuries market both nationally and globally and the role of the dollar as a reserve currency (or not) at the time also would be significant. For example, a default and restructuring of U.S. Treasury obligations could trigger economic crises in Europe and Asia and could result in systemic defaults on the sovereign debt of multiple states and financial institutions. The bottom line is that the U.S. would have to consider whether its default and restructuring would cause more harm to its economy (and other states' economies) than the benefits of reducing its debt on a (presumably) one-time basis.

The extent and nature of the impact of a U.S. default and restructuring also would be an important aspect of designing the exemptions from default contemplated by alternative approaches discussed in Part III.B. Determining which classes of beneficial holders would qualify for the exemption would require much care in analyzing ex ante the likely effects of the scheme if implemented. Exempting domestic holders might be politically essential in order to garner Congressional support. That would mean that foreign holders would bear the first-line brunt of a default and restructuring, which would pose political as well as diplomatic risks and also might impair the achievement of a successful restructuring.[7] Moreover, exempting too much of the U.S. debt would undermine the whole purpose of restructuring.

For the most part, this paper proceeds on the basis that the chief (and obvious) benefit of a restructuring for the U.S. would be the actual or de facto reduction in principal of U.S. Treasury obligations (whether in legal effect or by virtue of selective default).[8] As a general matter, it is better to owe less debt than more debt, especially if debt is reduced other than by way of payment of principal. But the central object of this essay is to explore how the U.S. might restructure its Treasury debt.

---

7 To reiterate, I make no claim here as to the likely benefits or costs of a restructuring that would discriminate against either foreign holders or domestic holders or that would instead adopt an approach of intercreditor equality. The goal here is to explore *whether* such discrimination would be possible and *how* it might be achieved. For a recent study on intercreditor equity in ten recent sovereign debt restructurings, see Aitor Erce & Javier Diaz-Cassou, *Selective Sovereign Defaults* (May 4, 2011), *available* at http://www.webmeets.com/files/papers/SAEe/2011/299/Erce_intercreditor_equity.pdf. Erce and Diaz-Cassou identify Belize, the Dominican Republic, Ecuador, and Pakistan as examples of restructurings that discriminated against external (foreign) creditors. *Id.* at 17-18. As examples of discrimination against domestic creditors, they identify Argentina, Russia, and ("to a lesser extent") Ukraine. *Id.* at 20-21. They identify Uruguay, Grenada, and Dominica as examples of a neutral approach. *Id.* at 19-20. The United States has it own history of discrimination against foreign creditors. *See, e.g.,* Wythe Holt, *The Origins of Alienage Jurisdiction*, 14 Okla. City U. L. Rev. 547, 553-62 (1989) (discussing discrimination by state legislatures against British creditors during the years following the Revolutionary War).

8 As explained below, under the Alternative 2 approach, the Treasuries obligations would not be reduced as a legal matter, but the U.S. would declare itself unwilling to pay X% of the principal obligations. Under Alternative 3, obligations would actually be reduced but only on a consensual basis.

An analysis of the likely impact of a U.S. default and restructuring as contemplated here is beyond the scope of this essay (and my expertise). Reducing the U.S. debt burden promises obvious benefits. But that is only one piece of the puzzle.

III. Outline of a Restructuring: Informational, Logistical, and Legal (Including Constitutional) Impediments

This part assumes that the U.S. might wish to restructure its debt in the future. It explores how the U.S. might go about this task and identifies various problems and impediments that would lie in the path of a restructuring. The restructuring of sovereign debt is necessarily complicated and difficult. This would be especially so in the case of U.S. debt.

A. Dynamics and Strategy.

Restructuring of U.S. obligations on Treasuries would face a significant and obvious complication. In general, the U.S. does not know the identity of the holders of its Treasuries that are held in the commercial book-entry system. (By "holders" of Treasuries, I mean the ultimate beneficial owners on the books of a Federal Reserve Bank or on the books of another intermediary with which the holder maintains a securities account, as discussed below.) It is true that we read about the large foreign holders of U.S. debt, including the Chinese and Japanese governments. But these data on holders of U.S. debt come from *surveys*.[9] With the exception of Treasuries held in the

---

9 See Major Foreign Holders of Treasury Securities (Jan. 2011 – Jan. 2012) *available at* http://www.treasury.gov/resource-center/data-chart-center/tic/Documents/mfh.txt (March 15, 2012) [hereinafter, Major Holders].
  Estimated foreign holdings of U.S. Treasury marketable and non-marketable bills, bonds, and notes reported under the Treasury International Capital (TIC) reporting system are based on annual Surveys of Foreign Holdings of U.S. Securities and on monthly data. These data help provide a window into foreign ownership of U.S. Treasury securities, but they cannot attribute holdings of U.S. Treasury securities with complete accuracy. For example, if a U.S. Treasury security purchased by a foreign resident is held in a custodial account in a third country, the true ownership of the security will not be reflected in the data. The custodial data will also not properly attribute U.S. Treasury securities managed by foreign private portfolio managers who invest on behalf of residents of other countries. In addition, foreign countries may hold dollars and other U.S. assets that are not captured in the TIC data. For these reasons, it is difficult to draw precise conclusions about changes in

"Treasury Direct" or "Legacy Treasury Direct" systems, all Treasuries must be held in an account with a Federal Reserve Bank.[10] In general, only depository institutions (banks) that are members of the Federal Reserve System and certain other depository institutions, including U.S. branches of foreign banks and foreign central banks, are eligible to have such accounts.[11] Other holders must hold through an intermediary that holds through a Federal Reserve Bank or through another intermediary. While the U.S. would have ready access to the books of Federal Reserve Banks, it would not have access to the underlying books of the depository institutions that hold through their accounts with the Federal Reserve Banks or to the books of other intermediaries down the chain.[12]

Consider a hypothetical example. Assume that Bank of America (BoA) holds Treasuries of a given issue in its account with the Federal Reserve Bank of New York. BoA, in turn, has credited some of its holdings of that issue to the securities accounts of its customers. BoA's customers include Banque Delen, a Belgian bank, and Societe Generale, a French bank. Banque Delen has credited some of its holdings of that issue to its customers, who include the National Bank of Pakistan. National Bank of Pakistan, likewise, has credited some of its holdings of that issue to its customers, who include the

---

the foreign holdings of U.S. financial assets by individual countries from TIC data. *Id.* at n.1.

10 Treasuries held in the Treasury/Reserve Automated Debt Entry System (or "TRADES") are governed by the TRADES Regulations, 31 C.F.R. Part 357. Treasuries also may be held in the Legacy Treasury Direct and the Treasury Direct Systems, in which case the U.S. would know the identity of the owners. But the Treasuries held in those systems outside of TRADES consist of less than 3% of the outstanding Treasuries and major holders are unlikely to use them. *See* note 136, *infra* (discussing Treasury Direct and Legacy Treasury Direct Systems).

11 *See* Federal Reserve Banks Operating Circular No. 7, Book-Entry Securities Account Maintenance and Transfer Services (August 19, 2005), ¶ 3.12 (defining "Participant" and listing institutions that are eligible to maintain securities accounts with a Federal Reserve Bank) *available at* www.frbservices.org/files/regulations/pdf/operating_circular_7.pdf. National banks are required to become members of the Federal Reserve System. 12 U.S.C. § 222. State-chartered depository institutions may apply for membership, which requires approval by the Board of Governors of the Federal Reserve System. 12 U.S.C. §§ 321, 322.

12 *Cf.* Steven L. Schwarcz, *Intermediary Risk in a Global Economy*, 50 Duke L.J. 1541, 1547-48 (2012) (explaining why it is difficult to ascertain the identity of investors holding securities through these intermediaries).

governments of Cuba, Iran, and North Korea. Societe Generale also has made credits to its customers, who include both individual holders and other banks—and so on. The example reflects the "tiered," "intermediated" securities holding systems.

The significance of the U.S. not knowing the identity of its Treasuries holders would depend on its approach to a possible restructuring. For example, were the U.S. to pursue bilateral negotiations with China and Japan, any resulting restructuring agreement would necessarily involve identification of the particular Treasuries held by the non-U.S. party. Such an approach would have several drawbacks, however. For example, it is plausible that neither China nor Japan would agree to treatment that is different from that afforded by the U.S. to other, similarly situated Treasuries holders. Moreover, and significantly, obtaining sufficient leverage in the negotiations might require the U.S. to be prepared to make a credible threat of default and restructuring absent an agreed solution. On any maturity date of an issue of Treasuries, because the U.S. could not determine which (if any) portion of the Treasuries were held by China or Japan, China and Japan would assume that the U.S. would be forced to default on the entire issue. Because the majority of the outstanding U.S. debt is held domestically, including by individuals and pension funds in the U.S., any threat of a general default might not be credible. In contrast, the U.S. would prefer a credible threat of a *selective* default to only certain Treasuries holders. Subpart B outlines a novel approach that could allow the U.S. to pose such a credible threat.

Even if the U.S. could present a credible threat of selective default, there are other difficulties with pursuing bilateral negotiations with only selected large Treasuries holders. Once a holder is made aware of a possible default, they could move quickly to exit the market (i.e., sell the Treasuries) based on the nonpublic information. Because huge holdings such as those of China and Japan could not be liquidated quickly, the U.S. would desire to avoid extended and lengthy negotiations. It probably would be necessary to present to selected holders finalized restructuring arrangements on a take-it-or-leave-it basis. The proposal probably would be enhanced by a plan to impose an across-the-board restructuring along the lines described in subpart B if the consensual bilateral or trilateral restructuring arrangements were declined.

Bilateral negotiations would present yet another set of problems. As a general matter it makes some sense for a distressed debtor to sit down with major creditors to discuss the debtor's situation, alternatives, and proposed solutions. But in the case of sovereign debt held by other sovereigns, political issues and concerns may flow from and dominate the purely economic considerations. For example, the second and third largest government holders of U.S. debt, Japan and the United Kingdom,[13] are states with which the U.S. has close ties and very friendly relations. The largest such holder, China,[14] is a powerful rival with which the U.S. aspires to have a stable and friendly relationship.[15] Would these governments view a restructuring plan that targets their holdings as a repudiation of these relationships or even as a hostile act akin to a blockade or boycott? Of course, the identities of the holders of U.S. Treasuries could change dramatically following a period such as that described in the fictional scenario in Part II or under any scenario that would give rise to the need for the U.S. to restructure its debt. But the concerns as to the political effects would be relevant regardless of the identities of the largest governmental holders of U.S. debt.

Difficulties notwithstanding, bilateral restructuring negotiations may be the only feasible alternative. The two most attractive restructuring approaches discussed in subpart B depend on the legal discharge and satisfaction of a portion of non-exempted Treasury obligations or on

---

13 *See* Major Holders, *supra* note 9.
14 *See id.*
15 One op-ed author proposed that the U.S. should abandon its alliance with Taiwan in exchange for China forgiving the U.S. debt that it holds. Paul V. Kane, *To Save our Economy, Ditch Taiwan*, N.Y. Times, Nov. 10, 2011 at A35. The suggestion was met with a flurry of on-line opposition. *See, e.g., On Paul V. Kane and His Stupid Op-Ed*, The China Hotline (Nov. 12, 2011), *available at* http://thechinahotline.wordpress.com/2011/11/12/on-paul-v-kane-and-his-stupid-op-ed/; *Ditching Taiwan to save U.S. Economy will be Myopic, Naïve*, Asian Conservatives (Nov. 11, 2011), *available at* http://asianconservatives.com/economy/ditching-taiwan-to-save-u-s-economy-will-be-myopic-naive/; Joshua Keating, *Decline Watch: Can we save America by ditching Taiwan?*, Passport (Nov. 11, 2011), *available at* http://blog.foreignpolicy.com/posts/2011/11/11/decline_watch_can_we_save_america_by_ditching_taiwan.

a selective default on such obligations and the ability of the U.S. to substantially shelter its offshore assets from execution by future judgment debtors. If neither of those situations could be established, by virtue of legal or practical constraints, then bilateral negotiations might be the only route forward. However, for this purpose, the restructuring proposals discussed in subpart B need not be airtight as a legal matter. They need only be adequate to present a credible threat of a selective default and restructuring so as to push major holders of Treasuries to the negotiating table.[16]

B. Anatomy of a U.S. Debt Restructuring.

This subpart outlines three alternative approaches. One is a selective default initiated by the U.S. in lieu of a bilateral or multilateral negotiated restructuring process. It is combined with unilaterally imposed restructuring terms that would replace and discharge a portion of the Treasury obligations with new non-debt securities (Prosperity Shares). A second is a selective default combined with the issuance of reduced-value Prosperity Shares on account of a portion of the Treasury obligations, but without discharging or otherwise affecting the legal status of the U.S. Treasury obligations. The third is an offer to swap Prosperity Shares for Treasuries on a consensual basis. None of the alternatives contemplates a selective default based solely on the nationality of Treasuries holders. The Treasuries on which a selective default would occur would be determined based instead on broader objective classifications. But the structure and logistics could be employed to effect a selective default on any objective basis.

1. Alternative 1: New Prosperity Shares in Satisfaction and Discharge of Debt.

The U.S. would issue to *all* holders of record of Treasuries in the commercial book-entry system on the books of the Federal Reserve Banks units of new Prosperity Shares. One unit of Prosperity Shares would be issued for each $10,000 of Treasuries. The Federal Reserve Banks would credit the Prosperity Shares on their books to the ac-

---

16 One participant at the Conference suggested that an actual default on the maturity date of one issue of Treasuries should be sufficient to bring the major holders to the table. Others thought the result of that approach would be market chaos.

count holders on the date of issue (Record Date) which should not be a date on which any Treasuries are maturing. The issuance and announcement of the issuance would be made on the Record Date with no previous information being released to the public. To avoid manipulation, the announcement would be made on a Saturday and the record date would be 12:01AM on the following Monday, in the time zone immediately west of the international date line. At the opening of business on Monday in the U.S., the Federal Reserve Banks would enter the credits of the Prosperity Shares on the book-entry accounts they maintain (or the credits entered over the weekend would become final). No corresponding debits of Treasuries would be made to the accounts of the holders of record.

The Federal Reserve Bank account holders would, to the extent they hold as intermediaries for their own account holders, credit the Prosperity Shares to the accounts of their account holders. Those account holders, if holding as intermediaries, would in turn credit the Prosperity Shares to the accounts of their account holders and so on down the chain. Because the Treasuries are book-entry, they must be held in some form of intermediated securities holding system somewhere in the world.

The terms of the Prosperity Shares would provide that the Prosperity Shares would discharge and satisfy a specified percentage (X%) of the aggregate Treasuries beneficially held by each account holder.[17] The terms of the remaining percentage (Y%) of the aggregate amount of Treasuries would remain unaffected. On the maturity date of each issue of Treasuries, the U.S. would pay Y% of the principal (and interest if applicable) of the maturing Treasuries and those funds would find their way to the accounts of the beneficial holders in the usual fashion.

---

17 In order to ensure the effectiveness of a selective default, Congress also should withdraw its consent to be sued in the Court of Federal Claims on account of the non-exempted Treasuries. See text at notes 141-44, *infra*. An alternative but less effective approach would be to eliminate the permanent indefinite appropriation, in effect since 1977, for payment of all judgments of the Court of Federal Claims. *See* 31 U.S.C. § 1304 (2000) ("permanent, indefinite appropriation" for payment of judgments as certified by the Secretary of the Treasury); 28 U.S.C. § 2517(a) (final judgments of the Court of Federal Claims to be paid by Secretary of the Treasury based on presentation of a certification of the judgment).

The discharge and satisfaction of X% of the Treasuries would be conditional. The Prosperity Shares would specify the types of beneficial holders whose Treasuries would be exempt from that discharge. It is the exemption which would accommodate the selective default aspect of the restructuring. The exemption would be conditioned on the submission of certifications (in a standard form provided by the U.S. and available online) demonstrating the exempt status of a beneficial holder *at and as of the Record Date*. The certifications would require specified evidence of the qualifications for exemption and would be subject to penalty of perjury under U.S. law. The exemption qualifications could be stated positively or negatively. For example, they could exempt specified holders (*e.g.*, U.S. domestic holders of all types and foreign holders that are individuals or pension-related funds or entities).[18] Or they could specify the non-exempted holders (*e.g.*, foreign governments and political subdivisions, foreign for-profit entities, and foreign mutual funds or similar investment vehicles). The exemption also might extend to Treasuries to the extent held by a foreign financial firm as required minimum capital or reserves or to meet liquidity requirements.[19]

The discharge and satisfaction would apply in practice as to the X% of Treasuries until holders of the securities on the books of the Fed submitted appropriate certifications of exemption. Upon acceptance of appropriate certification, the Prosperity Shares would be debited on the books of the Federal Reserve Banks (and down the line) and the X% of the Treasuries would be reinstated (if the Treasuries remained on the books) or additional Treasuries would be credited (and down the line through the tiers of intermediaries).

The U.S. would not pay the non-exempted Treasuries at their maturities and would selectively default on the non-exempted debt. If, on a maturity date, an exemption certification had been received and accepted, the Treasuries would be paid. Otherwise, the U.S. would

---

18 If the exemption structure were to discriminate against foreign holders, the U.S. should ensure that it would not run afoul of any of its most favored nation obligations that might exist under GATT or any applicable bilateral investment treaties. *See* Steven L. Schwarcz, Ch. 15 (this volume).

19 Such an exemption would impose at least some risk that financial firms could manipulate the system and even cover for non-financial firm clients.

default. If an exemption certificate were received after the maturity date, the U.S. then would pay the principal with additional interest to the Treasuries holder.[20]

The terms of the Prosperity Shares would be structured to provide periodic payments to the holders that reflect in some fashion the growth of the U.S. economy and positive increases in the fiscal health of the U.S. (taking into account the aggregate debt and annual budget deficits or surpluses).[21] Clearly, the Prosperity Shares would have a value of considerably less than the X% of debt they would replace, so in that sense this structure would be a restructuring under which the non-exempted holders would take a haircut on their outstanding holdings of Treasuries. That is the whole point of a scheme to clean up the balance sheet by discharging or defaulting on a material portion of outstanding Treasuries. But the design and economic structure of the Prosperity Shares would present a challenge. They should offer a feasible, if not probable, opportunity for meaningful future value while not obligating the U.S. to such an extent that it would obtain insufficient relief and benefit from the haircut or default. They should be structured so that the U.S. has incentives to improve its economy. Were too much of the upside benefits allocated to the Prosperity Shares, disincentives to improving the U.S. economy might arise.

---

20 In order to allow more flexibility, the legislation might delegate to the President (perhaps with the consent of the Secretary of the Treasury and a majority of the Federal Reserve Board) the decision to default and, perhaps, even the decision as to the percentage of non-exempted debt to be defaulted and the extent and nature of the exemptions.

21 While nothing as radical as Prosperity Shares has been proposed, the U.S. has shown increasing flexibility in the terms of Treasuries. Treasury inflation-protected securities (TIPS) bear a stated rate of interest and the principal is adjusted for inflation on semiannual interest payment dates. They are redeemed at maturity at the higher of par or the inflation-adjusted principal amount. See 31 C.F.R. §365.5(b)(2) (notes), (c)(2) (bonds). It now appears that beginning in the second half of 2012 the U.S. will begin issuing floating-rate notes for the first time. Susanne Walker, *Treasury Is to Sell Floating Rate Notes in Second Half, Bond Dealers Say*, Bloomberg (Feb. 9, 2012) *available at* http://www.bloomberg.com/news/2012-02-09/treasury-to-sell-floaters-in-second-half-of-year-dealers-say.html. Another proposal would be to tie the interest rate on certain Treasuries to the United States' gross domestic product. Mark J. Kamstra & Robert J. Shiller, *Trills Instead of T-Bills: It's Time to Replace Part of Government Debt with Shares in GDP*, The Economists' Voice (Sept. 2010) *available at* http://econpapers.repec.org/article/bpjevoice/v_3a7_3ay_3a2010_3ai_3a3_3an_3a5.htm.

2. Alternative 2: Selective Default and New Prosperity Shares as Additional Compensation.

Alternative 2 would operate essentially in the same manner as Alternative 1, with certain important exceptions. First, Alternative 2 would not discharge and satisfy any Treasury obligations. The legislation and the terms of the Prosperity Shares would clearly state that nothing in the law affects the validity of the public debt and that all existing public debt would remain valid, binding, and enforceable in accordance with its terms. Second, Congress would authorize the Executive Branch to selectively default on the same portion of Treasury obligations that would be satisfied under Alternative 1. For example, it could require Presidential finding of an emergency and the issuance of an executive order to implement the program. Assuming Congress adopted Alternative 1 as its first choice, Alternative 2 would differ in a third respect. The tenor of the Prosperity Shares under Alternative 2 would be structured to have a value of approximately one-half of the Alternative 1 Prosperity Shares. The enabling legislation also would provide that all payments received by the holders of Prosperity Shares would reduce the Treasury obligations dollar for dollar.

3. Alternative 3: Selective Default and Prosperity Shares Exchange Offering.

Instead of issuing the Prosperity Shares to compensate holders for a U.S. default on a percentage of the non-exempted Treasuries as under Alternatives 1 and 2, under Alternative 3, the U.S. would offer the Prosperity Shares to all non-exempted Treasuries holders. Acceptance of the offer would have the consequence of discharging and satisfying X% of the non-exempted Treasuries as under Alternative 1. But Alternative 3 would modify Treasury obligations only with consent of the relevant holders.

C. Selected Legal Issues.

Subpart B focused primarily on *how* the U.S. might go about restructuring of its debt. In particular, it explained how a selective default could be achieved through certification of exemptions, thereby overcoming the anonymous intermediated holding structure for Treasuries. It also explained how Treasuries could be partially replaced or supplemented by Prosperity Shares, either on a unilateral or voluntary exchange basis. This subpart focuses on examples of legal issues and impediments that would attend a restructuring along the lines presented in subpart B.

1. Legal and Constitutional Authority and Power to Default and Restructure U.S. Debt.

A default and restructuring of Treasuries as contemplated here would require the Department of Treasury and the Fed to work in tandem to achieve the restructuring. But none of Treasury, the Fed, or the President would have the inherent power to default on U.S. debt on a discretionary basis. Treasuries are issued pursuant to statutory authority and statutorily authorized regulations. Only Congress would have the power to authorize the Executive Branch to default on (*i.e.*, to refuse to pay) Treasuries.[22] This would likely be the chief legal (much less, political) impediment to a restructuring of Treasuries. Even if the requisite majorities in Congress could be persuaded on the merits to approve such a default, the process of debate and negotiation would be messy. Moreover, the public nature of the process

---

[22] Section 365.33 of the Department of Treasury's Uniform Offering Circular for Treasuries is captioned "Does the Treasury have any discretion in the auction process?" 31 C.F.R. § 356.33. Section 365.33(c) provides, "We reserve the right to modify the terms and conditions of new securities and to depart from the customary pattern of securities offerings at any time." It was suggested at the Conference that under this provision, Treasury could change the terms and conditions of issued and outstanding Treasuries. However, I believe the correct reading is that the provision refers to the terms of the new securities being auctioned. For purposes of the legal analysis presented here I disregard the possibility that the President has the unilateral power under current law to order a default, even in the face of the posited economic crisis. By way of analogy, I note that during the public debates about raising the debt ceiling in 2011 some argued that the President had the power to borrow in excess of the debt ceiling even without the approval of Congress. *See*, e.g., Eric A. Posner & Adrian Vermeule, *Obama Should Raise the Debt Ceiling on His Own*, The Opinion Pages (July 22, 2011), *available at* http://www.nytimes.com/2011/07/22/opinion/22posner.html. Also, I recognize that in such a crisis the President might order a default and that such an action might not present a justiciable issue. Nonetheless, the analysis proceeds on the more cautions assumption that Congressional approval would be necessary to effect a default and debt restructuring.

would present a serious, if not fatal, problem. The U.S. would lose the advantage of stealth and surprise, which would disrupt the market even before a completed restructuring were achieved (or worse, would block the possibility of a successful restructuring).

Consider some possible ways around this conundrum. The President, Treasury, and the Fed could implement the restructuring contingent upon post-hoc approval by Congress. Or, the President and Congressional Leaders could approach every member of Congress individually and confidentially. While unanimous agreement and support would be unlikely, the members' sense of patriotism and loyalty might be the basis for a pledge of strict confidentiality even by those who were not persuaded to approve the plan. At the appropriate time, a secret meeting of Congress could be called to approve the plan. Or, these approaches could be combined, with the first approach (an implementation contingent on subsequent Congressional approval) followed by an immediate Congressional approval based on earlier one-on-one confidential meetings.

The alternative approaches presented here are intended to illustrate examples of coherent restructurings that would proceed under the rule of law. If the President and Congress decide to default on the non-exempted Treasuries, Congress could simply fail to appropriate sufficient funds and payment of Treasuries in full would be impossible. That would be simple enough. The *unintentional* version of that scenario was the prospect that was the subject of so much discussion and debate during the 2011 debt ceiling impasse. In a restructuring mode, however, it would be wise for the U.S. to avoid the possibility of legal challenges in any U.S. courts that would have jurisdiction over the U.S. But it would also be desirable for the U.S. to take an approach that would not violate its own Constitution—whether or not the actions could be challenged in a court of law.

Alternatives 1 and 2 each might attract constitutional challenges. Depending on the terms of the Prosperity Shares, Alternative 3 might not be a feasible method of restructuring. Congress could at best hazard guesses at how legal challenges or market acceptance of Prosperity Shares might play out. Consequently, Congress could consider adopting all three alternatives as a hedge against future developments. It could give first priority to Alternative 1, with a savings clause to the effect that Alternative 2 would apply if Alternative 1 is not upheld. Alternative 3, then, would apply if Alternative 2 were to fail. Alternatively, if only one of the alternatives seems likely to be successful, Congress could opt for that approach. Once again, I should emphasize that these alternatives are illustrative only in order to provide a concrete setting for consideration of the various legal and practical issues that a restructuring would present.

a. Implementing Alternative 1.

Implementation of the Alternative 1 restructuring plan might be an unconstitutional exercise of Congressional power because it modifies the terms and relieves the U.S. of liability on the portion of the Treasury obligations replaced by the Prosperity Shares.[23] Unlike Alternative 2, which does not contemplate any discharge and satisfaction of the Treasury obligations as to which Prosperity Shares would be issued, and Alternative 3, which contemplates the substitution of Prosperity Shares for a portion of Treasuries debt only upon Treasuries holders' consent, Alternative 1 would unilaterally replace a portion of the Treasury obligations even in the absence of consent.

Section Four of the Fourteenth Amendment, provides in part: "The validity of the public debt of the United States . . . shall not be questioned."[24] Adopted in 1868, Section Four was originally written with an eye towards preventing challenges to Civil War debts,[25] but by its terms and as construed by the Supreme Court it applies to all federal debt.[26] An examination of the clause's structure and history

---

23 If the present option value of the Prosperity Shares could be shown to approximate the value of the putatively satisfied and discharged debt, that *might* solve the problem. But the terms of Prosperity Shares that could be so valued likely would not provide the debt relief contemplated by the restructuring.

24 U.S. Const. amend. XIV, §4.

25 Perry v. U.S., 294 U.S. 330, 354 (1935) ("this provision was undoubtedly inspired by the desire to put beyond question the obligations of the government issued during the Civil War.").

26 Id. (Perry held that the language of Section Four "indicates a broader connotation" than just covering Civil War debts, but "applies as well to the government bonds in question, and to others duly authorized by the Congress.") During the 2011 controversy over increasing the U.S. government debt ceiling, the scope of Section Four was the subject of sharp disagreement. *Compare* Laurence Tribe, *Guest*

has led one scholar to observe that "the intention was to lay down a constitutional canon for all time in order to protect and maintain the national honor and to strengthen the national credit."[27] A Congressional act that provides that the U.S. is not bound to pay a portion of its Treasuries debt as contemplated by Alternative 1 would, at least on its face, appear to "question[]" "[t]he validity of the public debt." The legislation would relieve the U.S. of its obligation to pay the portion of the Treasury obligations that would be replaced by the Prosperity Shares.

The only time the Supreme Court has construed Section Four was *Perry v. United States*, one of the *Gold Clause Cases*.[28] These cases concerned private corporate bonds, a U.S. gold certificate, and a U.S. government bond. The obligations each included a "gold clause" which stipulated that the relevant obligation was payable in gold

---

Post on the Debt Ceiling by Laurence Tribe, Dorf on Law (July 16, 2011) [hereinafter, Tribe, *Guest Post*], http://www.dorfonlaw.org/2011/07/guest-post-on-debt-ceiling-by-laurence.html. (arguing that the reference to "the public debt" in Section Four is limited to indebtedness such as bonds) with Neil H. Buchanan, *Borrowing, Spending, and Taxation: Further Thoughts on Professor Tribe's Reply,* Dorf on Law (July 19, 2011) [hereinafter, Buchanan, Borrowing], http://www.dorfonlaw.org/2011/07/borrowing-spending-and-taxation-further_19.html (arguing that it extends to all U.S. government obligations). For present purposes, it is clear enough that the public debt includes Treasuries that are the subject of this discussion. For a thorough analysis of the 2011 debt ceiling crisis and debates over legal issues, see Jeremy Kreisberg & Kelley O'Mara (under the supervision of Howell Jackson), [Appendix (this volume)] [*available at* http://finance.wharton.upenn.edu/conferences/debtconf/].

27 Phanor J. Eder, *A Forgotten Section of the Fourteenth Amendment,* 19 Cornell L.Q. 1, 15 (1933); see also Michael Abramowicz, *Beyond Balanced Budgets, Fourteenth Amendment Style,* 33 Tulsa L.J. 561, 585 (1997) ("A constitutional guarantee provided meaningful assurance to those who might purchase future government debt."); John McGuire, *The Public Debt Clause and the Social Security Trust Funds: Enforcement Mechanism or Historical Peculiarity?,* 7 Loy. J. Pub. Int. L. 203, 213-15 (2006) (explaining that the clause was designed to have a lasting influence and cover more than just Civil War debts). Donald Bernstein explained at the conference that the inflexibility that Section Four affords the U.S. in circumstances of financial distress has a very positive value. It forces "debtor discipline" which would be essential for a recovery. Donald S. Bernstein, Ch. 14 (this volume).

28 The cases are: *Perry v. U.S.,* 294 U.S. 330 (1935); *Nortz v. U.S.,* 294 U.S. 317 (1935); *Norman v. Baltimore & Ohio R.R. Co.,* 294 U.S. 240 (1935) (consolidated for review with *U.S. v. Bankers Trust Co.*). *See generally* Kenneth W. Dam, *From the Gold Clause Cases to the Gold Commission: A Half Century of American Monetary Law,* 50 U. Chi. L. Rev. 504, 514-18 (1983) (discussing the four major gold clause cases).

or gold coin. In 1933, early in the Roosevelt administration, Congress passed a Joint Resolution providing that a contractual requirement that payments be made in gold or specific coin or currency was against public policy, effectively nullifying such gold clauses.[29] The resolution further provided that any such obligations could be satisfied by the payment of any currency that was legal tender, dollar for dollar.[30]

Perry's plurality opinion on behalf of four Justices,[31] confirmed the unconstitutionality of a law that would relieve the U.S. from its obligation to pay federal debt according to its terms.[32] Mr. Perry was the holder of a U.S. government bond that made principal and interest "payable in United States gold coin of the present standard of value."[33] Perry sued to recover the amount in dollars equivalent to gold at earlier exchange rates under the gold clause term of the bond. The plurality opinion recognized that the Constitution empowers Congress to borrow money, which includes the right "to fix the amount to be borrowed and the terms of payment."[34] However, the plurality held the Joint Resolution to be unconstitutional insofar as it applied to gold clauses in federal obligations. The Court relied in part on Section Four. As it explained:

> We regard [Section Four] . . . as confirmatory of a fundamental principle, which applies as well to the government bonds in question, and to others duly authorized by the Congress, as to those issued before the Amendment was adopted. Nor can we perceive any reason for not considering the expression "the *validity* of the public debt" as embracing whatever concerns the integrity of the public obligations.[35]

The Court also relied directly on the fundamental principle confirmed by Section Four. It reasoned that "[h]aving this power to au-

---

29 H.R.J. Res. 192, 73d Cong., 48 Stat. 112-13 (1933) (enacted).
30 Id.
31 Mr. Justice Stone wrote a concurring opinion, discussed *infra,* thereby providing a 5-4 majority.
32 *Perry,* 294 U.S. at 353-54.
33 *See, e.g., Perry,* 294 U.S. at 347 (quoting bond terms).
34 *Perry,* 294 U.S. at 351.
35 *Id.* at 354.

thorize the issue of definite obligations for the payment of money borrowed, the Congress has not been vested with authority to alter or destroy those obligations."[36] The following discussion refers to this principle as the "non-abrogation principle." The Court further observed that "Congress was without power to reduce expenditures by abrogating contractual obligations" even in the face of a "great need of economy" and "widespread distress."[37]

While the use of language in *Perry's* plurality opinion as to the unconstitutionality of the Joint Resolution is quite clear, the actual holding of the case is quite astonishing. With reasoning that has been described as "baffling"[38] and "convoluted and suspect,"[39] the Court held that Perry was entitled to receive only the face amount of the bond *in dollars and not in gold coin*. The Court's holding left Perry in *exactly* the same position as would have been the case had the Court held the abrogation of gold clauses in U.S. bonds to be constitutional. Kenneth Dam explained the reasoning of the plurality opinion: [40]

> [T]he Court nonetheless relegated the holder of the government bond to receiving merely the face amount of $ 10,000 in legal tender currency. The Court reasoned that unlike the post-Civil War period, when coin and paper money floated in the marketplace at prices determined by supply and demand, the period of the Gold Clause Cases had a "single monetary system with an established parity of all currency and coins."[41] Even under the

---

36 *Id.* at 353; see also *Id.* at 352-53 (Congress "was without power to reduce expenditures by abrogating contractual obligations of the United States. To abrogate contracts, in the attempt to lessen government expenditure, would be not the practice of economy, but an act of repudiation.") (quoting *Lynch v. U.S.*, 292 U.S. 571, 580 (1934)).
37 *Id.* at 352. While the Court held the government's modification of its obligations to be unconstitutional, it is noteworthy that "the *Perry* Court appeared determined not to upset governmental policy and ultimately did not award Perry damages." Abramowicz, *supra* note 27, at 603.
38 Henry Hart, *The Gold Clause in United States Bonds*, 48 Harv. L. Rev. 1057 (1935).
39 Dam, *supra* note 28, at 517. Dam virtually destroys the factual underpinnings of the plurality opinion that the gold clauses interfered with the federal government's power over money and that enforcing the clauses would cause a dislocation of the economy. *Id.* at 518-525.
40 *Id.* at 517 (footnotes omitted).
41 Quoting from *Perry*, 294 U.S. at 357.

pre-1933 legislation, a gold coin could have been legal tender only for its face amount, not for the value of its gold content. Thus even if the bond had been paid in gold coin and even assuming that gold coin did not have to be surrendered to the government at the $ 20.67 price under the 1933 regulations, the bondholder could not have exchanged his gold coin at the thirty-five dollar price because no recipient would have been required to treat it as legal tender for more than its face amount. Moreover, he could not have exported the gold coin or sold it for its gold content. As a result, the holder had no legally cognizable loss of purchasing power. Since there was no "actual loss," recovery of money at the gold value—$ 1.69 per $ 1.00 face amount of the bonds—would "constitute not a recoupment of loss in any proper sense but an unjustified enrichment."[42]

The *Perry* plurality was clear that Congress has the power to deal with gold coin as a medium of exchange and that the requirement that gold be redeemed and the prohibition against export and sale of gold on the international market were lawful.[43] Thus, the Court held that the lawful acts of Congress permitted it to take an unlawful act—modification of the terms of its obligations—with impunity. The U.S. had modified its obligations *de facto*.[44] Mr. Justice Stone's concurring opinion made clear what the plurality opinion obfuscated (but clearly provided in result):

> While the Government's refusal to make the stipulated payment is a measure taken in the exercise of that power [to coin and regulate money], this does not disguise the fact that its action is to that extent a repudiation of its undertaking. As much as I deplore this refusal to fulfill the solemn promise of bonds of the United States, I cannot escape the conclusion, announced for the Court, that in the situation now presented, the Government, through the exercise of its sovereign power to regulate the

---

42 Quoting from *id.* at 358 (footnotes omitted).
43 *Perry*, 294 U.S. at 355-56.
44 Dam, *supra* note 28, at 518 ("The reasoning of the *Perry* plurality on the constitutional issue was, however, less important to the future of gold than was the result, which rendered gold clauses just as ineffective in government obligations as in private obligations.")

value of money, has rendered itself immune from liability for its action. To that extent it has relieved itself of the obligation of its domestic bonds, precisely as it has relieved the obligors of private bonds in *Norman v. Baltimore & Ohio R. Co.*, decided this day . . .[45]

Taking into account as well the four Justices who joined in the dissenting opinion, five of the nine Justices explicitly acknowledged that the government had effectively modified its obligations.[46]

With the result in *Perry* in mind, could Congress find a way to effectively implement Alternative 1 without running afoul of Section Four and the non-abrogation principle? Following is a sketch of one possible approach. It does not purport to be a definitive analysis but a point of departure for exploring this question.

It was quite convenient for the plurality and concurrence in *Perry* that the gold clause that Congress sought to override (albeit unconstitutionally, according to the plurality) was intimately related to the power over money that was lawfully exercised. Arguably, in the context of restructuring under Alternative 1, there is a Congressional power that might play a role somewhat analogous to that of Congressional power over money in *Perry*. It is the power conferred on Congress by the Bankruptcy Clause of the U.S. Constitution.[47] The Bankruptcy Clause provides that Congress has the power "To establish . . . uniform Laws on the subject of Bankruptcies throughout the United States."[48] Discussions of the Bankruptcy Clause often

---

45 *Perry*, 294 U.S. at 359. Stone's view was that it was sufficient to decide the case on the basis that there were no damages. He saw no need to go further. Unlike the plurality, he would not have reached the constitutional issue.

46 *Id.* at 377 (McReynolds, J., dissenting):
   The majority seem to hold that the Resolution of June 5th did not affect the gold clauses in bonds of the United States. Nevertheless we are told that no damage resulted to the holder now before us through the refusal to pay one of them in gold coin of the kind designated or its equivalent. This amounts to a declaration that the Government may give with one hand and take away with the other. Default is thus made both easy and safe!

47 U.S. Const. art. I, § 8, cl. 4.

48 *Id.* As understood at the time of the Framing of the Constitution, "insolvency laws under English law and the law of some colonies and states freed the debtor [from imprisonment] and distributed his assets among his creditors but did not re-

begin by noting the dearth of evidence concerning its origins and underlying purposes.[49] There is a good case to be made that its origins derive in substantial part from the federalism concerns that underlie diversity jurisdiction of the federal courts.[50] "[U]niform Laws on the subject of Bankruptcies throughout the United States,"[51] then, like federal courts in the diversity jurisdiction context, could provide a more neutral system that would be less biased in favor of local parties. While this federalism-related explanation carries significant weight, scholars continue to ponder the purposes and scope of the Bankruptcy Clause.[52]

I am aware of no evidence that the Framers considered the possibility that the Bankruptcy Clause might empower Congress to enact a law that would allow the U.S. government to discharge its debts. But surely that does not resolve the issue. I also am unaware of any sign that they considered municipal bankruptcies, but provisions for municipal bankruptcies have been on the books for more than

---

lieve him of his obligations to pay the underlying debts." Bruce H. Mann, Republic of Debtors: Bankruptcy in the Age of American Independence 80 (2002). On the other hand, "bankruptcy laws accomplished the same end [as insolvency laws] but also discharged the debtor from liability for unpaid debts." *Id.*, Within a few years, however, the Bankruptcy Clause was understood to empower Congress to enact either type of law. Jonathan C. Lipson, *Debt and Democracy: Towards a Constitutional Theory of Bankruptcy*, 83 Notre Dame L. Rev. 605, 633 (2008) [hereinafter, Lipson, Democracy]. Accordingly, I use the terms bankruptcy, bankruptcy law, and bankruptcy proceedings in this broad sense.

49 *See generally, e.g.,* David A. Skeel, Jr., *Debt's Dominion: A History of Bankruptcy Law in America* 3, 23-47 (2001) [hereinafter Skeel, *Debt's Dominion*], citing The Federalist No. 42 (James Madison) (Clinton Rossiter ed., 1961):

Almost the only contemporary evidence of the meaning or importance of uniform bankruptcy comes in the Federalist No. 42. Written by James Madison, Federalist No. 42 describes federal bankruptcy legislation as intimately connected with the regulation of commerce, and necessary to prevent debtors from fleeing to another state to evade local enforcement of their obligations.

50 *See* Charles W. Mooney, Jr., *A Normative Theory of Bankruptcy Law: Bankruptcy As (Is) Civil Procedure*, 61 Wash. & Lee L. Rev. 931, 982-90 (2004) [hereinafter, Mooney, *Normative Theory*].

51 U.S. Const. art. I, § 8, cl. 4.

52 *See, e.g.,* Skeel, *Debt's Dominion* at 23 (quoted *supra* note 49); Lipson, *Democracy, supra* note 48; Thomas Plank, *Bankruptcy and Federalism*, 71 Fordham L. Rev. 1063, 1090 n.106 (2002).; Charles Jordan Tabb, *The History of the Bankruptcy Laws in the United States*, 3 Am Bankr. Inst. L. Rev. 5, 7-11 (1995).

seventy-five years.[53] The current version is found in Chapter 9 of the Bankruptcy Code.[54] And recently a debate has emerged over whether federal bankruptcy law should be amended to permit states of the U.S. to become debtors.[55] Certainly nothing in the text of the Bankruptcy Clause itself would appear to limit the power of Congress to enact a bankruptcy law providing for discharge of the obligations of a government, including the federal government. Bankruptcy law is a branch of civil procedure law, the purpose of which is to protect and vindicate the rights of those with legal entitlements (*e.g.*, creditors) vis-a vis a debtor in financial distress.[56] As such, expanding bankruptcy law to embrace the U.S. federal government would be a coherent and logical extension of existing federal jurisdiction over claims against the U.S.[57]

The Bankruptcy Clause does not dictate to Congress the metes and bounds of a bankruptcy law; such a law need only deal with the "uniform Laws on the subject of Bankruptcies throughout the United States."[58] A bankruptcy law need not be situated in a stand-alone act denominated as a bankruptcy law,[59] although that has been the approach in the U.S.[60] Could a bankruptcy law that applied only to the U.S. government as debtor be a "uniform Law[] . . . throughout the United States"? The Supreme Court addressed "the nature of the uni-

---

[53] The first municipal bankruptcy act was enacted in 1934. Pub. L. No. 251, 73d Cong., 2d Sess., 48 Stat. 798 (1934).

[54] 11 U.S.C. §§ 901-946.

[55] *See, e.g.,* David Skeel, *Give States a Way to Go Bankrupt*, 16 The Weekly Standard No. 11 (Nov. 29, 2010), *available at* http://www.weeklystandard.com/articles/give-states-way-go-bankrupt_518378.html?page=1; David A. Skeel, Jr., *States of Bankruptcy*, 79 U. Chi. L. Rev. 677 (2012) (arguing in favor of a bankruptcy law for states); Joe Weisenthal, *More on Why the "State Bankruptcy" Idea Is Dangerous Nonsense*, Business Insider (Jan. 24, 2011), *available at* http://articles.businessinsider.com/2011-01-24/markets/30021798_1_state-bankruptcy-tax-hikes-spending-cuts.

[56] *See* Mooney, NORMATIVE THEORY, *supra* note 50, at 951-54.

[57] As discussed *infra*, claims against the U.S. government currently are subject to the jurisdiction of the Court of Federal Claims. See note 134, *infra*.

[58] U.S. Const. art. I, § 8, cl. 4.

[59] *See* Steven L. Schwarcz, *A Minimalist Approach to State "Bankruptcy,"* 59 UCLA L. Rev. 322, 336 (2011).

[60] *See* Act of April 4, 1800, chap. 19, 2 Stat. 19 (repealed 1803); Act of August 19, 1841, chap 9, 5 Stat. 440 (repealed 1843); Act of March 2, 1867, chap. 176, 14 Stat. 517 (repealed 1878); Bankruptcy Act of 1898, chap. 541, 30 Stat. 544 (repealed 1978); Bankruptcy Code, 11 U.S.C. §§ 101 *et seq.*

formity required by the Bankruptcy Clause" in *Railway Labor Executives' Association v. Gibbons*.[61] *Gibbons* held that an act enacted pursuant to the Bankruptcy Clause power was unconstitutional because it applied to only one named debtor and that debtor's creditors.[62] The act failed the uniformity requirement. As the Court explained:

> Our holding today does not impair Congress' ability under the Bankruptcy Clause to define classes of debtors and to structure relief accordingly. We have upheld bankruptcy laws that apply to a particular industry in a particular region. See 3R Act Cases, 419 U.S. 102 (1974). The uniformity requirement, however, prohibits Congress from enacting a bankruptcy law that, by definition, applies only to one regional debtor [the Chicago, Rock Island and Pacific Railroad Co.]. To survive scrutiny under the Bankruptcy Clause, a law must at least apply uniformly to a defined class of debtors. A bankruptcy law . . . confined as it is to the affairs of one named debtor can hardly be considered uniform. To hold otherwise would allow Congress to repeal the uniformity requirement from Art. I, § 8, cl. 4, of the Constitution.[63]

Of course, Congress did not write an entirely new bankruptcy law solely for the Rock Island Railroad, it only added a few special provisions. It follows that any provisions of a bankruptcy law that would apply only to the U.S. government as debtor would be suspect under *Gibbons*.

One way around the problem would be for the legislation to provide for bankruptcy relief for a "defined class of debtors," which could be the sovereigns consisting of the U.S. government or the government of any state of the U.S. Or the class could include any sovereign (although the likelihood of a foreign sovereign state's use of such a law seems fanciful). Even so, it is likely that some provisions of the law necessarily would apply only to the U.S. government. In that case, the fact that the U.S. government is so unlike any other debtor might be sufficient to overcome a uniformity objection. Congress could enact a new, special law for sovereign bankruptcy or amend

---

61 455 U.S. 457, 469.
62 *Gibbons*, 455 U.S. at 473.
63 *Id.*

the Bankruptcy Code[64] to allow the U.S. to propose a restructuring plan. Because the restructuring should be accomplished immediately on the record date, it would be necessary to propose the restructuring as contemplated by Alternative 1 at the commencement of the bankruptcy case.[65] The legislation might plausibly confer jurisdiction to handle a sovereign debtor case on any federal District Court in the case of the U.S. government and on any District Court sitting in a debtor state in the case of a state of the U.S.[66]

As to substance, Chapter 9 on Adjustment of Debts of a Municipality might provide a template or checklist of sorts inasmuch as it sets out markers on which provisions of the Bankruptcy Code are appropriate for a government debtor and which are not.[67] At least two of Chapter 9's requirements for confirmation of a plan of adjustment of a debtor's debts might be troublesome if applicable to a plan along the lines of Alternative 1. First, Plan confirmation requires acceptance by at least one class of impaired claims, not taking into account the claims of "insiders."[68] It is doubtful that the holders of impaired claims based on non-exempted Treasuries would accept a plan that offered the Prosperity Shares in lieu of more substantial payments or other value. Perhaps another class of claims could be impaired with a better chance of acceptance, such as claims held by Federal Reserve Banks. On the other hand, those claims might be considered insider claims.

Second, assuming that the classes of claims that include the holders of non-exempted Treasuries would not accept the plan, in order to invoke the cramdown provisions of Chapter 9 for confirmation notwithstanding such nonacceptance, the plan must "not discriminate unfairly" with respect to nonaccepting classes of claims.[69] Discrimi-

---

64 11 U.S.C. §§ 101-1530.
65 To reiterate, the alternatives presented here are illustrative so as to facilitate a concrete discussion.
66 I make no attempt here in these few pages to address the myriad details of such a bankruptcy law.
67 *See* 6 Collier on Bankruptcy (Alan N. Resnick & Henry J. Sommer, eds., 16th ed. 2011) ¶ 900.01[2][c] (discussing differences between Chapter 9 and Chapter 11 as to court involvement with operations of debtor).
68 11 U.S.C. §§ 901(a), 1129(a)(10).
69 11 U.S.C. §§ 901(a), 1129(b)(1).

nation based on the citizenship, residence, or principal place of business of Treasuries holders, as contemplated by Alternative 1, might constitute such unfair discrimination.[70] That is not to say that all unsecured creditors must be treated in the same fashion. Although Chapter 9 incorporates the priority for administrative expenses it does not incorporate the other priorities that apply in other chapters of the Bankruptcy Code.[71] It also does not adopt a baseline pro rata sharing distributional scheme as the Bankruptcy Code provides for liquidations under Chapter 7.[72] This leaves a debtor free to establish additional priorities pursuant to a plan. Presumably priorities with a rational, coherent basis, not unlike those established in Section 507 of the Bankruptcy Code, would not constitute unfair discrimination. Examples would include exempting from the Prosperity Share exchange (*i.e.*, affording priority to) claims below a specified dollar amount, claims of holders on behalf of pension funds, and claims necessary for a financial institution to maintain required minimum capital or reserves or to meet liquidity requirements.[73]

Notwithstanding the foregoing, in establishing a bankruptcy law that applied to the U.S. government, Congress would not be obliged to follow the Chapter 9 template.[74] For example, it could abandon

---

[70] An analysis of unfair discrimination in the cramdown process is beyond the scope of this paper. Suffice it to say that the substantial disparity in treatment under Alternative 1 between the non-exempted and exempt Treasury obligations, which have identical priority outside bankruptcy, strongly suggests unfair discrimination.

[71] 11 U.S.C. § 901(a) (incorporating 11 U.S.C. § 507(a)(2) on administrative expenses but not the other priorities established in section 507).

[72] *See* 11 U.S.C. § 726(a) (distributions in liquidation under Chapter 7).

[73] Lest I draw criticism for inconsistency or bias in favor of a U.S. federal government bankruptcy, I should emphasize that awarding such priorities under bankruptcy law is wrong. *See* Mooney, *Normative Theory, supra* note 50, at 1053-58. It would be (and in some respects is, under Bankruptcy Code section 507(a)) inconsistent with my position that, in general, bankruptcy law should not adopt rules on basic rights and obligations that differ from those applicable outside of bankruptcy. *Id.* at 957-1010. Exceptions are appropriate when based on a rational need for special rules in bankruptcy in order to achieve its goals. *Id.* at 1011-60. In the present discussion, I do not advocate such priorities. My goal instead is to explore the options that would be available to the U.S. government in order to implement Alternative 1 in bankruptcy.

[74] *See* Schwarcz, *supra* note 59, at 326. Indeed, following the Chapter 9 template arguably "can bring in a lot of excess baggage" because a sovereign debtor, such as the U.S. Government, is very different from municipalities. *Id.*

the concept of unfair discrimination in the new law. While that approach might be desirable for the U.S. government as debtor, it might be a very bad idea for state debtors. And treating the U.S. differently would again implicate the uniformity issue.

In addition to addressing the scope of the Bankruptcy Clause, it also is necessary to consider whether there would exist any conflict between implementation of Alternative 1 through the Bankruptcy Clause powers and any other Constitutional limitations. Under Section Four, for example, would such implementation "question[]" "the validity of the public debt"? Under any normal, accepted meaning of "validity" of debt the answer must be that it does not. "Valid" means "legal sufficiency"[75] and "binding" in the context of an obligation.[76] Bankruptcy provides remedies for and accommodates only valid obligations of the debtor, not invalid ones. Alternative 1 as implemented through a bankruptcy law would first determine the validity of a claim based on non-exempted Treasuries—an easy task for U.S. public debt, of course. Then the debt would be discharged and a distribution of Prosperity Shares would be made on account of the claim. In effect, there would be a novation that replaces a portion of

---

75 *See* Black's Law Dictionary (9th ed. 2009) (defining the adjective "valid" as "[l]egally sufficient; binding," indicating the related noun to be "validity," and giving as an example "a valid contract." Correspondingly, "invalid" means "not of binding force or legal efficacy" or "lacking in authority or obligation." *Id*.

76 As must be apparent, I am not a Constitutional law expert. But I have given hundreds of written legal opinions to the effect that an agreement is "a legal, valid and binding obligation of [an obligor] and enforceable against [the obligor] in accordance with its terms" or a similar variation. As Arthur Field has explained: "The language 'in accordance with its terms' as well as the word 'legal' are often omitted in current usage. They add nothing to the opinion. The word 'valid' is also sometimes omitted as adding nothing." Arthur Norman Field, Legal Opinions in Business Transactions § 6.15 (Practising Law Institute 2003). I think I understand "validity." However, Michael Abramowicz takes the position that, in Section Four, "validity" does not mean "legal" validity. Michael Abramowicz, *Train Wrecks, Budget Deficits, and the Entitlements Explosion: Exploring the Implications of the Fourteenth Amendment's Public Debt Clause*, GW Legal Studies Research Paper no. 575 [hereinafter, Abramowicz, *Train Wrecks*], *available at* http://papers.ssrn.com/sol3/papers.cfm?abstract_id=1874746. Perhaps his view of validity would make some sense if used in the instructions to a board game, for example. But to think "validity" as used in the United States Constitution does not mean "legal" validity seems more than far fetched. As noted, Field has explained that the "legal" modifier adds nothing. I take up Abramowicz's views on Section Four again in the discussion of Alternative 2. *See* pp. 44-46, infra.

the Treasury debt with the Prosperity Shares.[77] It is a truism that after discharge of the valid debt it would be transformed into Prosperity Shares and in that respect it would no longer be a valid debt for the former face amount. But that is the essence of a bankruptcy law. If Congress has the power under the Bankruptcy Clause to adopt a bankruptcy law that would apply to the U.S. government, then it necessarily has the power to provide for a discharge. Otherwise the Bankruptcy Clause power would be meaningless in this context.

From the foregoing, it appears that whether Congressional power to permit the implementation of Alternative 1under the Bankruptcy Clause conflicts with Section Four depends on whether a bankruptcy law applicable to the U.S. government as a debtor would be within the scope of the Bankruptcy Clause. As explained, if such a law is within the scope of the Bankruptcy Clause, it would prevail over any claim that it violates Section Four. In recent years, the Supreme Court has considered analogous potential conflicts between bankruptcy law and the Constitution apart from the Bankruptcy Clause, in particular sovereign immunity of the states of the U.S. under the Eleventh Amendment.[78]

In *Tennessee Student Assistance Corp. v. Hood*,[79] the Court held that a bankruptcy discharge of a student loan owed to a state "does not implicate a State's Eleventh Amendment immunity."[80] In effect, the majority opinion held that there is no Eleventh Amendment immunity from a discharge and, consequently, there was no conflict between that amendment and the discharge imposed by bankruptcy law. Two years later, in *Central Virginia Community College v. Katz*,[81] the Court held that a state's Eleventh Amendment sovereign immunity did not protect it against a suit to recover a pre-bankruptcy preferential payment made by the debtor to a state creditor. The principal

---

77 The statement in the text assumes that a bankruptcy law for the U.S. government would follow the pattern of discharge in Chapter 11. See 11 U.S.C. § 1141(d)(1).
78 U.S. Const. amend. XI. The Eleventh Amendment provides:
   The Judicial power of the United States shall not be construed to extend to any suit in law or equity commenced or prosecuted against one of the United States by Citizens of another State, or by Citizens or Subjects of any Foreign State.
79 541 U.S. 440 (2004).
80 *Id.* at 445.
81 546 U.S. 356 (2006).

rationale of the *Katz* majority opinion relied on the "*in rem*" nature of bankruptcy[82] and the "consent" of the states to suits in federal bankruptcy courts resulting from ratification of the Constitution.[83] The court further qualified its holding as applying only when the law under which Congress has permitted suit against the states is actually a bankruptcy law, i.e., a law "on the subject of Bankruptcies."[84] So, under *Katz*, there is a two-step model. First, examine the relevant nonbankruptcy legal entitlement—the Eleventh Amendment in *Katz*—to ascertain whether it is inconsistent with or would be contravened by the bankruptcy law involved. Second, determine whether the relevant bankruptcy law is actually one within the scope of the Bankruptcy Clause.

Applying this analysis to the present context, the discharge does affect the continued existence of the Treasury obligations, but only in the sense that the distribution in bankruptcy determines that valid debt is satisfied, not that it is invalidated. Moreover, it is clear enough that a law providing for a debtor's discharge is within the scope of the Bankruptcy Clause. As already noted, bankruptcy is part of civil procedure designed to provide remedies to holders of legal entitlements such as creditors. As to procedure, the Perry plurality opinion acknowledged:

> The fact that the United States may not be sued without its consent is a matter of procedure which does not affect the legal and binding character of its contracts. While the Congress is under no duty to provide remedies through the courts, the contractual obligation still exists and, despite infirmities of procedure, remains binding upon the conscience of the sovereign.[85]

If, as a *procedural* matter, Congress can lawfully fail to provide any remedy whatsoever for a breach of a U.S. contractual obligation, *a fortiori* it should have the power to provide a *procedural* remedy under the Bankruptcy Clause. This remedy posited here is the distribution of Prosperity Shares in satisfaction of the discharged portion of the Treasury obligations.

---

82 *Id.* at 362, 369-71.
83 *Id.* at 377-78.
84 *Id.* at 378-79.
85 *Perry*, 294 U.S. at 354.

Under any coherent distributional scheme of a bankruptcy law, the distributions to creditors must be grounded in a debtor's ability to pay. For purposes of confirming a plan under Chapter 11 of the Bankruptcy Code, for example, each holder of a claim of an impaired class must either accept the plan or receive property of a value not less than such holder would receive in a liquidation of the debtor—the "best interests" test. [86] But such a test is not feasible for a debtor that is a government. As explained in relation to a municipality debtor under Chapter 9:

> A municipality cannot be liquidated, its assets sold, and the proceeds used to pay its creditors. Nevertheless, the [best interests] concept is not without meaning in a municipal debt adjustment case. The concept should be interpreted to mean that the plan must be better than the alternative that creditors have. In the chapter 9 context, the alternative is dismissal of the case, permitting every creditor to fend for itself in the race to obtain the mandamus remedy and to collect the proceeds.[87]

In the present context, the alternative would likely be Alternative 2—a selective default and a race among holders to collect. As explained in Part III.C.3., the result probably would be uncollectible judgments (or no judgments at all, at least in the U.S., if non-exempted debt were removed from the jurisdiction of the Court of Federal Claims).[88] Presumably, the Prosperity Shares provided under Alternative 1 would offer a better result than uncollectible judgments and the less valuable Prosperity Shares provided under Alternative 2.

Although a discharge is a common feature of a bankruptcy regime, that does not end the inquiry as to the scope of the Bankruptcy Clause. One can easily imagine an unbiased, objective majority of the Supreme Court holding that a putative bankruptcy law that applies to the U.S. government as debtor is not within the scope of the Bankruptcy Clause. Such a holding likely would not be on the basis that the pattern and structure of the law is outside the common

---

86 11 U.S.C. § 1129(a)(7).
87 6 Collier on Bankruptcy (Alan N. Resnick & Henry J. Sommer, eds., 16th ed. 2011) ¶ 943.03[7][a].
88 *See* text at notes 141-44, *infra*.

understanding of the attributes of a bankruptcy law. Instead, it likely would be grounded on the proposition that the Framers never contemplated that the federal government itself would be an eligible and appropriate debtor to which a bankruptcy law could apply. Moreover, because the result of a bankruptcy discharge would frustrate the substance of Section Four, the later adopted Fourteenth Amendment could be construed to have revoked any power to discharge U.S. debt even if that power resided in the Bankruptcy Clause as originally adopted. But this is where the working assumption set out above would come into play.[89] It is assumed that the Court would be highly motivated to uphold the legislation in the face of an extreme financial crisis. There being no textual bar in the language of the Bankruptcy Clause itself, it provides a convenient opening for a willing Court.

Even if the Bankruptcy Clause could accommodate a bankruptcy law for the federal government, arguably implementation of Alternative 1 would face another constitutional hurdle. Would a discharge of the non-exempted Treasury obligations and the distribution of the Prosperity Shares constitute an unconstitutional taking "for public use without just compensation" under the Fifth Amendment?[90] Many bankruptcy scholars are of the view that the powers of Congress conferred by the Bankruptcy Clause are governed by that clause and not the Takings Clause of the Fifth Amendment, so long as such laws enacted under the Bankruptcy Clause are applied only prospectively.[91] Others have argued, however, that even powers that are within the scope of the Bankruptcy Clause must be tested under the Takings Clause. For example, Julia Forrester's careful study of takings in the

---

89 *See* text at notes 1-3, *supra*.

90 U.S. Const. amend. V ("nor shall property be taken for public use, without just compensation"); Julia Forrester, *Bankruptcy Takings*, 51 Fla. L. Rev. 851, *passim*; Thomas Plank, *Bankruptcy and Federalism*, 71 Fordham L. Rev. 1063, 1090 n.106 (2002).

91 James Steven Rogers, *The Impairment of Secured Creditor's Rights in Reorganization: A Study of the Relationship Between the Fifth Amendment and the Bankruptcy Clause*, 96 Harv. L. Rev. 973, 986-89, 1031 (1983) (arguing that prospective legislation under the Bankruptcy Clause could not constitute an unconstitutional taking under the Fifth Amendment and that the Bankruptcy Clause, and not the Fifth Amendment, controls limits on the power of Congress with respect to prospective legislation). As Julia Forrester has observed, "[p]rominent scholars have accepted his [Rogers'] conclusions without challenge." Forrester, supra note 90, at 855 & n.15 (collecting citations to articles relying on Rogers' conclusions) (1999).

context of bankruptcy provides a strong rebuttal of arguments that the exercise by Congress of its powers under the Bankruptcy Clause, even if prospective, is immune from attack as an unconstitutional taking.[92] Thomas Plank has reached the same conclusion.[93]

There would seem to be little question that the powers of Congress under the Bankruptcy Clause must yield to the Takings Clause. It is a fundamental constitutional principal that the general powers granted to Congress in the Constitution, including the Bankruptcy Clause, are subject to the Bill of Rights.[94] Surprisingly, however, scholars who have debated the issue have failed to take note of this general, overarching principle. In his thoughtful and thorough article, for example, James Rogers acknowledged and proceeded to rebut the prevailing view at the time that legislation under the Bankruptcy Clause is subject to the Takings Clause.[95] But neither Rogers nor Forrester explicitly took note of this general principle which appears to be dispositive of the question. Even so, it is doubtful that Alternative 1 would present an unconstitutional taking. If the Prosperity Shares distribution would pass muster under a Chapter 9-like best interests test, discussed above, that should constitute "just compensation" as it would under Chapter 9 itself.

The downside of implementing Alternative 1 through a sovereign bankruptcy regime is the involvement of a court. Even if handled by nonjudicial administrators, a system of appeals no doubt would be a necessary element of the system. That necessarily provides a forum for non-exempted Treasuries holders to attack the constitutionality of the scheme through a challenge to the scope of the Bankruptcy Clause or otherwise.

---

92 Forrester, *supra* note 90, at 854, 871-72, 885, 905, 911-12.
93 Plank, *supra,* note 90, at 1090 n.106.
94 *See, e.g.*, John E. Nowak & Ronald D. Rotunda, Constitutional Law 208 (7th ed. 2004) ("The commerce power, like all other federal powers, is subject to the restrictions of the Bill of Rights and other fundamental constitutional guarantees."); 1 Tribe, American Constitutional Law 851 (3d ed. 2000) ("There are, however, other limits on those [congressional] powers . . . One obvious example is the Bill of Rights, which forbids measures that might otherwise be thought to fall within Congress' Article I powers (*e.g.*, prohibiting those engaged in commerce from speaking on political subjects).").
95 Rogers, *supra* note 91

b. Implementing Alternative 2.

Under one possible statutory framework, Alternative 2 would become effective were Alternative 1 to be struck down. Alternatively, Congress might choose the Alternative 2 approach as the exclusive approach. Under Alternative 2, the validity of the public debt would be expressly preserved. However, the Executive Branch would be given discretion to selectively default on the non-exempted Treasuries, perhaps based upon specified Presidential findings and the declaration of an emergency. Congress also would approve the issuance of the (reduced value) Alternative 2 Prosperity Shares. The obvious question presented here is whether the selective default with Congressional authorization would pass muster as constitutional under Section Four and the non-abrogation principle.[96]

Under a purely textual analysis, Alternative 2 would not appear to "question[]" "[t]he validity of the public debt." Nor would it "alter or destroy those obligations" in contravention of the non-abrogation principle.[97] As already mentioned, as a legal term and concept, "validity" means "binding" and "enforceable.[98] Alternative 2, unlike Alternative 1, leaves the non-exempted Treasury obligations untouched. It would not affect their binding nature or enforceability. Holders would be free to pursue judgments and to seek enforcement against U.S. commercial assets around the world, subject to local laws on sovereign immunity. That is not to say that such enforcement efforts would not face substantial procedural hurdles. They certainly would, as discussed below in Part III.C.3. But the validity of the obligations would present no obstacles to enforcement. And Congress would not have altered or destroyed the obligations. Under Alternative 2, the U.S. would have no defense whatsoever as to its payment obligations.

The legislative history and historical context of Section Four offer support for this textual analysis.[99] Following the Civil War, Republi-

---
96 *Perry,* 294 U.S. at 354.
97 *Id.* at 353.
98 *See* text at note 76, *supra.*
99 For a concise exposition of this legislative history, see Jack Balkin, *The Legislative History of Section Four of the Fourteenth Amendment* (June 30, 2011) [hereinafter,

cans in Congress were concerned that a Democratic majority down the road might "repudiate" the debt incurred by the Union during the war.[100] While not free of doubt, it appears that the "repudiation" to be feared was the possibility that Congress might determine the wartime debt was not lawfully incurred—i.e., was invalid.[101] Michael Abramowicz, while explaining the phrase "authorized by law" in Section Four, observed that, without the phrase, Section Four "would have left open the possibility that a Democratic Congress could have repudiated the Union's Civil War bonds *as illegal and not part of the public debt.*"[102]

Senator Benjamin Wade of Ohio offered the initial proposal of what became the basis for Section Four. The proposal provided in pertinent part that "[t]he public debt . . . shall be inviolable."[103] Subsequently, Senator Howard introduced another proposal on the subject which provided: "The obligations of the United States, incurred in suppressing insurrection, or in defense of the Union, or for payment of bounties or pensions incident thereto, shall remain inviolate."[104] Howard's version was approved by the Senate.[105] Both versions differ substantially from Section Four as ultimately adopted—"[t]he va-

---

Balkin, *Legislative History*], http://balkin.blogspot.com/2011/06/legislative-history-of-section-four-of.html.
100 *Id.*
101 This is a somewhat unusual use of "repudiate" and "repudiation," which in the contract context are understood to mean merely a clear and unequivacal statement by a party that it will not perform. See, e.g., 23 *WILLISTON ON CONTRACTS* § 63:29 (Richard A. Lord, 4th ed.) ("A 'repudiation' is a statement by the obligor to the obligee indicating that the obligor will commit a breach that would itself give the obligee a claim for damages for total breach.") Of course, invalidity (or asserted invalidity) is one of many reasons why a party might choose to repudiate an obligation.
102 Abramowicz, *supra* note 27, at 588 (emphasis added).
103 Cong. Globe, 39th Cong., 1st Sess. 2768 (1866). Senator Wade revealed some concern about a future default in fact. For example, he asked if "open and hostile rebels" were to be seated in Congress "who can guaranty that the debts of the Government will be paid, or that your soldiers and the widows of your soldiers will not lose their pensions?" *Id.* at 2769. He argued that his proposal would "put the debt incurred in the civil war on our part under the guardianship of the Constitution." *Id.*
104 Cong. Globe, 39th Cong., 1st Sess. 2938 (1866).
105 *Id.* at 2941.

lidity of the public debt . . . shall not be questioned."[106] What does it mean for the "validity" of the public debt to be "questioned"? Is "validity . . . questioned" by a threat of default on the public debt? I believe not. Is it questioned by an actual default? Again, I believe not (or, at least, not *necessarily*).

Perry provides support for a strict textual analysis that explains what it means to "question" the public debt and that gives ordinary meaning to "validity." The plurality in *Perry* held that Congress lacks the authority to "alter or destroy" the U.S. government's obligations to repay borrowed funds. It also held that Section Four was "confirmatory" of this principle. This strongly suggests that to "question" the public debt would be an alteration or destruction of the terms of the debt. And, of course, that is exactly what the unconstitutional Congressional joint resolution had done by providing that the gold clauses in U.S. government bonds were against public policy and that the obligations could be satisfied with legal tender. The *Perry* Court also observed that "the validity of the public debt" embraces "whatever concerns the integrity of the public obligations." Equating "validity" with "integrity" also strongly suggests that the Court attributed the usual meaning to "validity"—binding and enforceable.[107] Under this analysis, Alternative 2, which leaves the non-exempted Treasuries valid and binding and enforceable under the original terms, would not "question[]" the "public debt."

Abramowicz has advanced an odd conception of "validity" which confounds the concept with that of "default." "The word 'validity' indicates that not merely the existence of the public debt, but also its binding force on the government 'shall not be questioned.'"[108] This statement seems at best incoherent. How can a debt or any obligation exist if it is not binding? It cannot. Abromowicz then argues:

---

106 U.S. Const. amend. XIV, §4.
107 Moreover, this understanding of validity is consistent with the last clause of the second sentence of Section Four, which *invalidates* debt incurred in aid of insurrection or for loss of slaves. The second sentence reads: "But neither the United States nor any State shall assume or pay any debt or obligation incurred in aid of insurrection or rebellion against the United States, or any claim for the loss or emancipation of any slave; but all such debts, obligations and claims shall be held illegal and void." U.S. Const. amend. XIV, §4.
108 Abramowicz, *supra* note 27, at 594.

The government thus may not acknowledge that the public debt exists but refuse to pay it. If the government fails to make a debt payment, the debt instrument is at least temporarily invalid for legal purposes. Moreover, there is no such thing as a valid debt that will nonetheless not be honored; a debt cannot be called 'valid' if existing laws will cause default on it. So as soon as Congress passes a statute that will lead to default in the absence of a change of course, the debt is invalid (or at least of questionable validity) and Congress has violated the original meaning of [Section Four].[109]

By conflating default with invalidity, the argument misses the point that a default can occur *only* with respect to valid debt. If putative debt is invalid it is not debt of a putative debtor and no default can occur. Under Alternative 2, the legal entitlements of holders of non-exempted Treasuries are unaffected. But Abramowicz's vision of default as invalidity clearly would consider Alternative 2 (and Alternative 1, of course) to be a violation of Section Four. Michael Stern also has taken strong exception to Abramowicz's suggestion that the threat of default would question the validity of the public debt.[110]

Abramowicz's more recent piece provides more detail on his views on validity. According to Abramowicz, Section Four:

> does not distinguish debts that are invalid for all practical purposes from debts that the law explicitly brands as invalid. The

---

109 *Id.* (footnotes omitted).
110 Michael Stern, "*Arrest Me: I Question the Validity of the Public Debt*," Point of Order (June 2, 2011), http://www.pointoforder.com/2011/06/02/arrest-me-i-question-the-validity-of-the-public-debt/:
  I think Abramowicz's argument here is weak. If the framers of the Fourteenth Amendment wanted to say that the government should take no action that would jeopardize the repayment of debt, surely there were more straightforward ways of saying so. . . . . If I conduct my financial affairs in such a way as to make it unlikely or impossible that I can repay all my creditors, I am acting irresponsibly, but I am not questioning the validity of my debts. Even a failure to pay a debt, if caused by inability rather than refusal to pay, cannot be said to question the debt's validity."
Stern does not explain his claim that refusal to pay a debt does question the debt's validity. In that sense, he joins Abramowicz in conflating validity with default.

word "validity" does not implicitly contain such a distinction, and it is not modified by the word "legal." Reading the distinction into [Section Four] . . . would allow the government to pass one statute providing that debts shall be legally valid, but another providing that the Treasury must not make payment on them. This perverse definition of validity would allow an end-run around . . . [Section Four] and would defy the Framers' intent to reassure debt-holders that their debts will be honored.[111]

Whether Section Four should be construed to permit Congress to take the approach that Abramowicz describes in his hypothetical is a fair question. But it hardly seems perverse to read the word "validity" as used in the Constitution to mean "legally valid." Indeed, it is reading "validity" to have a meaning *other* than legally valid which would be perverse.

The point made by Abramowicz can be reframed. It is true that a law that instructs the Executive Branch or gives it discretion to decline to pay obligations on Treasuries largely achieves the same result as invalidation.[112] (That is the point, of course, of Alternative 2.) But the analysis need not hinge on a misunderstanding of the meaning of "validity" as something other than legal validity. Giving "validity" its usual meaning, the argument would be that even if a law provides in so many words that debt is valid, but the same or another law also permits nonpayment of the debt, it is not legally valid construing the relevant law as a whole. This is a more plausible analysis than distorting the meaning of "validity" beyond recognition. In a proper case, this reasoning could plausibly justify equating default (or even a threat of default) with invalidity.

Jack Balkin also views a legislative threat of default as a questioning of the validity of the public debt. He considers Senator Wade's proposal and supporting speech to support this view.

---

111 Abramowicz, *Train Wrecks, supra* note 76, at 26 n.109.
112 This would be especially so if the consent of the U.S. to be sued were withdrawn, though the possibility of foreign judgments and process on foreign assets would remain. *See* text at notes 141-44, *infra*.

> If Wade's speech offers the central rationale for Section Four, the goal was to remove threats of default on federal debts from partisan struggle. . . . . The threat of defaulting on government obligations is a powerful weapon, especially in a complex, interconnected world economy. . . . Section Four was placed in the Constitution to remove this weapon from ordinary politics.[113]

Balkin has pointed out that the Republican supporters of Section Four feared a default or threat of default by the Democrats were they to return to power following the Civil War. He argues that if only a formal repudiation of public debt would violate Section Four, then "the section is practically meaningless."[114] In Balkin's view, individual members of Congress who would threaten a U.S. default on public debt to gain political advantage are themselves violating Section Four.[115] He argues that the proper interpretation of Section Four must take into account the assurances that the Republicans needed. But, it is interesting that Balkin's putative Section Four violation would not be susceptible to any sort of plausible judicial remedy. Indeed, it is Balkin's interpretation that renders Section Four impotent because it envisions a violation without a remedy. How could that provide assurances to anyone? Moreover, it is plausible that when Section Four was debated and adopted, an actual, intentional default on *valid* public debt was not in the consciousness of the legislators.[116] Certainly that rings true in what Senator Hendricks had to say in op-

---

113 Balkin, *Legislative History, supra* note 99. For a critique of Balkin's description, see Michael Stern, "*Threatening Default*": *A Response to Professor Balkin*, Point of Order (July 1, 2011), http://www.pointoforder.com/2011/07/01/threatening-default-a-response-to-professor-balkin/. Stern takes issue in particular with Balkin's reliance on Wade's proposal and speech while arguing that a threat of default does not amount to a prohibited repudiation. Balkin offered a detailed response defending his original analysis, pointing out that the final wording of Section Four was more similar to Wade's original proposal than to Howard's. Jack Balkin, *More on the Original Meaning of Section Four of the Fourteenth Amendment*, Balkinization (July 2, 2011) [hereinafter, Balkin, *More*], http://balkin.blogspot.com/2011/07/more-on-original-meaning-of-section.html.
114 Balkin, *More, supra* note 113.
115 *Id.* (post-Civil War setting); Jack Balkin, *Secretary Geithner understands the Constitution: The Republicans are violating the Fourteenth Amendment*, Balkinization (July 8, 2011), http://balkin.blogspot.com/2011/07/secretary-geithner-understands.html (2011 debt-ceiling crisis context).
116 This issue is worthy of further investigation.

position to Section Four.[117] On that view, protecting the public debt from invalidity would offer an effective method of protecting against actual default.

A lively debate about Section Four arose during the 2011 Congressional impasse over raising the debt limit. Almost fifteen years earlier, Abramowicz had argued that the federal debt-limit statute was unconstitutional as a violation of Section Four because it would lead to repudiation of the public debt absent Congressional action.[118] During the impasse, Neil Buchanan also took the position that the debt-ceiling statute is unconstitutional under Section Four.[119] However, Buchanan's position is that "[t]he debt limit is not unconstitutional because it increases the *risk* of default, but because it would actually require one."[120] Laurence Tribe was of the view that the debt-limit statute is not unconstitutional.[121] However, he conceded that what "makes more sense" is "a more modest interpretation of [Section Four] . . . under which only actual default (as opposed to any action that merely increases the risk of default) is impermissible."[122] Buchanan pointed out that in this respect Tribe agrees with him.[123]

A willing court could find additional substantial support and inspiration in *Perry* for adopting a strict textual analysis of Section Four that embraces "validity" in the normal sense and that supports the constitutionality of Alternative 2. *Perry* protected the validity and integrity of the U.S. government's promise to deliver gold coin by holding the attempt to eliminate the obligation unconstitutional. Like the hold-

---

117 Cong. Globe, 39th Cong., 1st Sess. 2940 (1866).
118 Abramowicz, *supra* note 27, at 578-80. For a more recent effort, see Abramowicz, *Train Wrecks, supra* note 76.
119 Neil H. Buchanan, *The Debt-Limit Crisis: A Problem That Will Keep Coming Back Unless President Obama Takes a Constitutional Stand Now*, Verdict (July 7, 2011), http://verdict.justia.com/2011/07/07/the-debt-limit-crisis; Neil H. Buchanan, *The Debt Ceiling Law is Unconstitutional: A Reply to Professor Tribe*, Verdict (July 11, 2011) [hereinafter, Buchanan, *Reply*], http://verdict.justia.com/2011/07/11/the-debt-ceiling-law-is-unconstitutional; Buchanan, *Borrowing, supra* note 26.
120 Buchanan, *Reply, supra* note 119.
121 Laurence Tribe, Op-Ed, *A Ceiling We Can't Wish Away*, N.Y. Times, July 7, 2011 [hereinafter, Tribe, *OpEd*, www.nytimes.com/2011/07/08/opinion/08tribe.html?_r=1&pagewanted=print; Tribe, *Guest Post, supra* note 26.
122 Tribe, Op-Ed, *supra* note 121.
123 Buchanan, *Reply, supra* note 119.

ing in *Perry*, Alternative 2 would leave the non-exempted Treasury obligations unaffected and would even reaffirm their validity and enforceability. As to remedies, in *Perry* the Court permitted the government to substitute the face amount of currency for its obligation to deliver gold coin. By a proper exercise of the government's powers over monetary policy, it had made it impossible for the holder of the gold clause bond to recover the original value of the gold. Under Alternative 2, the Prosperity Shares would be substituted for the actual payment of the non-exempted debt as called for under the terms of the Treasury obligations. As in *Perry*, Congress would have passed legislation authorizing the issuance of Prosperity Shares as a step toward rescuing the U.S. economy from an economic crisis. As in *Perry*, the value provided (the Prosperity Shares) to the non-exempted Treasuries holders would be less than the value originally promised (payment in full). But in *Perry*, the bond was paid and discharged by payment of the lesser value; Alternative 2 would leave the validity of the Treasury obligations intact and provide Prosperity Shares. In *Perry*, moreover, the offending joint resolution provided that gold clauses were "against public policy" and overtly changed the terms of U.S. obligations by providing that obligations could be satisfied not in gold but with legal tender.[124] Alternative 2 would not purport to change the terms of Treasuries, however. So long as the validity of the public debt remains pristine, arguably neither Section Four nor the non-abrogation principle (that Congress cannot alter or destroy U.S. obligations) would prohibit the U.S. from deciding not to pay the Treasury obligations voluntarily.

The power to decline to pay in the face of a national financial threat should not be confounded with the impairment of the validity or alteration of obligations. The exercise of monetary power relating to gold that was involved in *Perry* was, of course, closely related to the substance of the gold clause obligations. The relationship between the adoption of Alternative 2 as a general measure to ameliorate a financial crisis and the power of Congress over monetary policy is somewhat more attenuated. But there is a substantial connection nonetheless. Alternative 2 embraces a Congressional decision that continuing to print more money to pay U.S. obligations is bad mon-

---

124 *See* text at note 29, *supra*.

etary policy. A decision not to print money is as much an exercise over monetary policy as a contrary decision. As in *Perry*, under Alternative 2, the exercise by Congress of its power over monetary policy would leave non-exempt Treasury holders with less than the full benefit of their bargains. As in *Perry*, however, this result would prevent Section Four and the non-abrogation principle from overriding the power over monetary policy.

The discussion of Alternative 2 to this point has focused on the validity of the U.S. obligations, which Alternative 2 would not purport to affect. But the constitutionality of Alternative 2 also must be tested from another perspective that arises out of the sovereign nature of Treasuries. Certainly, holders of Treasuries have civil contractual claims based on the U.S. obligations to pay. But arguably they may have more than a contractual claim to the extent that U.S. law *requires* (other than by virtue of contractual obligation) the U.S. to pay. Current law provides with respect to Treasuries:

> (a) The faith of the United States Government is pledged to pay, in legal tender, principal and interest on the obligations of the Government issued under this chapter.
>
> (b) The Secretary of the Treasury shall pay interest due or accrued on the public debt. As the Secretary considers expedient, the Secretary may pay in advance interest on the public debt by a period of not more than one year, with or without a rebate of interest on the coupons.[125]

Subsection (a) does not directly require payment of principal, but that requirement might be implicit in "pledged to pay." Certainly, subsection (a) would authorize payment. Subsection (b) does directly require payment. Should these provisions, which are directed at the U.S. government, also be considered a part of the U.S. obligations to Treasury holders? Stated otherwise, are Treasury holders legal beneficiaries of these provisions? If so, then if Alternative 2 were implemented by a law that partially abrogated these provisions, that might well question the public debt and violate the non-abrogation principal.

---

125 31 U.S.C. § 3123(a), (b).

There would be no reason to modify the "faith of the United States Government" aspect of subsection (a) in order to implement Alternative 2. The faith of the U.S. would be unaffected inasmuch as the obligations would remain unaffected. Alternative 2 would, however, necessarily be at odds with an implicit directive to pay in subsection (a) and with subsection (b) in respect of interest payments on non-exempted Treasuries. But as directives to pay, these provisions provide no additional content to the U.S. obligations to holders of Treasuries. The terms of the Treasuries bind the U.S. to its payment obligations according to those terms. Nothing contained in section 3123 makes the U.S. any *more* obligated. Consequently, these provisions appear to be directives to the government and the Secretary rather than provisions intended to provide any additional substantive rights to holders.[126] Under this analysis, Alternative 2 would leave the U.S. obligations to holders of Treasuries intact, notwithstanding the decision of the executive branch to decline to pay obligations on the non-exempted Treasuries. It recognizes the difference between authorizing the Executive Branch to decline to pay, which would occur, and the elimination of the obligation of the U.S. to pay, which would not occur. On the other hand, it is clear enough that the Executive's

---

126 Section 365.30(a) of the Department of Treasury's Uniform Offering Circular for Treasuries provides:
  We will pay principal on bills, notes, and bonds on the maturity date as specified in the auction announcement. Interest on bills consists of the difference between the discounted amount paid by the investor at original issue and the par value we pay to the investor at maturity. Interest on notes and bonds accrues from the dated date. Interest is payable on a semiannual basis on the interest payment dates specified in the auction announcement through the maturity date. If any principal or interest payment date is a Saturday, Sunday, or other day on which the Federal Reserve System is not open for business, we will make the payment (without additional interest) on the next business day. If a bond is callable, we will pay the principal prior to maturity if we call it under its terms, which include providing appropriate public notice.
31 C.F.R. § 356.30(a). Like section 3123(a) and (b) discussed in the text, subsection (a) would not appear to establish an independent entitlement for the holders of Treasuries. Instead it is better seen as simply a term of the Treasuries inasmuch as the purpose of the Offering Circular is to establish the terms and conditions of Treasuries. See 31 C.F.R. §§ 356.0 ("Chapter 31 of Title 31 of the United States Code authorizes the Secretary of the Treasury to issue United States obligations, and to offer them for sale with the terms and conditions that the Secretary prescribes."); 356.1 ("The provisions in this part, including the appendices, and each individual auction announcement govern the sale and issuance of marketable Treasury securities issued on or after March 1, 1993.").

decision to default would in fact and law contravene the directives to pay in section 3123, so Alternative 2 would require Congress to provide an exception.

Notwithstanding the forgoing textual analysis distinguishing validity from default and the analysis of Section 3123(a) and (b) just advanced, defenders of Alternative 2's constitutionality would face an arguable flaw in these arguments. Although Alternative 2 would leave holders of non-exempted Treasuries with precisely the same legal entitlements vis-à-vis the U.S. as would have existed prior to its implementation, the actual judicial enforcement of Treasuries against the U.S. has never been a realistic expectation. Instead, confidence in the payment—and value—of Treasuries has been based on the "faith of the United States Government"[127] and the "contractual obligation . . . [that], despite infirmities of procedure, remains binding upon the conscience of the sovereign."[128] This seems to be the kernel of the argument advanced by Abramowicz and Balkin that legal validity with the prospect of nonpayment in fact violates Section Four.[129] But a contrary conclusion is also plausible, as discussed above. Neither Section Four nor the non-abrogation principle provides a positive command that the U.S. pay its obligations or a prohibition against nonpayment. The framers of Section Four might have chosen that approach but they did not. Section Four also does not condition the power of the government upon making a payment or giving other value as does the Fifth Amendment.[130] The non-exempted Treasuries would be valid obligations of the U.S. both before and after implementation of Alternative 2. Every day, obligors on valid obligations default and no one has ever thought such obligations are thereby invalidated. Finally, recall once again the holding in *Perry*. Notwithstanding the unconstitutionality of the attempt by Congress to abrogate the U.S. obligations under gold clauses, the Court allowed the *de facto* invalidation to stand.[131]

Given the working assumption of cooperative U.S. courts in a financial crisis, the ultimate constitutionality of Alternative 2 is plausible.

---

127 31 U.S.C. § 3123(a).
128 *Perry*, 294 U.S. at 354.
129 *See* text at notes 108-115, *supra*.
130 U.S. Const. amend. V (quoted in part *supra* note 90).
131 *See* text at notes 39-42, *supra*.

But that conclusion is far from clear. This underscores the importance of implementing Alternative 2 with steps to ensure that no U.S. court (i.e., no court with jurisdiction over the U.S.) would ever have the opportunity to examine the constitutionality of Alternative 2.[132]

c. Implementing Alternative 3.

The implementation of Alternative 3 would be straightforward. The U.S. would notify Treasuries holders of the exchange offer of Prosperity Shares in satisfaction of the specified percentage of Treasury obligations essentially on the same terms as under Alternative 1. However, unlike Alternative 1, the Prosperity Shares for Treasury obligations exchange would be strictly voluntary. Holders could choose to accept the offer or not to accept. This approach would avoid the legal difficulties and substantially reduce the political ramifications of the first two alternatives. It also would be more conducive for bilateral negotiations with major Treasuries holders, although the U.S. might not have sufficient leverage to succeed.

2. Credible Commitment Against Future Defaults.

Alternatives 1 and 2 would raise questions as to whether the U.S. might attempt serial restructurings. Such concerns would exacerbate the likely market fallout from either of these alternatives and might threaten future access of the U.S. to capital markets. How might the U.S. usefully assuage investors' concerns that the U.S. might repeat the process in the future? While a perfectly bulletproof prophylactic might not be possible, the issue is worth exploring. One approach would be to incorporate into the restructuring arrangement, possibly as a term of the Prosperity Shares, a poison pill-like feature. Such a feature might provide that any default on the non-defaulted portion of the Treasuries, or any future attempt to further restructure Treasuries, would *ipso facto* reinstate the status *quo ante*, impose a retroactive default interest rate, and provide for immediate payment of a penalty. Although such a provision could not prevent a future default, it might send a strong signal to the market that the restructuring is truly a one-time event.

---

132 *See* text at notes 141-44, *infra* (discussing withdrawal of consent by the U.S. to jurisdiction).

3. Post-Default Enforcement of Treasuries.

Consider next the legal rights of holders of Treasuries upon a U.S. default. Recall that references to "holders" are to the underlying beneficial owners of Treasuries in the commercial book-entry system. But some holders are more equal than others.

a. The Race to Judgment.

The offering circular for Treasuries provides with respect to the commercial book-entry system:

> [W]e do not have any obligations to any person or entity that does not have an account with a Federal Reserve Bank. We also will not recognize the claims of any person or entity:
>
> (i) That does not have an account at a Federal Reserve Bank, or
>
> (ii) with respect to any accounts not maintained at a Federal Reserve Bank.[133]

It follows that the *only* persons entitled to enforce Treasuries held in the commercial book-entry system are the depository institutions with securities accounts at a Federal Reserve Bank to which Treasuries have been credited. We can refer to these holders as "recognized holders." Absent default, this circumstance is innocuous enough. The U.S. satisfies its obligations by crediting accounts at a Federal Reserve Bank. A Federal Reserve Bank then credits the accounts of its account holders. If those account holders are acting as intermediaries, they credit their own account holders in turn with the payment and so on down the chain of intermediated holdings. The issue of enforcement against the issuer never arises.

Now consider the default scenario. Under the assumption that Congress would not withdraw its consent to suits against the U.S., upon a default, a recognized holder of Treasuries could sue the U.S. in the

---

[133] 31 C.F.R. § 356.30(c)(1). "We" is defined as "the Secretary of the Treasury and his or her delegates, including the Department of the Treasury, Bureau of the Public Debt, and their representatives. The term also includes Federal Reserve Banks acting as fiscal agents of the United States." 31 C.F.R. § 356.2.

Court of Federal Claims to recover a money judgment. That court has exclusive jurisdiction over claims against the U.S. based on contract.[134] But it is not clear what role the recognized holders would play after default in respect of the other holders (*i.e.*, the recognized holders' account holders to which they had credited Treasuries). In the intermediated holding system in the U.S., an intermediary has no duty to its account holders to pursue a defaulting issuer of debt securities. This is so whether the intermediary holds through a Federal Reserve Bank or through another intermediary (such as a central securities depository), or whether the intermediary is itself a central securities depository that is the registered owner of the securities on the books of the issuer. In the world of corporate and municipal debt securities, however, there normally is an indenture trustee charged with enforcement on behalf of the holders; it is not a holder's intermediary that is charged with that responsibility.

Recognized holders would have little motivation to take enforcement action following a U.S. default on Treasuries except to the extent that they hold Treasuries on their own behalf (*i.e.*, proprietary holdings) as opposed to holding for their account holders. Moreover, if U.S. domestic holders' Treasuries were exempted from default, domestic recognized holders would have no motivation to enforce, other than as a courtesy or for relationship reasons, on behalf of their account holders who hold nonexempt Treasuries. On the other hand, a holder of non-exempted Treasuries would be free to move the securities to an account with a recognized holder that would be willing to enforce on the holder's behalf. In particular, foreign recognized holders might be willing to act on behalf of their non-exempted foreign account holders.

---

134 28 U.S.C. § 1491(a)(1) (2011) ("The United States Court of Federal Claims shall have jurisdiction to render judgment upon any claim against the United States founded either upon the Constitution, or any Act of Congress or any regulation of an executive department, or upon any express or implied contract with the United States, or for liquidated or unliquidated damages in cases not sounding in tort."). *See also Gross v. Griffin*, 800 F. Supp. 2d 293, 299 (D. Me. 2011) ("This grant of jurisdiction to the Court of Federal Claims is exclusive, but 'only to the extent that Congress has not granted any other court authority to hear the claims that may be decided by the [Court of Federal Claims].'") (quoting *Bowen v. Mass.*, 487 U.S. 879, 910 n.48 (1988)); *Wagner v. U.S., Dep't of Hous. & Urban Dev.*, 835 F. Supp. 953, 958 (E.D. Ky. 1993), aff'd, 43 F.3d 1473 (6th Cir. 1994) (holding that the Court of Federal Claims has exclusive jurisdiction over breach of contract claims against the United States).

Unlike the situation of a trustee's enforcement under the terms of a bond indenture, currently there is no extant body of law or contractual arrangement that addresses enforcement by a recognized holder on behalf of its account holders (or account holders' account holders, etc.). It would be necessary to make such arrangements post-default. If a recognized holder wished to enforce its proprietary defaulted Treasuries, would it also be willing to enforce on behalf of its account holders? Inasmuch as the enforcement exercise would be a race to judgment and a subsequent race to locate and execute on assets not protected by sovereign immunity, such a recognized holder probably would not want to share recoveries with other holders. And holders probably would not be willing to subordinate their rights as a condition for their recognized holder to pursue their claims. It would be better to find another recognized holder without a proprietary claim that might be willing to enforce on behalf of other holders, subject to appropriate remuneration, indemnification, and the like. Presumably, counsel would be available to handle an enforcement action on a contingency basis.

As to Treasuries held in the commercial book-entry system, it is actually not surprising that the statutory and regulatory structure for actual enforcement is utterly unsuitable. No doubt it was created and has been operated on the unquestioned assumption that no default would ever occur. Action based on reasonable assumptions that turn out to be wrong is unfortunate. But action based on assumptions that are never questioned or examined may be considered careless. Even if it were absolutely clear that it would not be in the interest of the U.S. to default and attempt a restructuring of its Treasury obligations, having a clear and plausible means of enforcing the obligations should be a concern of holders of Treasuries. The occurrence of an "unintentional" default (*e.g.*, arising out of a Congressional impasse on raising the debt ceiling) or a default based on an inability to pay cannot be discounted entirely.

Some holders in the commercial book-entry system would have another alternative for enforcement. They could move their Treasuries from the commercial book-entry system to the Treasury Direct system.[135] This would provide a direct relationship with the U.S. and direct evidence of ownership of the Treasuries so held. But there are some limitations. Only recently have entities, as opposed to natural persons, been permitted to open Treasury Direct entity accounts.[136] Domestic U.S. governments are not eligible to open entity accounts.[137] One single named individual, the account manager, must be able to act alone with respect to the account. Most organizations must have a U.S. Employer Identification Number in order to open an account, which might be difficult or impossible for some foreign holders.[138] Moreover, because the holder would be identified to the U.S., it is unlikely that states such as Iran or Cuba would be willing to hold Treasuries through Treasury Direct.

Although the system is not enforcement friendly, one way or another the holder of defaulted Treasuries would find a way to pursue a claim

---

135 31 C.F.R. § 363.206(b) (2012) (explaining how to transfer Treasury securities to the TreasuryDirect system).

136 31 C.F.R. § 363.11 (2012) ("Only an individual or an entity is eligible to open a TreasuryDirect account."). The amendment to this regulation noted that: "To date, only individuals have been permitted to open a TreasuryDirect account. This final rule will permit certain specified entities to open accounts in TreasuryDirect and conduct transactions in eligible Treasury securities." Regulations Governing Securities Held in TreasuryDirect, 74 Fed. Reg. 19416-01 (final rule April 24, 2009) (codified at 31 C.F.R. pt. 363.11). An earlier direct registration system, now known as Legacy Treasury Direct, permits trusts, organizations, legal representatives of a decedent's estate, corporations, sole proprietorships, and partnerships to hold Treasuries. *See* Comparison of Legacy Treasury Direct with Treasury Direct, http://www.treasurydirect.gov/indiv/myaccount/comparisonltdandtd.htm. Legacy Treasury Direct is being phased out and new accounts cannot be opened. *Id.*

137 Regulations specify that registration of entities is limited to "sole proprietorship; partnership; corporation; limited liability company or professional limited liability company (LLC or PLLC); trust; decedent's estate; and estate of a living person such as an incompetent or a minor." 31 C.F.R. § 363.20(c) (2012). Moreover, the regulations specify that in the case of a trust, decedent's estate, or estate of a living person, registration is not available if the trust or legal representative of the estate "is acting on behalf of a federal, state, or local government." 31 C.F.R. § 363.20(c) (5)-(7) (2012). The regulation is silent as to registration if such an entity is acting on behalf of a foreign government.

138 31 C.F.R. § 363.11 (2012) ("In order to open a TreasuryDirect account, an . . . entity must have a valid SSN or employer identification number. The account owner must have a United States address of record and have an account at a United States depository financial institution that will accept debits and credits using the Automated Clearing House method of payment.").

in the Court of Federal Claims under current law. But as a part of implementing Alternatives 1 and 2, Congress might also withdraw its waiver of sovereign immunity and the jurisdiction of the Court of Federal Claims in respect of the non-exempted Treasury obligations. That would leave holders of defaulted non-exempted Treasury obligations without a U.S. forum in which to pursue a money judgment. If that approach is pursued, it also would be prudent to withdraw its waiver in connection with suits against U.S. government officials, as well.[139] That would deprive debt holders of a U.S. forum in which to challenge the constitutionality of Alternative 2.[140]

Arguably, Section Four itself could be construed as a waiver of sovereign immunity inasmuch as it protects the rights of the holders of public debt. But dictum in the plurality opinion in *Perry* indicates otherwise, stating clearly that Congress is not obliged to provide remedies for creditors of the U.S.[141] Justice Stone's concurring opinion is in accord.

> There is no occasion now to resolve doubts, which I entertain, with respect to these questions. At present they are academic. Concededly they may be transferred wholly to the realm of speculation by the exercise of the undoubted power of the Government to withdraw the privilege of suit upon its gold clause obligations.[142]

Months after *Perry* was decided, Congress did withdraw its consent to file suit against the U.S. based on gold clause obligations.[143] The only case to consider that withdrawal of consent upheld its validity and held that a claim under a gold clause bond was "barred by the doctrine of sovereign immunity."[144]

---

139 *See, e.g.*, 5 U.S.C. § 702 (permitting suits against officials and the U.S. for relief other than money damages).
140 As already explained, a bankruptcy law almost certainly would be subject to judicial scrutiny at some point, providing a means of challenging Alternative 1. *See* Part III.C.1.a., *supra* (discussing bankruptcy).
141 *Perry*, 294 U.S. at 354 (quoted *supra* text at note 85).
142 *Perry*, 294 U.S. at 360.
143 H. J. Res. 348, 74th Cong., 49 Stat. 938 § 2 (1935), *codified* at 31 U.S.C. 5118(c)(1)(B) & (C).
144 *Gold Bondholders Protective Council, Inc. v. United States*, 676 F.2d 643, 646 (Ct. Cl. 1982) ("In an unbroken line of decisions, it has been held that Congress

b. The Race to Recover.

Continuing the assumption that Congress would not withdraw its consent to suits against the U.S., now consider the means of enforcing a judgment against the U.S. obtained in the Court of Federal Claims.[145] The U.S. no doubt would assert an absolute sovereign immunity from execution in order to prevent enforcement of such a judgment against its assets located within U.S. territory. Whether such immunity from execution would be absolute under current U.S. law apparently has not been the subject of any reported decision. As with timely payment of Treasuries discussed above, it apparently has been assumed that judgments against the U.S. would be paid in due course and that Congress would always make necessary appropriations to do so.[146] In the absence of any controlling federal authority, it is virtually certain that a U.S. court would adopt absolute immunity from execution for domestic assets of the U.S. That would be consistent with laws enacted in other states with respect to domestic assets.[147] Inasmuch as the baseline for international law was

---

may withdraw its consent to sue the Government at any time.").

145 Of course, a recognized holder or a holder through Treasury Direct also might choose to sue in another jurisdiction outside the U.S. What follows concerning sovereign immunity (or not) from execution would also apply to judgments obtained outside the U.S.

146 Consistent with an absolute immunity from execution, the Rules of Procedure of the Court of Federal Claims, which are patterned after and numbered consistently with the Federal Rules of Civil Procedure, provide in part: "Rule 69. Execution [Not used]." Any exceptions to absolute immunity from execution would be those applicable under United States federal common law (including international law).

147 *See* Código de Procedimientos Civiles [CPC] [Civil Procedure Code] Article 4, Diario Oficial de la Federación [DO], 16 de Enero de 2012 (Mex.) (stating that Mexican courts may not attach property of Mexico in aid of execution); *Société X v. U.S.,* (Court of Cassation 1993) *cited in* August Reinisch, *European Court Practice Concerning State Immunity from Enforcement Measures,* 17 Eur. J. Int'l L. 803, 813 (2006) (explaining that under Turkish legislation, only assets of the Turkish state are immune from execution). Bond prospectuses of certain countries also reflect that property of the State that is within the State will be immune from execution. *See* $1,000,000,000 State Treasury of Republic of Poland 5¼% Notes due 2014 (Prospectus dated Aug. 20, 2003) (Prospectus Supplement dated Oct. 22, 2003), at 60, http://www.sec.gov/Archives/edgar/data/79312/000119312503066700/d424b5.htm (last visited Apr. 10, 2012) ("Under the laws of Poland, subject to certain exceptions, assets of Poland are immune from attachment or other forms of execution whether before or after judgment."); U.S.$600,000,000 Republic of Chile Floating Rate Notes due 2008 (Prospectus dated Jan. 16, 2004), at 1,

absolute immunity, it would appear that by virtue of the absence of any statutory waiver of immunity from execution and any case law relating to U.S. domestic assets, no relaxation of absolute immunity has occurred.

Glidden v. Zdanok[148] reflects the conventional wisdom that absolute immunity from execution for the recovery of money judgments applies under U. S. law. In *Glidden*, the issue presented was whether judges of the Court of Claims (now, Court of Federal Claims) were Article III constitutional judges.[149] The Court held that they were Article III judges. Writing for the plurality, Justice Harlan accepted the proposition that the Court of Claims lacked the power to enforce money judgments against the U.S.

> The problem was recognized in the Congress that created the Court of Claims, where it was pointed out that if ability to enforce judgments were made a criterion of judicial power, no tribunal created under Article III would be able to assume jurisdiction of money claims against the United States. Cong. Globe, 33d Cong., 2d Sess. 113 (1854) (remarks of Senator Stuart). The subsequent vesting of such jurisdiction in the District Courts . . . of course bears witness that at least the Congress has not thought such a criterion imperative.[150]

The issue here is not precisely one of immunity from execution, but rather one of the exclusive power of Congress over appropriations.[151]

---

http://www.sec.gov/Archives/edgar/data/19957/000119312504009460/d424b5.htm (last visited Apr. 10, 2012) ("Chile will not waive immunity from attachment prior to judgment and attachment in aid of execution under Chilean law with respect to property of Chile located in Chile and with respect to its movable and immovable property which is destined to diplomatic and consular missions and to the residence of the head of such missions or to military purposes . . . since such waiver is not permitted under the laws of Chile."). *See also* Philip R. Wood, Project Finance, Subordinated Debt and State Loans 154 (1995) ("A state can pass legislation, binding on its courts, immunising domestic assets from execution, and many have done so.").

148 370 U.S. 530 (1962).

149 The status of judges of the Court of Customs and Patent Appeals also was at issue.

150 *Glidden*, 370 U.S. at 570.

151 U.S. Const. art. I, § 9, cl. 7 ("No Money shall be drawn from the Treasury, but in Consequence of Appropriations made by Law . . ."). Recall the "permanent,

But, of course, absent immunity from execution, a court could reach assets without infringing on that exclusive power over the purse. This compels the conclusion that absolute sovereign immunity from execution is U.S. law with respect to assets of the U.S. government.

The U.S. codified restricted immunity in the federal Foreign Sovereign Immunities Act (FSIA) in 1976, and since that time issues of immunity of foreign sovereign states from execution, as well as adjudication, has been governed by that act.[152] Even prior to enactment of the FSIA, U.S. policy and case law had embraced restricted immunity for foreign states.[153] The principal relevant exception from

---

indefinite appropriation" currently in effect. *See* note 17, *supra*. On *Glidden* and related issues, *see* Vicki Jackson, *Suing the Federal Government: Sovereignty, Immunity, and Judicial Independence,* 35 Geo. Wash. Int'l L. Rev. 521, 594-605 (2003).

152 *See* 28 U.S.C. §§ 1330, 1332, 1391(f), 1441(d), 1602-11 (2012) (encompassing the various sections of the Act). Although the title of the act refers to "Foreign Sovereign Immunity," it is common to refer to "sovereign" immunity as immunity of a government from suit (or execution) in its own courts. Immunity of foreign states in another state's forum is usually referred to as "state" immunity. For convenience, this discussion refers to "sovereign" immunity in both contexts.

153 In 1952, the Acting Legal Adviser to the U.S. Department of State, Jack B. Tate, notified the Department of Justice of a shift in U.S. policy from support for absolute sovereign immunity to the restrictive theory of sovereign immunity, which would recognize immunity of foreign States for their public and governmental, but not their commercial, activities. Letter from Jack B. Tate, Acting Legal Adviser of the U.S. Dep't of State, to Acting Attorney General Phillip B. Perlman (May 19, 1952), *reprinted in*, 26 Dep't St. Bull. 984 (1952). This letter is commonly referred to as the Tate Letter. For a brief discussion of the historical importance of the Tate Letter, *see* Ruth Donner, *The Tate Letter Revisited*, 9 Willamette J. Int'l L. & Disp. Resol. 27, 27-30 (2001).

After its release, courts frequently referenced the Tate Letter in cases concerning sovereign immunity. *See Nat'l City Bank of N.Y. v. Republic of China*, 348 U.S. 356, 360 (1955) (citing the Tate Letter, the Supreme Court noted that "[a]s the responsible agency for the conduct of foreign affairs, the State Department is the normal means of suggesting to the courts that a sovereign be granted immunity from a particular suit. . . . Recently the State Department has pronounced broadly against recognizing sovereign immunity for the commercial operations of a foreign government . . ."). *See also Alfred Dunhill of London, Inc. v. Republic of Cuba*, 425 U.S. 682, 706 (1976) (referencing the Tate Letter, "We decline to extend the act of state doctrine to acts committed by foreign sovereigns in the course of their purely commercial operations."); *N.E. Shipping Corp. v. Gov't of Pak.*, 1975 A.M.C. 2005, 2007 (S.D.N.Y. 1975) (dismissing the issue of sovereign immunity in cases involving commercial actions of a State by recognizing the Department of State's application of the restrictive theory of sovereign immunity as announced in the Tate Letter); *Amkor Corp. v.*

immunity from execution under the FSIA would be "property in the United States of a foreign state . . . used for a commercial activity in the United States . . . if— . . . the property is or was used for the commercial activity upon which the claim is based."[154] It is now well accepted that the issuance of debt securities by a sovereign state is "commercial activity."[155] But the FSIA applies only to foreign states, not to the immunity (or not) of the U.S.

Assets of the U.S. that are used for commercial activity and located outside the U.S could be reached by judgment creditors to the extent permitted by the sovereign immunity rules applicable in a relevant foreign court.[156] In much of Europe, legislatures and courts

---

Bank of Korea, 298 F. Supp. 143, 144 (S.D.N.Y. 1969) (holding that the Department of State's decision to not extend sovereign immunity to Korea was binding under the restrictive theory of sovereign immunity and, moreover, the court agreed with this decision because entering into a contract for the purchase of machinery and equipment to be used in the construction of a soda plant was "private and commercial in nature rather than public or political acts . . . ."); *Victory Transp. Inc. v. Comisaria General de Abastecimientos y Transportes*, 232 F. Supp. 294, 296 (S.D.N.Y. 1963) (holding that sovereign immunity did not prohibit a private corporation from filing suit against a branch of the Spanish Ministry of Commerce because the agreement to charter petitioner's vessel was a "commercial operation of the Spanish government" and, in recognition of the Tate Letter, "the defense of sovereign immunity [was] not available.") *aff'd* 336 F.2d 354 (2d Cir. 1964).

154 28 U.S.C. § 1610(a)(2).

155 In *Republic of Argentina v. Weltover*, the Supreme Court held that a State's debt securities are commercial activities. 504 U.S. 607, 620 (1992). The Court noted that the FSIA "provides that the commercial character of an act is to be determined by reference to its 'nature'" and "that when a foreign government acts, not as regulator of a market, but in the manner of a private player within it, the foreign sovereign's actions are 'commercial' within the meaning of the FSIA." *Id.* at 614. *See also Mortimer Off Shore Servs., Ltd.* v. F.R.G., 615 F.3d 97, 107-08 (2d Cir. 2010) (holding that the commercial activity exception of the FSIA applied because agricultural bonds are commercial in nature and Germany had affirmatively assumed liability for these bonds); *Turkmani v. Republic of Bol.*, 193 F. Supp. 2d 165, 174-75 (D.D.C. 2002) (relying on *Weltover*, the court held that bonds issued by Bolivia constituted commercial activity under the FSIA).

156 England's foreign sovereign immunity legislation is typical of the law applicable to attachment of property of foreign states. State Immunity Act, 1978, c. 33, § 13(4) (U.K.). For discussion on immunity from execution see Hazel Fox, The Law of State Immunity 599-662 (2d ed. 2008); Dhisadee Chamlongrasdr, Foreign State Immunity and Arbitration 259-333 (2007); State Practice Regarding State Immunities 151-248 (Gerhard Hafner et al. eds., 2006); Ernest K. Bankas, The State Immunity Controversy in International Law: Private Suits Against Sovereign States in

have adopted restricted immunity from execution for assets used for commercial activity.[157] Most of these jurisdictions do not confine the commercial exception to immunity to assets that have a connection with the claim asserted against the state.[158] Some others, like the

---

Domestic Courts 182-84, 317-59 (2005).
157 *Banca Carige S.p.A Cassa Di Risparmio di Genova E Imperia v. Banco Nacional De Cuba*, [2001] Lloyd's Rep. 147, [153] (Eng.) ("The English common law adopted the 'restrictive' theory of sovereign immunity [regarding issues of attachment of a foreign State's property]."); *Société Sonotrach v. Migeon*, 77 I.L.R. 525, 527 (Fr. Court of Cassation 1985) ("The assets of a foreign State are, in principle, not subject to seizure, subject to exceptions in particular where they have been allocated for an economic or commercial activity . . . ."); *Condor & Filvem v. Nat'l Shipping Co. of Nigeria*, 33 I.L.M. 593 (It. Constitutional Court 1992), *sub nom Condor & Filvem v. Minister of Justice*, Case No. 329, 101 I.L.R. 394, 401-02 (It. Constitutional Court 1992) (holding that restrictive immunity for execution applied as long the property "is not destined to accomplish public functions," and allowing pre-judgment attachment on a vessel of the State-owned Nigerian shipping company for unpaid price of goods guaranteed by the Nigeria Central Bank and the State of Nigeria); *Abbott v. Republic of S. Afr.*, 113 I.L.R. 412, 425-26 (Spain Constitutional Court (Second Chamber) 1992) (holding that there was no longer a general rule of international law requiring foreign States to be granted absolute immunity from execution and allowing for execution of a State bank account for an unsatisfied judgment for salary arrears due to a foreign State employee, provided the funds were clearly and exclusively allocated for commercial or economic activities).
Restrictive immunity from execution is also generally observed outside of Europe. *See* Act on the Civil Jurisdiction of Japan with respect to a Foreign State, Act. No. 24 of 2009, art. 18(1) ("A Foreign State, etc. shall not be immune from jurisdiction with respect to proceedings of a civil execution procedures [sic] against the property held by said Foreign State, etc. that is in use or intended for use by said Foreign State, etc. exclusively for other than government non-commercial purposes."); *Cresh Co. v. Nauru Fin. Corp.*, Tokyo Chiho Saibansho [Tokyo Dist. Ct.] Nov. 30, 2000, 1740 HANREI JIHO [HANJI] 54, *translated in* 44 Japanese Ann. Int'l L. 204 (2001) (holding that the restricted theory had been adopted). *See also* State Immunity Act, R.S.C. 1985, c. S-18, §12(1)(b) (Can.) ("property of a foreign state that is located in Canada is immune from attachment and execution . . . except where. . . (b) the property is used or is intended for a commercial activity"); State Immunity Act 1979, §15(4) (Cap 313 1979) (Sing.) (stating that the Act "does not prevent the issue of any process in respect of property [of a State] which is for the time being in use or intended for use for commercial purposes."); Foreign States Immunities Act Act 87 of 1981 §14(3) (S. Afr.) (stating that the Act "does not prevent the issue of any process in respect of property [of a State] which is for the time being in use or intended for use for commercial purposes.").
158 Many sovereign immunity acts do not have a connection requirement. *See* State Immunity Act, 1978, c. 33, § 13(4) (U.K.) (State immunity "does not prevent the issue of any process in respect of property which is for the time being in use or intended for use for commercial purposes."); The State Immunity Ordinance, No. VI of 1981, § 14(2)(b) Pak. Code (1981) (Pak.) ("the property of a State, not be-

U.S., do have a form of connection requirement for the applicability of an exception from immunity from execution.[159] The United Na-

ing property which is for the time being in use or intended for use for commercial purposes, shall not be subject to any process for the enforcement of a judgment or arbitration award or, in an action in rem, for its arrest detention or sale."); State Immunity Act 1979, §15(4) (Cap 313 1979) (Sing.) ("Paragraph (b) of subsection (2) does not prevent the issue of any process in respect of property which is for the time being in use or intended for use for commercial purposes."); State Immunity Act, R.S.C. 1985, c. S-18, §12(1)(b) (Can.) ("property of a foreign state that is located in Canada is immune from attachment and execution . . . except where . . . (b) the property is used or is intended for a commercial activity;"); Foreign States Immunities Act, Act 87 of 1981 §14(3) (S. Afr.) ("Subsection (1)(b) shall not prevent the issue of any process in respect of property which is for the time being in use or intended for use for commercial purposes.").

See also *Nat'l Iranian Oil Co. Revenues from Oil Sales,* 65 I.L.R. 215, 242 (F.R.G. Federal Constitutional Court 1983) (rejecting the requirement of a connection between the claim and the property sought to be attached, noting that "[a] principle of international customary law forbidding a State where proceedings have been brought from taking measures of enforcement and safeguarding measures against assets of a foreign State which have no connection with the substantive claim being brought, cannot be established at present."); *Condor & Filvem v. Nat'l Shipping Co. of Nigeria,* 33 I.L.M. 593 (It. Constitutional Court 1992), *sub nom Condor & Filvem v. Minister of Justice,* 101 I.L.R. 394, 402 (It. Constitutional Court 1992) ("a further restriction is not generally recognized . . . that there be a specific link with the subject matter of the request . . . ."); *Abbott v. Republic of S. Afr.,* 113 I.L.R. 413, 426 (Spain Constitutional Court, Second Chamber 1992) ("it is not necessary that the property in respect of which execution is sought should be intended for the self-same activity jure gestionis as that which provoked the dispute. To hold otherwise would be to render illusory the right to enforcement of judgments in cases like the present one, involving the dismissal of an embassy employee.").

159 The French Court of Cassation held that the property in question had to be the subject matter of the claim in order to be attached, noting "immunity can be set aside in exceptional cases such as where the assets attached have been allocated for an economic or commercial activity of a private law nature, which has given rise to the claim at issue." *Islamic Republic of Iran v. Eurodif,* 77 I.L.R. 513, 515-16 (Court of Cassation, First Civil Chamber 1984) (noting that in this case "the debt originated in the very funds which had been allocated for the implementation of the Franco-Iranian programme for the production of nuclear energy, whose repudiation by the Iranian party gives rise to the application."). However, this holding may have been undermined by a more recent case. In 2001, a French Court of Appeal allowed for attachment of property of a foreign State relying on the ground that property was used or intended for use for commercial activity, but the court made no mention of the connection between the property sought to be attached and the underlying claim. *Creighton Ltd. v. Minister of Qatar,* Cour d'appel [CA] [regional court of appeal] Paris, 1st ch. G, Dec. 12, 2001, *reprinted* in Revue de l'Arbitrage 417, 418 (2003).

tions Convention on Jurisdictional Immunities of States and their Property (U.N. Convention) contains a somewhat curious connection requirement.[160] The U.N. Convention excepts from immunity from execution:

> property [that] is specifically in use or intended for use by the State for other than government non-commercial purposes and is in the territory of the State of the forum, provided that post-judgment measures of constraint may only be taken against property that has a connection with the entity against which the proceeding was directed.[161]

Under the U.N. Convention, a judgment creditor normally would not be permitted to execute against the property of one agency or instrumentality of a state to enforce a judgment against another, separate agency or instrumentality for want of a connection of the first entity's property with the second entity. That is consistent with the general rule that the assets of agencies and instrumentalities of a foreign state are immune from execution based on claims against

---

A required connection between the property sought for attachment and the underlying claim also appears in international conventions. *See* European Convention on State Immunity art 26, June 11, 1976, E.T.S. No. 74 ("a judgment rendered against a Contracting State . . . may be enforced in the State of the forum against property of the State against which judgment has been given, used exclusively in connection with such an activity . . . ."); International Law Association: Draft Convention on State Immunity art. 8(A)(2), March 1983, 22 I.L.M. 287 ("The property is in use for the purposes of commercial activity or was in use for the commercial activity upon which the claim is based"); International Law Commission Report on the Draft Articles Adopted at its Forty-Third Session art 18(1)(c), Sept. 11, 1991, 30 I.L.M. 1554 [*hereinafter Draft Articles on Jurisdictional Immunities of States and Their Property*] ("the property is specifically in use or intended for use by the State for other than government non-commercial purposes and is in the territory of the State of the forum and has a connection with the claim").

160 United Nations Convention on the Jurisdictional Immunities of States and Their Property, G.A. Res. 59/38, Annex, U.N. Doc. A/RES/59/38 (Dec. 2, 2004) (adopted without a vote) [hereinafter, U.N. Convention]. Resolutions of the General Assembly are *available at* http://www.un.org/documents/resga.htm. The U.N. Convention has 28 signatories and 13 parties, but 30 parties are required for it to enter into force. *Id.* Art. 30(1); http://treaties.un.org/Pages/ViewDetails.aspx?src=IND&mtdsg_no=III-13&chapter=3&lang=en.
161 U.N. Convention, Art. 19(c).

the state itself, assuming the necessary separateness of the agency or instrumentality exists.[162]

While restricted immunity from execution is the clear trend, many states continue to apply an absolute immunity from execution.[163] On

---

[162] The U.S. Supreme Court recognized this general rule by holding that "government instrumentalities established as juridical entities distinct and independent from their sovereign should normally be treated as such." *First Nat'l City Bank v. Banco Para El Comercio Exterior de Cuba*, 462 U.S. 611, 626-27 (1983). See also *De Letelier v. Republic of Chile*, 748 F.2d 790, 793-94 (2d Cir. 1984) (noting the presumption of separateness of juridical bodies from its State-parent government). But see *Weinstein v. Republic of Iran*, 609 F.3d 43, 51 (2d Cir. 2010) (noting that the Terrorism Risk Insurance Act (TRIA) overrode the presumption of independent status). The relevant provision of TRIA applies in the case of "a judgment against a terrorist party based on a claim based upon an act of terrorism." Terrorism Risk Insurance Act of 2002, § 201(a), Pub. L. No. 107-297, 116 Stat. 2337 (codified at 28 U.S.C. § 1610, Historical and Statutory Notes, Treatment of Terrorist Assets). British courts have also noted that "[t]he distinction between [state-controlled enterprises], and their governing state, may appear artificial: but it is an accepted distinction in the law of English and other states." *I Congreso del Partido*, [1983] 1 A.C. 244, 258 (H.L). Moreover, that court also held that commercial transactions entered into by state-owned organizations could not be attributed to the State, noting that "[t]he status of these organizations is familiar in our courts, and it has never been held that the relevant state is in law answerable for their actions." *Id.* at 271. On the other hand, when a separate entity of the State is found liable, the property of the entity is generally not immune unless the act by the entity is in exercise of sovereign authority. See State Immunity Act, 1978, c. 33, § 14 (U.K.) (English law distinguishes between the State sovereign and its organs and separate entities of the State; these separate entities are not immune and their property is subject to ordinary measures of execution unless the separate entity is performing an act in exercise of sovereign authority); The State Immunity Ordinance, No. VI of 1981, § 15(2) Pak. Code (1981) (Pak.) ("A separate entity is immune from the jurisdiction of the courts of Pakistan if, and only if: (a) the proceedings relate to anything done by it in the exercise of sovereign authority; and (b) the circumstances are such that a State would have been so immune."); State Immunity Act 1979, §16(2) (Cap 313 1979) (Sing.) ("A separate entity is immune from the jurisdiction of the courts in Singapore if, and only if: (a) the proceedings relate to anything done by it in the exercise of sovereign authority; and (b) the circumstances are such that a State would have been so immune."); *Société Sonotrach v. Migeon*, 77 I.L.R. 525, 527 (Fr. Court of Cassation, First Civil Chamber 1985) ("The assets of a foreign State are, in principle, not subject to seizure, subject to exceptions in particular where they have been allocated for an economic or commercial activity. . . . On the other hand, the assets of public entities, whether personalized or not, which are distinct from the foreign State, may be subjected to attachment by all debtors of that entity, of whatever type, where the assets form part of a body of funds which that entity has allocated for a principal activity governed by private law.").

[163] Ernest K. Bankas, The State Immunity Controversy in International Law 321

the other hand, at least one state does not recognize any immunity from execution.[164] Efforts to harmonize the law in this field over the years have been largely unsuccessful.[165] There is a fair amount of case (Springer 2005) ("And it is quite clear China, Brazil, Chile and Syria also follow the absolute sovereign immunity rule."). Other countries require authorization from the foreign State or their own government before any enforcement measures can be taken against a State. *See* Execution Act, art. 18, *translated in* Official Gazette of the Republic of Croatia, No. 88/2005, *available at* http://www.vsrh.hr/CustomPages/Static/HRV/Files/Legislation__Execution-Act.pdf ("Property of a foreign state in the Republic of Croatia may not be subject to execution or security without a prior approval by the Ministry of Justice of the Republic of Croatia, unless the foreign state consents to such execution or security."); Code of Arbitrazh Procedure of the Russian Federation art. 401 *translated* in 4 Russia & the Republics Legal Materials (William E. Butler ed., 2012) ("The filing of a suit in a court of the Russian Federation against a foreign state, involvement of a foreign State to participate in a case as a defendant or third person, imposition of arrest on property belonging to a foreign State and situated on the territory of the Russian Federation, and the adoption with respect to this property of other measures to secure a suit or levy execution against this property by way of enforcement of decisions of a court shall be permitted only with the consent of competent agencies of the respective State unless provided otherwise by an international treaty of the Russian Federation or a federal law."); Areios Pagos [A.P.] (Supreme Court, Plenary) 37/2002 (Greece) (reaffirming that article 923 of the Code of Civil Procedure requires the prior consent of the Minister of Justice to initiate enforcement proceedings against a foreign state); *Mirza Ali Akbar Kashani v. United Arab Republic*, 64 I.L.R. 489, 502 (India Supreme Court 1965) (holding that the effect of Section 86 of the Indian Code of Civil Procedure was "to modify" the doctrine of immunity whereby foreign States could not be sued without the consent of the Central Government).

164 Turkish courts generally deny any immunity from execution for foreign States. *See Société X v. U.S.,* (Court of Cassation 1993) *cited in* August Reinisch, *European Court Practice Concerning State Immunity from Enforcement Measures*, 17 Eur. J. Int'l L. 803, 813 (2006) (holding "that foreign states did not enjoy immunity from execution and that their property in Turkey could be seized because the applicable Turkish legislation exempted only assets of the Turkish state."). *See also Company X v. Embassy of Turkm.* (Tribunal de Grande Instance 2002) *cited in* Susan C. Breau, *Summary of State Practice Regarding State Immunities in the Council of Europe, in* State Practice Regarding State Immunities 240 (Gerhard Hafner et al. eds., 2006) (reaffirming that there is no immunity from execution in Turkish law); *Société v. La République Azerbaïdjan,* (Tribunal d'exécution 2001) *cited in* August Reinisch, *European Court Practice Concerning State Immunity from Enforcement Measures*, 17 Eur. J. Int'l L. 803, 813 (2006) (holding "that movable and immovable property of a foreign state could be seized.").

165 As mentioned, the U.N. Convention is not yet in force. The European Convention on State Immunity is in force, however, with eight states parties. European Convention on State Immunity, May 16, 1972, T.S. No. 74 (Signed in Basle on May 16, 1972, and entered into force June 11, 1976). The Convention has an optional (by a state's declaration) exception from immunity from execution for com-

law that addresses immunity from execution, but it reflects many conflicting holdings on the substance. For example, courts have taken various approaches to bank accounts that are in part used for sovereign, public activities and in part for commercial activities.[166]

---

mercial and industrial property. *Id.* at art. 26.

166 In the landmark *Philippine Embassy Bank Account* case, the plaintiff sought to attach a mixed bank account of a diplomatic mission. 65 I.L.R. 146 (F.R.G. Federal Constitutional Court 1977). Even though some of the account's transactions would have been considered commercial acts, the Court held that the account was immune from attachment because it was used to finance a diplomatic mission and prohibited courts from analyzing the specific uses of the funds. *Id.* at 185-89. The Court noted, however, that "international law does not prohibit asking the sending State to substantiate the fact that a given account is one that is used for the continued performance of the functions of its diplomatic mission." *Id.* at 189.

Similarly, the Italian Court of Cassation upheld prevailing case law that "[i]n the presence of mixed uses [of foreign State embassy bank accounts], the magistrate cannot be obliged to try and identify that portion of assets not used for sovereign purposes. Such intervention would be inadmissible as it would intrude into the exercise of sovereignty. Unless a non-sovereign use emerges clearly from the investigation and the evidence, the concept of immunity must prevail and be maintained." *Banamar-Capizzi v. Embassy of the Popular Democratic Republic of Algeria*, 87 I.L.R. 56, 61 (Italy Court of Cassation 1989). The House of Lords also followed suit by holding that a mixed bank account of an Embassy could not be dissected into commercial and sovereign purposes. *Alcom Ltd. v. Republic of Colom.*, 74 I.L.R. 170, 187 (Eng. House of Lords 1984). The court noted that the account is "one and indivisible; it is not susceptible of anticipatory dissection into the various uses to which moneys drawn upon it might have been put in the future if it had not been subjected to attachment by garnishee proceedings." *Id.* Because the foreign state certified its non-commercial use and the private party could not prove otherwise, the account was therefore immune from enforcement. *Id.* 187-88. The embassy bank account would, however, enjoy no immunity from execution if the account had been set aside "solely" to satisfy liabilities incurred in commercial transactions. *Id.* at 187.

Case law in France suggests that, with the exception of embassy bank accounts, mixed property may be attached. In 1969, the Court of Cassation held that, where a foreign State bank used the same account to settle commercial debts and to pay the expenses of its diplomatic services, the lower court erred in refusing execution on the chance of "risk originating in the impossibility of discriminating between the funds, a part of which only, as the court found, belongs to the State." *Englander v. Statni Banka Ceskoslovenska*, 52 I.L.R. 335, 336 (Fr. Court of Cassation 1969). However, in 1971, the Court created a sort of presumption that where the origin and destination of the funds of a foreign State could not be determined, then they would be immune from execution. *Clerget v. Banque Commerciale pour l'Europe du Nord*, 65 I.L.R. 54, 56 (Fr. Court of Cassation, First Civil Chamber 1971). In 2000, the Paris Court of Appeal held that diplomatic bank accounts could not be attached without an explicit waiver, suggesting that execution in other instances would be permissible against property of a foreign State used for both commercial and sovereign purposes.

If the U.S. conceivably might undertake a default and restructuring process, it would do well also to undertake well in advance some planning for asset protection and judgment proofing. It could maximize protection by utilizing separate, independent agencies and instrumentalities for as much of its commercial activity as is possible. Asset transfers to such entities on the eve of a default might invite courts to disregard their separateness.[167] The U.S. also should not

---

Russian Fed'n v. Noga, 127 I.L.R. 156, 160-61 (Fr. Paris Court of Appeal 2000).
The United States itself has flip-flopped on mixed bank accounts. In 1980, the D.C. District Court held that an analysis of the purposes of an embassy bank account was feasible and that the account was not immune from attachment. *Birch Shipping Corp. v. Embassy of the United Arab Republic of Tanz.*, 507 F.Supp. 311, 313 (D.D.C. 1980). The court also noted that if immunity were to be granted to a mixed account, it "would create a loophole, for any property could be made immune by using it, at one time or another, for some minor public purpose." *Id.* However, in 1987, the court refused to attach a mixed embassy bank account because the account was used for the functioning of a foreign State embassy and execution would undermine the Vienna Convention on Diplomatic Relations. *Liberian Eastern Timber Co. v. Gov't of the Republic of Liberia*, 659 F.Supp. 606, 610-11 (D.D.C. 1987) ("The Court, however, declines to order that if any portion of a bank account is used for a commercial activity then the entire account loses its immunity.").

167 In general, courts have noted multiple situations in which the presumption of separateness for juridical entities could be overcome. For instance, the U.S. Supreme Court held that the presumption of independent, separate juridical status had been overcome on "internationally recognized equitable principles." *First Nat'l City Bank v. Banco Para El Comercio Exterior de Cuba*, 462 U.S. 611, 621 (1983). In an action brought by a foreign state-owned bank against a private party, the court noted that Cuba was the real beneficiary because, without the bank, Cuba would be unable to obtain relief in the U.S. courts without waiving its sovereign immunity and answering for its liabilities from expropriation. *Id.* at 632. The court held that, under both international and national law, "Cuba cannot escape liability for acts in violation of international law simply by retransferring the assets to separate juridical entities" and the court "decline[d] to adhere blindly to the corporate form where doing so would cause such an injustice." *Id.* While not applied in the case, the Court also noted other areas in which the separateness of juridical bodies may be quashed, such as instances in which the relationship is that of principal and agent, or if equitable principles required it to prevent fraud and injustice. *Id.* at 629. *See also De Letelier v. Republic of Chile*, 748 F.2d 790, 794 (2d Cir. 1984) (While ultimately upholding the presumption of independent status, the court noted: "The broader message is that foreign states cannot avoid their obligations by engaging in abuses of corporate form. The *Bancec* Court held that a foreign state instrumentality is answerable just as its sovereign parent would be if the foreign state has abused the corporate form, or where recognizing the instrumentality's separate status works a fraud or an injustice."); *Kalamazoo Spice Extraction Co. v. Provisional Military Gov't of Socialist Eth.*, 616 F.Supp. 660, (W.D. Mich. 1985) (refused to uphold the presumption

take too much comfort from the jurisdictions that adhere to absolute immunity from execution. Facing a U.S. default on obligations owed to a foreign state and its citizens, the state's courts might be induced to embrace the trend toward restricted immunity. The U.S also should consider strategic relocations of assets well in advance of implementing any default and restructuring plan.[168] It also should

of separate juridical existence because the State exerted direct control over an entity in which the State became a majority shareholder through expropriation, and recognized that "the separate legal status of [the entity] under these circumstances would insulate the [State] from liability for its expropriation . . . while permitting the [State], through [the company], to profit from its commercial activities in the United States and to even assert a claim against KAL-SPICE to recover payment for assets of [the company] sold in this country."); *Walter Fuller Aircraft Sales Inc. v. Republic of the Philippines*, 965 F.3d 1375, 1380 (5th Cir. 1992) (enumerating factors to determine when the presumption of independent status should be overcome to allow for execution).

Whether entities should be viewed as separate from, or a part of the State, has also been illustrated in English law. See *Trendtex Trading Corp. v. Cent. Bank of Nig.*, 64 I.L.R. 111, 134 (Court of Appeal 1977) (holding that the Central Bank of Nigeria, separate legal entity with no clear expression of intent that it should have governmental status, was not an emanation, arm, alter ego or department of the State of Nigeria after looking to the functions and control of the organization and the evidence as a whole); *Baccus S.R.L. v. Servico Nacional Del Trigo*, 23 I.L.R. 160, 162-63 (Eng. Court of Appeal 1956) (whether a foreign department of State should lose its immunity because it conducts some of its activities by means of a separate legal entity depends on the nature of the activities and the foreign State's interest).

168 In general, military and diplomatic-related assets, Federal Reserve Bank assets, and other non-commercial assets should be protected by sovereign immunity from execution under most national laws and international law. U.N. Convention, art. 21 (listing property of a military character, for the performance of functions of the diplomatic mission of the State, central bank or other monetary authority of the State as property that should not be considered as property in use or intended for use by the State other than government non-commercial purposes).

The assets of diplomatic missions are generally immune from execution. *See, e.g.,* Vienna Convention on Diplomatic Relations, art. 22(3), April 18, 1961, 500 U.N.T.S. 95 ("The premises of the mission, their furnishings and other property thereon and the means of transport of the mission shall be immune from search requisition, attachment or execution."); Act on the Civil Jurisdiction of Japan with respect to a Foreign State, Act. No. 24 of 2009, art. 18(2)(i) (listing property that is exempted from execution as "Property which is used or intended for use in the performance of the functions of the diplomatic mission . . . ."); United States Foreign Sovereign Immunities Act, 28 U.S.C. § 1610(a)(4)(B) (2012) (stating that foreign State property shall not be immune, "*Provided*, That such property is not used for purposes of maintaining a diplomatic or consular mission or the residence of the Chief of such mission."). In the *Philippine Embassy Bank Account* case, the plaintiff sought to attach a mixed bank account of a diplomatic mission; however

pursue massive securitizations of its receivables on a regular basis, continually converting them into cash that can be more easily sheltered domestically. Debts owing to the Export-Import Bank of the United States, whose activities in supporting U.S. exports by private firms is singularly commercial in character, are a prime example. While these debts are held by an agency or instrumentality that has a separate existence, prudence would dictate securitizations nonetheless.[169]

Finally, it would be prudent for the U.S. to undertake in advance a thorough legal audit of its asset exposure under local laws on im-

the German Constitutional Court held that "[c]laims against a general current bank account of the embassy of a foreign State which exists in the State of the forum and the purpose of which is to cover the embassy's costs and expenses are not subject to forced execution by the State of the forum." 65 I.L.R. 146, 164 (F.R.G. Federal Constitutional Court 1977).
Property of a Central Bank or other monetary authority of a foreign State. See State Immunity Act, R.S.C. 1985, c. S-18, § 12(4) (Can.) ("property of a foreign central bank or monetary authority that is held for its own account and is not used or intended for a commercial activity is immune from attachment and execution."); State Immunity Act, 1978, c. 33, § 14(4) (U.K.) ("Property of a State's central bank or other monetary authority shall not be regarded . . . as in use or intended for use for commercial purposes."); State Immunity Act 1979, § 16(4) (Cap 313 1979) (Sing.) ("Property of a State's central bank or other monetary authority shall not be regarded . . . as in use or intended for use for commercial purposes;"); The Law of the People's Republic of China on Judicial Immunity from Compulsory Measures Concerning the Property of Foreign Central Banks (promulgated by the Standing Comm. Nat'l People's Cong., Oct. 25, 2005), arts. 1 & 2, *translated* in The National People's Congress of the People's Republic of China, http://www.npc.gov.cn/englishnpc/Law/2007-12/13/content_1384123.htm (last visited Feb. 17, 2012) (Article 1 states "The People's Republic of China grants to foreign central banks' property the judicial immunity from the compulsory measures of property preservation and execution . . . ."; however, Article 3 notes that "[w]here a foreign country grants no immunity to the property of the central bank of the People's Republic of China or to the property of the financial administration institutions of the special administrative regions of the People's Republic of China, or the immunity granted covers less items than what are provided for in this Law, the People's Republic of China shall apply the principle of reciprocity."); Foreign States Immunities Act, Act 87 of 1981 § 15(3) (S. Afr.) ("Property of the central bank or other monetary authority of a foreign state shall not be regarded . . . as in use or intended for use for commercial purposes . . . .").
Some assets, such as real property, would be impossible to relocate.
169 Moreover, any of the bank's loans made to Turkish borrowers likely would not be exempt from execution in Turkey. *See* note 164, *supra*.

munity from execution on a state-by-state basis around the world. Notwithstanding broad immunity from execution, experiences with recent efforts to enforce judgments against other sovereigns, such as Argentina and Iran, suggest that the U.S. could expect to battle many attempts to execute on commercial assets found outside the U.S. Moreover, given the likely dollar amounts of defaulted U.S. Treasuries, these battles could be massive in scale when compared to earlier experiences with other sovereign judgment debtors.

V. Conclusion

One goal of this paper has been to evaluate the feasibility of *any* type of restructuring of U.S. sovereign debt that would involve a material haircut (legal or *de facto*) of U.S. obligations. This essay has shown that a selective default and restructuring is feasible from logistical and informational perspectives and problematic but possibly feasible from a legal perspective. But this evaluation is only a first step in a discussion and analysis that should continue.

Further study of the circumstances—if any—under which a U.S. default and restructuring would be beneficial is important. When the national and global impact of such an approach is considered, it may be that default and restructuring is not, on balance, a realistic alternative. If that turns out to be so, it is nonetheless useful to know that and to know why it is so. The concern that sparked this essay derives from the apparent absence of evidence that anyone has explored the question in any depth. That failure, no doubt, was influenced by the failure to recognize that the new possible is the impossible. In the new normal, everything is thinkable.

Finally, there may be a kernel of a lesson in this paper for states other than the U.S. which may need to restructure sovereign debt in the future. The idea of a sovereign debt restructuring in an insolvency proceeding under the domestic laws of the sovereign debtor appears to be a novel concept. While there may be insurmountable constitutional impediments to such a proceeding under U.S. law, that may not be the case under the law of other states. An era of unprecedented judicial and administrative cooperation in the insolvencies of multinational debtors is emerging. This holds promise that future sovereign debt restructurings might be undertaken under the rule of law—that is, new regimes of insolvency designed for sovereign and other governmental debtors. But there is an important caveat to this suggestion. In order to inspire confidence, any such insolvency regime should be seen as fair to all concerned. It should be a real and recognizable insolvency regime with many of the traditional (in the relevant state) elements of such a regime. Ideally, moreover, it would be enacted in better times and not on the eve of a default.

14
A Comment on Professor Mooney's Thought Experiment: Can U.S. Debt Be Restructured?

Donald S. Bernstein[1]

I have been asked to comment on Professor Mooney's audacious "thought experiment" about how the public debt of the United States might be restructured, despite Section 4 of Amendment XIV to the United States Constitution, which states that the "validity of the public debt of the United States, authorized by law...shall not be questioned." Although we all hope the day never comes when the United States has to consider such a possibility, staring into the abyss, at least for a few moments, may help us see how best to avoid it. My perspective is that of a practicing corporate bankruptcy attorney, and, as you will see, I will draw upon analogies to the large corporate debtors I know so well. The analogies will, of course, be imperfect, because the United States is different not only from other sovereigns, but even more so from any debtor company, no matter its size. Still the comparisons are worth considering.

Any method of restructuring the debt of the United States must be speedy because of the chaos that would ensue if the restructuring process were to become drawn out, as most corporate restructurings

---
[1] The author is a partner and head of the insolvency practice at the law firm Davis Polk & Wardwell LLP and chair of the National Bankruptcy Conference.

do. The need for speed means that the restructuring method must bypass obtaining consents from the holders of the debt, even if an effective means of soliciting such consents could be devised. Any consensual restructuring faces the problem of "holdouts," and there is every reason to believe that many of the holders of cash-equivalent instruments like U.S. treasury securities will have little appetite to participate voluntarily in a debt restructuring.

Professor Mooney, seeking to bind the holders of U.S. debt to a speedy non-consensual restructuring that overcomes the constraints of the Fourteenth Amendment, suggests that the "bankruptcy clause" of Article I, Section 8, of the United States Constitution might provide the necessary authority for the federal government to repudiate (or in bankruptcy parlance "discharge") a portion of the principal obligations on its public debts. He acknowledges that this idea has its weaknesses and explores a second, alternative restructuring method: simply defaulting on the debt rather than repudiating it.

At least on its face, the Fourteenth Amendment seems to make a partial or complete debt repudiation by the United States extremely problematic.[2] Professor Mooney posits, however, that the overriding power to modify indebtedness under the bankruptcy clause of the Constitution might extend to *all* debtors, including the United States. As we know from Chapter 9 of the federal Bankruptcy Code, governmental units, like states and municipalities, can go bankrupt – if they consent to doing so. Why shouldn't the same apply to the United States itself?

Invoking the bankruptcy clause, of course, does not end the discussion because doing so merely creates a conflict between two competing constitutional provisions. Professor Mooney resolves this conflict in favor of the bankruptcy clause because the Fourteenth Amendment only bars questioning the *validity* of the public debt of the United States, and it is indisputably true that a debt can be *valid* but nevertheless be rendered *unenforceable* by bankruptcy. In fact, that

---

[2] While, as Professor Mooney points out, the Supreme Court, in *Perry v. United States*, 294 U.S. 330 (1935), allowed the U.S. to refuse to honor the "gold clause," if the U.S. had sought to walk away from the debts themselves the result presumably would have been different.

is what most bankruptcies do. They permit a distressed debtor to free itself from its valid debts to restore the debtor's financial health.[3] On this view, there is nothing inconsistent between the Fourteenth Amendment and the discharge of debts of the United States pursuant to the bankruptcy power conferred on Congress.

As a corporate reorganization lawyer, nothing appeals to me more than the idea that the bankruptcy clause of the Constitution, my stock in trade, trumps all, and, from the point of view of a commercial law expert, Professor Mooney's distinction between validity and enforceability rings true. I was for a number of years the Chair of the TriBar Opinion Committee, which is the leading bar organization setting standards for third-party legal opinions rendered by law firms, and the idea that bankruptcy affects the enforceability of a debt but not its validity is consistent with customary legal opinion practice.

Still, I have misgivings about Professor Mooney's broad reading of the bankruptcy clause of the Constitution. The proposition that, in the face of the Fourteenth Amendment, the United States can pass a law to declare itself bankrupt and then impose a "bankruptcy repudiation" of its own debts feels like "bootstrapping." Though there is scant historical record, it appears that the bankruptcy clause was intended to permit Congress to preempt the hodgepodge of laws the several states applied to their own bankrupt citizens, allowing the marshaling of debtors' assets and resolution of debts across state lines. This undoubtedly accounts for the reference to "uniform laws" in the text of the clause.[4] It is difficult to see how the bankruptcy

---

3 This of course is typically in the interest of the debtor's creditors in a reorganization case under Chapter 11 of the federal Bankruptcy Code because the going concern value of the enterprise is preserved and made available in the form of equity to the holders of discharged claims.

4 That the Fourteenth Amendment was directed at allowing Congress to reconcile the differences among the states' bankruptcy laws is apparent from the brief reference to the bankruptcy clause in *The Federalist Papers*. In Federalist No. 42, Madison states that:

> "The power of establishing uniform laws of bankruptcy is so intimately connected with the regulation of commerce, and will prevent so many frauds where the parties or their properties may lie or be removed into different States, that the expediency of it seems not likely to be drawn into question."

The Federalist No. 42 (James Madison) (the powers conferred by the Constitution further considered).

clause could have been intended to apply to the United States itself when, before the Fourteenth Amendment, there was no real need to have a bankruptcy power to adjust the debts of the federal government. Even if our farsighted founding fathers were conscious of the possibility that the United States might someday issue mounds of its own debt, they almost certainly would have taken the view that, as a sovereign, the United States had all the power it needed to walk away from its debts. Considered in this light, it seems, at least to this bankruptcy lawyer, implausible that the bankruptcy clause of Article I of the Constitution could be construed to trump the subsequently passed Fourteenth Amendment.

That leaves Professor Mooney's other non-consensual restructuring method: simply defaulting. Does the Fourteenth Amendment prohibit the United States from barring debtholders' collection remedies if the United States defaults on its debts or otherwise defers paying them? The argument that a mere default would not call into question the validity of the debt of the United States sounds plausible. A debt default is not, on its face, an outright repudiation of the debt, and would seem not to question the debt's validity. Certainly, a default by a corporate debtor does not call into question the validity of the company's debt. The sovereign stands ready to hold the debtor accountable by enforcing the debt. The fact that the debt is enforced by the sovereign through its courts is the very characteristic that demonstrates the debt's validity. The distinction between validity and enforceability breaks down, however, when it comes to debts of the sovereign itself. Obligations of the sovereign can be enforced only at the sovereign's own sufferance, so the validity of the debt and the debt's enforceability merge to become a single concept. Where an issuer can fail to pay its debts with impunity, can it really be said that the debts are "valid" in the first place? If Congress were to withdraw the waiver of sovereign immunity with respect to U.S. public debt, thereby leaving creditors without any remedy if the U.S. defaulted, wouldn't that action call into question the debt's validity?

In sum, it is hard for me to accept that the bankruptcy clause of the Constitution can do the work that Professor Mooney would like it to do or that the United States can, consistent with the Fourteenth

Amendment, simply default on its debts without making a default remedy available to its creditors.

Even though, however, we are unlikely to find a bankruptcy silver bullet to help restructure the debts of the United States, experience from corporate bankruptcies and reorganizations can teach us much. Bankruptcy accomplishes two fundamental things for a distressed company. First, it helps the company restore its profitability by giving it breathing space and helping it eliminate costs (through, among other things, discontinuing unprofitable operations, rejecting executory contracts and leases, and eliminating interest expense). Second, through the discharge of claims, it permits the company to right-size its debt load so it fits the company's income generating capacity. The costs and debts eliminated in a typical bankruptcy reorganization include not only those arising out of debt for borrowed money but also day-to-day operating payables and long term payment commitments. From a financial point of view, operating payables and long term commitments are just other forms of debt, and if they are above the level that can be sustained by the company over time, they have to be reduced for the company to survive.

To successfully restructure, the cost of the company's financial survival must be spread among the company's stakeholders, including shareholders, lenders, suppliers, current employees and retirees. Our bankruptcy laws and the parties' relative non-bankruptcy entitlements set the parameters for the allocation of costs among the relevant parties.

Financially strapped sovereigns, like business enterprises, must spread the cost of their restructuring among their relevant stakeholders to achieve sustainability. The stakeholders are, of course, somewhat different from those in a private enterprise. In addition to the holders of the sovereign's debt, the stakeholders include the users of government services (the public), the beneficiaries of government support (such as social security and medicare recipients) and taxpayers. Increasing taxes, reducing services, and reducing debt and long term commitments are the devices available to the sovereign to achieve sustainability. However, in the case of sovereigns, there is no bankruptcy law to mediate how the costs are allocated. The allocation is purely a political question.

Corporate debtors often lack the discipline to make the choices they have to make to successfully restructure. We all remember how, prior to the bankruptcies of General Motors and Chrysler, the federal Automotive Task Force required those companies to rewrite their restructuring plans because their initial efforts failed to grapple effectively with the issues they were facing. The experience of the auto companies reminds me of the story of the senior officer of another large public company that went bankrupt many years ago who was asked why the company did not see the firm's financial problems coming. He responded by saying "the mind when faced with brutal reality retreats into fantasy." This very human reaction is common: management of the typical debtor is not equipped to deal with adversity. Their minds "retreat into fantasy" rather than face and address the hard choices. One of the functions of our corporate reorganization laws is to require a debtor to make hard choices by superimposing creditors committees, the court or, if necessary, a trustee on the company's decision making process, threatening liquidation of the business, and limiting the privilege of confirming a plan of reorganization to entities that meet a test of sustainability -- Chapter 11's so-called "feasibility" requirement.[5]

Because sovereigns typically are outside the bankruptcy system, the discipline to make hard choices has to be imposed in other ways. Commonly, another sovereign or group of sovereigns (or a proxy, like the IMF) will offer financial support on the condition that the distressed sovereign meet certain goals in terms of debt reduction and fiscal austerity. Such conditional assistance provides the debtor country's government officials with the "political cover" they need to take necessary, but unpopular, actions. There is, however, no "other sovereign" who can offer conditional assistance to a reserve currency country with the largest economy in the world, so it is difficult to see where our own government officials can find political cover from the

---

[5] To meet the "feasibility" requirement, the debtor must show there will not be a need for liquidation or further financial reorganization of the debtor. *See* 11 U.S.C. 1129(a)(11).

fallout of allocating the burden of a restructuring of the finances of the United States. There is, as a result, every political incentive not to make the hard choices, but instead to kick the can down the road. The hard choices are, however, unavoidable, and they eventually will have to be made.

Many years ago, I represented a storied Milwaukee-based industrial company -- Allis-Chalmers Corporation. Allis-Chalmers had two principal businesses: they made extremely durable (in fact all too durable) farm equipment and enormous hydro-turbines, like those used by the Tennessee Valley Authority and in the "Big Allis" power generation facility that to this day supplies much of New York City's electric power. During the 1980s, the company was forced to sell its farm equipment business, and, after the sale closed, the chief financial officer made a presentation to the company's lenders showing the company's income statement after the divestiture. A cost item that had seemed small when the company was larger loomed large on the pro forma income statement. It was the cost of healthcare and pension payments to retired employees. As the company was getting smaller, these legacy costs were continuing to grow, and the payments still had to be made. As the CFO looked up at the figures, he said to the audience, "As the water in the river has gone down, the rocks have begun to show." Ultimately, the company's growing payment obligations were not sustainable, and Allis-Chalmers had to be liquidated. The company's creditors and retirees received only a tiny fraction of what they were owed -- far less than they would have received had the hard choices been made sooner, permitting the company to survive.

The lesson for the United States is at once blindingly obvious and one that none of us wants to hear. Either revenue (taxes) must continue to grow or the cost of government services and benefits, and other national financial commitments, must be reduced. While it is nice to talk about restructuring treasury obligations, in the long run, fiscal sustainability will depend on our willingness to make even harder choices about our nation's other financial commitments and how to share the pain of restructuring them. Finding clever ways to address the nation's existing public debt simply will not solve the problem.

Perhaps in this light it may not be such a bad thing that the public debt of the United States is difficult to repudiate. Rather than kicking the can down the road, we will have to grapple with and solve the real, far larger, issues; and, as with most restructurings, putting off the day of reckoning will only make the inevitable choices more painful and difficult. We can only "retreat into fantasy" for so long if we want to avoid the abyss.

15
Direct and Indirect U.S. Government Debt

Steven L. Schwarcz[1]

My presentation focuses on two issues. First, I comment on the draft paper by Professor Charles W. Mooney, Jr., "United States Sovereign Debt: A Thought Experiment on Default and Restructuring," which explores the restructuring of U.S. Treasury Securities ("Treasuries")—the classic form of direct U.S. government debt. Second, I discuss an important type of indirect U.S. government debt—financing raised by the federal government through special-purpose entities (SPEs)—and the possible consequences of such indirect financing.

I. Comments On Professor Mooney's Paper

A. *Specific Comments.*

Let me begin with specific comments, most critically what terms of the debt should be restructured. Prof. Mooney's paper only mentions restructuring the principal amount of Treasuries, ignoring their interest rate and maturities. Extending debt maturities, however, could help the government avoid default by readjusting debt repayment

---

[1] Stanley A. Star Professor of Law & Business, Duke University School of Law, and Founding Director, Duke Global Capital Markets Center; schwarcz@law.duke.edu. These comments are copyright © 2012 by Steven L. Schwarcz. I thank Feroz Ali Khader for valuable research assistance.

to revenues. At the same time, it arguably would be more constitutionally permitted than reducing the principal amount,[2] especially if the extended maturities accrue interest at a market rate so that, economically, there would be no "actual loss."[3] Extending debt maturities would also be less politically and commercially disruptive than reducing the principal amount, because the debt would eventually be honored.

Prof. Mooney may wish to compare the ability of large Treasuries holders to quickly exit the market with the increasing corporate debt-restructuring problem caused by distressed-debt trading. Not only are large investors able to quickly divest their claims, at a discounted price. More significantly, buyers of those claims often include opportunistic investors, such as hedge funds, who increasingly have been trying to "game" the system for short-term advantage. This has been undermining some of the long-term debtor restructuring goals of the federal Bankruptcy Code.[4]

Regarding post-default enforcement of Treasuries, Prof. Mooney's paper observes that the offering circular for Treasuries provides, with respect to the commercial book-entry system, that the federal government does not "have any obligation to any person or entity that does not have an account with a Federal Reserve Bank." But query whether that restriction might itself be unconstitutional because it "questions" enforceability of the debt. Moreover, if that restriction were held to be unconstitutional, at least two additional questions would arise: Would investors be deemed to, and could they even, waive the unconstitutionality?

I am not convinced, as is Prof. Mooney, that default should be equated with invalidity. Section Four of the Fourteenth Amendment provides that the "validity of the public debt of the United States . . . shall not be questioned."[5] Prof. Mooney observes that the plurality

---

2 *Cf. infra* note 5 and accompanying text.
3 *Perry v. United States*, 294 U.S. 330, 358 (1935).
4 *See* Harvey Miller, *Keynote Address: Bankruptcy And Reorganization, Through The Looking Glass Of 50 Years (1960 – 2010)*, presented March 12, 2012, at the annual Induction of Fellows of the American College of Bankruptcy, United States Supreme Court, at 12-13 (expressing concern over distressed-debt trading).
5 U.S. CONST. amend. XIV, §4.

in Perry held that Congress lacks the authority to "alter or destroy" the federal government's obligations to repay borrowed funds. But to question the "validity" of public debt appears more closely tied to questioning the premise of the debt. One could distinguish that from changing when the debt is payable or paid, for example. When a debtor refuses to pay, it acknowledges the debt but does not pay. In contract law, a parallel to this would be the distinction between the legality of a contract and breach of a contract.

Finally, Prof. Mooney raises the possibility of the federal government selectively defaulting on debt held by some but not all foreign nations. Query whether that might constitute unfair discrimination by the federal government in violation of the Most-Favored-Nation clause of the WTO agreement, resulting in trade sanctions under the WTO dispute settlement regime?[6]

Next, I consider more general questions raised, or at least inspired, by Prof. Mooney's paper.

B. More General Comments.

A critical question is the extent to which the federal government might be able to achieve a consensual restructuring of its Treasuries. The biggest obstacle to a debtor attempting to consensually restructure its debt is the holdout problem: that one or more creditors may strategically hold out from agreeing to a reasonable debt-restructuring plan, hoping they either will receive full payment of their claims or that the imperative of other creditors to settle will persuade those creditors to allocate to the holdouts more than their fair share of the settlement.[7]

In order to help solve the holdout problem, sovereign nations often insert so-called collective action clauses (CACs) into their debt instruments. These clauses permit a super-majority vote by holders of

---

[6] It also should be noted that some recent bilateral Free Trade Agreements negotiated by the U.S. government have included Most-Favored-Nation (MFN) treatment clauses with regard to sovereign debt issued by the parties.
[7] Steven L. Schwarcz, *A Minimalist Approach to State "Bankruptcy,"* 59 UCLA L. REV. 322, 328 (2011).

those instruments to change the key terms of the instruments.[8] I have found no evidence, however, that Treasuries contain collective action clauses.[9] The federal government might wish to consider the pros and cons of including these types of clauses in future issuances of Treasuries—a potential negative being that even acknowledging the possibility of the need to restructure its debt (by including CACs) might increase financing cost and panic the Treasuries market.

Absent collective action clauses, the federal government can still solve the holdout problem at a later date, if and when needed. In a state-debt context, I have argued that a "minimalist" approach to government debt restructuring could be used to help solve this problem (possibly without significantly increasing the cost of debt) by legislatively imposing supermajority voting by classes of claims.[10] Logically, the federal government could legislate a similar solution to the holdout problem.

The federal government should be able, constitutionally, to enact such legislation. The Constitution's Contracts Clause applies only to state, not federal, action. And, as explained below, I do not believe such legislation—even if retroactively applied to Treasuries or other forms of federal government debt—would constitute a "taking" under the Fifth Amendment.

Certainly Congress has power under the Bankruptcy Clause of the Constitution to retroactively impair contractual obligations.[11] I would not rely on that power, however, because it is questionable (as Professor Mooney acknowledges) whether the Bankruptcy Clause

---

8 Steven L. Schwarcz, *Sovereign Debt Restructuring Options: An Analytical Comparison*, HARV. BUS. L. REV. 301 (Fall 2011 issue), also available at http://ssrn.com/abstract=1872552.

9 Although one conference participant had vaguely recollected that federal law under which Treasuries are issued might reserve the federal government's right to amend the terms of outstanding Treasuries, neither that participant nor I could find the source of that right. *Cf.* 31 C.F.R. §356.33(c) (enabling the federal government to change the terms, pre-issuance, of new issues of Treasuries). Newly issued Treasuries could include provisions that enable the federal government to amend their terms, but that likely would greatly increase government financing costs.

10 *See A Minimalist Approach to State "Bankruptcy," supra* note 7.

11 Hanover Nat'l Bank v. Moyses, 186 U.S. 181, 188 (1902).

would apply to federal government debt. But even without that power, the legislation's retroactive application should not violate the Fifth Amendment because retroactive federal legislation is constitutional (and not a "taking") so long as it does not completely destroy property rights in a way that the affected parties could not have anticipated.[12] The consensual relinquishment of rights under supermajority voting should not constitute complete destruction of creditor rights. The only right that is completely destroyed is an individual creditor's right to be a holdout; that right, however, is arguably an unreasonable private expectation that should not be protected.[13]

My other general comment responds to questions raised in the conference of how the federal government might accelerate revenues in order to pay maturing Treasuries. One such approach might be securitization, in which the government securities—or monetizes—future revenues. In a famous example, David Bowie securitized the revenues coming due under his future song royalties. The federal government might similarly consider securitizing future tax revenues, for example.[14] To the extent a federal-revenue securitization is structured under specific enabling legislation, the legislative certainty would reduce financing costs compared to corporate securitizations, which rely on an imperfect patchwork of case-law, statutes, scholarly articles, and soft law.[15]

Next consider an important type of *indirect* U.S. government debt—financing raised by the federal government through special-purpose entities.

---

12 *See* E. Enters. v. Apfel, 524 U.S. 498, 528–29 (1998) ("[L]egislation might be unconstitutional if it imposes severe retroactive liability on a limited class of parties that could not have anticipated the liability . . . ."); United States v. Riverside Bay Homes, 474 U.S. 121, 128 n.5 (1985); Speckmann v. Paddock Chrysler Plymouth, Inc., 565 F. Supp. 469 (E.D. Mo. 1983).
13 *See* Jan G. Laitos, *Legislative Retroactivity*, 52 WASH. U. J. URB. & CONTEMP. L. 81, 100 (1997).
14 By way of analogy, my experience is that some municipalities, over the past decade, have been securitizing their tax revenues.
15 *See generally* STEVEN L. SCHWARCZ, STRUCTURED FINANCE, A GUIDE TO THE PRINCIPLES OF ASSET SECURITIZATION (3d ed. 2002 & supplements).

II. Federal Government Financing Through SPEs

A. *Introduction.*

Restructuring Treasuries would be only part of the U.S. government debt-restructuring picture. I have been examining the growth of federal government financing through the use of special-purpose entities ("national SPEs").[16] It is possible this growth not only will continue but accelerate. By way of analogy, most U.S. state debt is no longer in the form of general obligation bonds but debt issued by state-sponsored SPEs.[17]

Consider the following examples of national SPEs.

B. *Taxonomy.*

1. Government Sponsored Enterprises (GSEs).

The most prominent national SPEs are the so-called government sponsored enterprises, such as Fannie Mae and Freddie Mac (used for promoting home ownership).

2. SPEs Used in the 2008 Financial Crisis.

In order to stabilize and bring liquidity back to the commercial paper markets during the 2008 financial crisis, the U.S. Federal Reserve created, among other facilities, the Commercial Paper Funding Facility ("CPFF") to operate as a lender of last resort for those markets. Because the Fed traditionally used its lender-of-last-resort powers

---

16 Steven L. Schwarcz, "Special-Purpose Entities in National Finance" (draft on file with author).

17 *Cf.* Steven L. Schwarcz, *The Use and Abuse of Special-Purpose Entities in Public Finance*, 97 MINN. L. REV. (forthcoming 2012, issue no. 2) (discussing SPEs used for state-government financing); Cheryl D. Block, *Congress and the Accounting Scandals: Is the Pot Calling the Kettle Black?*, 82 NEB. L. REV. 365, 435-42 (2003) (identifying the problem of national SPEs). Also compare Jonathan Rosenbloom, *Can a Private Corporate Analysis of Public Authority Administration Lead to Democracy*, 50 N.Y.L. SCH. L. REV. 851 (2005-2006) (raising normative questions about state SPEs).

under Section 13(3) of the Federal Reserve Act to only make loans to banks, it structured the CPFF as a series of Fed loans to State Street Bank and Trust Company, which then made back-to-back loans to a newly-created special-purpose entity, CPFF LLC. CPFF LLC used the back-to-back loan proceeds to purchase commercial paper from corporations and other commercial paper issuers.[18]

Similarly, the Money Market Investor Funding Facility (MMIFF) was designed to provide liquidity to U.S. money market investors during the financial crisis. Under the MMIFF, the Federal Reserve Bank of New York could provide senior secured funding to a series of special-purpose entities to facilitate an industry-supported private-sector initiative to finance the purchase of eligible assets from eligible investors.[19]

3. Other National SPEs.

I also have been examining the Tennessee Valley Authority (TVA) and other "authorities" and "public benefit corporations," as well as SPEs used to finance military aircraft, including through leasing.

C. Identifying Possible National-SPE Abuses.

National-SPE financing can strike at the very heart of our system of representative government, placing into question the fiscal integrity of public governance. I have been analyzing, both descriptively and normatively, their monitoring, governance, and accountability and the transparency of their debt liabilities.[20] Although the use of national SPEs is not inherently wrongful, SPEs have at least as great, if not greater, potential to be abused in public finance than in corporate finance. Several factors contribute to this.

---

18 Tobias Adrian, Karin Kimbrough, & Dina Marchioni, *The Federal Reserve's Commercial Paper Funding Facility,* FRBNY ECON. POLICY REV. 423 (June 2010). See also FRB: OTHER LENDING FACILITIES - CREDIT AND LIQUIDITY PROGRAMS AND THE BALANCE SHEET, http://www.federalreserve.gov/monetarypolicy/bst_lendingother.htm (last visited Apr 24, 2012).
19 FRB: MONEY MARKET INVESTOR FUNDING FACILITY, http://www.federalreserve.gov/monetarypolicy/mmiff.htm (last visited Apr 24, 2012).
20 I have not considered, however, national-SPE debt restructuring questions per se.

Reduced transparency of national SPEs, like corporate SPEs, can undermine financial integrity. Because national-SPE debt is not technically a legal obligation of the federal government, the government does not have to disclose that debt in its financial statements and budget. This lack of disclosure can be misleading; the federal government may have compelling economic and reputational motivations to stand behind that debt, especially if the national SPEs engage in providing critical government services—as occurred when the federal government recently backstopped Fannie Mae and Freddie Mac's obligations—or if the federal government's failure to backstop the debt might cause a downgrading of ratings on federal government debt. Because of these motivations, the federal government effectively is making undisclosed de facto guarantees.

Off-balance-sheet financing can also trigger systemic consequences.[21] Its use by corporate SPEs is seen, for example, as a contributing cause of the 2008 financial crisis.[22] The lack of transparency can also have other serious consequences, such as preventing debt from being priced correctly based on national fiscal risk. Moreover, unlike corporate SPEs, reduced transparency of national SPEs can undermine constitutional and democratic legitimacy.

---

21 *Cf.* Iman Anabtawi & Steven L. Schwarcz, *Regulating Systemic Risk: Towards an Analytical Framework*, 86 NOTRE DAME L. REV. 1349, 1359 (2011) (observing that Enron's use of SPEs could have triggered a systemic financial crisis if Enron's viability had more closely correlated with the viability of other financial institutions).
22 *See, e.g.,* Joint Economic Committee, U.S. Congress, *The U.S. Housing Bubble and the Global Financial Crisis: Vulnerabilities of the Alternative Financial System (2008)*, available at http://jec.senate.gov/republicans/public/?a=Files.Serve&File_id=b54b89ff-649e-4e45-93f0-395d1f507762; *What Went Wrong*, ECONOMIST, Mar. 22, 2008, at 79, *available at* http://www.economist.com/node/10881318; Niall Ferguson, *Wall Street Lays Another Egg*, Vanity Fair, Dec. 2008, at 190; Mark Jickling, *CRS Report for Congress: Averting Financial Crisis* (2008), available at http://fpc.state.gov/documents/organization/103688.pdf; Martin Neil Baily et al., *The Origins of the Financial Crisis* (2008), available at http://www.brookings.edu/~/media/research/files/papers/2008/11/origin%20crisis%20baily%20litan/11_origins_crisis_baily_litan

D. Assessing the Propensity for Abuse.

The federal government may have a greater inherent propensity than corporations to want to use SPEs to raise off-balance-sheet and off-budget debt: unlike corporations, the federal government cannot "fail" in the sense of being forced to liquidate, so it lacks that deterrent against non-transparent use of SPEs.

National SPEs are also more likely to be misused than corporate SPEs because, as I explain in my forthcoming publication, public finance is more susceptible than corporate finance to monitoring failures.[23]

E. Restraining National-SPE Abuses.

How should national-SPE abuses be restrained and, whatever the restraints, how should they be implemented? Regarding the first question, regulatory efforts to reform state and corporate SPEs suggest four overarching organizing principles: improving transparency of the SPE debt; improving monitoring of the SPEs; limiting the SPE debt; and improving SPE governance.[24] I elsewhere explain how these principles could, and arguably should, be applied to national SPEs.[25]

Regarding the second question (How should restraints be implemented?), the clearest approach would be for the federal government to enact an oversight law for its own SPEs. But why would the federal government do that if the result is, effectively, to more clearly publicize its financial problems?

---

23 See "Special-Purpose Entities in National Finance," *supra* note 16. In that article, I explain that the federal government is monitored by citizens and creditors whereas corporations are monitored by shareholders and creditors. Creditors monitor only to the limited extent of their negotiated covenants but, unlike corporate debt, there are no covenants in federal debt. Therefore creditor monitoring of national-SPE debt is likely to be de minimis compared to creditor monitoring of corporate SPE debt. The federal government is also monitored by citizens, who have even less incentive to monitor than most creditors because, unlike creditors, few if any citizens are likely to have sufficient amounts at stake to justify the cost of monitoring. In contrast, corporations are also monitored by shareholders, who can have concentrated holdings.

24 *The Use and Abuse of Special-Purpose Entities in Public Finance*, *supra* note 17.

25 "Special-Purpose Entities in National Finance," *supra* note 16.

One answer is that the federal government would be doing the "right thing."[26] Another answer, perhaps more pragmatic, is that as the problem of national-SPE debt becomes more publicly known, the federal government will face reputation costs. Improving national-SPE accountability might then help the federal government save money.[27]

---

[26] Query whether the federal government, at least under the current Congress, really wants to do the right thing. One wag observed at the conference that politicians might know what is right but they don't seem to know how acting right can get them re-elected.

[27] Cf. *The Use and Abuse of Special-Purpose Entities in Public Finance, supra* note 17 (observing a savings resulting from improving state-SPE accountability).

Appendix
The 2011 Debt Limit Impasse: Treasury's Actions & The Counterfactual – What Might Have Happened if the National Debt Hit the Statutory Limit

Jeremy Kreisberg & Kelley O'Mara
(Under the Supervision of Professor Howell Jackson)

Introduction 258
I: 2011 Debt Limit Impasse 258
  A. Political Backdrop to the 2011 Debt Limit Impasse 258
  B. Treasury Undertook Extraordinary Measures to Reduce the Debt Subject to the Limit 260
    1. Issuance of State and Local Government Series Treasury Securities Suspended 261
    2. Debt Issuance Suspension Period Declared 261
      a. G-Fund: Reinvestments Suspended 262
      b. Civil Fund: Reinvestments Suspended and Existing Securities Redeemed 263
    3. Reinvestment in the Exchange Stabilization Fund Suspended 265
    4. Federal Financing Bank Swaps Not Utilized 266
    5. Selling Assets to Raise Revenue Not Seriously Considered 267
  C. Resolution: The Budget Control Act of 2011 268

II. The Counterfactual: What Would Have Happened if the United States Hit the Debt Limit in August 2011? 272

    A. Legal Background 272

        1. The Fourteenth Amendment 272

        2. The Duty to Fulfill Statutory Spending Obligations 274

    B. Legal Theories for Executive Action if the National Debt Hits the Statutory Limit 276

Theory 1: The President Is Bound by the Debt Limit, and Treasury Must Follow "First In, First Out" Procedures 277

    A. The President Is Bound by the Debt Limit 277

    B. The President Cannot Prioritize Spending Obligations; Therefore, Treasury Must Follow "First In, First Out" Procedures 281

    C. 2011 Impasse: Treasury Appears to Favor FIFO Approach 284

Theory 2: The President Is Bound by the Debt Limit, but Treasury Can Prioritize Spending Obligations 287

    A. The President Can Prioritize at His Discretion 287

    B. The President Must Prioritize Bondholder Payments 291

    C. The President Must Prioritize Bond Payments and Other "Obligations" 295

    D. Social Security and Medicare Trust Fund Redemptions Could Enable Payments After Reaching the Statutory Debt Limit 297

Theory 3: The President Can Ignore the Debt Limit 300

    A. The Debt Limit Is Unconstitutional 300

    B. The President's Emergency Powers Justify Further Borrowing 302

    C. The President Must Obey Statutory Spending Commitments Rather Than the Debt Limit 303

    D. 2011 Impasse: Debt Limit Would Not Likely Have Been Repudiated 304

Theory 4: The President Is Bound by the Debt Limit and Statutory Spending Obligations 306

    A. Congressional Silence Implies a Pro Rata Approach 306

    B. Treasury Should Look to Statutes for Guidance 308

        1. Legislative Prioritization 308

        2. Government Shutdown 309

Conclusion 310
Appendix A: Timeline of Actions During the 2011 Debt Limit
 Impasse 313
Appendix B: Relevant August 2-31, 2011 Financials 314
Appendix C: History of the Public Debt Clause 315
Appendix D: Perry v. United States 316

Introduction

During the summer of 2011, as the nation's outstanding debt approached the statutory limit, political leaders in Washington came to an impasse during negotiations to extend the country's borrowing authority. The statutory debt limit,[1] first established in 1917, acts as a ceiling to the amount of debt the U.S. Treasury can borrow in order to finance deficit expenditures.[2] When appropriated expenses are greater than incoming revenues, failures to raise the limit could cause the United States to default on its obligations. The debt limit has been raised by Congress 78 times since 1960,[3] typically without controversy. In the last two decades, however, it has increasingly been used as a bargaining chip in broader negotiations between the political parties. In 2011, as tensions about the nation's increasing debt and annual deficits came to the fore of political discussion, the debt limit was once again invoked as a forcing mechanism in broader policy negotiations.

Part I of this paper will explore the Department of Treasury's efforts to extend the nation's borrowing authority during the 2011 impasse in order to provide political leaders more time for negotiations and to prevent the country from reaching the statutory limit. Part II will discuss what the Executive Branch might have done if the limit had been reached, including both the legal justifications and practical implications of the unprecedented choices.

I: 2011 Debt Limit Impasse

A. Political Backdrop to the 2011 Debt Limit Impasse

On May 16, 2011, the national debt reached the statutory limit of $14.294 trillion,[4] amounting to more than 250% of the same

---

[1] 31 U.S.C. § 3101(b).
[2] *See generally* D. Andrew Austin & Mindy R. Levit, *The Debt Limit: History and Recent Increases*, CONG. RESEARCH SERV. (Feb. 2, 2012), *available at* http://www.hsdl.org/?view&did=707321.
[3] Dep't of Treasury, *Debt Limit: Myth v. Fact* (available at http://www.treasury.gov/initiatives/Documents/Debt%20Limit%20Myth%20v%20Fact%20FINAL.pdf).
[4] Austin & Levit, *supra* note 2, at 1. Feb. 12, 2010 legislation (Pub. L. No. 111-139) increased the statutory debt limit to $14.29 trillion.

figure only ten years prior.[5] The nation's debt increased rapidly over the course of the decade due to substantial cuts in tax revenue,[6] the costs of fighting two wars,[7] economic stimulus packages,[8] and the rising cost of entitlements.[9] When the Republican Party, with the help of the Tea Party movement, recaptured a majority in the House of Representatives in the midterm elections of 2010, deficit and debt reduction became a focal point of their agenda.[10] Additionally, early in 2011, several bipartisan commissions studied the problem of structural deficits and the increasing national debt.[11] Against this backdrop, Treasury Secretary Timothy Geithner notified Congress on January 6, 2011, that the outstanding debt subject to the limit stood at $13.95 trillion, leaving only $335 billion of borrowing authority.[12] Secretary Geithner urged Congress to raise the limit by the first quarter of 2011, warning it could be reached as early as March 31 or as late as May 16.[13] Before agreeing to an extension of the debt

---

[5] Treasury Direct, *Monthly Statement of the Public Debt of the United States*, DEP'T OF TREASURY, May 31, 2001 (available at ftp://ftp.publicdebt.treas.gov/opd/opds052001.pdf). Debt subject to the limit equaled $5.573 trillion in May 2001.

[6] *See* Cong. Budget Office (CBO), *CBO's 2011 Long Term Budget Outlook* 65 (June 21, 2011) (available at http://www.cbo.gov/sites/default/files/cbofiles/attachments/06-21-Long-Term_Budget_Outlook.pdf). Expiration of 2001 tax cuts estimated to generate additional tax revenue amounting to 2.9% of GDP.

[7] *See Id.* at 58. Defense spending increased from 3% of GDP in 2000 to 4.7% of GDP in 2009-2010 "mainly as a result of operations in Iraq and Afghanistan and related activities."

[8] *See* Letter from Cong. Budget Office to Nancy Pelosi regarding the American Recovery and Reinvestment Act of 2009, (Feb. 13, 2009) (available at http://www.cbo.gov/sites/default/files/cbofiles/ftpdocs/99xx/doc9989/hr1conference.pdf). American Recovery and Reinvestment Act of 2009 was scored by CBO at $787 billion cumulative impact on federal deficits.

[9] *See* CBO, *supra* note 6, at 7-10. CBO estimates that "growth in noninterest spending as a share of gross domestic product (GDP) is attributable entirely to increases in spending on several large mandatory programs: Social Security, Medicare, Medicaid, and (to a lesser extent) insurance subsidies that will be provided through the health insurance exchanges established by the March 2010 health care legislation."

[10] *See* Jennifer Steinhauer, *Debt Bill Is Signed, Ending a Fractious Battle*, N.Y. TIMES, Aug. 2, 2011, http://www.nytimes.com/2011/08/03/us/politics/03fiscal.html.

[11] For example, President Obama established a commission on deficit reduction led by former Senator Alan Simpson and former White House Chief of Staff Erskine Bowles. The Bipartisan Policy Center established a deficit reduction task force led by former Senator Pete Domenici and former Director of OMB Alice Rivlin. *See* Bipartisan Policy Center, *Side-by-Side Comparison: Simpson-Bowles Commission, BPC Domenici-Rivlin Task Force, President Obama, and Chairman Ryan*, Apr. 22, 2011, http://www.bipartisanpolicy.org/library/staff-paper/side-side-comparison-simpson-bowles-commission-bpc-domenici-rivlin-task-force-pr.

[12] Letter from Timothy Geithner, Secretary of the Treasury, to Harry Reid, Majority Leader, US Senate (January 6, 2011) (available at http://www.treasury.gov/initiatives/Pages/debtlimit.aspx).

[13] *Id.*

limit, House Republicans insisted on matching spending cuts to correspond with any debt limit increase and advanced a Balanced Budget Amendment.[14] President Obama and congressional Democrats pushed to include revenue increases in a deficit reduction measure and sought to protect entitlements.[15] Despite extensive negotiations between President Obama and leaders of the House Republicans, an extension of the debt limit remained in doubt[16] until its ultimate resolution on August 2, 2011.[17]

B. Treasury Undertook Extraordinary Measures to Reduce the Debt Subject to the Limit

In anticipation of reaching the statutory debt limit, Treasury Secretary Geithner undertook a variety of financial maneuvers to extend the nation's borrowing authority. On February 3, 2011, Treasury began to draw down its $200 billion Supplementary Financing Account at the Federal Reserve,[18] freeing up funds to pay for appropriated expenses without new borrowing against the debt limit.[19] This maneuver provided a reprieve before the debt limit of $14.294 trillion was reached on May 16, 2011.[20] Approaching and reaching the debt limit prompted Treasury Secretary Geithner to take several "extraordinary measures," including the suspension of new debt issuances, the suspension of the investment of select government trust funds, and the redemption of securities invested in one government trust fund. These maneuvers provided Congress

---

[14] *See* WASH. POST, *How the Parties Fared in the Debt-Ceiling Deal*, Aug. 1, 2011, http://www.washingtonpost.com/wp-srv/special/politics/debt-ceiling/debt-ceiling-deal/.
[15] *Id.*
[16] *See* Andrew Taylor, *Passing Major Debt Deal by Aug. 2 Seems Doubtful*, ASSOCIATED PRESS, July 2, 2011, http://www.azcentral.com/arizonarepublic/news/articles/20110702debt0702.html.
[17] Austin & Levit, *supra* note 2, at 2
[18] Press Release, Dep't of Treasury, *Treasury Issues Debt Management Guidance on the Supplementary Financing Program* (Jan. 27, 2011) (available at http://www.treasury.gov/press-center/press-releases/Pages/tg1037.aspx).
[19] *See* Treasury Direct, *Daily Treasury Statements*, DEP'T OF TREASURY, Feb 2, 2011 - May 15, 2012, (available at http://www.fms.treas.gov/dts/index.html). On Feb. 2, 2011 the balance of the Supplementary Financing Program account was $199,963,000,000. On the day of the announcement, the balance dropped to $174,967,000,000, reflecting a $25 billion withdrawal. Periodic withdrawals continued until the balance hit $5 billion on March 24, 2011, where it remained until July 28, 2011 when the remaining money was withdrawn. As of May 15, 2012, this account has not been restored and it retains a $0 balance.
[20] Austin & Levit, *supra* note 2, at 21.

and the Executive Branch an additional eleven weeks to reach an agreement before the country would exhaust all borrowing authority and face potential default on August 2, 2011.[21]

1. Issuance of State and Local Government Series Treasury Securities Suspended

On May 6, 2011, ten days before reaching the statutory debt limit, Secretary Geithner suspended the issuance of State and Local Government Series Treasury Securities ("SLGS").[22] SLGS are special purpose securities issued to state and local governments to provide them with a method for investing cash proceeds from their issuance of bonds in compliance with federal tax laws and Internal Revenue Service ("IRS") arbitrage rules.[23] The suspension of SLGS sales is common in anticipation of a debt impasse, as these outstanding securities count against the debt limit and no statute requires their issuance.[24] Suspending sales of these securities did not create any headroom under the ceiling, but it did slow the increase in the outstanding debt, providing incremental time for negotiation.[25] Following the increase in the debt limit on August 2, SLGS issuances resumed.[26]

2. Debt Issuance Suspension Period Declared

When the outstanding debt subject to the statutory limit reached $14.294 trillion on May 16, 2011, Secretary Geithner notified

---

[21] Letter from Timothy Geithner, Secretary of the Treasury, to Harry Reid, Democratic Leader, U.S. Senate (May 16, 2011) (available at http://www.treasury.gov/initiatives/Pages/debtlimit.aspx).

[22] Letter from Timothy Geithner, Secretary of the Treasury, to Harry Reid, Democratic Leader, U.S. Senate (Apr. 4, 2011) (available at http://www.treasury.gov/initiatives/Pages/debtlimit.aspx).

[23] Dep't of Treasury, *State & Local Government Series – Frequently Asked Questions* (May 2, 2011) (available at http://www.treasury.gov/connect/blog/Documents/05.02%20SLGS%20EXTERNAL%20QA%20FINAL.pdf).

[24] *Id.* Issuance of SLGS have been suspended previously during debt limit impasses in 1995-1996, 2002, 2003, 2004, 2006, and 2007.

[25] *Id.*

[26] See Treasury Direct, SLGS FAQs, Dep't of Treasury (available at http://www.treasurydirect.gov/govt/resources/faq/faq_slgs.htm), stating that SLGS issuances were suspended from May 6, 2011 – Aug. 2, 2011. *See also* Treasury Direct, *Daily Treasury Statement*, Dep't of Treasury, Aug. 2, 2011, https://fms.treas.gov/fmsweb/viewDTSFiles?dir=a&fname=11080200.pdf (showing that on Aug. 2, $3.6 billion in SLGS securities were issued).

Congress that a Debt Issuance Suspension Period ("DISP") would begin and last until August 2, 2011, when the "Department of Treasury project[ed] that the borrowing authority of the United States [would] be exhausted."[27] This declaration enabled the Secretary to take certain actions with regard to the Government Securities Investment Fund ("G-Fund"), and the Civil Service Retirement System Fund ("Civil Fund") to create headroom under the debt limit.[28] Given the use of these measures in the previous debt limit impasses of 1996, 2002, 2003, 2004 and 2006,[29] it was widely assumed that Secretary Geithner would undertake these actions without controversy. Notably, the Treasury Secretary is precluded from taking similar actions with regard to the Social Security and Medicare trust funds.[30]

a. G-Fund: Reinvestments Suspended

Enabled by the declaration of the DISP, Secretary Geithner notified Congress on May 16, 2011, that he would be "unable to invest fully" the G-Fund in interest-bearing securities of the United States.[31] The entire balance of the G-Fund, a retirement fund for government

---

[27] Geithner, May 16, 2011, *supra* note 21.
[28] *Id.*
[29] Dep't of Treasury, *Frequently Asked Questions on the Civil Service Retirement and Disability Fund and Government Securities Investment Fund Related to the Debt Limit* (May 16, 2011) (available at http://www.treasury.gov/connect/blog/Documents/20110516%20CSRDF%20 and%20G-FUND%20FAQ.pdf).
[30] 42 U.S.C. § 1320b-15 expressly precludes the Secretary or other officers from (1) delaying deposits or credits to Social Security and Medicare trust funds, (2) refraining from investing Social Security or Medicare trust funds in public debt obligations and (3) redeeming any public debt obligations held by the Social Security or Medicare trust funds prior to maturity for any purpose other than the payment of benefits or administrative expenses. This provision was passed on Mar. 29, 1996 as a part of Pub. L. No. 104-121, which also raised the debt limit. The bill's sponsor, Rep. Bill Archer, explained that the section "codifie[d] Congress' understanding that the Secretary of Treasury and other Federal officials are not authorized to use Social Security and Medicare funds for debt management purposes under any circumstances." He further elaborated "[i]t is the purpose of this legislation to clarify that any limitation on the public debt shall not be used as an excuse to avoid the full and timely investment of the Social Security trust funds." In a separate statement, Rep. Archer said, "There are no circumstances envisioned under which the investments of the trust funds will not be made in a timely fashion in accordance with the normal investment practices of the Treasury, or under which the trust funds are drawn down prematurely for the purpose of avoiding limitations on the public debt or to make room under the statutory debt limit for the Secretary of the Treasury to issue new debt obligations in order to cover the expenditures of the Government." 142 CONG. REC. H2987-01, 38-40 (Mar. 28, 1996) (statement of Rep. Archer).
[31] Geithner, *supra* note 21. Notification to Congress required by 5 U.S.C. § 8438(h)(2) (2009).

employees, matures daily and is reinvested in special-issue Treasury securities, which count against the debt limit.[32] However, during a declared DISP, the Secretary of the Treasury can suspend issuance of additional amounts of obligations into the G-Fund "if issuances could not be made without causing the public debt of the United States to exceed the public debt limit."[33] Under this authority, on the first day of the DISP, $19 billion in principal and $1.5 million in interest was suspended from investment in securities for the G-Fund, instantly creating headroom beneath the limit.[34] Over the eleven weeks of the DISP, $137.5 billion was suspended from investment in Treasury securities, allowing the nation to continue to borrow the corresponding amount without exceeding the statutory debt limit.[35] On August 2, 2011, when the debt limit was raised, $137.5 billion in principal was restored to the G-Fund;[36] on August 3, 2011, $378 million in deferred interest[37] was paid to the Fund to make it whole.[38]

b. Civil Fund: Reinvestments Suspended and Existing Securities Redeemed

As with the G-Fund, Secretary Geithner announced on May 16, 2011 that he would "be unable to invest fully the portion of the Civil Fund not needed immediately to pay beneficiaries."[39] During a DISP, new contributions to the Civil Fund, which provides defined benefits to retired and disabled federal employees, need

---

[32] FAQs, *supra* note 29.
[33] 5 U.S.C. § 8438(g)(1) (2009).
[34] Dep't of Treasury, *Report on the Operation and Status of the Government Securities Investment Fund May 16, 2011 to August 3, 2011* (Aug. 24, 2011) (available at http://www.treasury.gov/initiatives/Documents/G%20Fund%20Letters.pdf). Report pursuant to 5 U.S.C. § 8438(h) (2009).
[35] *Id.* Total suspended daily investments from May 16, 2011 – Aug. 1, 2011 equaled $137,543,151,298.
[36] *Id.* Repayment pursuant to provision 5 U.S.C, § 8438(g)(3) (2009): "Upon expiration of the debt issuance suspension period, the Secretary of the Treasury shall *immediately* issue to the [G-Fund] obligations . . . as are necessary to ensure that . . . the holdings of obligations of the . . . [G-Fund] *will replicate the obligations* that would then be held by the [G-Fund] . . . *if the suspension of issuances . . . had not occurred.*" (emphasis added).
[37] *Id.* Payment pursuant to 5 U.S.C. § 8438(g)(4) (2009), which states that Treasury must repay interest, as if the DISP had not occurred.
[38] 5 U.S.C. § 8348(g)(2) (2009): "Any issuances of obligations to the [G-Fund] which, solely by reason of the public debt limit are not issued, *shall be issued . . . as soon as such issuances can be issued without exceeding the public debt limit.*" (emphasis added).
[39] Geithner, *supra* note 21. Discretionary decision pursuant to 5 U.S.C. § 8348(j)(1) (2006).

not be invested in special issue Treasury securities.[40] Instead, these investments can be suspended, effectively reducing the debt subject to the limit and creating additional borrowing authority. Over the course of the DISP, suspension of these new investments totaled $5.5 billion.[41] Additionally, this allowed the Treasury to create more than $80 billion in headroom on June 30, by (1) not reinvesting $63 billion in maturing securities eligible for rollover, and (2) declining to invest $17.4 billion in semi-annual interest.[42]

In conjunction with the authority to suspend investment of the Civil Fund, the Secretary of the Treasury has the ability to suspend investment in the Postal Service Retiree Health Benefit Fund ("Postal Fund").[43] During the DISP, Secretary Geithner invoked this discretionary authority, declining to reinvest $8.7 billion of maturing securities and $800 million in accrued interest in Treasury securities.[44]

In addition to the suspension of investments, Secretary Geithner authorized the redemption of a portion of the securities held by the Civil Fund.[45] During a DISP, the Treasury Secretary has the authority to redeem existing Treasury securities held by the Civil Fund in the amount equal to the civil service benefit payments authorized to be made by the Fund during the declared period.[46] Using this delegated authority, Secretary Geithner redeemed $17.1 billion in Treasury securities from the Civil Fund, immediately lowering the outstanding debt subject to the limit by the same amount.[47]

---

[40] 5 U.S.C. § 8348(j)(1) (2006) authorizes the Secretary to "suspend additional investment of amounts in the [Civil Fund] if such additional investment could not be made without causing the public debt of the United States to exceed the public debt limit."

[41] Dep't of Treasury, *Report on Fund Operations and Status From May 16, 2011 to December 30, 2011* (Jan. 27, 2012) (available at http://www.treasury.gov/initiatives/Documents/Debt%20Limit%20CSRDF%20Report%20to%20Reid.pdf). Total suspended daily investments from May 16, 2011 - Aug. 2, 2011 equaled $5,487,140,000.

[42] *Id.* Treasury did not invest $63,062,518,000 in securities maturing and eligible for rollover or $17,416,286,000 in semi-annual interest payable on June 30, 2011.

[43] *Id.* Discretionary authority pursuant to 5 U.S.C. § 8909a(c) (2011), which states that investments of the Postal "shall be made in the same manner" as investments for the Civil Fund under 5 U.S.C. § 8348 (2006).

[44] *Id.* On June 30, 2011, Treasury did not invest $8,724,468,000 in securities maturing and eligible for rollover or $808,879,000 in semi-annual interest payable to the Postal Fund.

[45] Geithner, *supra* note 21.

[46] FAQs, *supra* note 29. Discretionary authority pursuant to 5 U.S.C. § 8348(k)(1) (2006).

[47] Report on Civil Fund, *supra* note 41. Treasury redeemed $17.1 billion from a 2-7/8 percent bond maturing in 2025. Against this amount, Treasury did not redeem $5.7 billion on June 1, $5.7 billion on July 1, and $5.3 billion on Aug. 1, which represented a portion of the payments authorized to be made by the Civil Fund during the period of the DISP. Treasury also

When the debt limit was raised on August 2, 2011, the Secretary issued obligations to make the Civil Fund whole, conforming to the statutory requirement of the Secretary of the Treasury to invest the amount suspended during the DISP "as soon as such investments can be made without exceeding the public debt limit."[48] This necessitated investing nearly $86 billion to account for the suspended investments and reinvestments during the DISP.[49] Similarly, Treasury invested $9.5 billion in the Postal Fund to account for the suspended reinvestment of maturing securities and interest.[50] The Treasury Department also reinvested $17.1 billion of securities redeemed at the outset of the DISP from the Civil Fund.[51] The Civil Fund and Postal Fund were made whole on December 30, 2011, when Treasury paid $516 million to the Civil Fund and $22 million to the Postal Fund, representing the interest foregone during the suspension period and accrued since August 2.[52]

3. *Reinvestment in the Exchange Stabilization Fund Suspended*

In keeping with precedent set during past debt limit negotiation periods,[53] Secretary Geithner suspended reinvestments of the portion of the Exchange Stabilization Fund ("ESF") held in U.S. dollars on July 15.[54] Congress appropriates funds to the ESF for a variety of

---

redeemed $462 million on Aug. 1, which represented the amount needed to make the remainder of the benefit payment from the Fund that day.

[48] 5 U.S.C. § 8348(j)(2) (2006). "Any amounts in the Fund which, solely by reason of the public debt limit, are not invested *shall be invested* by the Secretary of the Treasury *as soon as such investments can be made without exceeding the public debt limit*." (emphasis added).

[49] Report on Civil Fund, *supra* note 41. $86 billion comprised of $84,109,884,000 of principal (rollover investment planned for June 30, 2011) and $1,856,060,000 of interest accrued between July 1 and Aug. 1. Payment pursuant to 5 U.S.C. § 8348(j)(3) (2006), requiring the Secretary of the Treasury "to replicate to the maximum extent practicable the obligations that would then be held by the [Civil Fund] if the suspension of investment . . . and any redemption or disinvestment . . . had not occurred."

[50] *Id.* Actions pursuant to 5 U.S.C. § 8909a(c) (2011) and 5 U.S.C. § 8348(j)(3) (2006). On Aug. 2, Treasury invested $9,533,347,000 of principal in the Postal Fund, representing the June 30 payments not reinvested.

[51] *Id.*

[52] *Id.* Payment subject to 5 U.S.C. § 8348(j)(4) (2006), which requires the Secretary to pay the funds the interest that would have been earned during the DISP on the first normal interest payment date after the expiration of the DISP.

[53] Dep't of Treasury, *Exchange Stabilization Fund Q&A* (July 15, 2011) (available at http://www.treasury.gov/press-center/press-releases/Documents/07%2013%20ESF%20QA%202.pdf). Government previously suspended daily reinvestment of Treasury securities held in the ESF during the debt limit impasses in 1996, 2003, 2004, and 2006.

[54] Press Release, Dep't of Treasury, *Update: As Previously Announced, Treasury to Employ Fi-*

purposes, including the stabilization of international financial markets through the purchase and sale of foreign currencies.[55] Similar to the G-Fund, the portion of the ESF held in U.S. dollars is invested in special-issue Treasury securities, the entire balance of which matures and is reinvested daily.[56] However, no statute requires the investment of the ESF in Treasury securities.[57] By declining to reinvest the securities in this Fund, Treasury effectively lowered the outstanding debt of the United States by $23 billion, providing much needed headroom under the statutory debt limit.[58] This final maneuver sent an important signal that the country was close to exhausting its borrowing authority. The date of this maneuver was concerning to at least one analyst, who predicted this final "extraordinary measure" would not be made until August 1, 2011.[59] When the debt limit was raised on August 2, 2011, this portion of the ESF was reinvested in Treasury securities, but the ESF is not entitled to, and did not receive, foregone interest.[60]

4. *Federal Financing Bank Swaps Not Utilized*

In contrast to the 1996, 2003 and 2004 impasses, the Department of Treasury did not elect to use the Federal Financing Bank ("FFB") in order to extend the nation's borrowing authority.[61] Relevant statutes allow the Secretary to issue up to $15 billion in FFB obligations in exchange for other federal debt, including securities held by the Civil Fund.[62] Since FFB securities do not count against the debt limit, this

---

nal Extraordinary Measure to Extend U.S. Borrowing Authority Until August 2 (July 15, 2011) (available at http://www.treasury.gov/press-center/press-releases/Pages/tg1243.aspx).

[55] ESF Q&A, *supra* note 53.
[56] *Id.*
[57] *Id.*
[58] *Id.*
[59] Austin & Levit, *supra* note 2, at 26.
[60] Gov't Accountability Office (GAO), *Financial Audit: Bureau of Public Debt's Fiscal Years 2011 and 2010* 21 (Nov. 2011). As of Sept. 2011, the affected portion of the ESF amounted to $22,721,204,000.
[61] Gov't Accountability Office (GAO), *Debt Limit: Delays Create Debt Management Challenges and Increase Uncertainty in the Treasury Market* 9 (Feb. 2011). 5 U.S.C. § 8348(e) (2006) authorizes the Secretary of the Treasury to invest Civil Fund obligations in "other interest-bearing obligations of the United States, if the Secretary determines that the purchases are in the public interest."
[62] *Id.* at 7. 12 U.S.C. § 2288 (1973), "The Bank is authorized, with the approval of the Secretary of the Treasury, to issue publicly and have outstanding at any one time not in excess of

measure could have created some additional breathing room as the nation approached the ceiling.[63] However, the outstanding balance of FFB securities already amounted to $10.2 billion in May 2011,[64] leaving less than $5 billion of opportunity for potential swaps. On this ground, Secretary Geithner dismissed the option of using FFB securities in a swap as a valid extraordinary measure in April 2011.[65] Additionally, the prudence of this maneuver has been questioned, as Treasury officials now say that they can no longer reverse these FFB transactions once the debt limit is raised because of the potential substantial costs that both the FFB and its counterparties could incur due to unexpected interest rate changes.[66]

5. Selling Assets to Raise Revenue Not Seriously Considered

To fund appropriated expenditures without raising new taxes or issuing new debt, some suggested that the United States should sell its financial assets.[67] In May 2011, a Morgan Stanley report estimated

---

$15,000,000,000, or such additional amounts as may be authorized in appropriations Acts, of obligations having such maturities and bearing such rate or rates of interest as may be determined by the Bank."

[63] GAO, *supra* note 61, at 7.

[64] Treasury Direct, *Monthly Statement of the Public Debt of the United States*, DEP'T OF TREASURY (May 31, 2011) (available at http://www.treasurydirect.gov/govt/reports/pd/mspd/2011/opds052011.pdf). FFB balance totaled $10.239 billion.

[65] Geithner, *supra* note 22, at fn. 14, stating "The potential to use such an exchange transaction is of limited use at this time because the FFB has a limited amount of obligations available to the exchange."

[66] GAO *supra* note 61, at 11-12. *See also* General Accounting Office, *Analysis of Actions Taken during 2003 Debt Issuance Suspension Period* 12, 25-29 (May 2004), stating that the risks, such as unforeseen interest rate changes, related to transactions between the FFB and Civil Fund may be substantial. "According to FFB estimates, the Civil Service fund lost interest of over $1 billion on a $15 billion transaction in October 2002 when the FFB decided to redeem early its 9(a) obligations that were issued to the Civil Service Fund. These obligations related to Treasury's efforts to manage the debt during the 1985 debt ceiling crisis, and the losses occurred because of (1) the unexpected early redemption by FFB and (2) unforeseen interest rate changes." The Secretary of the Treasury does not have statutory authority to restore these types of losses. Further gains and losses are hard to estimate.

[67] *U.S. Should Sell Assets Like Gold to Get Out of Debt, Conservative Economists Say*, WASH. POST, May 12, 2011, http://www.washingtonpost.com/national/economy/us-should-sell-assets-like-gold-to-get-out-of-debt-economists-say/2011/05/12/AFIvmI4G_story_1.html. In addition to gold, some commentators suggested that the United States sell land, interstate highway property, or utilities.

that the nation's gold reserves[68] and student loan portfolio[69] were each worth $400 billion, while Treasury's mortgage-backed securities[70] amounted to $125 billion.[71] Secretary Geithner stated that selling these assets was "not a viable option."[72] He suggested that a "fire sale" of assets would undercut confidence in the United States and cause damage to financial markets and the economy.[73] This view was further espoused by Mary J. Miller, Assistant Secretary of the Treasury for Financial Markets, who stated that selling such assets "would be extremely destabilizing to the world financial system."[74] Addressing calls to sell Treasury's portfolio of MBS faster than currently scheduled,[75] Secretary Geithner stated that flooding the market with such securities could damage the value of similar assets held by private investors without making "an appreciable difference in when the debt limit must be raised."[76]

C. Resolution: The Budget Control Act of 2011

On August 2, 2011, the debt limit impasse officially ended when President Obama signed the Budget Control Act of 2011 ("BCA").[77]

---

[68] See 31 U.S.C. § 5116(a)(1)(A) (2002), which grants the Treasury Secretary the authority, with the approval of the President, to "sell gold in the way, in amounts, at rates, and on conditions the Secretary considers most advantageous to the public interest." See also 31 U.S.C. §5116(a)(2): "Amounts received from the sale of gold shall be deposited by the Secretary in the general fund of the Treasury and shall be used for the sole purpose of reducing the national debt."

[69] See 20 U.S.C. § 1087i (1998), which grants the Secretary of Education, in consultation with the Secretary of the Treasury, the authority to sell loans "on such terms as the Secretary determines are in the best interest of the United States."

[70] See 12 U.S.C. § 5211(c)(4), which grants the Treasury Secretary the authority to sell TARP assets.

[71] David Greenlaw, et al., Morgan Stanley, *US Economics - Debt Ceiling Showdown: An Update* 3 (May 2011). Figure for MBS estimated lower in Austin & Levit, *supra* note 2, at 5, which states that at the end of Apr. 2011, the U.S. Treasury had sold $121 billion of its $225 billion portfolio.

[72] Geithner, *supra* note 22.

[73] *Id.*

[74] Mary J. Miller, Assistant Secretary of the Treasury for Financial Markets, *Federal Asset Sales Cannot Avoid Need for Increase in Debt Limit*, Dep't of Treasury (May 6, 2011) (available at http://www.treasury.gov/connect/blog/Pages/Federal-Asset-Sales-Cannot-Avoid-Need-for-Increase-in-Debt-Limit.aspx).

[75] *Id.* "Treasury is gradually selling these assets, at the rate of up to $10 billion per month, in order to maximize value to taxpayers without hurting the market or mortgage rates."

[76] Geithner, *supra* note 22.

[77] Austin & Levit, *supra* note 2, at 2. Pub. L. No. 112-25: House approval 269-161, and Senate approval 74-26.

In addition to providing for a debt limit increase, the BCA established caps on discretionary spending[78] and created the Joint Select Committee ("Super Committee"), which had the stated goal of achieving at least $1.5 trillion in savings over 10 years.[79] Though the threat of default was no longer looming, market reactions to the resolution of the impasse were not positive.[80] The protracted negotiations showcased Washington's fractious partisan politics and created a crisis of confidence.[81] The price on one-year U.S. CDSs more than doubled during the summer of 2011, reflecting the increased speculation that an agreement would not be reached and a "credit event" would take place.[82] On August 5, 2011, Standard & Poor's downgraded the long-term sovereign debt credit rating for U.S. Treasuries from AAA to AA+, stating that "the political brinksmanship of recent months highlights what we see as America's governance and policymaking becoming less stable, less effective, and less predictable than what we previously believed."[83] Additionally, the lengthy negotiations served to increase borrowing costs in FY 2011 by $1.3 billion.[84]

---

[78] Budget Control Act of 2011, Title 1. *See* Letter from Cong. Budget Office, to John Boehner and Harry Reid regarding Budget Control Act Analysis (Aug. 1, 2011), which estimated that this part of the legislation would reduce budget deficits by $917 billion between 2012 and 2021.

[79] Budget Control Act of 2011, Title 4. Austin & Levit, *supra* note 2, at 3, states that failure to meet this goal triggers $1.2 trillion in automatic cuts, for a resulting total of at least $2.1 trillion in cuts over the 2012-2021 period.

[80] *See e.g.,* Michael Krebs, *Global Markets Crash as Congressional Job Disapproval Hits High,* Digital Journal, Aug. 5, 2011, http://www.digitaljournal.com/article/309962.

[81] *See e.g.,* Timothy Geithner, Editorial, *Compromise Achieved, Reform's the Next Chapter,* Wash. Post, Aug. 2, 2011, http://www.washingtonpost.com/opinions/compromise-achieved-reforms-the-next-chapter/2011/08/02/gIQAXQBMqI_story.html ("It should not be possible for a small minority to threaten catastrophe if the rest of the government decides not to embrace an extreme agenda of austerity and the dismantling of programs for the elderly and the less fortunate.").

[82] The Economist, *The Mother of All Tail Risks,* June 23, 2011, http://www.economist.com/node/18866851 ("One-year protection is now almost as expensive as five-year protection. This is more often seen in distressed markets where investors are pricing in an imminent default than with otherwise healthy borrowers with long-term problems.").

[83] Standard & Poor's, Press Release, *United States of America Long-Term Rating Lowered To 'AA+' Due To Political Risks, Rising Debt Burden; Outlook Negative* (Aug. 5, 2011) (available at http://www.standardandpoors.com/ratings/articles/en/us/?assetID=1245316529563) ("We lowered our long-term rating on the U.S. because we believe that the prolonged controversy over raising the statutory debt ceiling and the related fiscal policy debate indicate that further near-term progress containing the growth in public spending, especially on entitlements, or on reaching an agreement on raising revenues is less likely than we previously assumed and will remain a contentious and fitful process.").

[84] Gov't Accountability Office (GAO), *Debt Limit: Analysis of 2011-2012 Actions Taken and*

To resolve the debt limit impasse, the BCA provided for new procedures[85] to raise the debt limit between $2.1 trillion and $2.4 trillion in three stages.[86] The first extension of the debt limit occurred at enactment. On August 2, 2011, President Obama certified that the debt was within $100 billion of its legal limit, prompting an immediate $400 billion increase in the limit.[87] On that day, the debt subject to the limit increased by $238 billion[88] (60% of the new borrowing authority), due largely to the restoration of suspended investments during the DISP. This initial presidential certification also triggered a potential $500 billion increase in the debt limit, scheduled to be effective only if Congress failed to pass a joint resolution of disapproval using special expedited procedures[89] within 50 calendar days.[90] On September 22, 2011, the second increase went into effect, despite a House vote of disapproval.[91]

After the initial $900 billion increase, the BCA authorized the President to once more submit a written certification to Congress that the outstanding national debt was within $100 billion of the limit.[92] The BCA provided both the House and the Senate

Effect of Delayed Increase on Borrowing Costs 2 (July 2012); *see also* Ed O'Keefe, *GAO: Debt fight cost at least $1.3 billion*, Wash. Post, July 23, 2012, http://www.washingtonpost.com/politics/gao-debt-fight-cost-at-least-13-billion/2012/07/23/gJQAZdOE5W_story.html (in addition to the increased borrowing costs, the impasse created 5,570 hours of work for employees of the Bureau of Public Debt and 500 hours of work for the Government Accountability Office).
[85] Bill Heniff Jr., *Legislative Procedures for Adjusting the Public Debt Limit: A Brief Overview*, Cong. Research Serv. 1 (Aug. 4, 2011), http://www.fas.org/sgp/crs/misc/RS21519.pdf. Typically the limit can be raised in two ways: (1) under regular legislative procedures in both chambers, either as freestanding legislation or as a pert of a measure dealing with other topics; or (2) as part of the budget reconciliation process provided for under the Congressional Budget Act of 1974.
[86] Austin & Levit, *supra* note 2, at 2.
[87] *Id.*
[88] Treasury Direct, *Daily Treasury Statements*, Dep't of Treasury, Aug. 1, 2011 - Aug. 2, 2011 (available at http://www.fms.treas.gov/dts/index.html). Debt subject to the limit on Aug. 1 equaled $14,293,975,000,000 Aug. 2 it equaled $14,532,332,000,000. An increase in intergovernmental holdings of the public debt (including Civil Fund, Postal Fund, ESF) accounted for 48% ($113.6 billion) of this increase. 52% ($124.7 billion) was an increase in debt held by the public, which includes the G-Fund. These figures are not in alignment with the sum of reinvested DISP funds because of other public debt issues and redemptions.
[89] 31 U.S.C. §§ 3101A(c) – 3101A(d) (2011).
[90] 31 U.S.C. § 3101A(a)(1)(B) (2011).
[91] Austin & Levit, *supra* note 2, at 2. Increase on Sept. 22, 2011. Disapproval measure passed the House (H.J. Res. 77) on a 232-186 vote. Senate rejected a separate disapproval measure on a 45-52 vote.
[92] 31 U.S.C. § 3101A(a)(2)(A) (2011).

with special expedited procedures[93] to adopt a joint resolution of disapproval to prevent a further increase in the limit within 15 days of this certification.[94] As provided for in the BCA, the amount of the third increase was to be $1.2 trillion.[95] However, if the Senate submitted to the states a proposed balanced budget amendment for their ratification, the debt limit would be raised by $1.5 trillion.[96] Alternatively, if the Super Committee achieved deficit reduction exceeding $1.2 trillion, the increase would be equal to the amount of that reduction, up to $1.5 trillion.[97] Ultimately, the third increase was limited to $1.2 trillion, as a balanced budget amendment was not submitted for ratification, and the Super Committee failed to achieve deficit reduction.[98]

On January 28, 2012, the debt limit was increased by $1.2 trillion to $16.394 trillion,[99] despite another House disapproval measure.[100] As currently projected by the BiPartisan Policy Center, the nation will reach its new debt limit between late November 2012 and early January 2013.[101] If "extraordinary measures" are again relied upon, the nation's borrowing authority is predicted to be exhausted in February 2013 without a further increase to the debt limit.[102]

---

[93] 31 U.S.C. §§ 3101A(c) – 3101A(d) (2011).
[94] 31 U.S.C. § 3101A(b) (2011). 31 U.S.C. § 3101A(f)(6) (2011) provides that if such a resolution were passed over a likely presidential veto, the debt limit would not be increased and the Office of Management and Budget ("OMB") would sequester budgetary resources on a "pro rata" basis. Effectively, this would mean across-the-board spending cuts to both defense and non-defense programs, not already exempt based on the Balanced Budget and Emergency Deficit Control Act of 1985.
[95] 31 U.S.C. § 3103(A)(a)(2)(i) (2011).
[96] 31 U.S.C. § 3103(A)(a)(2)(ii) (2011).
[97] 31 U.S.C. § 3103(A)(a)(2)(iii) (2011).
[98] Heidi Przybyla, *Supercommittee Failure Threatens Recovery as Rating Affirmed*, BLOOMBERG BUSINESSWEEK, Dec. 3, 2011, http://www.businessweek.com/news/2011-12-03/supercommittee-failure-threatens-recovery-as-rating-affirmed.html.
[99] Austin & Levit, *supra* note 2, at 1. Debt outstanding at the end of Jan. 2012 was $15,214 trillion. Raise followed a Jan. 12, 2012 certification by the President that the debt was within $100 billion of the limit.
[100] *Id.* Disapproval measure passed the House on Jan. 18, 2012 (H.J. Res. 98), 239-176 vote.
[101] Steve Bell, Loren Adler & Shai Akabas, *The Debt Ceiling Slouches Toward 2012*, BIPARTISAN POLICY CENTER (Feb. 24, 2012) (available at http://www.bipartisanpolicy.org/blog/2012/02/debt-ceiling-slouches-toward-2012).
[102] *Id.*

II. The Counterfactual: What Would Have Happened if the United States Hit the Debt Limit in August 2011?

Despite the protracted negotiations, political leaders were able to reach a compromise to raise the debt limit just before the government exhausted all borrowing authority. Therefore, it is unclear what events may have transpired if an agreement was not reached by August 2, 2011. The following discussion considers the alternatives the President may have elected to pursue, and the legal grounds on which such decisions could have been defended, if the public debt hit the statutory limit and spending obligations exceeded projected revenues.

The Constitution grants Congress the power to spend, the power to tax, and the power to borrow. The Executive enforces congressional action in these areas by spending the money Congress appropriates, raising revenue within the bounds of the tax code, and borrowing money to fulfill any projected shortfalls. However, just as the tax code presents a limit on the Executive's authority to raise revenue through taxation, the debt limit provides an upper boundary on how much the Executive can borrow. These revenue-raising constraints are coupled with the President's longstanding obligation to spend all money appropriated by Congress. Thus, when the country reaches the debt limit, the Executive faces a dilemma: assuming that the President cannot unilaterally raise taxes, the Executive must either spend less than Congress appropriated or borrow more than the debt limit permits. Something must give.

A. Legal Background

1. *The Fourteenth Amendment*

Any decision the President may have made if borrowing authority had been exhausted before a compromise was reached would have been made in light of section four of the Fourteenth Amendment ("Public Debt Clause"[103]). The Clause states: "The validity of the

---
[103] The "Public Debt Clause" was coined by Professor Michael Abramowicz. Michael B. Abramowicz, *Train Wrecks, Budget Deficits, and the Entitlements Explosion: Exploring the Implications of the Fourteenth Amendment's Public Debt Clause* (GWU Law School Public Law

public debt of the United States, authorized by law, including debts incurred for payment of pensions and bounties for services in suppressing insurrection or rebellion, shall not be questioned."[104] The Supreme Court has only addressed the Public Debt Clause once, in *Perry v. United States*,[105] leaving a significant interpretive gap as to the full meaning of the Clause. Various academic commentators have attempted to fill this gap with a range of interpretations of the phrase, "public debt," and the word, "questioned," which, if adopted, would serve to stretch the meaning of the Public Debt Clause. The meaning of "public debt" could determine the scope of the obligations that the Executive is bound to fulfill if the national debt hits the limit. For instance, if "public debt" only includes bond payments, then the Public Debt Clause would not protect Social Security, Medicare, Medicaid, or discretionary spending.[106] On the other end of the spectrum, "public debt" might be said to refer to all statutory obligations, including mandatory programs and other appropriations.[107]

The meaning of "questioned" could determine the threshold at which the Public Debt Clause is triggered. Some legal academics have argued that the debt limit itself is unconstitutional because its existence allows for the possibility that the United States would default.[108] Others have taken the view that the debt limit is only unconstitutional when the national debt exceeds the statutory limit because the validity of the public debt will be in doubt only when the

---

Research Paper No. 575) (June 29, 2011), http://ssrn.com/abstract=1874746.
[104] U.S. Const. amend. XIV, § 4 states, in full: "THE VALIDITY OF THE PUBLIC DEBT OF THE UNITED STATES, AUTHORIZED BY LAW, INCLUDING DEBTS INCURRED FOR PAYMENT OF PENSIONS AND BOUNTIES FOR SERVICES IN SUPPRESSING INSURRECTION OR REBELLION, SHALL NOT BE QUESTIONED. BUT NEITHER THE UNITED STATES NOR ANY STATE SHALL ASSUME OR PAY ANY DEBT OR OBLIGATION INCURRED IN AID OF INSURRECTION OR REBELLION AGAINST THE UNITED STATES, OR ANY CLAIM FOR THE LOSS OR EMANCIPATION OF ANY SLAVE; BUT ALL SUCH DEBTS, OBLIGATIONS AND CLAIMS SHALL BE HELD ILLEGAL AND VOID."
[105] 294 U.S. 330 (1935). *See infra* Appendix D.
[106] *See, e.g.*, Gerard Magliocca, *Could the 14th Amendment End Debt Ceiling Negotiations?*, WASH. POST, Live Chat, July 7, 2011, http://live.washingtonpost.com/14th-Amendment-debt-ceiling-chat.html.
[107] *See, e.g.*, Neil H. Buchanan, *Borrowing, Spending, and Taxation: Further Thoughts on Professor Tribe's Reply*, DORF ON LAW, July 19, 2011, http://www.dorfonlaw.org/2011/07/borrowing-spending-and-taxation-further_19.html.
[108] *See, e.g.*, Abramowicz, *supra* note 103, at 37.

United States technically defaults.[109] This broad reading of the word "questioned" under the Public Debt Clause is, however, problematic because many governmental actions, including perennial deficits, might be said to question the validity of the public debt.[110]

2. *The Duty to Fulfill Statutory Spending Obligations*

The President's course of action, had the statutory limit been reached, must also have been chosen in consideration of his duty to spend money as appropriated by Congress. Congress has the power "to borrow money on the credit of the United States."[111] While the debt limit constrains executive borrowing authority by delegating borrowing power to the Executive up to the statutory debt limit,[112] a different statutory and judicial scheme limits Executive authority to curtail spending of appropriated obligations. In 1972, President Nixon asserted his authority to impound, or refuse to pay a congressionally-allotted sum, but the courts[113] consistently[114] ordered the President to spend the full allotment when beneficiaries of impounded programs brought claims.[115] In response, Congress passed the Impoundment Control Act of 1974,[116] the current version[117] of which prescribes the rules for the rescission or deferral of spending obligations.[118]

---

[109] *See, e.g.*, Neil H. Buchanan, *The Debt Ceiling Law is Unconstitutional: A Reply to Professor Tribe*, VERDICT, July 11, 2011, http://verdict.justia.com/2011/07/11/the-debt-ceiling-law-is-unconstitutional.

[110] *See, e.g.*, Laurence Tribe, Op-Ed, *A Ceiling We Can't Wish Away*, N.Y. TIMES, July 7, 2011, www.nytimes.com/2011/07/08/opinion/08tribe.html?_r=1&pagewanted=print.

[111] U.S. Const. Art. I, Sec. 8, Cl. 2. Power delegated to the Secretary of the Treasury pursuant to 31 U.S.C. 3101(b).

[112] *See* Anita S. Krishnakumar, *In Defense of the Debt Limit Statute*, 42 HARV. J. ON LEGIS. 135 at 135-36.

[113] For example, in *Train v. City of New York*, 420 U.S. 35, 44 (1975), the Supreme Court held that the President could not withhold a portion of an appropriation; rather, he would have to allot the entire sum.

[114] Cathy S. Neuren, *Addressing the Resurgence of Presidential Budgetmaking Initiative: A Proposal to Reform the Impoundment Control Act of 1974*, 63 TEX. L. REV. 693, 697-98 (1984).

[115] *Id.* at 702-03. President Nixon used impoundment to refuse to fulfill an obligation if it would push spending to levels exceeding his proposed $250 billion ceiling for the following fiscal year. He used this authority to cancel Democratic programs and advance his agenda.

[116] 2 U.S.C. §§ 681-688. The Impoundment Control Act is Title X of the Congressional Budget and Impoundment Control Act, 2 U.S.C. §§ 601-688. The full text of the Impoundment Control Act can be found *infra* in Appendix E.

[117] The original deferral procedures were struck down in *City of New Haven v. United States*, 809 F.2d. 900 (D.C.C. 1987), due to its unconstitutional use of the legislative veto, *see INS v. Chadha*, 462 U.S. 919 (1983).

[118] Neuren, *supra* note 114, at 703.

If the President wishes to defer spending obligations, he must submit a "special message" to Congress regarding his proposed rescission;[119] however, the President must spend the money that he proposed to rescind unless, within forty-five days, Congress passes[120] a rescission bill.[121] The President cannot propose to rescind an obligation more than once,[122] and he can only propose rescissions of discretionary spending authority.[123] The President may defer spending until the end of the fiscal year under three circumstances: "(1) to provide for contingencies; (2) to achieve savings made possible by or through changes in requirements or greater efficiency of operations; or (3) as specifically provided by law."[124] The Comptroller General, and not private individuals,[125] may bring suits pursuant to the Act.[126]

In *Clinton v. City of New York*,[127] the Supreme Court affirmed the President's duty to spend the full allotment of money authorized by Congress. After Congress enacted the Line Item Veto Act[128] in 1996, plaintiffs challenged President Clinton's authority to cancel spending provisions of the Balanced Budget Act of 1997 and the Taxpayer Relief Act of 1997.[129] Specifically, President Clinton canceled section 4722(c) of the Balanced Budget Act of 1997, which would have exempted New York from returning certain Medicaid subsidies to the federal government,[130] and section 968 of the Taxpayer Relief Act of 1997, which provided a tax benefit to "owners of certain food

---

[119] See 2 U.S.C. § 683(a) (1987).
[120] The Senate cannot filibuster a rescission bill because debate on rescission bills is limited by 2 U.S.C. § 688(d) (1974). See Jim Cooper, Op-Ed, *Rescission Time in Congress*, N.Y. TIMES, March 11, 2005, http://query.nytimes.com/gst/fullpage.html?res=980CE6D8173CF932A25750C0A9639C8B63.
[121] See 2 U.S.C. § 683(b) (1987).
[122] Id.
[123] Gov't Accountability Office, *Impoundment Control Act: Use and Impact of Rescission Procedures* 7 (Dec.16, 2009), Statement of Susan A. Poling, Managing Associate General Counsel, Office of General Counsel, Before the Subcommittee on Federal Financial Management, Government Information, Federal Services, and International Security, Committee on Homeland Security and Governmental Affairs, U.S. Senate.
[124] 2 U.S.C. § 684(b) (1987).
[125] See Rocky Ford Hous. Auth. v. U.S. Dept. of Agric., 427 F. Supp. 118, 134 (D.D.C. 1977).
[126] 2 U.S.C. § 687 (1987).
[127] 524 U.S. 417 (1998).
[128] Id. at 437. The Line Item Veto Act allowed the President to cancel spending authority unless Congress passed a disapproval bill. The President retained the authority to veto the disapproval bill.
[129] Id. at 420-21.
[130] Id. at 422-23.

refiners and processors . . . if they sell their stock to eligible farmers' cooperatives."[131]

Although Justice Stevens' majority opinion struck down the Line Item Veto Act on the narrow ground that it violated the Presentment Clause[132] of the Constitution,[133] Justice Kennedy's concurrence provided a separation of powers argument against the Line Item Veto Act on the basis that unilateral, presidential cancellation of budget authority threatens individual liberties.[134] According to Justice Kennedy, "if a citizen who is taxed has the measure of the tax or the decision to spend determined by the Executive alone, without adequate control by the citizen's Representatives in Congress, liberty is threatened. Money is the instrument of policy, and policy affects the lives of citizens. The individual loses liberty in a real sense if that instrument is not subject to traditional constitutional constraints."[135] However, Justice Scalia disagreed, arguing that, while the Line Item Veto Act was an impermissible delegation of legislative authority to "'cancel' an item of spending," the Act would have been constitutional if it "authorized the President to 'decline to spend' any item of spending."[136]

B. Legal Theories for Executive Action if the National Debt Hits the Statutory Limit

If the national debt hit the statutory limit, the legal ambiguities surrounding the Fourteenth Amendment and the Executive's duty to fulfill statutory spending obligations could be resolved in numerous ways. The section below outlines several courses of action the Executive might take if borrowing authority is exhausted, and explores the legal rationale on which each theory could be grounded.

---

[131] *Id.* at 423-25.
[132] U.S. Const. Art. I, Sec. 7.
[133] 524 U.S. at 448-49.
[134] *See id.* at 449-52.
[135] *Id.* at 451.
[136] *Id.* at 468-69.

Theory 1: The President is Bound by the Debt Limit, and Treasury Must Follow "First In, First Out" Procedures

A. The President is Bound by the Debt Limit

The debt limit may prevent the President from borrowing more money. Proponents of this view argue that the Public Debt Clause does not invalidate the debt limit based on their interpretations of "questioned" and "public debt," and several arguments exist to rebut the applicability of *Perry* to the debt limit.

First, the word "questioned" may have a narrow interpretation, which protects repudiation but does not protect default.[137] Professor Michael Stern argues that the legislative history is either unsettled[138] or demonstrates that the Public Debt Clause was intended to prevent repudiation based on floor speeches by the framers of the amendment.[139] Professor Laurence Tribe contends that the lack of a clear threshold for triggering the Public Debt Clause illustrates the absurdity of applying the Clause to the debt limit because, if any act that increases the risk of default is unconstitutional, then a "budget deficit, tax cut, or spending increase" may be unconstitutional.[140]

Second, the Public Debt Clause may not apply to the debt limit if non-borrowing revenues are sufficient to fulfill all payments included within the scope of "public debt."[141] In response to an interpretation of "public debt" that includes all statutory spending commitments,

---

[137] *See* Michael Stern, *"Threatening Default": A Response to Professor Balkin*, POINT OF ORDER, July 1, 2011, http://www.pointoforder.com/2011/07/01/threatening-default-a-response-to-professor-balkin/.
[138] *See infra* Appendix C.
[139] *See id.* Senator Ben Wade said of his proposal, "[i]t puts the debt incurred in the civil war on our part under the guardianship of the Constitution of the United States, so that a Congress cannot *repudiate* it." (emphasis added).
[140] Tribe, *supra* note 110. Professor Tribe points out that, if acts that increase the risk of default are unconstitutional, "the absence of a debt ceiling could likewise be attacked as unconstitutional — after all, the greater the nation's debt, the greater the difficulty of repaying it, and the higher the probability of default."
[141] *See* Calvin Massey, *The Debt Limit and the Fourteenth Amendment*, THE FACULTY LOUNGE, June 30, 2011, http://www.thefacultylounge.org/2011/06/the-debt-limit-and-the-fourteenth-amendment.html. Professor Massey argues that "public debt" protects principal and interest payments to bondholders, as well as "old-age pensions under Social Security, military pensions, and other federal pensions."

Professor Stern points to the second sentence of the Public Debt Clause[142] to show that only "debt" obligations fall within the scope of "public debt" because "debt" and "obligations" are separate entities in the rest of the Clause.[143] Professor Tribe argues that the usage of "debt" in the original Constitution cannot refer to all statutory obligations.[144] Moreover, a proposed floor amendment[145] would have replaced "public debt" with "obligations," but failed to be adopted. Therefore, the Framers of the Fourteenth Amendment may have "deliberately decided to exclude 'obligations' from the Public Debt Clause."[146]

Third, it is unclear how a court would evaluate the Public Debt Clause today. When given the opportunity in 1989 and 1990, several federal appellate courts did not apply the Clause. With respect to the Court's only interpretation of the Public Debt Clause, Professor Abramowicz notes that "*Perry* was decided at the height of the constitutional crisis between the Roosevelt Administration and the Court over new Deal legislation,"[147] and "[i]n post-1937 cases, the Court backed away from earlier activist stances limiting the government's ability to craft economic policy."[148]

---

[142] "But neither the United States nor any State shall assume or pay any debt or obligation incurred in aid of insurrection or rebellion against the United States, or any claim for the loss or emancipation of any slave; but all such debts, obligations and claims shall be held illegal and void." U.S. Const. amend. XIV, § 4.

[143] Michael Stern, *"Arrest Me. I Question the Validity of the Public Debt."* POINT OF ORDER, June 2, 2011, http://www.pointoforder.com/2011/06/02/arrest-me-i-question-the-validity-of-the-public-debt/.

[144] Laurence Tribe, *Guest Post on the Debt Ceiling by Laurence Tribe*, DORF ON LAW, July 16, 2011, http://www.dorfonlaw.org/2011/07/guest-post-on-debt-ceiling-by-laurence.html.

[145] *See infra* Appendix C. Senator Howard's amendment is as follows: "The obligations of the United States, incurred in suppressing insurrection, or in defense of the Union, or for payment of bounties or pensions incident thereto, shall remain inviolate."

[146] Stern, *supra* note 143. In response to this argument, Professor Jack Balkin points out that Senator Howard's wording appears narrower than the final version of the Public Debt Clause because it is limited to the obligations enumerated in the proposed amendment. Jack Balkin, *More on the Original Meaning of Section Four of the Fourteenth Amendment*, BALKINIZATION, July 2, 2011, http://balkin.blogspot.com/2011/07/more-on-original-meaning-of-section.html.

[147] *Id.*

[148] *Id.* at 15-16. However, it is debatable whether an application of the Public Debt Clause to the debt limit debate would be an "activist interpretation."

Perry was decided on the same day as four other cases[149] relating to the constitutionality of the Joint Resolution of June 5, 1933 (the "Joint Resolution"), which permitted the government to satisfy its obligations with any legal currency when the bondholder's contract required payment in gold.[150] The Supreme Court in *Perry* stated, "[h]aving this power to authorize the issue of definite obligations for the payment of money borrowed, the Congress has not been vested with authority to alter or destroy those obligations."[151] However, the plaintiff did not collect the value of his contract in gold because he did "not show[] . . . that in relation to buying power he has sustained any loss whatever."[152]

While some academics interpret the decision in *Perry* as prohibiting the government from breaching its obligations,[153] Professor Henry Hart questioned how the bondholder could have suffered no damage if the Joint Resolution was unconstitutional.[154] Professor Hart did not have a "conviction" of what was the proper interpretation of the *Perry* decision.[155] However, he reconciles the conflicting messages from Chief Justice Hughes by noting that "it was not easy to come out baldly and announce that the public credit has no integrity," but when the Court had to decide on an ultimate resolution of whether the United States would have to satisfy its obligations in gold, "different considerations solicited its judgment."[156] While Professor Hart considered the remedy as "manifestly useless" for the bondholder in *Perry*, he argued that it "may not always be useless" under different circumstances.[157]

If the Public Debt Clause is insufficient, the President's emergency powers may not permit unilateral executive action. Congress has

---

[149] These five cases are known as the "gold clause cases." Henry M. Hart, Jr., *The Gold Clause in United States Bonds*, 48 Harv. L. Rev. 1057, 1057-58 n.2 (1935). The cases are: *Norman v. Baltimore & Ohio R. R.*, 294 U.S. 240 (1935), *United States v. Bankers Trust Co.*, 294 U.S. 240 (1935) (two cases), and *Nortz v. United States*, 294 U.S. 317 (1935).
[150] *See infra* Appendix D.
[151] 294 U.S. at 353.
[152] *Id.* at 357.
[153] Abramowicz, *supra* note 103, at 13.
[154] Hart, *supra* note 149, at 1060.
[155] *Id.* at 1094.
[156] *Id.*
[157] *Id.* at 1096.

the power "to borrow money on the credit of the United States."[158] According to Professor Tribe, "[n]othing in the 14th Amendment or in any other constitutional provision suggests that the President may usurp legislative power to prevent a violation of the Constitution."[159] In support of this argument, Professor Tribe cites Justice Jackson's concurrence in *Youngstown Sheet & Tube Co. v. Sawyer*[160] and argues that the President's power to borrow would be at its "lowest ebb" of legitimacy.[161] In addition, Professor Tribe reasons that the "debt limit statute merely limits *one source of revenue* that the government might use to pay its bills"; therefore, it is unclear why the debt limit statute is unconstitutional while the tax code and other revenue limits are not.[162] The President may be bound to use legal revenue sources[163] before he can breach a statutory obligation.[164]

Professor Neil Buchanan argues that the President must choose to breach the obligation to borrow within the debt limit rather than levy additional taxes or spend less than Congress appropriated.[165] Professor Tribe responds by framing the debate as one between (1) the power to spend money and (2) the power to raise revenues.[166] Thus, the authority to borrow money is grouped with the power to tax, sell assets, and print money. As between these two powers, "the principle that must yield is the one barring executive control over spending, not the one barring executive control over revenue-raising."[167] In

---

[158] U.S. Const. Art. I, Sec. 8

[159] Tribe, *supra* note 110.

[160] 343 U.S. 579, 637-38 (1952).

[161] Tribe, *supra* note 110.

[162] Tribe, *supra* note 144.

[163] *See* Magliocca, *supra* note 106. For example, the United States can legally sell its assets to raise money. *See supra* notes 68, 69, 70. Another potential legal solution outlined by Brad Plumer, *Can A Giant Platinum Coin Save Our Credit?*, Wash. Post, July 30, 2011, http://www.washingtonpost.com/blogs/ezra-klein/post/can-a-giant-platinum-coin-save-our-credit/2011/07/11/gIQA2VAPjI_blog.html?hpid=z1, would have been minting trillion dollar coins. Technically, Treasury could mint platinum coins of any value, which could be deposited in the Federal Reserve. This authority is derived from 31 U.S.C. § 5112(k) (2010), which states, "The Secretary may mint and issue platinum bullion coins and proof platinum coins in accordance with such specifications, designs, varieties, quantities, denominations, and inscriptions as the Secretary, in the Secretary's discretion, may prescribe from time to time." The Fed could then transfer the balance to Treasury, allowing for full payment of all expenses. The potential inflationary effects are questionable, but some argue this would be a fully legal strategy. However, it is not likely to be seen popularly as a legitimate exercise of executive power in this situation.

[164] Tribe, *supra* note 144.

[165] *See* Buchanan, *supra* note 107.

[166] Tribe, *supra* note 144.

[167] *Id.*

support of his argument, Professor Tribe tracks the admonition of executive revenue-raising from England through the "battle cry of the American Revolution . . . 'No taxation without representation!'"[168] In addition, Professor Tribe cites various examples of Presidents who refused to spend money[169] in contrast to zero examples of a President who unilaterally raised revenue and a "deeply-rooted tradition of prioritizing personal liberty from government imposition over affirmative expectations of government payment."[170]

B. The President Cannot Prioritize Spending Obligations; Therefore, Treasury Must Follow "First In, First Out" Procedures

If the President is bound by the debt limit, he may not have the legal authority to unilaterally prioritize spending obligations. As a result, Treasury may have to continue to pay its bills as they come due using a "First In, First Out" ("FIFO") procedure.[171]

The 1985 Senate Finance Committee, under the leadership of Bob Packwood, espoused this theory.[172] The Committee found, based on the "best available information," that the President and the Secretary of the Treasury have no authority to prioritize payments.[173] It stated, "each law that authorizes expenditures or makes appropriations stands on equal footing, and there are no grounds for the Administration to distinguish a payment for any one program over any other program."[174] The report expected the Secretary of the Treasury to fulfill its spending obligations "as they come due while cash remains in the till."[175]

In response to Senator Packwood and the Senate Finance Committee, the Government Accountability Office wrote, "[w]e are aware of no

---
[168] *Id.*
[169] *Id.* E.g. Ulysses Grant, Franklin D. Roosevelt, Harry Truman, and Richard Nixon.
[170] *Id.*
[171] *See* Mindy R. Levit, Clinton T. Brass, Thomas J. Nicola, Dawn Nuschler, & Alison M. Shelton, *Reaching the Debt Limit: Background and Potential Effects on Government Operations*, Cong. Research Serv. 7-8 (July 27, 2011).
[172] S. Rep. No. 99-144, at 5 (Sept. 26, 1985).
[173] *Id.*
[174] *Id.*
[175] *Id.*

statute or any other basis for concluding the Treasury is required to pay outstanding obligations in the order in which they are presented for payment unless it chooses to do so. Treasury is free to liquidate obligations in any order it finds will best serve the interests of the United States."[176] However, Treasury has maintained that it does not have the authority to prioritize spending obligations.[177] The Congressional Research Service reconciles the differing opinions of GAO and Treasury by noting that they "offer two different interpretations of Congress's silence with respect to a prioritization system for paying obligations."[178]

The 1995-1996 impasse may act as a precedent, forcing Treasury to follow a FIFO procedure unless Congress passes a bill providing prioritization guidelines.[179] During the 1995-1996 impasse, Treasury adopted the interpretation of the 1985 Senate Finance Committee and notified Congress that, absent an extension of the debt limit,

---

[176] Letter from U.S. Government Accountability Office to Bob Packwood, Chairman, Committee on Finance, United States Senate (Oct. 9, 1985) (available at http://redbook.gao.gov/14/fl0065142.php). The letter, addressed to Senator Packwood states in full: "YOU HAVE REQUESTED OUR VIEWS ON WHETHER THE SECRETARY OF THE TREASURY HAS AUTHORITY TO DETERMINE THE ORDER IN WHICH OBLIGATIONS ARE TO BE PAID SHOULD THE CONGRESS FAIL TO RAISE THE STATUTORY LIMIT ON THE PUBLIC DEBT OR WHETHER TREASURY WOULD BE FORCED TO OPERATE ON A FIRST IN-FIRST-OUT BASIS. BECAUSE OF YOUR NEED FOR AN IMMEDIATE ANSWER, *OUR CONCLUSIONS MUST, OF NECESSITY, BE TENTATIVE,* BEING *BASED ON THE LIMITED RESEARCH* WE HAVE BEEN ABLE TO DO. IT IS OUR CONCLUSION THAT THE SECRETARY OF THE TREASURY DOES HAVE THE AUTHORITY TO CHOOSE THE ORDER IN WHICH TO PAY OBLIGATIONS OF THE UNITED STATES. ON A DAILY BASIS THE TREASURY DEPARTMENT RECEIVES A NORMAL FLOW OF REVENUES FROM TAXES AND OTHER SOURCES. AS THEY BECOME AVAILABLE IN THE OPERATING CASH BALANCE, TREASURY MAY USE THESE FUNDS TO PAY OBLIGATIONS OF THE GOVERNMENT AND TO REISSUE EXISTING DEBT AS IT MATURES. SEE GENERALLY H.R. REPT. NO. 31, 96TH CONG., 1ST SESS. 9-10 (1979). WE ARE AWARE OF NO STATUTE OR ANY OTHER BASIS FOR CONCLUDING THAT TREASURY IS REQUIRED TO PAY OUTSTANDING OBLIGATIONS IN THE ORDER IN WHICH THEY ARE PRESENTED FOR PAYMENT UNLESS IT CHOOSES TO DO SO. TREASURY IS FREE TO LIQUIDATE OBLIGATIONS IN ANY ORDER IT FINDS WILL BEST SERVE THE INTERESTS OF THE UNITED STATES. UNLESS IT IS RELEASED EARLIER OR WE HEAR OTHERWISE FROM YOU, THIS LETTER WILL BE AVAILABLE FOR RELEASE TO THE PUBLIC 30 DAYS FROM TODAY." (emphasis added).

[177] *See* Levit, *supra* note 171, at 7-8.

[178] *Id.* at 8.

[179] *See* Bruce Bartlett, *How Will the Debt Limit "Game of Chicken" End?*, The Fiscal Times, May 20, 2011, http://www.thefiscaltimes.com/Columns/2011/05/20/How-Will-the-Debt-Limit-Game-of-Chicken-End.

Social Security payments could not be completed.[180] In response, Congress passed temporary exemptions[181] from the debt limit in order to allow the President to issue new debt to the Social Security Trust Funds, and to pay Social Security beneficiaries.[182]

Absent congressional authorization, the Supreme Court's decision in *Clinton*[183] may provide an implicit prohibition on executive discretion regarding the satisfaction of statutory spending obligations.[184] Professor Buchanan writes that the *Clinton* Court "held that the president may not cancel appropriations that Congress has authorized."[185] As compared to the line item veto at issue in *Clinton*, Professor Buchanan argues that prioritization is more "extreme" because it allows the President to reduce levels of spending within

---

[180] General Accounting Office, *Debt Ceiling: Analysis of Actions During the 1995-1996 Crisis* 10 (1996).

[181] Pub. L. No. 104-103 (Feb. 8, 1996) and Pub. L. No. 104-115 (Mar. 12, 1996). These two provisions had the effect of temporarily exempting some newly issued Treasury securities from being counted against the debt limit. This allowed "Treasury to (1) raise $29 billion to pay March 1996 Social Security benefits and (2) in March 1996, invest $58.2 billion from government trust fund receipts and maturing securities." General Accounting Office, *supra* note 180 at 6. *See* 42 Cong. Rec. H1197-01, 1-2 (Feb. 1, 1996) (statement of Rep. Archer). The Act's sponsor Rep. Bill Archer stated that this bill was enacted "in an effort to reassure our seniors." He further stated, "[w]ith the passage of this bill, President Clinton has no excuse not to send out Social Security checks."
Note: This provision was limited to new debt *issuances* and is distinct from the issue discussed *infra* in Theory 2D, which would allow for Social Security Trust Fund *redemptions* in order to pay beneficiaries. Pub. L. No. 104-103 specifically addressed the monthly process of crediting the Trust Funds with new debt securities equal to the amount of incoming Social Security revenues received by the Treasury. Rep. Smith contended that "[Treasury has] no legal authority to withhold payments for Social Security or any other trust fund when there are surpluses coming into those trust funds." However, Social Security currently runs a current account deficit, which may change this evaluation. Without an Act similar to this 1996 measure, the Secretary may be forced to violate either 42 U.S.C. § 1320b-15, which prohibits a delay of deposits into the Trust Funds, or the Debt Limit.

[182] *See* Gov't Accountability Office, *supra* note 61, at 9; 142 Cong. Rec. H1197-01, 4 (Feb. 1, 1996) (statement of Rep. Smith). "Under normal circumstances Treasury would sell bonds a few days before benefit payments are due with a settlement date the same as the benefit payment date. Then the trust fund is disinvested and the debt limit has returned to what it was. Because we are at the debt limit Treasury cannot use this normal procedure. Because the Social Security Trust is void of any cash, Treasury must sell securities to make benefit payments that come due. This bill will allow these securities to be sold outside the debt limit, then as the benefit payments are met the trust fund securities will be redeemed. The securities which were sold will then come under the debt limit, so by March 15, when all benefit checks have been paid, the debt will be the same as it was before."

[183] 524 U.S. 417. *See supra* Section II.A.2 – The Duty to Fulfill Statutory Spending Obligations.

[184] *See* Buchanan, *supra* note 107.

[185] *Id.*

each obligation, while the line item veto only allows the President to cancel an entire spending item.[186] Professor Buchanan further contends that the Impoundment Control Act "establishes that Congress has aggressively disapproved of presidential encroachment on its spending authority -- encroachment of precisely the type that prioritization represents."[187]

C. 2011 Impasse: Treasury Appears to Favor FIFO Approach

Throughout the 2011 impasse, Treasury officials implied in their statements that the Department would most likely employ the FIFO method of making payments if the outstanding debt reached the statutory limit. In his May 2 letter, Secretary Geithner stated that, upon default, "a broad range of payments would have to be limited or delayed, including military salaries, Social Security and Medicare payments, interest on debt, unemployment benefits and tax refunds,"[188] suggesting a *pari passu* approach.[189] Further, Treasury repeatedly expressed a bias against prioritizing payments, implicating the use of the FIFO method instead. For example, in responding to Senator Jim DeMint's suggestion that interest payments be prioritized, Secretary Geithner called such a proposal "a radical and deeply irresponsible departure from the commitment by Presidents of both parties, throughout American history, to honor all of the commitments our Nation has made."[190] In a separate statement, Deputy Secretary of the Treasury Neal Wolin contended that prioritizing bond payments would be "unworkable" and "unacceptable to American servicemen and women, retirees, and all Americans who would rightly reject the notion that their payment has been deemed a lower priority by their government."[191] Even

---

[186] *Id.*
[187] *Id.*
[188] Letter from Timothy Geithner, Secretary of the Treasury, to John Boehner, Speaker of the House, US House of Representatives (May 2, 2011) (available at http://www.treasury.gov/initiatives/Pages/debtlimit.aspx).
[189] Meaning that payments would be put on an "equal footing," as in bankruptcy proceedings.
[190] Letter from Timothy Geithner, Secretary of the Treasury, to Jim DeMint, Senator, US Senate (June 28, 2011) (available at http://www.treasury.gov/initiatives/Pages/debtlimit.aspx).
[191] Neal Wolin, Deputy Secretary of the Treasury, *Proposals to "Prioritize" Payments on U.S. Debt Not Workable; Would Not Prevent Default*, Dep't of Treasury, Jan. 21, 2011 (available at http://www.treasury.gov/connect/blog/Pages/Proposals-to-Prioritize-Payments-on-US-Debt-Not-Workable-Would-Not-Prevent-Default.aspx).

President Obama seemed to deny plans to prioritize, saying that he could not "guarantee" that Social Security checks would go out if the country hit the statutory debt limit.[192] On July 27, 2011, a New York Times article cited Treasury officials' repeated statements that they did not have "the legal authority to pay bills based on political, moral or economic considerations," and suggested that these statements imply that "the government will need to pay bills in the order that they come due."[193]

The FIFO approach would not only have been a legally permissible explanation,[194] but also may have been more politically expedient for the Executive Branch than making difficult choices about which payable accounts should "win" and "lose" in a unilateral prioritization scheme. Such decisions with limited resources would upset various political constituencies. Further, adherence to a FIFO approach may have served to apply pressure to Congressional Republicans. As one commentator observed, certain members of Congress may have been more likely to negotiate in the face of "soldiers going without pay."[195] Lastly, it can be argued that a default FIFO prioritization scheme may have been more practical[196] than comprehensively prioritizing 80 million payments per month.[197] Despite superficial plausibility, however, a FIFO payment scheme is not without complexity, since Treasury does not control 100% of payments.[198]

---

[192] Politifact, *Barack Obama said Social Security and other federal checks may not go out on Aug. 3 if the debt ceiling is not increased*, TAMPA BAY TIMES, July 12, 2011, http://www.politifact.com/truth-o-meter/statements/2011/jul/13/barack-obama/barack-obama-said-social-security-and-other-federal/.

[193] Binyamin Applebaum, *Treasury to Weigh Which Bills to Pay*, N.Y. TIMES, July 27, 2011, http://www.nytimes.com/2011/07/28/business/economy/treasury-to-weigh-which-bills-to-pay.html?_r=1.

[194] *See* Senate Report, *supra* note 172.

[195] Felix Salmon, *Can Treasury Prioritize Bond Payments?*, REUTERS, July 29, 2011, http://blogs.reuters.com/felix-salmon/2011/07/29/can-treasury-prioritize-bond-payments/.

[196] Jay Powell, *How Will the Federal Government Decide Who Gets Paid after August 2?*, BIPARTISAN POLICY CENTER (July 25, 2011) (available at http://www.bipartisanpolicy.org/blog/2011/07/how-will-federal-government-decide-who-gets-paid-after-august-2).

[197] Jerome Powell, *Real Implications of Debt Debate*, POLITICO, June 29, 2011, http://www.politico.com/news/stories/0611/58026.html.

[198] Ease of FIFO method should not be assumed, as Treasury's Financial Management Service only disburses 85% of government payments. *See* Financial Management Service, *Fact Sheet: Payment Management* (available at http://www.fms.treas.gov/news/factsheets/pmt_mgmt.html). The Department of Defense, the Postal Service and other independent agencies disburse the remaining sum. Coordinating receipt of bills among the various agencies for a FIFO disbursement of moneys may have presented significant difficulties.

A FIFO approach would have led to a de facto prioritization of accounts based on temporal payment. On August 2, when all borrowing authority would have been exhausted, expenses exceeded revenue by almost $3 billion.[199] Therefore, $3 billion in expenses would have carried over to August 3 to be paid before new incoming bills. On August 3, $22 billion in Social Security payments[200] would have become subject to temporal ordering, and could not have been paid in full by the end of the day, likely unleashing a political firestorm. Potentially more concerning would be the technical default on sovereign debt obligations, which would have occurred on August 5, when $1 million in interest expense came due but could not have been satisfied due to backlogged payments from August 3.[201] While delay of these relatively diminutive daily interest payments may have been excused, failing to make $32 billion in interest payments due on August 15 would have certainly qualified as a technical default.[202] Even if these payments were the first expense of the day, the obligations could not have been satisfied in full until August 25.[203] By August 31, the accumulated expense carryover figure would have amounted to $127 billion, and Treasury would have been eleven days delinquent on appropriated expenditures.[204]

---

[199] Treasury Direct, *Daily Treasury Statements*, DEP'T OF TREASURY, Aug. 2, 2011 – Aug. 31, 2011. Reflects actual figures. Aug. 3, 2011 Non-debt inflows = $6.287 billion, Expenses = $9.686 billion.
[200] *Id.*
[201] *Id.*
[202] *Id.*
[203] *Id.*
[204] *Id.* Unpaid expenses by August 31 based on inflows alone would have been equal to $127.16 billion. The first among these delinquent obligations would have been incurred on August 17, 2011. *See infra* Appendix B.

THEORY 1: THE PRESIDENT IS BOUND BY THE DEBT LIMIT, AND TREASURY MUST FOLLOW "FIRST IN, FIRST OUT" PROCEDURES	
Status of Funds utilized during DISP	DISP likely would have been extended; Funds would not have been made whole on Aug. 2
Interest Payments to Bondholders (Aug. 2 – Aug. 31)	Interest payments delayed on a FIFO basis, treated equally with all other obligations. Technical default on debt obligations as of August 5 as a result of delinquency on a $1 million interest payment.[205]
Mandatory Spending on Entitlements (Aug. 2 – Aug. 31)	Payments delayed on a FIFO basis, treated equally with all other obligations.
Appropriated Discretionary Spending (Aug. 2 – Aug. 31)	Payments delayed on a FIFO basis, treated equally with all other obligations.
Proportion of total expenses paid Aug. 2 – Aug. 31	59% [206]
Outstanding Debt on Aug. 31	$14.294 trillion, as approved in Feb. 2010 legislation

Theory 2: The President is Bound by the Debt Limit, but Treasury Can Prioritize Spending Obligations

A. The President Can Prioritize at His Discretion

If the national debt hits the statutory limit, the President may have the authority to breach his obligation to spend the money appropriated by Congress. The primary justification for prioritization is the aforementioned position of the Government Accountability Office, which reasoned that Treasury could prioritize its obligations in the public interest because no law requires a FIFO procedure.[207] In order to effectively prioritize spending obligations, OMB may "apportion" funding pursuant to the Antideficiency Act.[208]

---

[205] *Id.*
[206] *Id.* During Aug. 2 – Aug. 31, 2011: Inflows = $186.404 billion, Expenses = $313.564 billion.
[207] GAO, *supra* note 176.
[208] *See* 31 U.S.C. § 1512 (1982). The Antideficiency Act, composed of multiple statutory provisions, provides rules for federal employees with respect to appropriations. Gov't Accountability Office, *Antideficiency Act Background* (2006) (available at http://www.gao.gov/legal/

Professor Tribe argues that the President would have the authority to prioritize spending if the national debt hit the statutory limit because (1) the existing revenue sources would not allow the President to fulfill all spending obligations and (2) he does not have the power to raise revenues without congressional authorization.[209] As a result, the President's only option would be to cut spending in order to avoid a breach of the debt limit or the rules of the tax code. According to Professor Tribe, the President may be under some constraints when he chooses which obligations to prioritize. Importantly, the spirit of the impoundment crisis and its legal backlash provide an implicit prohibition against prioritizing obligations for political allies.[210]

Prioritization is a de facto choice to *not* fulfill some appropriated obligations; therefore, the President may be able to justify temporary prioritization by using the rescission or deferral provisions of the Impoundment Control Act.[211] When a spending obligation comes due that the President does not want to pay, he may propose to rescind the obligation.[212] Congress would then have forty-five days to pass a rescission bill; otherwise, the President must fulfill the obligation. Thus, even if Congress does not pass a rescission bill, the rescission proposal could buy the President forty-five days until he must spend the undesired allotment.[213] The deferral provisions of the Act would permit the President to defer spending obligations until the end of the fiscal year.[214] However, the President would have to show that the deferral proposal fits into one of the three permitted purposes stated in the Act: "(1) to provide for contingencies; (2) to achieve savings made possible by or through changes in requirements or greater efficiency of operations; or (3) as specifically provided by law."[215]

If the President attempted to achieve prioritization through deferral, he would likely seek to justify it as a provision for "contingencies"

---

lawresources/antideficiencybackground.html). *See also* Levit et al. *supra* note 171, at 8.
[209] *See* Tribe, *supra* note 144. *See also supra* Theory I.A – *The President is Bound by the Debt Limit.*
[210] *See id.*
[211] *See* Levit, et al., *supra* note 171, at 8-9.
[212] *See* 2 U.S.C. § 683(a) (1987).
[213] *See* 2 U.S.C. § 683(b) (1987).
[214] 2 U.S.C. § 684(b) (1987).
[215] *Id.*

under the Impoundment Control Act. When the D.C. Circuit in *City of New Haven v. United States* reviewed the original deferral language, it upheld "routine 'programmatic' deferrals . . . to meet the inevitable contingencies that arise in administering congressionally-funded agencies and programs," but it declared that "'policy' deferrals, which are intended to advance the broader fiscal policy objectives of the Administration," are unconstitutional.[216] The Act was amended with the "contingencies" language to reflect this distinction and permit only "programmatic" deferrals.[217] Therefore, "[d]eferrals for policy reasons are not authorized."[218]

Professor Peter Shane writes that prioritization through "programmatic deferral" would be "deeply ironic" because "the President could select expenditures to defer or not defer only by making policy judgments about spending levels that are different from the policy judgments that Congress enacted in its appropriations Acts."[219] However, Professor Shane argues that the President would have no other option and he "would have to decide, on his own initiative, what projects and activities to put on hold to keep from violating the law. Congress would thus have tacitly abdicated to the executive branch a huge swath of the power over government fiscal policy that the Framers quite deliberately vested in Congress."[220]

Partially due to the Administration's hesitance to discuss the issue during debt limit negotiations, it is unknown if the Executive Branch would have acted on this putative prioritization authority. However, it is clear that Treasury had a distaste for prioritizing.[221] Secretary

---

[216] 809 F.2d at 901. "The critical distinction between 'programmatic' and 'policy' deferrals is that the former are ordinarily intended to *advance* congressional budgetary policies by ensuring that congressional programs are administered efficiently, while the latter are ordinarily intended to *negate* the will of Congress by substituting the fiscal policies of the Executive Branch for those established by the enactment of budget legislation."

[217] See Letter from Milton J. Socolar for the Comptroller General of the United States, to the President of the Senate and the Speaker of the House of Representatives (Mar. 6, 1990) (available at http://www.gao.gov/assets/220/212244.pdf).

[218] U.S. General Accounting Office, *Principles of Federal Appropriations Law: Third Edition*, Volume I, 1-32 fn. 61.

[219] Peter M. Shane, *What May a President Do if He Cannot Pay Our Bills Without Borrowing and Borrowing More Money is Unlawful?*, SHANE REACTIONS, July 19, 2011, http://shanereactions.wordpress.com/2011/07/19/what-may-a-president-do-if-he-cannot-pay-our-bills-without-borrowing-and-borrowing-more-money-is-unlawful/.

[220] *Id.*

[221] *See, e.g.,* Geithner, *supra* note 22; Wolin, *supra* note 191.

Geithner stated that prioritization would be "unwise, unworkable, unacceptably risky, and unfair to the American people."[222] In addition to a likely political backlash that would result from any prioritization choice,[223] the markets expressed their opposition to any such scheme.[224]

If the Executive Branch had decided to prioritize, however, it would have faced an endless number of intricate political decisions in choosing which of over 80 million monthly payments[225] should be "winners" and "losers." From August 2 - August 31, 2011, revenues amounted to over $186 billion,[226] while expenses totaled almost $314 billion,[227] leaving a shortfall of $127 billion, which would normally have been provided for through continued debt issuances. There are an unlimited number of prioritization schemes that could have been chosen. For example, the President could have paid-in-full bondholders, Social Security, Medicare, Medicaid, Unemployment, Active Duty Military, Veteran's Administration, TANF, SNAP, TSA and HUD with $742 million remaining.[228] However, he would not have been able to satisfy other appropriations, including payments to Defense vendors, the Department of Education, or Federal Employee Salary and Benefits.[229]

---

[222] Salmon, *supra* note 195.
[223] *See* Greenlaw, *supra* note 71, at 3.
[224] *See, e.g.*, Jennifer Saba & Walter Brandimarte, *S&P Warns Against Prioritizing Debt Payments: Report*, REUTERS, July 26, 2011, http://www.reuters.com/article/2011/07/27/us-usa-debt-sp-idUSTRE76Q0DR20110727.
[225] Powell, *supra* note 197.
[226] Treasury Direct, *supra* note 199. Sum of Non-Debt Issuance inflows.
[227] *Id.* Sum of Outflows, excepting public debt cash redemptions.
[228] *Id.* This approach assumes revenue smoothing over the course of the month. Not all chosen expenses could have been paid on their given due date.
[229] *Id.*

Theory 2A: The President is Bound by the Debt Limit, but Can Prioritize at His Discretion	
Status of Funds utilized during DISP	DISP likely would have been extended; Funds would not have been made whole on Aug. 2
Interest Payments to Bondholders (Aug. 2 – Aug. 31)	Likely to be prioritized and paid as scheduled ($38 billion)[230]
Mandatory Spending on Entitlements (Aug. 2 – Aug. 31)	Likely to be prioritized and paid as scheduled (Social Security: $51 billion; Medicare: $32 billion)[231]
Appropriated Discretionary Spending (Aug. 2 – Aug. 31)	34%[232] of discretionary expenses could have been prioritized for payment at the Executive's discretion, after payment on interest and entitlements.
Proportion of total expenses paid Aug. 2 – Aug. 31	59%[233]
Outstanding Debt on Aug. 31	$14.294 trillion, as approved in Feb. 2010 legislation

B. The President Must Prioritize Bondholder Payments

If the President is bound by the debt limit, the Public Debt Clause may provide a directive to prioritize "public debt."[234] Most academics agree that "public debt" includes bond payments.[235] However, others advocate a broader interpretation of "public debt" to include statutory spending commitments or all contractual obligations.[236] A concern arising from a broader interpretation is that, if "public debt" includes all statutory spending commitments, the Public Debt

---

[230] *Id.*

[231] *Id.*

[232] *Id.* Inflows of $186.404 billion - $37.951 billion in interest payments - $31.793 billion in Medicare expenses - $51.214 billion in Social Security expenses = $65.446 billion in remaining revenue for $192.606 billion in expenses

[233] *Id.* Inflows = $186.404 billion, Expenses = $313.564 billion during Aug. 2 – Aug. 31, 2011.

[234] *See* Tribe, *supra* note 144. Various interpretations of "public debt" would determine which payments must be prioritized. While the government would not be able to fulfill all obligations pursuant to a broad interpretation, inclusive of all obligations, it may be able to prioritize "public debt" if it includes only bond payments or bond payments and "contractual" obligations.

[235] *See, e.g.,* Abramowicz, *supra* note 103, at 20.

[236] *See, e.g.,* Buchanan, *supra* note 107.

Clause may prevent Congress from rescinding or altering a statutory appropriation;[237] an interpretation that allowed for such a conclusion would not be plausible. Using the same logic, Professor Tribe argues that "public debt" cannot include Social Security payments because, in *Flemming v. Nestor*,[238] "the Supreme Court held that Congress could revise or repeal Social Security Act benefits even though they had already been promised by prior legislation."[239] While some academics argue that "public debt" protects all contractual obligations,[240] Social Security beneficiaries contributed taxes, rather than voluntary payments pursuant to an agreement, and they have not signed a written contract.[241]

In response to the argument that current "pensions" are part of the "public debt," proponents of a narrow interpretation contend that, due to the fear that southern Democrats would refuse to pay back war debts, the "pensions and bounties" phrase[242] was only necessary to provide an unambiguous indication that those debts could not be questioned.[243] On that view, the "including" phrase is limited to those unique situations that involve the Civil War or, in a broader view, the suppression of insurrections.

This narrow construction of the Fourteenth Amendment to support favoring only bondholder payments was widely discussed as a valid form of prioritization throughout the 2011 impasse.[244] On April 25, 2011, in anticipation of reaching the debt limit, Matthew Zames, Chairman of the Treasury Borrowing Advisory Committee and a Managing Director at J.P. Morgan Chase, wrote Secretary Geithner, warning that "any delay in making an interest or principal payment by Treasury even for a very short period of time . . . could trigger

---

[237] *See* Abramowicz, *supra* note 103, at 43-44.
[238] 363 U.S. 603 (1960).
[239] Tribe, *supra* note 144.
[240] *See* Abramowicz, *supra* note 103, at 20-21.
[241] *Id.* at 43-44. Although the contributions to Social Security and Medicare are tied to the benefits received, they are a tax rather than a contractual agreement. *Id.*
[242] U.S. Const. amend. XIV, § 4: "The validity of the public debt of the United States, authorized by law, *including debts incurred for payment of pensions and bounties for services in suppressing insurrection or rebellion*, shall not be questioned." (emphasis added).
[243] *See* Abramowicz, *supra* note 103, at 20.
[244] Letter from Jim DeMint, et. al., U.S. Senate, to Timothy Geithner, Secretary of the Treasury (May 26, 2011) (available at http://www.demint.senate.gov/public/index.cfm?ContentRecord_id=7371d3a9-9435-4277-87ef-330fcf689087&p=PressReleases).

another catastrophic financial crisis."[245] However, it is unclear if Treasury would have acted on its presumptive authority to prioritize these payments. In responding to Senator Jim DeMint's suggestion that inflows should be used to pay interest only, Secretary Geithner wrote that the "idea is starkly at odds with the judgment of every previous Administration, regardless of party, that has faced debt limit impasses."[246] Deputy Secretary of the Treasury Neal Wolin insisted that prioritizing bondholders would simply cause "default by another name" and would be recognized by the world as a "failure by the U.S. to stand behind its commitments."[247]

Despite this purported stance, on July 28, 2011, a report, based on a statement from an anonymous administration official, asserted that Treasury would give priority to bondholder interest payments if lawmakers failed to raise the debt limit.[248] The statement was likely made to reassure the markets.[249] However, it is unclear if Treasury would have followed through on this plan, and it is unknown if and how they would have further prioritized payments, as the administration was reluctant to discuss such plans for fear it would relieve pressure on Congress to reach an agreement.[250]

Prioritizing bondholder payments alone would have prevented technical default, as inflows were sufficient to satisfy this obligation. From August 2 - August 31, Treasury paid $38 billion of interest

---

[245] Letter from Matthew Zames, Chairman of the Treasury Borrowing Advisory Committee, to Timothy Geithner, Secretary of the Treasury (Apr. 25, 2011), (http://www.treasury.gov/resource-center/data-chart-center/quarterly-refunding/Documents/Geithner_Debt_Limit_Letter_4_25_11E.pdf. Zames cited fears of contagion, possibly prompting runs on money market funds, and warned of potential increases in Treasury borrowing costs over the long term. Zames' concerns regarding increased borrowing rates for taxpayers are supported by D. Andrew Austin & Rena S. Miller, *Treasury Securities and the U.S. Sovereign Credit Default Swap Market*, CONG. RESEARCH SERV. 15 (Aug. 15, 2011), http://www.fas.org/sgp/crs/misc/R41932.pdf. In fact, one study cited claims that after the U.S. missed a payment on T-bills in 1979, the government borrowed at a 60bp premium for years afterward.

[246] Geithner, *supra* note 190. Further, Geithner wrote, "[y]our letter is based on an untested and unacceptably risky assumption: that if the United States were to continue to pay interest on its debt – yet failed to pay legally required obligations to its citizens, servicemen and women, and businesses – there would be no adverse market reaction and no damage to the full faith and credit of the United States."

[247] Wolin, *supra* note 191.

[248] Peter Cook and Cheyenne Hopkins, *U.S. Contingency Plan Said to Give Priority to Bondholders*, BLOOMBERG, July 28, 2011, http://www.bloomberg.com/news/2011-07-28/u-s-contingency-plan-gives-bondholders-priority.html.

[249] *See id.*

[250] *Id.*

on government bonds,[251] leaving $148 billion in inflows to pay $276 billion in obligations.[252] Presumably, the remainder of these obligations would have been made using a FIFO approach.[253] Notably, protecting from technical default alone may not have been sufficient to prevent a negative market reaction, especially in light of the CDS definition of "credit event," which includes failure to pay any "obligation."[254]

Theory 2B: The President Must Prioritize Bondholder Payments	
Status of Funds utilized during DISP	DISP likely would have been extended; Funds would not have been made whole on Aug. 2
Interest Payments to Bondholders (Aug. 2 – Aug. 31)	Paid, as scheduled ($38 billion)[255]
Mandatory Spending on Entitlements (Aug. 2 – Aug. 31)	With no authority to prioritize, entitlements would likely be subject to a FIFO payment scheme
Appropriated Discretionary Spending (Aug. 2 – Aug. 31)	With no authority to prioritize, discretionary expenses would likely be subject to a FIFO payment scheme
Proportion of total expenses paid Aug. 2 – Aug. 31	59% (54% of non-interest expenses)[256]
Outstanding Debt on Aug. 31	$14.294 trillion, as approved in Feb. 2010 legislation

---

[251] Treasury Direct, *supra* note 199.
[252] *Id.*
[253] *See supra* Theory 1. Prioritizing interest would have presented a unique difficulty under a FIFO approach in that $32 billion was due to be paid on Aug. 15. Inflows from that day alone would have been insufficient to make such a payment. Therefore, funds would have to have been set-aside in advance, prioritizing a future payment over payments already due.
[254] *See* Austin & Miller, *supra* note 245 at 11-12; *see also* International Swaps and Derivatives Association, *CDS on US Sovereign Debt Q&A*, http://www2.isda.org/news/cds-on-us-sovereign-debt-qampa. "A CDS is triggered when a Credit Event occurs. There are three Credit Events that are typically used for Sovereigns such as the United States. They are: Failure to Pay; Repudiation/Moratorium and Restructuring . . . . 'Failure to Pay means, after the expiration of any applicable Grace Period . . . . the failure by a Reference Entity to make, when and where due, any payments in an aggregate amount of not less that the Payment requirement under one or more *Obligations*, in accordance with the terms of such Obligation at the time of such failure.'" (emphasis added). The grace period for U.S. CDS is 3 days. The U.S. CDS market is relatively small, and exposures are limited, so the triggering of CDS alone would not be a large threat to the economy at this time. However, if the U.S. CDS market grows, or if the broader market is afflicted with contagion concerns upon a triggering event, the danger to the U.S. economy could be large, despite continued payment on the reference entity (Treasury securities).

C. The President Must Prioritize Bond Payments and Other "Obligations"

"[P]ublic debt" may refer to certain obligations with a wider scope than mere bond payments and a narrower scope than all statutory obligations. Professor Abramowicz proposes a definition of "public debt" which is limited to statutory "agreements" and excludes "gratuitous promises."[257] Social Security may be included because the trust fund is constituted in part by recipients' tax payments, and future beneficiaries may rely on these payments.[258] It is unclear whether Medicare fits the form of an agreement because its contributions and benefits are more attenuated than Social Security.[259] Under this interpretation, the Public Debt Clause would also protect the discretionary programs that represent contractual obligations, such as payments owed to contractors or pension funds.[260]

Professor Calvin Massey argues that the "pensions and bounties" phrase of the Public Debt Clause[261] provides an indication of what is included within the scope of "public debt."[262] Under this interpretation, the President has a constitutional obligation to prioritize bond payments and "old-age pensions under Social Security, military pensions, and other federal pensions."[263]

---

[255] Treasury Direct, *supra* note 199.

[256] *Id.* During Aug. 2 – Aug. 31, 2011: Inflows = $186.404 billion, Expenses = $313.564 billion, Interest Expense = $37.951 billion.

[257] Abramowicz, *supra* note 103, at 19-21. Professor Abramowicz explains, "[f]irst, a government promise is "authorized by law" only if it is contained in a congressional statute. Second, a debt is "[a] sum of money due by certain and express agreement." Applying this definition to the Public Debt Clause, the United States incurs a public debt only if a statute embodies an agreement, or, more restrictively, only if the government issues a written agreement. Since a gratuitous promise does not ordinarily constitute a legally enforceable agreement, the Clause would be further limited to governmental promises made in exchange for good consideration." *Id.* at 20-21.

[258] *Id.* at 36.

[259] *Id.* Medicare "Part B, offering supplemental medical insurance, is funded primarily through general tax revenues." *Id.* at 36 n.156.

[260] *Id.* at 35-36. "For example, government civil-service pension payments and money owed to independent contractors represent unambiguous obligations that the government owes because of past agreements in which the debt-holders have already fulfilled their part of the bargains."

[261] U.S. Const. amend. XIV, § 4: "The validity of the public debt of the United States, authorized by law, *including debts incurred for payment of pensions and bounties for services in suppressing insurrection or rebellion*, shall not be questioned." (emphasis added).

[262] *See* Massey, *supra* note 141.

[263] *Id.*

Prioritizing Social Security payments became a key flashpoint of the public debate between the President and congressional Republicans during the 2011 debt impasse. While some in Washington contended that the President had the legal authority to at least prioritize Social Security payments,[264] the President stated, "I cannot guarantee that [Social Security] checks go out on August 3 if we haven't resolved this issue, because there may simply not be the money in the coffers to do it."[265] In response, Speaker of the House John Boehner stated "the Treasury Secretary is going to have options in terms of who should be paid and who shouldn't . . . . [T]here are some debts that have to be rolled over. But there's going to be money available on August 3, and I think it's way too early to be making some types of veiled threats like that."[266]

Even if payment were restricted only to interest and Social Security, this interpretation of "obligations" would have created challenges just one day after all borrowing authority was exhausted. On August 3, 2011, when $22 billion of Social Security payments were due, Treasury would have been $3.5 billion short of paying these two line items in full.[267] This gap would have been filled the next day through new inflows;[268] however, damage from such a "default" already may have been done. At the end of the month, under this prioritization scheme, Treasury could have made all required payments on interest and Social Security if inflows were smoothed, with only $97 billion remaining to pay $224 billion in other obligations.[269]

---

[264] *See, e.g., Social Security Checks Could Be Delayed Without Debt-Ceiling Deal*, FOXNEWS.COM, July 13, 2011, http://www.foxnews.com/politics/2011/07/13/report-backs-obama-warning-that-social-security-checks-at-risk-in-debt-crisis/#ixzz1pu12fdjo ("Rep. Tim Huelskamp, R-Kansas, said Wednesday that if the administration were to withhold Social Security payments, it would be a 'political decision' because there are 'sufficient receipts' to cover the checks.").
[265] *See, e.g.* Politifact, *supra* note 192.
[266] FOXNEWS.COM, *supra* note 264.
[267] Treasury Direct, *supra* note 199. Non-Debt revenues for Aug. 2 & Aug. 3 = $18.537 billion. Interest and Social Security Expense = $22.023 billion.
[268] *Id.* Aug. 4 Revenues = $3.546 billion. Aug. 4 new Social Security and Interest Expense = $64 million.
[269] *Id.* Other payments likely to be made under a FIFO approach. Non-prioritized payments would be delayed in favor of the prioritized programs.

THEORY 2C: PRESIDENT MUST PRIORITIZE BONDHOLDER PAYMENTS AND OTHER "OBLIGATIONS"	
Status of Funds utilized during DISP	DISP likely would have been extended; Funds would not have been made whole on Aug. 2
Interest Payments to Bondholders (Aug.2 – Aug. 31)	Paid, as scheduled ($38 billion)[270]
Mandatory Spending on Entitlements (Aug. 2 – Aug. 31)	Social Security likely to be paid as scheduled ($51 billion).[271] Medicare less likely to be deemed an "obligation."
Appropriated Discretionary Spending (Aug. 2 – Aug. 31)	Expenses deemed "obligations" would be paid (e.g., government pensions, previously incurred contractual expenses)
Proportion of total expenses paid Aug. 2 – Aug. 31	59% (43% of non-interest and Social Security expenses)[272]
Outstanding Debt on Aug. 31	$14.294 trillion, as approved in Feb. 2010 legislation

D. Social Security and Medicare Trust Fund Redemptions Could Enable Payments After Reaching the Statutory Debt Limit

The President may not be forced to develop a prioritization scheme that ensures payments to Social Security beneficiaries after reaching the debt limit; instead, the Executive Branch may provide for such payments by redeeming obligations possessed by the Social Security Trust Funds.[273] In November 1985, when the government reached the debt limit, Secretary of the Treasury James Baker redeemed nearly $15 billion of Treasury securities held by the Social Security Trust Funds in order to pay beneficiaries.[274] This maneuver lowered the outstanding debt subject to the limit by the amount of the redemption, and simultaneously allowed for new borrowing at that

---
[270] *Id.*
[271] *Id.*
[272] *Id.* Inflows – Interest and Social Security = $97.239 billion. Outflows – Interest and Social Security = $224.399 billion.
[273] Nancy Altman & Mark S. Scarberry, *Disentangling Social Security from the Debt Ceiling*, HUFFINGTON POST, July 20, 2011, http://www.huffingtonpost.com/nancy-altman/disentangling-social-secu_b_905227.html.
[274] Letter from Charles Bowsher, Comptroller General of the United States, to James R. Jones, Chairman, Subcommittee on Social Security, Committee on Ways and Means, House of Representatives (Dec. 5, 1985) (available at http://archive.gao.gov/d12t3/128621.pdf).

amount in order to pay beneficiaries.[275] The Comptroller General later investigated the validity of this maneuver and implicitly upheld the principle of Trust Fund redemptions to pay Social Security benefits, as long as such redemptions are undertaken at the precise amount and speed "absolutely necessary" to effect benefit payments.[276] The following year, in a proposed debt limit increase bill, the Senate Finance Committee introduced a provision that would have expressly "prohibit[ed] the Secretary of the Treasury, in his role as Managing Trustee of the Social Security trust funds, from engaging in premature redemption of securities held by the trust funds during a debt limit crisis *even if such redemption were required in order to pay beneficiaries.*"[277] This bill was not passed.[278]

Following the 1995-1996 debt limit impasse, Congress enacted a provision that effectively codified the Comptroller General's opinion.[279] The "Protection of Social Security and Medicare Trust Funds" provision proscribes the use of these Funds to create general "headroom" during a DISP,[280] but ostensibly allows for public debt obligations held by the Trust Funds to be redeemed prior to maturity for the purpose of "payment of benefits or administrative expenses."[281] This authority, however, does not give the Secretary the legal authority to continue to invest incoming Social Security receipts in Treasury securities if the debt limit has been reached.[282]

---

[275] Michael McConnell, *Three Common Legal Misunderstandings About the Debt Ceiling*, ADVANCING A FREE SOCIETY, THE HOOVER INSTITUTION, July 28, 2011, http://www.advancingafreesociety.org/2011/07/28/three-common-legal-misunderstandings-about-the-debt-ceiling/.

[276] Bowsher, *supra* note 274. The Comptroller found that "it appears, on the basis of the information now available, that the Secretary redeemed or failed to invest the Trust Funds' assets in amounts and for periods of time greater than *absolutely necessary* to pay social security benefits." (emphasis added). The Comptroller, however, found that such actions by the Secretary were reasonable under these specific circumstances.

[277] S. Rep. No 99-335, at 7 (1986). Emphasis added.

[278] H.R.J.Res.668, 99th Cong. (1986).

[279] McConnell, *supra* note 275.

[280] 42 U.S.C. § 1320b–15, *supra* note 30.

[281] *Id.* Statute precludes "redeem[ing] prior to maturity amounts. . . . which are invested in public debt obligations *for any purpose other than* the payment of benefits or administrative expenses." (emphasis added).

[282] Jeffrey Kunkel, Social Security Administration Chief Actuary, *Social Security Trust Fund Investment Policies and Practices, Actuarial Note No. 142*, 3. *See supra* note 181, 182. In 1996, Congress passed a bill to allow for continued investment of these receipts in excess of the debt limit. Without similar legislation enabling investment of receipts, the Secretary would be violating 42 U.S.C. 1320b-15 by not investing receipts immediately.

The use of Trust Fund redemptions in order to make Social Security beneficiary payments was not widely discussed during the 2011 impasse. Both the President and Secretary Boehner discussed Social Security in the context of prioritization[283] and indicated that it was possible that Social Security benefit payments would be interrupted.[284] However, it is possible that the Executive Branch could have invoked this redemption exception in order to create the borrowing authority necessary to guarantee Social Security benefit payments without exceeding the statutory debt limit.[285]

THEORY 2D: SOCIAL SECURITY AND MEDICARE TRUST FUND REDEMPTIONS COULD ENABLE PAYMENTS AFTER REACHING THE STATUTORY DEBT LIMIT	
Status of Funds utilized during DISP	DISP likely would have been extended; Funds would not have been made whole on Aug. 2
Interest Payments to Bondholders (Aug. 2 – Aug. 31)	May be subject to either prioritization or FIFO procedures
Mandatory Spending on Entitlements (Aug. 2 – Aug. 31)	Social Security Trust Fund obligations redeemed to pay beneficiaries as scheduled ($51 billion).[286] Medicare Trust Fund obligations redeemed to pay beneficiaries as scheduled ($32 billion).[287]
Appropriated Discretionary Spending (Aug. 2 – Aug. 31)	May be subject to either prioritization or FIFO procedures
Proportion of total expenses paid Aug. 2 – Aug. 31	86% (100% of Social Security and Medicare expenses; 81% of non-Social Security and Medicare expenses)[288]
Outstanding Debt on Aug. 31	$14.294 trillion, as approved in Feb. 2010 legislation. No difference, in overall debt. As the balance held by the Trust Funds decreases, an off-setting increase in Debt held by the Public would occur.

---

[283] *See supra* Theory 2C.
[284] Altman & Scarberry, *supra* note 273.
[285] Thomas Saving, Op. Ed., *Obama's Debt Ceiling Scare Tactics*, WALL ST. J., July 22, 2011, http://online.wsj.com/article/SB10001424053111903554904576458294273264416.html?mod=opinion_newsreel ("[M]eeting Social Security obligations in August, September and all future months in this fashion would add nothing to the gross government debt subject to the debt limit. Not, at least, until the $2.4 trillion Trust Fund is exhausted in 2038.").
[286] Treasury Direct, *supra* note 199.
[287] *Id.* Assumes that Medicare Trust Fund would operate in the same fashion as Social Security Trust Fund redemptions, given that the Medicare trust fund is included in 42 U.S.C. § 1320b-15.
[288] *Id.* Assumes that none of the incoming revenues would be put toward Social Security or

Theory 3: The President Can Ignore the Debt Limit

Several legal mechanisms exist to justify further borrowing in excess of the debt limit.

A. The Debt Limit is Unconstitutional

The constraints of the Public Debt Clause may require the President to breach the debt limit. The President may argue that the debt limit is unconstitutional because it "question[s]" the "validity of the public debt" either (1) on its face because its existence makes default possible; or (2) at the point that the national debt hits the statutory limit because the debt limit prevents further borrowing to satisfy statutory obligations.[289] Alternatively, the President may argue that a strategy of threatening to refuse to extend the debt limit is unconstitutional.[290]

The argument for the unconstitutionality of the debt limit depends on an interpretation of "questioned" that is broader than "repudiation" and inclusive of either "default" or acts that jeopardize[291] the "validity

---

Medicare payments to beneficiaries. Thus, Social Security and Medicare trust funds would be depleted by the amount needed for beneficiary payments, as would the outstanding debt subject to the limit. Treasury could then use the additional "headroom" to borrow the corresponding amount to pay beneficiaries. This would increase the percentage of general expenses that could be paid using inflows.

[289] See supra Section II.A.2 – *The Fourteenth Amendment.*

[290] See Jack Balkin, *Secretary Geithner understands the Constitution: The Republicans are violating the Fourteenth Amendment*, BALKINIZATION, July 8, 2011, http://balkin.blogspot.com/2011/07/secretary-geithner-understands.html. During the debt limit impasse in 2011, Professor Balkin argued that the "strategy of congressional leaders in the Republican Party violates the Constitution because they are threatening to take us over a cliff in order to push their radical policy agenda." Professor Balkin suggested that the argument against the constitutionality of the threat could be a political boon for the President and a means of applying pressure on Congress to extend the debt limit without further threats. However, he warned that the constitutional argument must be made early and often, and a failure to clarify this point may "virtually guarantee[] that this same hostage taking strategy will be used repeatedly whenever a House of Congress controlled by one party wants to stick it to a White House controlled by the other." Professor Balkin substantiates his point by referring to Senator Wade's speech about his proposed amendment, *see infra* Appendix C, to demonstrate that the purpose of the Public Debt Clause was to "remove threats of default on federal debts from partisan struggles." Jack Balkin, *The Legislative History of Section Four of the Fourteenth Amendment*, BALKINIZATION, June 30, 2011, http://balkin.blogspot.com/2011/06/legislative-history-of-section-four-of.html.

[291] See Abramowicz, *supra* note 103, at 24.

of the public debt."[292] Proponents of this interpretation point to the political context after the Civil War[293] to show that the northern Republicans framed the Public Debt Clause to prevent the southern Democrats from excusing their war debts, and the distinction between repudiation and default was irrelevant to their goal.[294] They also argue that an interpretation which limits "questioned" to "repudiation" is redundant because the Court in *Perry* reasoned that debt repudiation is unconstitutional without the Public Debt Clause.[295] Finally, they look to linguistic hints within the Public Debt Clause, including its passive construction,[296] and to the change from the initial proposed language,[297] which used "inviolable" instead of "questioned,"[298] to suggest a broad reading of "questioned."

In response to the argument that a broad interpretation of "questioned" presents a slippery slope in which any act that increases the risk of default might be unconstitutional,[299] Professor Neil Buchanan responds that "[a]n increase in the nation's level of debt does nothing to increase the probability of default because the definition of default is the inability to repay obligations on the terms to which the parties have agreed. No matter how large the debt, the possibility of default remains zero, so long as there is no debt limit."[300]

---

[292] If the national debt hit the statutory limit and the United States was no longer able to satisfy its interest payments to bondholders, the likely consequence would be that the government would "default" on its debt until the government raised the debt limit rather than openly "repudiate" its obligations. "Roughly speaking, to repudiate a debt means that you state that you are not going to pay it and that you don't owe the money. Defaulting on a debt means that you aren't able to perform, but you still acknowledge that you owe the money." Balkin, *supra* note 146.

[293] *See infra* Appendix C.

[294] *See* Balkin, *supra* note 290.

[295] *See infra* Appendix D. *See also* Abramowicz, *supra* note 103, at 15.

[296] Professor Abramowicz argues, "[q]uestioning a proposition is not equivalent to insisting that the proposition is false but merely entails suggesting that it might be." *Id.* at 24. The passive construction of the Public Debt Clause may also "allow[] for a reading . . . containing a reassuring promise from the Framers to bondholders" and "make[] the Clause more evocative than descriptive, more like an announcement of a general principle of debt validity than like a technical rule barring failure to make debt payments." *Id.* at 25.

[297] This was the proposal by Senator Ben Wade. *See infra* Appendix C.

[298] The replacement of "inviolable" with "questioned" may "sugges[t] a preference for phraseology that protects the public debt so strongly as to put the government's commitment to it beyond question" by "precluding government action that makes default possible." Abramowicz, *supra* note 103, at 27.

[299] *See* Tribe, *supra* note 110.

[300] Buchanan, *supra* note 109. Professor Buchanan's argument is dependent on the combination of statutes through which appropriations bills and mandatory spending programs outpace

Depending on the revenues relative to spending obligations,[301] the argument for the unconstitutionality of the debt limit may depend on a broad reading of "public debt." The "pensions and bounties" phrase of the Public Debt Clause[302] may bolster the argument that "public debt" includes more than bond payments.[303] The *Perry* Court indicates that the Public Debt Clause protects "the integrity of the public obligations,"[304] which may include all statutory spending obligations.[305] Professor Buchanan cites *United States v. Winstar Corp.*[306] and *Cherokee Nation of Oklahoma v. Leavitt*[307] to support the proposition that "statutory spending obligations are legally binding commitments that the government . . . cannot ignore once it has committed to pay the funds."[308]

B. The President's Emergency Powers Justify Further Borrowing

The President may justify unilateral borrowing by asserting his emergency powers.[309] If the market responds negatively to the debt limit, the President may argue that he must borrow money to allay the concerns of investors. In support of this general proposition,

---

other revenue streams. As a result (on the assumption that the President cannot unilaterally raise taxes), borrowing money would be the only way to avoid the possibility of default if the national debt hits the statutory limit.

[301] If tax revenues allow the President to fulfill all of the obligations protected by the Public Debt Clause, the debt limit may not present constitutionality issues.

[302] U.S. Const. amend. XIV, § 4: "The validity of the public debt of the United States, authorized by law, *including debts incurred for payment of pensions and bounties for services in suppressing insurrection or rebellion*, shall not be questioned." (emphasis added).

[303] *See* Abramowicz, *supra* note 103, at 19. Professor Abramowicz states, "the 'including' phrase indicates that the Framers conceived the 'public debt' as including not just financial instruments, but also such promises as war pensions and bounties." *Id.* He further argues that "[t]he word 'debts' draws a parallel with the phrase 'public debt,' suggesting that the Framers naturally thought of pensions and bounties as being part of the 'public debt.'"

[304] *See infra* Appendix D.

[305] *See* Neil H. Buchanan, *The Debt-Limit Crisis: A Problem That Will Keep Coming Back Unless President Obama Takes a Constitutional Stand Now*, VERDICT, July 7, 2011, http://verdict.justia.com/2011/07/07/the-debt-limit-crisis.

[306] 518 U.S. 839 (1996).

[307] 543 U.S. 631 (2005).

[308] Buchanan, *supra* note 107. Professor Buchanan further asserts that a narrow interpretation of "public debt" is less logical because the debt we currently owe would not include interest payments, which are "simply a contractual commitment," while the principal payments would remain the only debt already incurred.

[309] The President is vested with the "executive Power," U.S. Const. Art. II, Sec.1, swears that he will "preserve, protect, and defend the Constitution of the United States," *id.*, serves as the Commander-in-Chief, U.S. Const. Art. II, Sec. 2, and "take[s] Care that the Laws be faithfully executed," U.S. Const. Art. II, Sec. 3.

Professor Balkin[310] and Professors Eric Posner and Adrian Vermeule[311] cite the suspension of habeas corpus by President Abraham Lincoln during the Civil War. Professor Richard Pildes responded to Professors Posner and Vermeule by arguing that unilateral borrowing by the President would cause similar consequences to a default.[312] According to Professor Pildes, unilateral borrowing could result in economic turmoil both domestically and in the world economy because "the country would have been tied in knots for a year or more about whether the President had acted unconstitutionally; impeachment surely would have loomed; and it is unclear who would have bought U.S. debt, and at what price, given all the legal uncertainty that would have existed about whether the President had issued the debt lawfully."[313] Professor Balkin warned that "the President has the power to act *as a default rule* in emergencies," but "he must ask Congress for retroactive authorization of what he has done" and, "without subsequent authorization, it would be illegal."[314]

C. The President Must Obey Statutory Spending Commitments Rather Than the Debt Limit

The President may base his authority to borrow on a theory of statutory interpretation. Because Congress has passed an appropriations bill and has set revenue levels with a tax code and a debt limit, the President must breach one of the following if the national debt hits the statutory limit: (1) the obligation to spend all money appropriated by Congress; (2) the obligation to tax at the levels provided by Congress; or (3) the obligation to borrow money without hitting the debt limit.[315] The President may be able to breach his duty to borrow within the debt limit because the spending

---

[310] *See* Jack Balkin, *Under What Circumstances Can the President Ignore the Debt Ceiling?*, BALKINIZATION. July 6, 2011, http://balkin.blogspot.com/2011/07/under-what-circumstances-can-president.html.
[311] *See* Eric A. Posner and Adrian Vermeule, Op-Ed, *Obama Should Raise the Debt Ceiling on His Own*, N.Y. TIMES, July 22, 2011, http://www.nytimes.com/2011/07/22/opinion/22posner.html. "[President Lincoln] said that it was necessary to violate one law, lest all the laws but one fall into ruin."
[312] Richard H. Pildes, *Book Review: Law and the President*, 125 HARV. L. REV. 1381, 1411 (2012).
[313] *Id.*
[314] Balkin, *supra* note 310.
[315] *See* Buchanan, *supra* note 107.

obligations have been defended through the impoundment crisis and the decision in *Clinton*,[316] and the prohibition on unilateral taxation is foundational in our country's history.[317] An alternative statutory argument holds that an appropriations bill, if later in time than the most recent debt limit increase, may implicitly supersede the debt limit.[318]

D. 2011 Impasse: Debt Limit Would Not Likely Have Been Repudiated

It is unclear whether or not President Obama would have invoked any of these arguments to repudiate the debt limit statute, if the BCA had not been passed on August 2, 2011, but it appears unlikely. On May 25, 2011, Secretary Geithner read the 14th Amendment aloud at a public event when discussing the debt limit negotiations,[319] signaling to some that the Executive Branch was considering invoking this authority.[320] However, in an official statement on July 8, Treasury General Counsel George Madison stated that Secretary Geithner "never argued that the 14th Amendment to the U.S. Constitution allows the President to disregard the statutory debt limit."[321] Instead,

---

[316] *See id.* Professor Buchanan argues that, as between the power to borrow money and spend money, Congress has more zealously guarded its power to control appropriations. In contrast to the Impoundment Control Act and its subsequent protection by the courts, debt limit extensions were relatively routine occurrences before 2011. Furthermore, Professor Buchanan asserts that a "reasonable Congress" would prefer that the President continue to borrow money in excess of the debt limit rather than cancel spending to vital programs, including Medicaid.

[317] *See* Tribe, *supra* note 144.

[318] *See* Zachary A. Goldfarb, *Obama, Democrats not ready to play 14th Amendment card with debt ceiling*, WASH. POST, July 6, 2011, http://www.washingtonpost.com/business/economy/obama-democrats-not-ready-to-play-14th-amendment-card-with-debt-ceiling/2011/07/06/gIQAVU1O1H_story.html. The argument is set forth by Professor Larry Rosenthal.

[319] *Tim Geithner: 14th Amendment Says Debt 'Shall Not Be Questioned'*, HUFFINGTON POST first posted June 30, 2011, updated on Aug. 30, 2011 (available at http://www.huffingtonpost.com/2011/06/30/tim-geithner-14th-amendment_n_887925.html). The clip can be viewed in the C-SPAN video at the 39-minute mark. After reading the Public Debt Clause, he criticized the tactics of Republican leaders, which he characterized as follows: "If you don't do things my way, I'm going to force the United States to default--not pay the legacy of bills accumulated by my predecessors in Congress." Geithner responded to this perception, stating that "it's not a credible negotiating strategy, *and it's not going to happen.*" (emphasis added).

[320] *See e.g.,* Tribe, *supra* note 110.

[321] Erika Gudmundson, *FACT CHECK: Treasury General Counsel George Madison Responds to New York Times Op-Ed on 14th Amendment Statement*, DEP'T OF TREASURY, (July 8, 2011) (available at http://www.treasury.gov/connect/blog/Pages/FACT-CHECK-Treasury-General-Counsel-George-Madison-Responds-to-New-York-Times-Op-Ed-on-14th-Amendment.aspx).

Madison wrote, "[l]ike every previous Secretary of the Treasury who has confronted the question, Secretary Geithner has always viewed the debt limit as a binding legal constraint that can only be raised by Congress."[322] On June 29, when asked about invoking the Fourteenth Amendment if negotiations to raise the debt limit proved unsuccessful, President Obama responded, "I'm not a Supreme Court Justice, so I'm not going to put my constitutional law professor hat on here."[323] However, it appears that a decision to invoke the Public Debt Clause in order to repudiate the statutory limit may have been supported by several political leaders, including House Minority Leader Nancy Pelosi and former President Bill Clinton.[324]

If the President repudiated the debt limit statute as unconstitutional on any legal theory, Treasury presumably would have continued to spend on August 2 as authorized under the appropriations continuing resolution.[325] Effectively, such a decision would have required no departure from the actual inflows, outflows, or borrowing observed when the BCA was enacted. The Funds utilized to create headroom through "extraordinary measures" would likely have been made whole, new debt auctions would have proceeded, and spending presumably would have been unaffected. Therefore, as seen in reality, the debt would have increased to $238 billion on August 2 after repaying the Funds, and would have continued to increase to $14.639 trillion by the end of August 2011.[326] The President's decision to repudiate the debt limit statute would not have been without predictable adverse consequences. At the very least, the cloud of uncertainty surrounding such unprecedented, unilateral executive action may have significantly raised interest rates on new debt issued.[327]

---

[322] Gudmundson, *supra* note 321.
[323] Huffington Post, *supra* note 319.
[324] Matthew Yglesias, *Nancy Pelosi Calls for Constitutional Abrogation of the Debt Ceiling*, SLATE. COM, June 20, 2012, http://www.slate.com/blogs/moneybox/2012/06/20/pelosi_says_14th_amendment_makes_the_debt_ceiling_unconstitutional.html.
[325] Pub. L. No. 112-10: Department of Defense and Full-Year Continuing Appropriations Act, 2011 became law on Apr. 15, 2011.
[326] Treasury Direct, *supra* note 199. Reflects the actual increase in the debt after the BCA was passed and the debt limit was increased.
[327] *See e.g.,* Kathy A. Ruffing & Chad Stone, *Separating the Debt Limit from the Deficit Problem*, CENTER ON BUDGET AND POLICY PRIORITIES 1 (July 21, 2011) ("History shows that even the uncertainty surrounding a debt limit increase can raise interest rates.").

THEORY 3: THE PRESIDENT CAN IGNORE THE DEBT LIMIT	
Status of Funds utilized during DISP	With repudiation of debt limit, Funds likely would have been made whole on Aug. 2
Interest Payments to Bondholders (Aug. 2 – Aug. 31)	Paid as scheduled, with no interruptions
Mandatory Spending on Entitlements (Aug. 2 – Aug. 31)	Paid as scheduled, with no interruptions
Appropriated Discretionary Spending (Aug. 2 – Aug. 31)	Paid in conformity with continuing resolution
Proportion of total expenses paid Aug. 2 – Aug. 31	100%
Outstanding Debt on Aug. 31	$14.639 trillion ($345 billion above the debt limit)[328]

Theory 4: The President is Bound by the Debt Limit and Statutory Spending Obligations

If the President is bound by the debt limit, and Treasury does not use a First In, First Out approach, some alternative legal theories may allow the President to ground his decisions through implicit statutory preferences or directives.

A. Congressional Silence Implies a Pro Rata Approach

The President may elect to use a pro rata spending approach in which the Executive Branch calculates the projected revenues relative to spending obligations and cuts the same percentage from each obligation. Although OMB typically uses its apportionment authority to prevent agencies from exhausting their budget authority, it may attempt to use apportionment procedures to issue funds at a lower rate pursuant to the Antideficiency Act.[329] However, apportionment authority is under the same constraints as deferral authority, and

---

[328] Treasury Direct, *supra* note 199.
[329] *See* 31 U.S.C. § 1512 (1982); Levit, *supra* note 171, at 8.

OMB would have to justify the apportionment procedure as a provision for "contingencies."[330] The pro rata theory is predicated on the idea that Congress' statutory scheme provides the President with an implicit order to spend less than Congress appropriated in an amount that can be discerned by looking to the revenue limits and spending appropriations passed by Congress. However, by using a pro rata approach, the President would de facto decide to default on interest payments because the government would pay only a portion of its obligations to bondholders. The pro rata approach may also amount to a breach of the President's duty to spend the money appropriated by Congress, unless he rescinds or defers a portion of each obligation pursuant to the Impoundment Control Act.[331]

Following a pro rata interpretation, the government could have disbursed funds to outstanding accounts in proportion to receipts. In FY2011, receipts accounted for 64% of outlays.[332] Therefore, using a yearly pro rata approach, all expenses would receive a 36% haircut. If the allocation was done on a daily basis, this could result in accounts being paid at as low as 35%[333] of the amount due or as high as 100%, depending on the day.[334] There would have been a technical default on August 2, when $2 million in interest was payable, but only 64% of it could have been paid on a yearly pro rata allocation, and only 70% on a daily pro rata allocation.[335]

---

[330] 31 U.S.C. § 1512(c); *see* Theory 2A – *The President Can Prioritize at His Discretion.*
[331] *See supra* Section II.A.2 - *The Duty to Fulfill Statutory Spending Obligations; see also* Levit, *supra* note 171, at 8-9.
[332] Press Release, Department of Treasury, *Joint Statement of Timothy Geithner, Secretary of the Treasury, and Jacob Lew, Director of the Office of Management And Budget, on Budget Results for Fiscal Year 2011*, (Oct. 14, 2011) (available at: http://www.treasury.gov/press-center/press-releases/Pages/tg1328.aspx). Budget results for FY2011: Receipts = $2,301 billion, Outlays = $3,601 billion, Deficit = $1,299 billion.
[333] Treasury Direct, *supra* note 199. On Aug. 4, inflows accounted for only 35% of outflows. On Aug. 23, this figure was 27%. However, on Aug. 22, there were excess inflows, that would be rolled-over, effectively allowing for a 53% pro rata allocation on Aug. 23. Similarly on Aug. 9 and Aug. 30, 30% and 29% pro rata rates, respectively, would have effectively been higher due to excess inflows on previous days.
[334] *Id.* On Aug. 8, Aug. 11, Aug. 27, and Aug. 29 revenues exceeded expenses, so 100% of expenses could have been paid.
[335] *Id.* On August 2, non-debt inflows totaled $6.287 billion, while outflows totaled $9.686 billion.

THEORY 4A: CONGRESSIONAL SILENCE IMPLIES A PRO RATA APPROACH	
Status of Funds utilized during DISP	DISP likely would have been extended; Funds would not have been made whole on Aug. 2
Interest Payments to Bondholders (Aug. 2 – Aug. 31)	Yearly pro rata allocation: 64% Daily pro rata allocation: 51%[336]

Mandatory Spending on Entitlements (Aug. 2 – Aug. 31)	Yearly pro rata allocation: 64%
	 Daily pro rata allocation: [337]
	    Social Security = 43%
	    Medicare = 63%.

Appropriated Discretionary Spending (Aug. 2 – Aug. 31)	Yearly pro rata allocation: 64%
	 Daily pro rata allocation, e.g.: [338]
	    Defense vendor = 65%
	    Medicaid = 64%
	    Unemployment = 63%

Proportion of total expenses paid Aug. 2 – Aug. 31	59% [339]
Outstanding Debt on Aug. 31	$14.294 trillion, as approved in Feb. 2010 legislation

B. Treasury Should Look to Statutes for Guidance

1. *Legislative Prioritization*

The President and Congress may attempt to create legislative, stopgap solutions. For instance, during the 1995-1996 impasse Congress passed temporary exemptions[340] from the debt limit in order to allow the President to issue new debt to the Social Security Trust

---

[336] *Id.* Between Aug. 2, 2011 – Aug. 31, 2011, interest paid on a daily pro rata basis would have totaled $19.418 billion, 51% of $37.951 billion in interest expense due over that time.

[337] *Id.* Between Aug. 2, 2011 – Aug. 31, 2011, Social Security paid on a daily pro rata basis would have totaled $21.767 billion, 43% of $51.214 billion Social Security payments due over that time. During the same period, Medicare paid on a daily pro rata basis would have totaled $20.131 billion, 63% of $31.793 billion in Medicare payments due.

[338] *Id.* Between Aug. 2, 2011 – Aug. 31, 2011, Defense Vendor expenses paid on a daily pro rata basis would have totaled $21.381 billion, 65% of $32.923 billion in Defense Vendor payments due over that time. During the same period, Medicaid paid on a daily pro rata basis would have totaled $11.566 billion, 64% of $18.122 billion in Medicaid payments due. Unemployment payments would have totaled $5.541 billion, 63% of $8.757 billion in Unemployment payments due over that time.

[339] *Id.* During Aug. 2 – Aug. 31, 2011: Inflows = $186.404 billion, Expenses = $313.564 billion.

[340] *See, e.g.*, Pub. L. No. 104-103 (Feb. 8, 1996).

Funds in order to credit the accounts for incoming revenues.[341] Several similar bills were proposed in 2011. Legislation introduced by Senator Pat Toomey and Representative Tom McClintock[342] would prioritize principal and interest payments.[343] Senator David Vitter and Representative David Heller's proposal[344] would prioritize "all obligations on the debt held by the public and Social Security benefits," while Representative Martin Stutzman[345] would add some military expenditures to the Vitter/Heller proposal.[346] These bills did not pass.

2. *Government Shutdown*

In order to ground his prioritization strategy in statutory guidelines, the President could use government shutdown procedures to direct his decisions. When Congress and the President fail to pass a timely[347] appropriations bill or continuing resolution, government shutdown procedures define the guidelines for running the government.[348] The Antideficiency Act prohibits voluntary services for the government "except for emergencies involving the safety of human life or the protection of property" or those services otherwise "authorized by law."[349] Pursuant to the Antideficiency Act and several opinions by Attorneys General,[350] the Office of Management and Budget's most recent Circular No. A-11[351] instructs agencies to prepare for a government shutdown by planning to retain only those employees that fall within specified categories.[352] Government shutdown

---

[341] Pub. L. No. 104-103 (Feb. 8, 1996). *See supra* note 181. "In addition to any other authority provided by law, the Secretary of the Treasury may issue under chapter 31 of title 31, United States Code, obligations of the United States before March 1, 1996, in an amount equal to the monthly insurance benefits payable under title II of the Social Security Act in March 1996."

[342] S. 163/H.R. 421; 112th Congress.

[343] Levit, *supra* note 171, at 13.

[344] S. 259/H.R. 568; 112th Congress.

[345] H.R. 728; 112th Congress.

[346] Levit, *supra*, note 171, at 13.

[347] A timely budget or continuing resolution is passed by the end of the fiscal year.

[348] *See* Puja Seam & Brad Shron, *Government Shutdowns* 1 (Harvard Law School Federal Budget Policy Seminar, Briefing Paper No. 10, 2005) (available at http://www.law.harvard.edu/faculty/hjackson/GovernmentsShutdowns_10.pdf).

[349] 31 U.S.C. § 1342 (1996).

[350] *See* Seam & Shron, *supra* note 348, at 15.

[351] *Id.*

[352] Office of Mgmt. & Budget, Circular No. A-11 (2011), available at http://www.whitehouse.gov/sites/default/files/omb/assets/a11_current_year/a_11_2011.pdf, at 2, Section 124. "Their compensation is financed by a resource other than annual appropriations; [t]hey are necessary

procedures are distinct from a debt limit crisis because a government shutdown occurs due to a lack of appropriations authority, while the debt limit involves a lack of borrowing authority.[353] However, the President may use the government shutdown procedures to justify a preference for spending obligations that are essential to protect "life and property."[354]

Conclusion

It remains unclear how the President and the Treasury Department would have responded if the national debt had hit the statutory limit on August 2, 2011. While legal concerns may have impacted the decision-making of the Executive Branch, practical and political considerations were the most likely catalyst for actions taken during the impasse. The specter of defaulting on the debt, rising interest rates, and late Social Security payments pushed the nation's political leaders to an agreement, but the mounting national debt may provoke political stalemates prior to future extensions of the debt limit. Treasury's actions before August 2, while allowing a buffer zone before the outstanding debt hit the limit, appeared to soften the urgency in Washington, and may offer a dangerous precedent for future negotiations.

The BiPartisan Policy Center projects that the nation will reach its $16.394 trillion debt limit[355] between late November 2012 and early January 2013.[356] If "extraordinary measures" are again relied upon, the nation's borrowing authority is predicted to be exhausted

---

to perform activities expressly authorized by law; [t]hey are necessary to perform activities necessarily implied by law; [t]hey are necessary to the discharge of the President's constitutional duties and powers; or [t]hey are necessary to protect life and property."

[353] Levit, *supra* note 171, at 10 ("Alternatively stated, in a situation when the debt limit is reached and Treasury exhausts its financing alternatives, aside from ongoing cash flow, an agency may continue to obligate funds. However, Treasury may not be able to liquidate all obligations that result in federal outlays due to a shortage of cash. In contrast to this, if Congress and the President do not enact interim or full year appropriations for an agency, the agency does not have budget authority available for obligation. If this occurs, the agency must shut down non-excepted activities, with immediate effects on government services.").

[354] *See id.*

[355] Austin & Levit, *supra* note 2, at 1.

[356] Steve Bell, Loren Adler & Shai Akabas, *The Debt Ceiling Slouches Toward 2012*, BiPartisan Policy Center, (Feb. 24, 2012) (available at http://www.bipartisanpolicy.org/blog/2012/02/debt-ceiling-slouches-toward-2012).

in February 2013 without a further increase to the debt limit.[357] Concurrently, major budgetary changes will take place at the end of 2012 without congressional action. The expiration of the Bush tax cuts, which is projected to increase revenues by $3.7 trillion over the next decade, is set to take place on December 31, 2012.[358] On January 2, 2013, sequestration cuts from the Budget Control Act will trigger $1.2 trillion in deficit reduction over nine years, divided between defense and non-defense programs.[359] This combination of wide-scale tax increases, substantial cuts to defense, and another potential gridlock over the debt limit may provide an impetus for all sides to negotiate a long-term deficit reduction plan.

On May 15, 2012, Speaker John Boehner voiced his willingness to leverage this upcoming debt limit increase, stating, "[w]e shouldn't dread the debt limit. We should welcome it. It's an action-forcing event in a town that has become infamous for inaction."[360] Boehner announced, "When the time comes, I will again insist on my simple principle of cuts and reforms greater than the debt limit increase. This is the only avenue I see right now to force the elected leadership of this country to solve our structural fiscal imbalance."[361] Boehner's words prompted Secretary Geithner to respond, warning that "[t]his commitment to meet the obligations of the nation, this commitment to protect the creditworthiness of the country, is a fundamental commitment that you can never call into question or violate."[362] Geithner expressed his hope that Congress can resolve the next debt limit increase "without the drama and the pain and the damage they caused the country last July."[363]

[357] *Id.* See Congressional Budget Office, *The Budget and Economic Outlook: Fiscal Years 2012-2022* (January 2012) (available at http://www.cbo.gov/sites/default/files/cbofiles/attachments/01-31-2012_Outlook.pdf). Notably, CBO baseline assumptions for FY2013 project deficit spending at 16%, and CBO's alternative fiscal scenario project deficit spending at 26.8%. These projections fall far short of the 41% of deficit spending observed in August 2011.

[358] Jeanne Sahadi, *Bush tax cuts: The real endgame*, CNN MONEY, Nov. 28, 2011, http://money.cnn.com/2011/11/28/news/economy/bush_tax_cuts/index.htm.

[359] *Id.*

[360] John Boehner, Speaker of the House, *Address on the Economy, Debt at the Peter G. Peterson Foundation 2012 Fiscal Summit* (May 15, 2012) (available at http://www.speaker.gov/speech/full-text-speaker-boehners-address-economy-debt-limit-and-american-jobs).

[361] *Id.*

[362] Erik Wasson, *Geithner warns Boehner not to play with next deal to increase the debt ceiling*, THEHILL.COM, May 15, 2012, http://thehill.com/blogs/on-the-money/budget/227393-geithner-warns-boehner-not-to-play-with-debt-ceiling-again.

[363] *Id.*

Speaker Boehner's recent comments highlight a potential reality in American politics—that debt limit increases may no longer be routine. The possibility of future crises underscores the impact of legal uncertainties that surround these issues. As a result, the 2011 debt limit impasse may properly act as a call for legal clarity, specifically with regard to the Executive Branch authority to prioritize spending obligations. While prior debates over the debt limit have been clouded by disagreements over the legal consequences of inaction, a clear legislative scheme might inform both political leaders and the public during future negotiations.

Jeremy Kreisberg & Kelley O'Mara (Under the Supervision of Professor Howell Jackson)

APPENDIX A: TIMELINE OF ACTIONS DURING 2011 DEBT LIMIT IMPASSE

Date	Event
February 12, 2010	• Congress passes legislation raising the debt limit to $14.29 trillion.
January 6, 2011	• Secretary Geithner writes Congress that the outstanding debt stood at $13.95 trillion, leaving only $335 billion of borrowing authority.
February 3, 2011	• Treasury began to draw down its $200 billion Supplementary Financing Account at the Federal Reserve
April 15, 2011	• After long negotiations, Congress passes the Department of Defense and Full-Year Continuing Appropriations Act, 2011 to fund the government for the rest of the fiscal year, narrowly averting government shutdown for the second time in 8 days.
May 6, 2011	• Secretary Geithner suspended the issuance of State and Local Government Series Treasury Securities ("SLGS") to slow the increase in the outstanding debt.
May 16, 2011	• National debt reaches debt limit of $14.29 trillion. • Secretary Geithner declares a "Debt Issuance Suspension Period," to enable actions affecting the G-Fund, Civil Fund, and Postal Fund.
July 12, 2011	• In a CBS interview, President Obama warns that he cannot "guarantee" that Social Security checks will go out if the limit is reached.
July 15, 2011	• Secretary Geithner suspends reinvestments in the portion of the ESF held in US Dollars.
August 2, 2011	• Budget Control Act becomes law and debt limit is raised instantly by $400 billion to $14.69 trillion, following a Presidential Certification. • G-Fund, Civil Fund and Postal Fund suspended principal investments were reinvested in Treasury securities. • SLGS issuances resumed.
August 3, 2011	• Interest due to the G-Fund was invested in Treasury securities.
August 5, 2011	• Standard & Poor's downgraded the long-term sovereign debt credit rating for U.S. Treasuries from AAA to AA+, citing the political brinksmanship observed during the impasse.
September 22, 2011	• Debt limit was raised by $500 billion to $15.19 trillion, as called for by BCA, despite a House disapproval measure.
December 30, 2011	• Interest earned by Civil Fund and Postal Fund during impasse was restored and invested in Treasury securities.
January 12, 2012	• President Obama certified that the outstanding debt subject to the limit was within $100 billion of the statutory limit.
January 28, 2012	• Debt limit was raised by $1.2 trillion to $16.39 trillion, despite a House disapproval vote.

Appendix B: Relevant August 2-31, 2011 Financials[364]

Figure 1. Actual Non- Debt Inflows ($186bn) and Outflows ($314bn) (in $ billions)

$22 billion - Social Security

$32 billion - Interest Expense

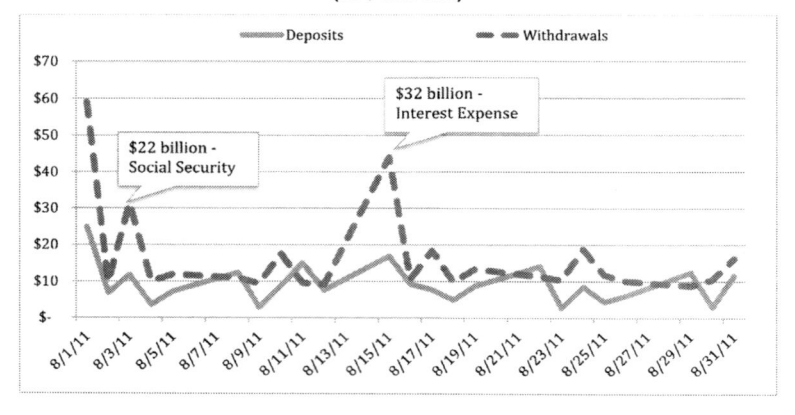

Figure 2. Accumulation of Delinquent Payments Under FIFO Approach (in $ billions)

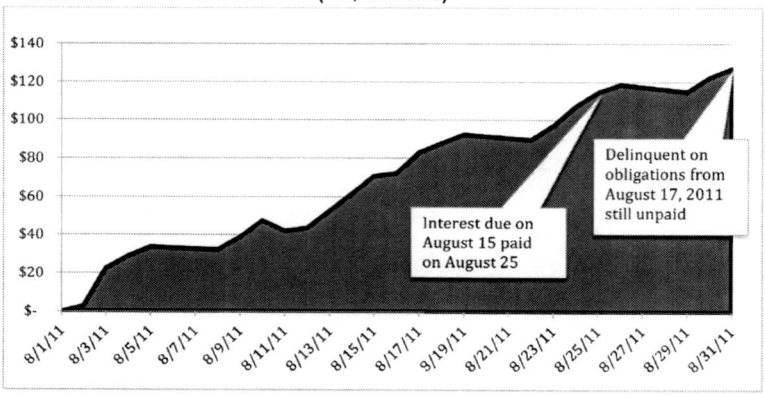

Interest due on August 15 paid on August 25

Delinquent on obligations from August 17, 2011 still unpaid

---

[364] Treasury Direct, *Daily Treasury Statements*, August 2, 2011 – August 31, 2011. Amounts reflect actual figures observed in August 2011, as stated in 30 days of Daily Treasury Statements. Figure 1: "Deposits" calculated as Gross Deposits minus deposits from Public Debt Cash Issuances, which were only enabled due to the BCA. "Withdrawals" are displayed as gross Withdrawals minus Public Cash Redemptions, which were rolled over in new debt issuances. Figure 2 displays accumulated net withdrawals minus net deposits over the course of August.

APPENDIX C: HISTORY OF THE PUBLIC DEBT CLAUSE

Political Backdrop of the 14th Amendment	Despite the Union victory in the Civil War, the Emancipation Proclamation "unraveled the Three-Fifths Compromise and thus increased the population base that determined the South's representation."[365] The purpose of the Public Debt Clause "was to prevent the Democrats, once they regained political power, from repudiating the Union debt."[366]
Economic Context of the Public Debt Clause	Financial instruments in the 1860's were risky, the value of American debt had fallen during the Civil War, and the possibility remained that the United States would default on its debt in the aftermath of the war.[367] The Thirty-Ninth Congress, which passed the Fourteenth Amendment, had an "almost religious commitment to hard-money principles."[368] Congress rolled back the wartime maneuvers allowing the issuance of greenbacks, which were not backed by gold or silver, by a vote of 144-6.[369]
Legislative History of the Public Debt Clause	Senator Ben Wade, whose proposal may have motivated the final version of the Public Debt Clause,[370] said of his proposal that "[i]t puts the debt incurred in the civil war on our part under the guardianship of the Constitution of the United States, so that a Congress cannot repudiate it."[371] Senator Wade's proposal states, in part, "[t]he public debt of the United States . . . shall be inviolable."[372] Others believe[373] that the motivation for the Public Debt Clause came from Senator Jacob Howard's proposed amendment,[374] which replaced "public debt" with "obligations." Senator Wade "was a key Republican leader during this period . . . and was soon to be elected President pro tempore of the Senate."[375] Senator Wade's status as President pro tempore would make him, "in effect, the Vice-President in waiting."[376]

---

[365] Abramowicz, *supra* note 103, at 11-12.
[366] Balkin, *supra* note 146.
[367] Abramowicz, *supra* note 103, at 10.
[368] *Id.* at 11.
[369] *Id.*
[370] See Balkin, *supra* note 290.
[371] Congressional Globe, 39th Cong., 1st session 2769 (May 23, 1866), available at http://memory.loc.gov/ammem/amlaw/lwcglink.html.
[372] *Id.* at 2768.
[373] See Stern, *supra* note 137.
[374] Senator Howard's amendment is as follows: "The obligations of the United States, incurred in suppressing insurrection, or in defense of the Union, or for payment of bounties or pensions incident thereto, shall remain inviolate." Congressional Globe, *supra* note 371, at 2938.
[375] Balkin, *supra* note 146.
[376] *Id.*

Appendix D: *Perry v. United States*[377]

Context	*Perry* was decided on the same day as four other cases[378] relating to the constitutionality of the Joint Resolution of June 5, 1933, which declared that "'every obligation . . .' shall be discharged 'upon payment, dollar for dollar, in any coin or currency which at the time of payment is legal tender for public and private debts.'"[379]
Facts	The plaintiff purchased a bond for $10,000 which stated, "[t]he principal and interest hereof are payable in United States gold coin of the present standard of value."[380] After an appreciation of the value of gold relative to the value of the dollar,[381] the United States invoked the Joint Resolution of June 5, 1933 and "refused to redeem the [plaintiff's] bond 'except by the payment of 10,000 dollars in legal tender currency.'"[382]
Reasoning	The Constitution, absent the Public Debt Clause, does not permit the repudiation of payment to bondholders.[383] Chief Justice Hughes stated, "[h]aving this power to authorize the issue of definite obligations for the payment of money borrowed, the Congress has not been vested with authority to alter or destroy those obligations."[384] The Court viewed the Public Debt Clause as "confirmatory of a fundamental principle" rather than merely applicable to the "obligations . . . issued during the Civil War."[385] Regarding the scope of the Public Debt Clause, the Court could not "perceive any reason for not considering the expression 'the validity of the public debt' as embracing whatever concerns the integrity of the public obligations."[386]
Holding	Plaintiff cannot recover because he has "not shown . . . that in relation to buying power he has sustained any loss whatever."[387]
Relevance	*Perry* is the only time the Supreme Court has addressed the Public Debt Clause.

---

[377] 294 U.S. 330 (1935).
[378] These five cases are known as the "gold clause cases." Hart, *supra* note 149, at 1057-58 n.2. The cases are: *Norman v. Baltimore & Ohio R. R.*, 294 U.S. 240 (1935), *United States v. Bankers Trust Co.*, 294 U.S. 240 (1935) (two cases), and *Nortz v. United States*, 294 U.S. 317 (1935). *Id.*
[379] 294 U.S. at 349.
[380] *Id.* at 346-47.
[381] Abramowicz, *supra* note 103, at 13
[382] 294 U.S. at 347
[383] Congress' power to borrow money cannot include the power to repudiate its obligations because the Constitution does not "contemplate[] a vain promise." *Id.* at 351.
[384] *Id.* at 353
[385] *Id.* at 354
[386] *Id.* at 354
[387] *Id.* at 357